Unum

William Sutherland ed.

Order this book online at www.trafford.com
or email orders@trafford.com

Most Trafford titles are also available at major online book retailers.

Printed in the United States of America.

ISBN: 978-1-4669-1573-2 (sc)
ISBN: 978-1-4669-1659-3 (e)

Library of Congress Control Number: 2012902716

Trafford rev. 03/23/2012

 www.trafford.com

North America & international
toll-free: 1 888 232 4444 (USA & Canada)
phone: 250 383 6864 ◆ fax: 812 355 4082

Dedicated to God for all that He has done (especially for seeing my wife through successful heart surgery and sparing her from post-operative suffering), is doing, and will do, for His enduring unconditional love and salvation, and for His inspiration and guidance, to my beautiful, wife, Angella, my step-children Ralfston "Chase" and Avagail Meek, and Anna-Kay Smikle, my brother Don Sutherland, his wife Qiong, their son Alex, my sisters Michelle, Malane and Minette Gargurevich, my mother Roberta Sutherland, my father Herbert Gargurevich, my step-mother Betty Gargurevich, my grandparents John and Irene Sutherland, (Auntie) Christine Jones, and Daniel Goldstein, MD, my wife's heart surgeon and the entire Albert Einstein Hospital medical team.

Table of Contents

Introduction

More wars have been fought over nationalism and religion than anything else. Such wars have taken place since the dawn of humanity. With regard to the latter, throughout history religious intolerance has been used to justify discrimination, genocidal violence, the Holocaust (1933-1945) and other crimes against humanity, in which up to 800+ million lives[1] have been lost and no group has been spared – not even saints (e.g. St. Joan of Arc (1412-1431) was burned at the stake on May 30, 1431) even though God is not a bigot; He *is* love. Why? Because many have characterized religion by extremism and violence and continue to do so to this day. With this in mind is it any wonder that secularism and atheism have become palatable alternatives and the media views religion negatively even though more than 200 million[2] have died in the name of reason and enlightenment over the last two centuries?

Consequently, because of fierce competition for power and influence that has existed throughout the ages due to human fallibility, too many unnecessary differences still exist whether intra-or-inter sectarian between Christians, Muslims, Jews, and East and West. Approximately 110,000 were killed in the Bosnian War (1992-1995) that pitted Serbs (Orthodox Christians), Croats (Roman Catholics), and Bosniaks (Muslims) against each other shortly after the Yugoslavian breakup in 1991, 13,000 have died in Nigeria since 1999 in Christian-Muslim strife, regimes in China, North Korea and Vietnam consistently suppress and persecute independent religious groups (Buddhists, Christians, Jews, Muslims alike), Muslim-dominated regimes in the Middle-East impose Islamic principles on religious minorities (e.g. through inhumane "shari'a" and repressive "blasphemy" laws for which progressives Salman Tasmeer (1944-2011), Governor of Punjab and Shahbaz Bhatti (1968-2011), Minister of Minority Affairs were assassinated in Pakistan because of their stated opposition) and/or fail to prosecute crimes committed against religious minorities (when not committing them – e.g. Iran executed 10 Baha'i women including 17 year-old Mona Mahmúdnizhád (1965-1983) in June 1983 for merely practicing their faith), tens of thousands have died in intra-Muslim strife (between Sunnis and Shi'ites and targeting of the minority Ahmadi and Sufi sects) since 2002 in Iraq, Iran, and Pakistan, several thousand have died in Hindu-Muslim clashes since 1992 in India where de facto religious discrimination permeates large swaths of society and the Hindutva movement seeks to create a de jure "Hindu" nation, the current Israeli government refuses to lease State-owned land to non-Jewish organizations and citizens – these are only a few recent examples of the religious intolerance that plagues today's world. In fact per <u>Global Restrictions of Religion</u> (Pew Research Center, 16 December 2009) "nearly 70% of the world's 6.8 billion people live in countries with heavy restrictions on religion, the brunt of which often falls on religious minorities... religious groups must register with the government in ([nearly] 90% [of the world's countries]) in [which such] registration requirements [have] resulted in major problems for, or outright discrimination against, certain faiths, [and] tensions between religious groups were reported in [approximately] 87% of [the world's] countries [during] the period studied (mid-2006 through mid-2008)." Because of this "[i]t is assumed that religions must be in conflict with each other [and]... with the secular" while their "positive potential" is viewed as "naïve" and "a form of apostasy."[3]

The mysteries of God are too complex and too profound for a single religion or people to monopolize. Accordingly John wrote – "*Jesus did many other things as well. If every one of them were written down... the whole world would not have room for the books that would be written.*" [John 21:25] To expand, if this passage only pertains to Jesus the Christ (c. 5

BCE-c. 33 CE until his ascension), imagine how much more exists when God in His totality is considered. If God is considered in His totality, there would not be enough room in all the universes to record everything!

In the same spirit it is a mistake to believe that one may only attain salvation through acceptance of a single doctrine or that certain dogma are not subject to interpretation. God provides each of us who welcome Him into our heart a multi-dimensional personal relationship such that His message, though consistent with His loving nature and scripture, will be different. His message is individualized towards our personal needs to enhance our spiritual growth, to facilitate our personal journey of discovery and to broaden our path to salvation.

We are all branches on the same vine and no branch should be broken and trampled to give precedence to another. Accordingly, it is hardly likely that God can be pleased with intra-and-inter sectarian religious strife since no creator whether a painter, sculptor, or author could rejoice at the destruction of their masterpiece. This is especially true pertaining to God's masterpiece – the human being, notably because of the sanctity of life.

"Human life is sacred because from its beginning it involved the creative action of God and it remains for ever in a special relationship with the Creator, who is its sole end..."[4] "All life is sacred, as we all have a part of the divine soul ("*atman*") in us."[5]

> "*[H]ave neither male nor female slaves, see all people as equal...*" [The "Luminous" Religion]

The purpose of this book, a collection of scripture, psalms, and proverbs is to promote tolerance since the world's religions have greater unity than is apparent – all lead to the same Creator whether one calls Him Yahweh, Jehovah, Allah, Brahman or by another name.

The "Luminous" religion (c. 635-1399) came closest to uniting. Per Martin Palmer, The Jesus Sutras (Ballantine Wellspring, New York, 2001) it "presented [a] peaceful, insightful interaction between Eastern and Western cultures... unit[ing] the wisdom and moderation of Taoism and the humanism and compassion of Christianity." Sadly, it was stamped out by oppression and persecution in mid-to-late 14th century China. Nevertheless, even though the "Luminous" religion is extinct per se, some of its sutras still exist providing corroborative, insightful texts applicable and inspirational to this day, which are included in "*Unum*."

Even when the various religions appear to diverge greatly – everything (virtues, prophesies, teachings) even when not recognized, leads to Jesus the Christ, the epitome of God's *agape* (unconditional) love and to God, the Loving Creator.

> "*For God so loved the world that He gave His only begotten Son, that whoever believes in Him should not perish but have everlasting life*" [John 3:16] and "*Love is the reflection of God's unity in the world... It constitutes the entire significance of creation.*" [Meher Baba (1894-1969)][6]
>
> "*[The Messiah], 'the raft of salvation and compassion,' suffered terrible woes so that all should be freed from karma. All of us are saved by his works... [H]e will not leave you without qi (life)... So have no fear, not even of death; you will live as the Messiah lives... raised after death... [There] will be such joy and happiness...*" [The "Luminous" Religion]

19th Century Russian Icon

Sometimes mere insights lead to Jesus. For example piece fragments of three Buddhist psalms together and Jesus the Savior is revealed:

> [54] *He who is of [God]...* [71] *[the] Lord that was made flesh...* [54] *ordain[ed] that His saving grace should be made manifest.* [126] *...[T]hrough [Him] we attain... the final deliverance that destroyed... sin.*[7]

With the theme of this book focusing on God's love and mercy, the very traits that prompted St. Thérèse of Lisieux (1873-1897) to write – "*How can I fear a God Who is nothing but mercy and love?*"[8] – selected scriptures exclude elements of violence, nationalism, and chauvinism. God's infinite wisdom, awesome power, and wondrous deeds do not need to be reinforced by cruelty, war and bloodshed. In fact, when God's unconditional love and enduring mercy are combined with examples of righteousness and virtue, they more than suffice.

Besides love is more appealing than coercion. The latter can only serve to alienate people from their Creator, which was vividly portrayed in a letter by Carmine Masucci – "Separation of church and state is essential... God could not generate what is written in all the 'sacred' documents... Only man could be so vindictive of his fellow man."[9] At the same time, God's *agape* love can encourage us to freely seek and embrace our Maker as we grow intellectually and spiritually, probing the very meaning and purpose of our existence. God would have it no other way – otherwise we would be slaves instead of "*heirs of the kingdom*" [James 2:5].

Religion is not intended to exclude, divide or subvert but to include, invite, and since in reality "There is no difference in the realization of the Truth... The difference is only in words and terms..." as stated by Indian mystic Meher Baba.[10] Buddhist spiritual leader, Tenzin Gyatso (b. 1935), the 14th Dalai Lama captured the true essence of religion when he stated, "The whole purpose of religion is to facilitate love and compassion, patience, tolerance, humility, forgiveness."[11]

> "*There is no compulsion in religion...*" [Quran, The Cow 2:256]

> "*Be kind and merciful to humanity, for all are [God's] creatures; do not oppress them... Always work for the good of mankind. Never unduly assert yourselves... over others... Be humble in spirit, kind and gentle, and forgiving, sympathetic towards all...*" [Mirza Ghulam Ahmad (1835-1908)]

Religious freedom is even more imperative when the current state of the world is considered in which God and religion are being de-emphasized and de-legitimized. Although The Good

<u>Book: A Secular Bible</u> by A.C. Grayling (Walker & Company, New York, 2011) offers beautiful, inspirational material to unite humanity through science and philosophy, the absence of salvation and thus hope is palpable. Despite an atheist's best intentions and efforts, moral corruption, social disorder, and spiritual ignorance will be the consequences if God is purged from society.

Nevertheless, regardless of social trends or whether one recognizes it or not, God, infallibly remains the beginning and end of everything and the author of all creation:

> "*I am the Alpha and the Omega, the First and the Last, the Beginning and the End* " [Revelation 22:13] and "*...Shall what is formed say to the One Who formed it, 'You did not make me?'*" [Isaiah 29:16]

It is my hope that "*Unum*" ("One" in Latin) can bridge our differences and inspire and initiate positive change and a strengthening of faith and love for God, thus serving as a light to illuminate today's darkness of intolerance, persecution, and rejection. To enhance the prospects of religious tolerance it would be constructive if New Testament scripture was edited to provide a more accurate and concise account of the crucifixion (Jesus was killed by humanity, not by the Jews or to a lesser extent, the Romans as illustrated in 1 Corinthians 2:7-9 – "the crucifixion was pre-ordained by God as a ransom for our sins") and the Talmud was purged of its negative depictions of Jesus (He was not a criminal who practiced witchcraft). In "*Unum*" both New Testament scripture and the Talmud with reference to Jesus have been edited to illustrate the true message of God's loving mercy and salvation especially since too much hatred in the form of anti-Semitism and genocide has already been propagated in God's name.

Only through appreciation of the unity of faiths through their rich, autonomous diversity can humanity be enlightened enough to recognize we are ALL the creation of the SAME, REAL, LIVING God and progress towards the Japanese concept of "*ittai*" (to become one), the very essence of Christ's mystical body. After all, we ARE one and as one suffers, we all suffer and as one rejoices, we all rejoice.

Consequently when God's message is embraced in totality by the heart and soul, free of human subjectivity – a beautiful unity (free of racism and other forms of discrimination) through diversity can ensue consistent with the Quran –

> *Al-Sajdah 32:7 He is the One who... started the creation of the human from clay. Al-Sajdah 32:9 He shaped him and blew into him from His spirit. And He gave you the hearing, the eyesight, and the brains... The Romans 30:22 and the diversity of your tongues and colors.*

We are all brothers and sisters belonging to the same human family with the same Father, God our Creator. This is why Sufi poet Nur ad-Din Abd ar-Rahman Jami (1414-1492) wrote, "Who is man? The reflection of the Eternal Light"[12] and Indian leader Mahatma Gandhi (1869-1948) said, "I consider myself a Hindu, Christian, M[u]sl[i]m, Jew, Buddhist and Confucian."[13]

Religion can be a beautiful thing if practiced, as God so desires in which the two greatest commandments: *"Love the Lord your God with all your heart and with all your soul and with all your mind"* and *"Love your neighbor as yourself"* [Matthew 22:37,39] are followed. Per St. Clement of Alexandria (c. 150-215), "When you see your brother [or sister], you see God."[14]

Accordingly, religion need not be judgmental. We are all imperfect, each with our own faults. Consequently, it is counterproductive for some to condemn the sins of others while justifying their own indiscretions as somehow more palatable.

> *"He who is without sin among you, let him throw a stone at her first"* [John 8:7], *"For God did not send his Son into the world to condemn the world, but to save the world through him"* [John 3:17] and *"I take this suffering upon myself provided that not one person… shall perish…"* [Pesikta Rabbati, Piska 36.1; Zohar II. 212a]

In addition religious tolerance can enhance and broaden our understanding of God's love and His will. For example we can learn that "God does not punish thousands of innocent human beings for the acts, good, bad or indifferent of a few."[15]

> *"Those eighteen who died when the tower in Siloam fell on them — do you think they were more guilty than all the others living in Jerusalem? I tell you, no!"* Jesus said. [Luke 13:4-5]

Statements that attribute natural disasters to divine punishment are inaccurate and counterproductive. They only serve to alienate people from God as evidenced by one person who wrote of the 2011 Joplin, MO. tornado disaster, "...[G]od kills over a hundred people but spares… a cross."[16] Consequently, the message of hope and God's redeeming love exhibited by three miracles – the standing cross, the survival of the twenty persons who cried out to God while sheltered in a "Dollar Store" freezer, and appearance of a double rainbow – were overlooked.

Based on Sikh scripture, "the [c]reative [p]ower of the Universe" is responsible for natural disasters since the very essence of nature, unlike that of God, is indifferent and unfeeling. Biblical scripture further corroborates this fact in 1 Kings 19:11-12: "*...a great and powerful wind tore the mountains apart and shattered the rocks… but the LORD was not in the wind. After the wind there was an earthquake, but the LORD was not in the earthquake. After the earthquake came a fire, but the LORD was not in the fire...*"

And if we adhered to Eastern traditions (Buddhism, Shinto) with regard to adversity and tragedy, we could be more productive and even healthier due to lowered stress levels, since we would place emphasis "on [our] behavior in reaction to [such adversity or] tragedy"[17] in lieu of casting blame or attempting to discern the "Whys?"

"All nations form but one community" since we share a common origin and common destiny, namely the same God, Who desires to save all, and because "goodness and truth" can be found in all religions.[18]

When this is recognized, religion can actually play a constructive role in conflict resolution. This is critical since "[i]f humanity is to survive and flourish in an environment that renders cultural and geographic isolation impossible, it is essential that the world['s] religions… become active forces for compassion, love, and justice without which global peace cannot be achieved [especially since we have] to deal with 'others' who live by very different belief systems and principles."[19] This is so because religion "addresses the most profound existential issues of human life [of which] individual and social conceptions of peace [are paramount]."[20] Accordingly religion must also serve as a means of reconciliation when differences exist especially during times of conflict.

Let not the angels continue to be right when they protested God's plan to create the human race:

> *"What! [W]ilt Thou place in it such as shall make mischief in it and shed blood, and we celebrate Thy praise and extol Thy holiness?"* [Quran, The Cow 2:30]

In the spirit of the 1986 World Day of Prayer for Peace in Assisi, Italy, in which an unprecedented number of Jewish, Muslim, Buddhist, Shinto, Zoroastrian, Hindu, Unitarian, and traditional African and American Indian spiritual leaders "prayed, side by side"[21] at the behest of Pope John Paul II (1920-2005), let "*Unum*" facilitate the dawning of a new era in which, with our rich diversity, we not only coexist but interact with love, compassion, and righteousness such that the world is transformed into a holier, more sanctified place as we make our individual journeys to our inheritance – God's heavenly kingdom and eternal life – made possible only through His unconditional love and His only Son's passion, death, and resurrection.

Perhaps one day all religions, despite their de facto autonomy, may be able to hold a cohesive, combined service in which unifying, corroborative scripture from each can be read as leaders and laity pray together to magnify God's unconditional love for ALL humanity with whom He has entered into an everlasting Covenant.

Let the religions stand together in solidarity. Let all worship the one and only God, our Creator and heavenly Father for "*(All) people are a single nation.*" [Quran, The Cow 2:213]. After all, it is the wish of God as expressed through Jesus "that [all] may be one..." [John 17:11].

We all have a calling to "[m]ake every effort to keep the unity of [God] through the bond of peace." [Ephesians 4:3] In fact, in the words of Meher Baba, "...the more [one] becomes spiritually minded or advances towards God, the more tolerant [they] become and the less differentiation [they] see."[22]

Let there be interaction, peace, harmony, compassion, and love between all to enhance righteousness and truth and facilitate our ultimate goal – blissful eternity in paradise described as immensely "more beautiful than [one] can say or imagine [because of the limitation of] worldly similes and words" when a disciple asked, "Is the promise [of paradise – [a] 'Holy Land exquisitely adorned with gold and silver and precious gems [that consists of] pure waters with golden sands, surrounded by pleasant walks covered with lotus flowers [in which] [j]oyous music is heard... flowers rain down three times a day [and the] birds sing... harmonious notes [in praise of God]' – vain talk and a myth?"[23]

Let immersion in the scriptural passages within "*Unum*" bring across the hope and love that only God can provide. And when it does, may it help each of us to practice the simple way of St. Benedict (480-547):

"[P]ursue... what [is] better for someone else... show... pure [and humble] love [towards each other and] loving fear [to God]. Let [all] prefer nothing whatever to [God]..." [Adaptation of Benedictine Rule 72:7-11].

Furthermore, let "*Unum*" and the beautiful scriptures within unite so that we can all live the prayer of St. Francis of Assisi (1181-1226):

St. Francis of Assisi Preaches to the Birds by Giotto c. 1297-1299

Lord, make me an instrument of [Y]our peace.
Where there is hatred, let me sow love.
Where there is injury, pardon.
Where there is doubt, faith.
Where there is despair, hope.
Where there is darkness, light.
that we are born to Eternal Life.Where there is sadness, joy.

O Divine Master, grant that I may not so much seek to be consoled, as to console; to be understood, as to understand; to be loved, as to love. For it is in giving that we receive. It is in pardoning that we are pardoned, and it is in dying

Then we can have the world God so desires as we make our Earthly journeys and bide our time, all the while enriching the physical and spiritual lives of ourselves and others until we attain the everlasting life God seeks for each and every one of us:

> "[T]he Heavenly Honored One sends the [Pure Wind] (Holy Spirit) to all places to save everyone." [The "Luminous" Religion] and "*My Father's house has many rooms; if that were not so, would I have told you that I am going there to prepare a place for you?*" [John 2:14]

In addition, the purpose of "*Unum*" is to rebut the attacks on Jesus' reputation and to set the record straight with regard to Mary Magdalene. She was *never* a prostitute, which is clear in the gospels, despite Pope Gregory's (c. 540-604) 591 declaration that was made to preserve the status quo of the male-centric world of his era. To accomplish this, the Gospel of John, Synoptic (Luke, Matthew, and Mark) and Gnostic gospels are all included in Book XXVIII: "The Gospels: Jesus The Christ." Furthermore, when sutras from the Luminous Religion are added, it is apparent that not only does Book XXVIII illustrate God's unconditional love for humanity and Jesus' ultimate sacrifice to redeem us, it also unveils the beautiful love between him and an attractive young woman from the prosperous fishing village of Magdala (located on the northwest side of the Sea of Galilee).

It began when Mary Magdalene (c. 6-78) impulsively went to listen to a sermon by Jesus in c. 30. Afterwards, she gave up her lust for extravagance and the material things of the world, fell in love with Jesus and became his most devoted and beloved disciple. She was always at his side — during good times and bad. He confided in her and returned her affection, often kissing her. He knew she had *agape* love for him. At the same time, she knew and understood him completely and willingly embraced a celibate spiritual loving relationship so that Jesus could fulfill his Father's will. Therefore instead of objecting to his mission, she put God first and supported Jesus. She stayed with him during his humiliation and crucifixion when just about everyone else whom he was associated with fled and/or denied him. She did not care if the Roman soldiers and hostile crowd were watching. She was ready to die with her Jesus.

**Jesus and Mary Magdalene by Stephen Adam 1906,
Kilmore Church, Dervaig, Isle of Mull, Scotland, UK**

Consequently, she was the first person Jesus appeared to following his resurrection since their bond of love was unbreakable and her broken heart was in greatest need of consolation. And when Jesus appeared to Mary Magdalene, she instinctively embraced him and could not let go. Only after he instructed her to do so since his mission was not complete, did she comply. Then following his ascension, she fearlessly helped spread the Good News and even went where no one else would dare go — straight to the Roman Emperor in c. 35 (just two years after the resurrection). Instead of imposing a death sentence, the incredulous Tiberius (42 BCE-37 CE), known as an intellectual who detested power, listened and questioned her. Then, following the miracle Jesus made possible, he went to the Senate and when they rejected his efforts to accept her teachings, he provided protection for the apostles for the remainder of his rule. He warned that persecutors would face serious consequences.

The purpose of "*Unum*" is not to undermine or replace the Bible, Torah, Quran, and the other holy books. It is intended to serve as a scholarly supplement that illustrates the beautiful unity through diversity that exists between the world's faiths, nationalities, and races that ultimately leads to eternal salvation with the same loving Creator. Let "*Unum*" promote inclusion and love and bring people to God. Let it also add to the spirit of the 1986 World Day of Prayer for Peace, and the 2006 and 2011 Global Conferences on World Religions, the latter two which featured prominent scholars, writers, and religious leaders, in which the attendees agreed on three progressive resolutions – "religious schools (seminary, yeshiva, madrasah, etc.) should teach a course in world religions, violating the sanctity of the scripture of one religion amounts to violating the sanctity of the scriptures of all religions, and... the [world's] religions should come together to formulate a Universal Declaration of Human Rights" pertaining to religious belief since "religions are not entities unto themselves; they are [in reality] part of the [daily] experience of the people living them." In essence "the world's religions are living entities"[24] and thus when broken down into their purest and simplest form – individual human beings within whom God resides – "*Do you not know that your bodies are temples of the Holy Spirit, who is in you, whom you have received from God?*" [1 Corinthians 6:19]. Last, let it bring people to God and help create a better world.

May God in His loving mercy bless and keep you and your friends and family always,

William

[1] seehowtheyrun. Huffington Post. 22 July 2006. http://www.huffingtonpost.com/social/seehowtheyrun/general-david-petraeus-co_n_706718_59632884.html

[2] seehowtheyrun. Huffington Post. 22 July 2006. http://www.huffingtonpost.com/social/seehowtheyrun/general-david-petraeus-co_n_706718_59632884.html

[3] Mark Reynolds. In defense of religion. McGill News Alumni Magazine. Fall/Winter 2011. 11.

[4] 2258. Catechism of the Catholic Church. Liberia Editrice Vaticana. Vatican City. 1994. 544

[5] Hindu Doctrine of Ahimsa.

[6] Unity in Diversity Quotes. 6 May 2011. http://dropsoul.com/mystic-quotes.php

[7] Shinran Shonin. Project Gutenberg EBook of Buddhist Psalms. 2004.

[8] Patrick Ahern. Maurice and Thérèse: The Story of Love. Image Publishing, Inc., Memphis, TN. 2001.

[9] Carmine Masucci. Separation of church and state is essential. The Sound And Town Report. 6 May 2011.

[10] Unity in Diversity Quotes. 6 May 2011. http://dropsoul.com/mystic-quotes.php

[11] Unity in Diversity Quotes. 6 May 2011. http://dropsoul.com/mystic-quotes.php

[12] Sufi Poetry. Living from the Heart. Wahiduddin's Web. 13 August 2010. http://wahiduddin.net/sufi/sufi_poetry.htm

[13] Unity in Diversity Quotes. 6 May 2011. http://dropsoul.com/mystic-quotes.php

[14] Unity in Diversity Quotes. 6 May 2011. http://dropsoul.com/mystic-quotes.php

[15] Ahmed Rehab. God is Not a Terrorist. About.com. 16 March 2011.

[16] Priest and his church's cross survive Joplin tornado destruction. Catholic News & Info. 23 May 2011.

[17] Dan Gilgoff. How Japan's religions confront tragedy. CNN. 14 March 2011.

[18] 842-843. Catechism of the Catholic Church. Liberia Editrice Vaticana. Vatican City. 1994. 223

[19] Ingrid Shafer. Global Conflict and Religious Intolerance -- Is Religion Compatible with Genuine Morality? Can Faithful Christians be Religious Pluralists? Crosstimbers: A Multicultural, Interdisciplinary Journal. Spring/Summer 2005.

[20] Abdul Aziz Said and Nathan C. Funk. The Role of Faith in Cross-Cultural Conflict Resolution. Presented at the European Parliament for the European Centre for Common Ground. September 2001.

[21] Jerry Filteau. Pope made important overtures to non-Christian religions. CNS. 2005.

[22] Unity in Diversity Quotes. 6 May 2011. http://dropsoul.com/mystic-quotes.php

[23] Buddhist Prophesies Fulfilled. 28 March 2011. http://www.bci.org/prophecy-fulfilled/Buddha.htm

[24] Mark Reynolds. In defense of religion. McGill News Alumni Magazine. Fall/Winter 2011. 11.

I. Creation

Christianity/Judaism:

Genesis 1:

[1] In the beginning God created the heavens and the earth. [2] The earth was without form, and void; and darkness *was* on the face of the deep. And the Spirit of God was hovering over the face of the waters. [3] Then God said, "Let there be light;" and there was light. [4] And God saw the light, that *it was* good; and God divided the light from the darkness. [5] God called the light Day, and the darkness He called Night. So the evening and the morning were the first day. [6] Then God said, "Let there be a firmament in the midst of the waters, and let it divide the waters from the waters." [7] Thus God made the firmament, and divided the waters which *were* under the firmament from the waters which *were* above the firmament; and it was so. [8] And God called the firmament Heaven. So the evening and the morning were the second day.

[9] Then God said, "Let the waters under the heavens be gathered together into one place, and let the dry *land* appear;" and it was so. [10] And God called the dry *land* Earth, and the gathering together of the waters He called Seas. And God saw that *it was* good. [11] Then God said, "Let the earth bring forth grass, the herb *that* yields seed, *and* the fruit tree *that* yields fruit according to its kind, whose seed *is* in itself, on the earth;" and it was so. [12] And the earth brought forth grass, the herb *that* yields seed according to its kind, and the tree *that* yields fruit, whose seed *is* in itself according to its kind. And God saw that *it was* good. [13] So the evening and the morning were the third day. [14] Then God said, "Let there be lights in the firmament of the heavens to divide the day from the night; and let them be for signs and seasons, and for days and years; [15] and let them be for lights in the firmament of the heavens to give light on the earth;" and it was so. [16] Then God made two great lights: the greater light to rule the day, and the lesser light to rule the night. *He made* the stars also. [17] God set them in the firmament of the heavens to give light on the earth, [18] and to rule over the day and over the night, and to divide the light from the darkness. And God saw that *it was* good. [19] So the evening and the morning were the fourth day.

[20] Then God said, "Let the waters abound with an abundance of living creatures, and let birds fly above the earth across the face of the firmament of the heavens." [21] So God created great sea creatures and every living thing that moves, with which the waters abounded, according to their kind, and every winged bird according to its kind. And God saw that *it was* good. [22] And God blessed them, saying, "Be fruitful and multiply, and fill the waters in the seas, and let birds multiply on the earth." [23] So the evening and the morning were the fifth day. [24] Then God said, "Let the earth bring forth the living creature according to its kind: cattle and creeping thing and beast of the earth, *each* according to its kind;" and it was so. [25] And God made the beast of the earth according to its kind, cattle according to its kind, and everything that creeps on the earth according to its kind. And God saw that *it was* good.

[26] Then God said, "Let [Me] make man in [My] image, according to [My] likeness..." [27] So God created man in His *own* image... male and female He created them. [28] Then God blessed them, and God said to them, "Be fruitful and multiply..." [29] And God said, "See, I have given you every herb *that* yields seed which *is* on the face of all the earth, and

every tree whose fruit yields seed; to you it shall be for food. [30] Also, to every beast of the earth, to every bird of the air, and to everything that creeps on the earth, in which *there is* life, *I have given* every green herb for food"; and it was so. [31] Then God saw everything that He had made, and indeed *it was* very good. So the evening and the morning were the sixth day.

Genesis 2:

[1] Thus the heavens and the earth, and all the host of them, were finished. [2] And on the seventh day God ended His work… and He rested on the seventh day from all His work, which He had done. [3] Then God blessed the seventh day and sanctified it, because in it He rested from all His work… [4] This *is* the history of the heavens and the earth when they were created, in the day that the LORD God made the earth and the heavens, [5] before any plant of the field was in the earth and before any herb of the field had grown. For the LORD God had not caused it to rain on the earth, and *there was* no man to till the ground; [6] but a mist went up from the earth and watered the whole face of the ground.

[7] And the LORD God formed man *of* the dust of the ground, and breathed into his nostrils the breath of life; and man became a living being. [18] And the LORD God said, "*It is* not good that man should be alone; I will make him a helper comparable to him." [19] Out of the ground the LORD God formed every beast of the field and every bird of the air, and brought *them* to Adam to see what he would call them. And whatever Adam called each living creature that *was* its name. [20] So Adam gave names to all cattle, to the birds of the air, and to every beast of the field. But for Adam there was not found a helper comparable to him.

[21] And the LORD God caused a deep sleep to fall on Adam, and he slept; and He took one of his ribs, and closed up the flesh in its place. [22] Then the rib, which the LORD God had taken from man He made into a woman, and He brought her to the man. [23] And Adam said: "This *is* now bone of my bones And flesh of my flesh; She shall be called woman, because she was taken out of Man." [24] Therefore a man shall leave his father and mother and be joined to his wife, and they shall become one flesh.

Islam:

Beneficient 55:1,14, The Rock 15:26, and Al-Baqarah 30 The Beneficient God… created man from dry clay like earthen vessels… from altered black mud [declaring] Lo! I am about to place a viceroy in the earth… The Believers 23:14 Then [He] made the seed a clot, then [He] made the clot a lump of flesh, then [He] made the lump… bones, then [He] clothed the bones with flesh [and] caused [them] to grow into… creation. The Companions 39:6 He has created you from a single being, then made its mate of the same [kind].

Al-Sajdah 32:4 God is the One who created the heavens and the earth, and everything between them in six days, then assumed all authority. Al-Sajdah 32:7 He is the One who perfected everything He created, and started the creation of the human from clay. Al-Sajdah 32:9 He shaped him and blew into him from His spirit. And He gave you the hearing, the eyesight, and the brains… The Romans 30:22 and the diversity of your tongues and colors.

The Rock 15:22 and The Companions 39:6 [I]ndeed, it is [H]e who give[s] life… The Ant 27:64 [and] reproduces it… in the wombs of your mothers and gives… sustenance from the heaven and the earth. Yasin 36:33-35 [He] gave life [to the dead earth] and [brought] forth from it grain so they [can] eat of it. And [He made] therein gardens of palms and grapevines… and [made] springs to flow forth in it [t]hat they may eat of the fruit thereof. ^{The Sandhills 46:33} [He] is able to give life to the dead… He has surely power over all things.

^{Beneficient 55:7} [T]he heaven, He raised it high [a]nd the earth, He has set it for living creatures. ^{The Rock 15:22} [H]e sen[t] the winds fertilizing… [and] water down from the cloud… ^{Beneficient 10-12} Therein is fruit and palms, having sheathed clusters, [a]nd the grain with husk and fragrance. ^{Beneficient 55:19-20 and Prophets 21:31} He has made the two seas to flow freely that they meet together. Between them is a barrier, which they cannot pass. He made [great] mountains… and foods. ^{Prophets 21:33} He created the night and the day and the sun and the moon; all travel along swiftly in their celestial spheres. ^{Yasin 36:38-39} And the sun runs on to a term appointed for it… Neither is it allowable to the sun that it should overtake the moon, nor can the night outstrip the day; and all float on in a sphere. ^{The Kingdom 67:3} [Y]ou see no incongruity… can you see any disorder? ^{Yasin 36:37} [A] sign is… the night: We draw forth from it the day.

^{Ha Mim 41:10-11} Then He directed Himself to the heaven and its vapor, so He said to it and to the earth: Come both willingly or unwillingly. They both said: We come willingly.

Bahaism:

Source: Bahá'u'lláh:

"[God] created… all from the same dust…"

Confucianism:

"There has never been a birth without the collaboration of Heaven. God is the creator of all…"

Hinduism:

Rig Veda Hymn LXXXI. Visvakarman:

^{3,7} He, the Sole God, whose works are righteous, produc[ed] earth and heaven…

Rig Veda Hymn LXXXII. Visvakarman:

¹ The Father… created both these worlds… Then when the eastern ends were firmly fastened, the heavens and the earth were far extended.

Rig Veda Hymn CXXIX. Creation:

¹ [Before there] was not non-existent nor existent: there was no realm of air, no sky… ² Death was not then nor was there aught immortal: [N]o sign was there, the day's and night's divider: [A]part from [God there] was nothing whatsoever. ³ Darkness [and indiscriminant chaos] there was.

Upanishads:

^{Katha Upanishad Part 6} In the beginning [when there was nothing], the Creator longed for the joy of creation… He remained in meditation, and then came… matter and life. The Universe

is a manifestation of God.

Mundaka Upanishad Chapter 1, Part 1 He is the Eternal… the source of all creation.

Maitri Upanishad Part 6 [God] supreme is immeasurable, inapprehensible, beyond conception, never-born, beyond reasoning, beyond thought. His vastness is the vastness of space. At the end of the worlds, all things sleep: He alone is awake in Eternity. Then from [H]is infinite space new worlds arise and awake, a universe which is a vastness of thought. In the consciousness of [God] the universe is, and unto [H]im it returns… The end is immortality, union and peace.

Sikhism:

Sri Guru Granth Sahib:

How can you forget the One who created your soul… the breath of life? …All are made of the same clay. The One Lord has fashioned the vessels… The actions of the Creator… are marvelous and wonderful… The One… God, prevails everywhere. All the creation comes from this One.

The Lord Himself creates, He Himself gives… From the Lord God, everything was created. The Lord alone is the One Creator… [He Himself] created the earth, and the two lamps of the sun and the moon. He created the [c]reative [p]ower of the Universe… [He is] the Universal Father of all. He created everyone.

The "Luminous" Religion:

Source: **Martin Palmer. The Jesus Sutras (Ballantine Wellspring, New York, 2001):**

The True Lord of the Primordial Void, in absolute stillness and constant naturalness, crafted and nourished all things. He raised the earth and established the sky… The sun rises; darkness is banished… Every living thing comes from… [God]… [Who has] no beginning and no end… Everything visible and invisible is [created by God]…

[God]… appointed [humanity] as the guardians of all creation.

Scientology:

All living organisms are composed of matter and energy existing in space and time, [created] by God… [L]ife is… neither accidental nor purposeless.

Mayan Religion:

Source: **Allen J. Christensen. Popol Vuh: Literal Translation. Mesoweb Publications. 29 November 2011. http://www.mesoweb.com/publications/Christensen/PV-Literal.pdf:**

[36-37] Protector, Shelterer… [80-82] Life, Creation, Giver of breath… [91] To everything, [92] Whatever exists [93-96] Sky, Earth, Lake, Sea… [173] Beneath light then… [4880-4881] People framed, People shaped… [174] [God] gave birth to… people. [4981-4982] There was their breath, they became… [5031] We were created… [5252-5254] Black people, White people, Many forms [of] people… [4985] [He] [c]ompleted their sight, [4986] [He] [c]ompleted their knowledge… [4890] [He] rejoiced.

II. The Fall of Adam and Eve

Christianity/Judaism:

Genesis 2:

[8] The LORD God planted a garden eastward in Eden, and there He put the man whom He had formed. [9] And out of the ground the LORD God made every tree grow that is pleasant to the sight and good for food. The tree of life *was* also in the midst of the garden, and the tree of the knowledge of good and evil.

[16] And the LORD God commanded the man, saying, "Of every tree of the garden you may freely eat; [17] but of the tree of the knowledge of good and evil you shall not eat, for in the day that you eat of it you shall surely die." [25] And they were both naked, the man and his wife, and [they] were not ashamed.

Genesis 3:

[1] Now the serpent was more cunning than any beast of the field, which the LORD God had made. And he said to the woman, "Has God indeed said, 'You shall not eat of every tree of the garden?'" [2] And the woman said to the serpent, "We may eat the fruit of the trees of the garden; [3] but of the fruit of the tree which *is* in the midst of the garden, God has said, 'You shall not eat it, nor shall you touch it, lest you die.'"

[4] Then the serpent said to the woman, "You will not surely die. [5] For God knows that in the day you eat of it your eyes will be opened, and you will be like God, knowing good and evil." [6] So when the woman saw that the tree *was* good for food, that it *was* pleasant to the eyes, and a tree desirable to make *one* wise, she took of its fruit and ate. She also gave to her husband with her, and he ate. [7] Then the eyes of both of them were opened, and they knew that they *were* naked; and they sewed fig leaves together and made themselves coverings.

[8] And they heard the sound of the LORD God walking in the garden in the cool of the day, and Adam and his wife hid themselves from the presence of the LORD God among the trees of the garden. [9] Then the LORD God called to Adam and said to him, "Where *are* you?"

[10] So he said, "I heard Your voice in the garden, and I was afraid because I was naked; and I hid myself." [11] And He said, "Who told you that you *were* naked? Have you eaten from the tree of which I commanded you that you should not eat?" [12] Then the man said, "The woman whom You gave *to be* with me, she gave me of the tree, and I ate." [13] And the LORD God said to the woman, "What *is* this you have done?" The woman said, "The serpent deceived me, and I ate." [14] So the LORD God said to the serpent: "...[O]n your belly you shall go, and you shall eat dust all the days of your life. [15] And I will put enmity between you and the woman, and between your seed and her seed; he shall bruise your head, and you shall bruise his heel."

[16] To the woman He said: "...[I]n pain you shall bring forth children..." [17] Then to Adam He said, "Because you have heeded the voice of your wife, and have eaten from the tree

of which I commanded you, saying, 'You shall not eat of it': Cursed *is* the ground for your sake; In toil you shall eat *of* it all the days of your life. [18] Both thorns and thistles it shall bring forth for you, and you shall eat the herb of the field. [19] In the sweat of your face you shall eat bread till you return to the ground, for out of it you were taken; for dust you *are*, and to dust you shall return."

[21] …[F]or Adam and his wife the LORD God made tunics of skin, and clothed them. [22] Then… [23] the LORD God sent him out of the garden of Eden to till the ground from which he was taken. [24] So He drove out the man; and He placed cherubim at the east of the garden of Eden, and a flaming sword which turned every way, to guard the way to the tree of life.

Adam and Eve by Cranach the
Elder 1526

Islam:

The Elevated Places 7:19-25 And [God said]: O Iblis (Adam)! Dwell you and your wife in the garden; so eat from where you desire, but do not go near this tree, for then you will be of the unjust.

Ta Ha 20:117-120 [He also] said: O Iblis is an enemy to you and to your wife, therefore let him not drive you both forth from the garden so that you should be unhappy; surely it is for you that you shall not be hungry therein nor bare of clothing; and that you shall not be thirsty therein nor shall you feel the heat of the sun.

But the Shaitan (Satan) made an evil suggestion to him; he said: O Iblis! Shall I guide you to the tree of immortality and a kingdom, which decays not?

The Elevated Places 7:21-25 and The Cow 2:36 And he swore to them both: Most surely I am a sincere adviser to you. Then he caused them to fall by deceit; so when they tasted of the tree, their evil inclinations became manifest to them, and they both began to cover

6

themselves with the leaves of the garden; and their Lord called out to them: Did I not forbid you both from that tree and say to you that the Shaitan is your open enemy?

They said: Our Lord! We have been unjust to ourselves, and if [You] forgive us not, and have [not] mercy on us, we shall certainly be of the losers. He said: ...[T]here is for you in the earth an abode and a provision for a time... Therein shall you live, and therein shall you die, and from it shall you be raised.

The Elevated Places 7:26 [He also said]: O children of Iblis! [I] have indeed sent down to you clothing to cover your shame, and for beauty and clothing that guards [against evil], that is the best. Ta Ha 20:123 [W]hoever follows My guidance, he shall not go astray nor be unhappy.

The "Luminous" Religion:

Source: Martin Palmer. The Jesus Sutras (Ballantine Wellspring, New York, 2001):

Their minds were empty; they were content; and their hearts were simple and innocent. Originally they had no desire... Under the influence of Satan, they abandoned their pure and simple goodness...

III. The Great Flood

Christianity/Judaism:

Genesis 6:

[18] I will establish My covenant with you; and you shall go into the ark — you, your sons, your wife, and your sons' wives with you. [19] And of every living thing of all flesh you shall bring two of every *sort* into the ark to keep *them* alive… they shall be male and female. [20] Of the birds after their kind, of animals after their kind, and of every creeping thing of the earth after its kind, two of every *kind* will come to you to keep *them* alive. [21] And you shall take for yourself of all food that is eaten, and you shall gather *it* to yourself; and it shall be food for you and for them."

Genesis 7:

[1] Then the LORD said to Noah, "Come into the ark, you and all your household because I have seen *that* you *are* righteous… [5] And Noah did according to all that the LORD commanded him. [6]

[7] So Noah, with his sons, his wife, and his sons' wives, went into the ark because of the waters of the flood. [8] Of animals… birds, and of everything that creeps on the earth – [15] of all flesh in which *is* the breath of life, [9] two by two they went into the ark… male and female. [10] And it came to pass after seven days that the waters of the flood were on the earth [11] [when] all the fountains of the great deep were broken up, and the windows of heaven were opened. [12] And the rain was on the earth forty days and forty nights.

[17] The waters increased and lifted up the ark, and it rose high above the earth. [18] The waters prevailed and greatly increased on the earth, and the ark moved about on the surface of the waters. [19] And the waters prevailed exceedingly on the earth, and all the high hills under the whole heaven were covered. [24] And the waters prevailed on the earth one hundred and fifty days.

Genesis 8:

[1] Then God remembered Noah, and every living thing, and all the animals that *were* with him in the ark. And God made a wind to pass over the earth, and the waters subsided. [2] The fountains of the deep and the windows of heaven were also stopped, and the rain from heaven was restrained. [3] And the waters receded… [4] Then the ark rested… on the mountains of Ararat. [5] And the waters decreased continually [until] the tops of the mountains were seen.

[6] So it came to pass, at the end of forty days, that Noah opened the window of the ark which he had made. [7] Then he sent out a raven, which kept going to and fro until the waters had dried up from the earth. [8] He also sent out a dove, to see if the waters had receded from the face of the ground. [9] But the dove found no resting place for the sole of her foot, and she returned into the ark to him, for the waters *were* on the face of the whole earth. [10] And he waited yet another seven days, and again he sent the dove out from the ark. [11] Then the dove came to him in the evening, and behold, a freshly plucked olive leaf *was* in her mouth; and Noah knew that the waters had receded from

the earth. [12] So he waited yet another seven days and sent out the dove, which did not return again to him anymore.

[13] And it came to pass… that the waters were dried up from the earth; and Noah removed the covering of the ark and looked, and indeed the surface of the ground was dry.

[15] Then God spoke to Noah, saying, [16] "Go out of the ark, you and your wife, and your sons and your sons' wives with you. [17] Bring out with you every living thing of all flesh that *is* with you: birds and cattle and every creeping thing that creeps on the earth, so that they may abound on the earth, and be fruitful and multiply on the earth." [18] So Noah went out, and his sons and his wife and his sons' wives with him. [19] Every animal, every creeping thing, every bird, *and* whatever creeps on the earth, according to their families, went out of the ark.

Genesis 9:

[8] Then God spoke to Noah and to his sons with him, saying: [9] "And as for Me, behold, I establish My covenant with you and with your descendants after you, [10] and with every living creature that *is* with you: the birds, the cattle, and every beast of the earth… [11][N]ever again shall there be a flood to destroy the earth." [13] I set My rainbow in the cloud [as] the sign of the covenant between Me and the earth. [14] It shall be, when I bring a cloud over the earth, that the rainbow shall be seen in the cloud; [15] and I will remember My covenant, which *is* between Me and you and every living creature.

Noah's Ark by Edward Hicks 1846

Islam:

Nuh 71:1-3 [I] sent Nuh (Noah) to his people, saying: Warn your people… He said: O my people! Surely I am a plain warner to you: That you should serve [God].

Nuh 71:15-17 Do you not see how [God] has created the… heavens… [a]nd made the moon therein a light, and made the sun a lamp? And [God] has made you grow out of the earth as a growth[?]

^{Nuh 71:11-12, 19-20} He [sent] down upon you the cloud, pouring down abundance of rain: And help[ed] you with wealth and son, and ma[de] for you gardens, and rivers. And [He] has made for you the earth a wide expanse, that you may go along therein in wide paths.

^{Nuh 71:7} [W]henever [Nuh] called them… they put their fingers in their ears, cover[ed] themselves with their garments, and persist[ed]… puffed up with pride.

^{The Holy Prophet 11:36-37,40} And it was revealed to Nuh: That none of your people will believe except those who have already believed, therefore do not grieve at what they do: And make the ark [according to] [My] revelation… Carry in it two of all things, a pair, and your own family…

^{The Holy Prophet 11:38,40} And he began to make the ark; and whenever the chiefs from among his people passed by him they laughed… [u]ntil… water came forth from the valley.

^{The Holy Prophet 11:41-42} And [Nuh] said: Embark… [I]n the name of [God] be its sailing and its anchoring; most surely my Lord is Forgiving [and] Merciful. And it moved on with them amid waves like mountains.

^{The Holy Prophet 11:44-45} And it was said: O earth, swallow down your water, and O cloud, clear away; and the water was made to abate and the affair was decided, and the ark rested on the Judi… And Nuh said: My Lord! [You are] the most just of judges.

^{The Holy Prophet 11:52} O my people! [A]sk forgiveness of your Lord, then turn to Him; He will send on you clouds pouring down abundance of rain and add strength to your strength, and do not turn back guilty.

^{The Holy Prophet 11:123} [T]herefore serve Him and rely on Him [for] your Lord is not heedless of what you do.

Hinduism:

Satapatha-Brahmana and The Mahabharata/Book 1: Adi Parva/Section LXXV:

One morning Manu, [who was] imbued with great wisdom and devoted to [piety and] virtue was [instructed by God, through a fish] – "…Build a ship; when the flood comes, go inside." He took [the] advice and built the ship. When the flood came, [Manu carried] the seed of every plant [inside while] one pair of each kind of animal [entered].

[The flood lasted 40 days causing the waters to rise. The water grew so high that the entire earth was covered]. Afterwards, when the waters subsided] the ship [came to rest on] a nearby mountain-side [where Manu tied it] to a tree [so that it would not drift].

[He was then instructed], "Come down the mountain slowly, as the water level drops." Manu did exactly what he was told… The flood destroyed every[thing] [but Manu [and everything in the ark], protected by God [survived]. [Afterwards Manu] was rewarded with a wife, with whom he began to repopulate the earth.

Additional Sources:

Manu. Myth Encyclopedia: Myths and Legends of the World.
http://www.mythencyclopedia.com/Le-Me/Manu.html

MANU AS THE INDIAN VERSION OF NOAH. 8 February 2010.
http://genesisflood.blog.com/2010/02/08/manu-as-the-indian-version-of-noah/

Antiquity of the Vedic Civilization- the Great Deluge. 10 February 2011.
http://biguniverse.co.cc/antiquity-of-the-vedic-civilization-the-great-deluge

Mayan Religion:

Source: Allen J. Christensen. **Popol Vuh: Literal Translation.** Mesoweb Publications. 29 November 2011. **http://www.mesoweb.com/publications/Christensen/PV-Literal.pdf:**

[729] It began darkened rain... [5584] blackened rain... [730-731] Day rain, Night rain... [5600-5601] Sorrowful their mouths, Sorrowful their faces... [5710] At [the sun's] coming out [5667] Then they were warmed... [4523] Greatly they rejoiced... [6164] Great joy there was...

Nahuan Religion:

Source: Flood Legends from Around the World. Northwest Creation Network. 4 December 2011.
http://www.nwcreation.net/noahlegends.html

A man named Tapi lived a long time ago. Tapi was a very pious man. The [C]reator told Tapi to build a boat that he would live in. He was told that he should take his wife, a pair of every animal that was alive into this boat. ...[E]veryone thought he was crazy. Then the rain started and the flood came. ...[T]he mountains became flooded as well. Finally the rain ended. Tapi decided that the water had dried up when he let a dove loose that did not return.

North American Indian:

Kaska:
Source: Mythical origins of language. Wikipedia.org. 19 November 2011:

"Before the flood, there was but one cent[er]; for all the people lived together in one country, and spoke one language."

IV. The Tower of Babel

Christianity/Judaism:

Genesis 11:

¹ Now the whole earth had one language and one speech. ² And it came to pass, as they journeyed from the east, that they found a plain in the land of Shinar, and they dwelt there. ³ Then they said to one another, "Come, let us make bricks and bake *them* thoroughly." They had brick for stone, and they had asphalt for mortar. ⁴ And they said, "Come, let us build ourselves a city, and a tower whose top *is* in the heavens; let us make a name for ourselves…"

⁵ But the LORD came down to see the city and the tower which the sons of men had built. ⁶ And the LORD said, "Indeed the people *are* one and they all have one language, and this is what they begin to do; now nothing that they propose to do will be withheld from them. ⁷ Come, let [Me] go down and there confuse their language, that they may not understand one another's speech." ⁸ So the LORD scattered them… over the face of all the earth, and they ceased building the city. ⁹ Therefore its name is called Babel, because there the LORD confused the language of all the earth; and from there the LORD scattered them abroad over the face of all the earth.

Islam:

Jonah 10:17 Who is then more unjust than who forges a lie against [God] or gives the lie to His communications? Surely the guilty shall not be successful. The Believer 40:35 Thus does [God] set a seal over the heart of every proud, haughty one.

The Narratives 28:38 Firon (Pharaoh) said: O chiefs! I do not know of any god for you besides myself; therefore kindle a fire for me, O Haman, for brick, then prepare for me a lofty building… The Believer 40:36-37 …[B]uild for me a tower that I may attain the means of access, to the heavens, then reach the God of Musa (Moses) [for] The Narratives 28:38 I surely think him to be a liar.

The Narratives 28:39 And he was unjustly proud in the land, he and his hosts… The Narratives 28:38 [a]nd thus the evil of his deed was made fairseeming to Firon, and he was turned away from the way; and the struggle of Firon was not in aught but destruction.

The Narratives 28:37 And Musa said: My Lord knows best who comes with guidance from Him, and whose shall be the good end of the abode; surely the unjust shall not be successful.

Jonah 10:19 And people are naught but a single nation, so they disagree; and had not a word already gone forth from your Lord, the matter would have certainly been decided between them in respect of that concerning which they disagree.

Hinduism:

Source: A. Dickson-White. The Warfare of Science With Theology – Chapter XVII – From Babel To Comparative Philology. 1995. 4 December 2011.

There grew in the cent[er] of the earth the wonderful `world tree,' or `knowledge tree.' It was so tall that it reached almost to heaven. It said in its heart, `I shall hold my head in heaven and spread my branches over all the earth, and gather all men together under my shadow, and protect them, and prevent them from separating.' But [God], to punish the pride of the tree, cut off its branches and cast them down on the earth…and made differences of belief and speech and customs to prevail on the earth, to disperse [the people] upon its surface.

V. The Patriarch Abraham

Christianity/Judaism:

Genesis 12:

[1] The LORD said to Abram: "[Go] [t]o a land that I will show you. [2] I will make you a great nation; I will bless you and make your name great..."

Genesis 14:

[18] Melchizedek king of Salem brought out bread and wine; he *was* the priest of God Most High. [19] And he blessed [Abram] and said: "Blessed be Abram of God Most High, Possessor of heaven and earth; [20] [a]nd blessed be God Most High..."

Genesis 12:

[4] So Abram [and his family] departed as the LORD had spoken to him... [5] [and] came to the land of Canaan.

Genesis 13:

[14] And the LORD said to Abram: "Lift your eyes now and look from the place where you are — northward, southward, eastward, and westward; [15] for all the land which you see I give to you and your descendants forever. [16] And I will make your descendants as the dust of the earth; so that if a man could number the dust of the earth, *then* your descendants also could be numbered."

Genesis 15:

[2] But Abram said, "Lord GOD, what will You give me, seeing I go childless?" [4] And behold, the word of the LORD *came* to him, saying, [5] "Look now toward heaven, and count the stars if you are able to number them... [s]o shall your descendants be."

Genesis 16:

[1] Now Sarai, Abram's wife, had borne him no *children*. And she had an Egyptian maidservant whose name was Hagar. [2] So Sarai said to Abram, "See now, the LORD has restrained me from bearing *children*. Please, go in to my maid; perhaps I shall obtain children by her." And Abram heeded the voice of Sarai. [3] Then Sarai, Abram's wife, took Hagar her maid, the Egyptian, and gave her to her husband Abram to be his wife... [4] So he went in to Hagar, and she conceived.

[9] The Angel of the LORD said to [Hagar]: [11] "Behold, you *are* with child, and you shall bear a son. You shall call his name Ishmael. [10] I will multiply your descendants exceedingly, so that they shall not be counted for multitude." [15] So Hagar bore Abram a son; and Abram named his son, whom Hagar bore, Ishmael.

Genesis 17:

[1] [T]he LORD appeared to Abram and said to him, "I *am* Almighty God; walk before Me and be blameless. [2] And I will make My covenant between Me and you, and will multiply you exceedingly." [3] Then Abram fell on his face, and God talked with him, saying: [4] "As for Me, behold, My covenant is with you, and you shall be a father of many nations. [5] No longer shall your name be called Abram, but your name shall be Abraham; for I have made you a father of many nations. [6] I will make you exceedingly fruitful; and I will make nations of you, and kings shall come from you. [7] And I will establish My covenant between Me and you and your descendants after you in their generations, for an everlasting covenant, to be God to you and your descendants after you."

[15] Then God said to Abraham, "As for Sarai your wife, you shall not call her name Sarai, but Sarah *shall be* her name. [16] And I will bless her and also give you a son by her; then I will bless her, and she shall be *a mother of* nations; kings of peoples shall be from her." [7] Then Abraham fell on his face and laughed, and said in his heart, "Shall *a child* be born to a man who is one hundred years old? And shall Sarah, who is ninety years old, bear *a child?*" [18] And Abraham said to God, "Oh, that Ishmael might live before You!"

[19] Then God said: "No, Sarah your wife shall bear you a son, and you shall call his name Isaac; I will establish My covenant with him for an everlasting covenant, *and* with his descendants after him. [20] And as for Ishmael, I have heard you. Behold, I have blessed him, and will make him fruitful, and will multiply him exceedingly. He shall beget twelve princes, and I will make him a great nation." [22] Then He finished talking with him, and God went up from Abraham.

Genesis 18:

[1] Then the LORD appeared to [Abraham] by the terebinth trees of Mamre, as he was sitting in the tent door in the heat of the day. [2] So he lifted his eyes and looked, and behold, three men were standing by him; and when he saw *them,* he ran from the tent door to meet them, and bowed himself to the ground, [3] and said, "My Lord, if I have now found favor in Your sight, do not pass on by Your servant. [4] Please let a little water be brought, and wash your feet, and rest yourselves under the tree. [5] And I will bring a morsel of bread, that you may refresh your hearts. After that you may pass by, inasmuch as you have come to your servant."

They said, "Do as you have said." [6] So Abraham hurried into the tent to Sarah and said, "Quickly, make ready three measures of fine meal; knead *it* and make cakes." [7] And Abraham ran to the herd, took a tender and good calf, gave *it* to a young man, and he hastened to prepare it. [8] So he took butter and milk and the calf, which he had prepared, and set *it* before them; and he stood by them under the tree as they ate.

[9] Then they said to him, "Where *is* Sarah your wife?" So he said, "Here, in the tent." [10] And He said, "I will certainly return to you according to the time of life, and behold, Sarah your wife shall have a son." [11] Now Abraham and Sarah were old, well

advanced in age; *and* Sarah had passed the age of childbearing. [12] Therefore Sarah laughed within herself, saying, "After I have grown old, shall I have pleasure, my lord being old also?"

[13] And the LORD said to Abraham, "Why did Sarah laugh, saying, 'Shall I surely bear *a child,* since I am old?' [14] Is anything too hard for the LORD? At the appointed time I will return to you, according to the time of life, and Sarah shall have a son."

Genesis 21:

[1] And the LORD visited Sarah as He had said, and the LORD did for Sarah as He had spoken. [2] For Sarah conceived and bore Abraham a son in his old age, at the set time of which God had spoken to him. [3] And Abraham called the name of his son who was born to him — whom Sarah bore to him — Isaac. [8] So the child grew and was weaned. And Abraham made a great feast on the same day that Isaac was weaned.

[14] …Abraham rose early in the morning, and took bread and a skin of water; and putting *it* on her shoulder, he gave *it* and the boy to Hagar, and sent her away. Then she departed and wandered in the Wilderness of Beersheba. [15] And the water in the skin was used up, and she placed the boy under one of the shrubs. [16] Then she went and sat down [a distance] from *him*… for she said to herself, "Let me not see the death of the boy." So she sat opposite *him,* and lifted her voice and wept.

[17] And God heard the voice of the lad. Then the angel of God called to Hagar out of heaven, and said to her, "What ails you, Hagar? Fear not, for God has heard the voice of the lad where he *is.* [18] Arise, lift up the lad and hold him with your hand, for I will make him a great nation." [19] Then God opened her eyes, and she saw a well of water. And she went and filled the skin with water, and gave the lad a drink. [20] So God was with the lad…

Genesis 22:

[1] Now it came to pass after these things that God tested Abraham, and said to him, "Abraham!" And he said, "Here I am." [2] Then He said, "Take now your son, your only *son* Isaac, whom you love, and go to the land of Moriah, and offer him there as a burnt offering on one of the mountains of which I shall tell you."

[3] So Abraham rose early in the morning and saddled his donkey, and took two of his young men with him, and Isaac his son; and he split the wood for the burnt offering, and arose and went to the place of which God had told him. [5] And Abraham said to his young men, "Stay here with the donkey; the lad and I will go yonder and worship, and we will come back to you."

[6] So Abraham took the wood of the burnt offering and laid *it* on Isaac his son; and he took the fire in his hand, and a knife, and the two of them went together. [7] But Isaac spoke to Abraham his father and said, "My father!" And he said, "Here I am, my son." Then he said, "Look, the fire and the wood, but where *is* the lamb for a burnt offering?" [8] And Abraham said, "My son, God will provide for Himself the lamb for a burnt offering." So the two of them went together.

⁹ Then they came to the place of which God had told him. And Abraham built an altar there and placed the wood in order; and he bound Isaac his son and laid him on the altar, upon the wood. ¹⁰ And Abraham stretched out his hand and took the knife to slay his son.

¹¹ But the Angel of the LORD called to him from heaven and said, "Abraham, Abraham!" So he said, "Here I am." ¹² And He said, "Do not lay your hand on the lad, or do anything to him; for now I know that you fear God, since you have not withheld your son, your only *son,* from Me."

¹³ Then Abraham lifted his eyes and looked, and there behind *him was* a ram caught in a thicket by its horns. So Abraham went and took the ram, and offered it up for a burnt offering instead of his son.

¹⁵ Then the Angel of the LORD called to Abraham a second time out of heaven, ¹⁶ and said: "By Myself I have sworn, says the LORD, because you have done this thing, and have not withheld your son, your only *son* — ¹⁷ blessing I will bless you, and multiplying I will multiply your descendants as the stars of the heaven and as the sand which *is* on the seashore… ¹⁸ In your seed all the nations of the earth shall be blessed, because you have obeyed My voice."

Genesis 24:

¹ [T]he LORD had blessed Abraham in all things.

Islam:

The Cow 2:124 And when [the] Lord tried Ibrahim (Abraham) with certain words, he fulfilled them. He said: Surely I will make you an Imam of men. The Holy Prophet 11:69-70 And certainly [My] messengers came to Ibrahim with good news. They said: Peace. Peace, said he, and he made no delay in bringing a roasted calf. But when he saw that their hands were not extended towards it, he deemed them strange and conceived fear of them. They said: Fear not...

The Holy Prophet 11:71-73 And his wife was standing (by), so she laughed, then [I] gave her the good news of Ishaq (Isaac) and after Ishaq of (a son's son) Yaqoub (Jacob). She said: O wonder! [S]hall I bear a son when I am an extremely old woman and this my husband [is] an extremely old man? Most surely this is a wonderful thing. They said: Do you wonder at [God's] bidding? The mercy of [God] and His blessings are on you, O people of the house, surely He is Praised, Glorious.

Abraham 14:39 Praise be to [God], Who has given me in old age Ismail (Ishmael) and Ishaq; most surely my Lord is the Hearer of prayer.

The Rangers 37:102 And when [Ibrahim] attained to working with [Ishaq], he said: O my son! [S]urely I have seen in a dream that I should sacrifice you; consider then what you see. [Ishaq] said: O my father! [D]o what you are commanded; if [God] please[s], you will find me of the patient ones.

The Rangers 37:103-105 So when they both submitted and he threw him down upon his forehead, [a]nd [God] called out to him saying: O Ibrahim! You have indeed shown the truth of the vision; surely thus do [I] reward the doers of good.

The Rangers 37:109-113 Peace be on Ibrahim. Thus do [I] reward the doers of good. Surely he was one of [My] believing servants. And [I] gave him the good news of Ishaq, a prophet among the good ones. And [I] showered [My] blessings on him and on Ishaq; and o[n] their offspring.

Marium 19:54 And mention Ismail in the Book; surely he was truthful in (his) promise, and he was an apostle, a prophet. The Cattle 6:86-87 And Ismail… and every one [I] made to excel (in) the worlds: And from among their fathers and their descendants and their brethren, and [I] chose them and guided them into the right way.

The Cow 2:125-128 And [God] enjoined Ibrahim and Ismail saying: Purify My House for those who visit and those who abide for devotion and those who bow down (and) those who prostrate themselves. And when Ibrahim said: My Lord, make it… secure …and provide its people with fruits… And when Ibrahim and Ismail raised the foundations of the House: Our Lord! [A]ccept from us; surely [You are] the Hearing, the Knowing: Our Lord! [M]ake us both submissive to [You] and (raise) from our offspring a nation submitting to [You], and show us [Y]our ways…

The Cow 2:131-132 I submit myself to the Lord of the worlds. And the same did Ibrahim enjoin on his sons and (so did) Yaqoub.

VI. Joseph

Christianity/Judaism:

Genesis 37:

[3] [Jacob named "Israel' by an angel] loved Joseph more than all his children... [4] [W]hen his brothers saw that their father loved him more than all his brothers, they hated him and could not speak peaceably to him.

[5] Now Joseph had a dream, and he told *it* to his brothers: [7] "There we were, binding sheaves in the field. Then behold, my sheaf arose and also stood upright; and indeed your sheaves stood all around and bowed down to my sheaf." [8] And his brothers said to him, "Shall you indeed reign over us? Or shall you indeed have dominion over us?" So they hated him even more...

[9] Then he dreamed still another dream and told it to his brothers, and said, "Look, I have dreamed another dream. And this time, the sun, the moon, and the eleven stars bowed down to me."

[10] So he told *it* to his father and his brothers; and his father rebuked him and said to him, "What *is* this dream that you have dreamed? Shall your mother and I and your brothers indeed come to bow down to the earth before you?" [11] And his brothers envied him, but his father kept the matter *in mind.*

[12] Then his brothers went to feed their father's flock. [13] And Israel said to Joseph, "Are not your brothers feeding *the flock*? Come, I will send you to them." So he said to him, "Here I am."

[14] Then he said to him, "Please go and see if it is well with your brothers and well with the flocks, and bring back word to me." [17] So Joseph went after his brothers and found them...

[18] Now when they saw him afar off, even before he came near them, they conspired to kill him. [19] Then they said to one another, "Look, this dreamer is coming! [20] Come therefore, let us now kill him and cast him into some pit; and we shall say, 'Some wild beast has devoured him.' We shall see what will become of his dreams!"

[21] But Reuben heard *it,* and he delivered him out of their hands, and said, "Let us not kill him. [22] And Reuben said to them, "Shed no blood, *but* cast him into this pit which *is* in the wilderness, and do not lay a hand on him" — that he might deliver him out of their hands, and bring him back to his father.

[23] So it came to pass, when Joseph had come to his brothers, that they stripped Joseph *of* his tunic... [24] Then they took him and cast him into a pit. And the pit *was* empty; *there was* no water in it.

[25] And they sat down to eat a meal. Then they lifted their eyes and looked, and there was a company of Ishmaelites, coming with their camels, bearing spices, balm, and myrrh, on their way to carry *them* down to Egypt. [26] So Judah said to his brothers,

"What profit *is there* if we kill our brother and conceal his blood? ^{27} Come and let us sell him to the Ishmaelites, and let not our hand be upon him, for he *is* our brother *and* our flesh." And his brothers listened. ^{28} Then Midianite traders passed by; so *the brothers* pulled Joseph up and lifted him out of the pit, and sold him to the Ishmaelites for twenty *shekels* of silver. And they took Joseph to Egypt. ^{29} Then Reuben returned to the pit, and indeed Joseph *was* not in the pit; and he tore his clothes. ^{30} And he returned to his brothers and said, "The lad *is* no *more;* and I, where shall I go?"

^{31} So they took Joseph's tunic, killed a kid of the goats, and dipped the tunic in the blood. ^{32} Then they sent the tunic of *many* colors, and they brought *it* to their father and said, "We have found this. Do you know whether it *is* your son's tunic or not?" ^{33} And he recognized it and said, "*It is* my son's tunic. A wild beast has devoured him. Without doubt Joseph is torn to pieces." ^{34} Then Jacob tore his clothes, put sackcloth on his waist, and mourned for his son many days. ^{35} And all his sons and all his daughters arose to comfort him; but he refused to be comforted, and he said, "For I shall go down into the grave to my son in mourning." Thus his father wept for him.

Genesis 39:

^{1} Now Joseph had been taken down to Egypt. And Potiphar, an officer of Pharaoh, captain of the guard, an Egyptian, bought him from the Ishmaelites who had taken him down there. ^{2} The LORD was with Joseph, and he was a successful man; and he was in the house of his master the Egyptian. ^{3} And his master saw that the LORD *was* with him and that the LORD made all he did to prosper in his hand. ^{4} So Joseph found favor in his sight, and served him. Then he made him overseer of his house, and all *that* he had he put under his authority. ^{5} So it was, from the time *that* he had made him overseer of his house and all that he had, that the LORD blessed the Egyptian's house for Joseph's sake; and the blessing of the LORD was on all that he had in the house and in the field. ^{6} Thus he left all that he had in Joseph's hand, and he did not know what he had except for the bread which he ate.

Now Joseph was handsome in form and appearance. ^{7} And it came to pass after these things that his master's wife cast longing eyes on Joseph, and she said, "Lie with me."

^{8} But he refused and said to his master's wife, "Look, my master does not know what *is* with me in the house, and he has committed all that he has to my hand. ^{9} *There is* no one greater in this house than I, nor has he kept back anything from me but you, because you *are* his wife. How then can I do this great wickedness, and sin against God?" ^{10} So it was, as she spoke to Joseph day by day, that he did not heed her, to lie with her *or* to be with her.

^{11} But it happened about this time, when Joseph went into the house to do his work, and none of the men of the house *was* inside, ^{12} that she caught him by his garment, saying, "Lie with me." But he left his garment in her hand, and fled and ran outside. ^{16} So she kept his garment with her until his master came home. ^{17} Then she spoke to him saying, "The Hebrew servant whom you brought to us came in to mock me; ^{18} so it happened, as I lifted my voice and cried out, that he left his garment with me and fled outside."

¹⁹ So it was, when [Potiphar] heard the words [of] his wife that his anger was aroused. ²⁰ Then Joseph's master took him and put him into the prison... ²¹ But the LORD was with Joseph and showed him mercy, and He gave him favor in the sight of the keeper of the prison. ²² And the keeper of the prison committed to Joseph's hand all the prisoners who *were* in the prison; whatever they did there, it was his doing. ²³ The keeper of the prison did not look into anything *that was* under *Joseph's* authority, because the LORD was with him; and whatever he did, the LORD made *it* prosper.

Genesis 41:

¹ Then it came to pass, at the end of two full years, that Pharaoh had a dream. ⁵ He slept and dreamed a second time... ⁸ Now it came to pass in the morning that his spirit was troubled... but *there was* no one who could interpret them for Pharaoh.

⁹ Then the chief butler spoke to Pharaoh – ¹² [T]here *was* a young Hebrew man with us [in prison], a servant of the captain of the guard. And we told him, and he interpreted our dreams for us; ¹³ [a]nd [they] came to pass, just as he interpreted for us.

¹⁴ Then Pharaoh sent and called Joseph, and they brought him quickly out of the dungeon; and he shaved, changed his clothing, and came to Pharaoh. ¹⁵ And Pharaoh said to Joseph, "I have had a dream, and *there is* no one who can interpret it. But I have heard it said of you *that* you can understand a dream, to interpret it." ¹⁶ So Joseph answered Pharaoh, saying, "*It is* not in me; God will give Pharaoh an answer of peace."

¹⁷ Then Pharaoh said to Joseph: "Behold, in my dream I stood on the bank of the river. ¹⁸ Suddenly seven cows came up out of the river, fine looking and fat; and they fed in the meadow. ¹⁹ Then behold, seven other cows came up after them, poor and very ugly and gaunt, such ugliness as I have never seen in all the land of Egypt. ²⁰ And the gaunt and ugly cows ate up the first seven, the fat cows. ²¹ When they had eaten them up, no one would have known that they had eaten them, for they *were* just as ugly as at the beginning. So I awoke. ²² Also I saw in my dream, and suddenly seven heads came up on one stalk, full and good. ²³ Then behold, seven heads, withered, thin, *and* blighted by the east wind, sprang up after them. ²⁴ And the thin heads devoured the seven good heads."

²⁵ Then Joseph said to Pharaoh, "The dreams of Pharaoh *are* one: ²⁶ The seven good cows *are* seven years, and the seven good heads *are* seven years; the dreams *are* one. ²⁷ And the seven thin and ugly cows which came up after them *are* seven years, and the seven empty heads blighted by the east wind are seven years of famine. ²⁹ Indeed seven years of great plenty will come throughout all the land of Egypt; ³⁰ but after them seven years of famine will arise, and all the plenty will be forgotten in the land of Egypt; and the famine will deplete the land. ³¹ So the plenty will not be known in the land because of the famine following, for it *will be* very severe.

³³ "Now therefore, let Pharaoh select a discerning and wise man, and set him over

the land of Egypt. ³⁴ Let Pharaoh do *this,* and let him appoint officers over the land, to collect one-fifth *of the produce* of the land of Egypt in the seven plentiful years. ³⁵ And let them gather all the food of those good years that are coming, and store up grain under the authority of Pharaoh, and let them keep food in the cities. ³⁶ Then that food shall be as a reserve for the land for the seven years of famine which shall be in the land of Egypt, that the land may not perish during the famine."

³⁷ So the advice was good in the eyes of Pharaoh and in the eyes of all his servants. ³⁸ And Pharaoh said to his servants, "Can we find *such a one* as this, a man in whom *is* the Spirit of God?"

³⁹ Then Pharaoh said to Joseph, "Inasmuch as God has shown you all this, *there is* no one as discerning and wise as you. ⁴⁰ You shall be over my house, and all my people shall be ruled according to your word; only in regard to the throne will I be greater than you." ⁴¹ And Pharaoh said to Joseph, "See, I have set you over all the land of Egypt."

⁴⁵ So Joseph went out over *all* the land of Egypt.

⁴⁷ Now in the seven plentiful years the ground brought forth abundantly. ⁴⁸ So he gathered up all the food of the seven years, which were in the land of Egypt, and laid up the food in the cities; he laid up in every city the food of the fields which surrounded them. ⁴⁹ Joseph gathered very much grain, as the sand of the sea, until he stopped counting, for *it was* immeasurable.

⁵³ Then the seven years of plenty which were in the land of Egypt ended, ⁵⁴ and the seven years of famine began to come, as Joseph had said. The famine was in all lands, but in all the land of Egypt there was bread. ⁵⁵ So when all the land of Egypt was famished, the people cried to Pharaoh for bread. Then Pharaoh said to all the Egyptians, "Go to Joseph; whatever he says to you, do." ⁵⁶ The famine was over all the face of the earth, and Joseph opened all the storehouses and sold to the Egyptians. And the famine became severe in the land of Egypt. ⁵⁷ So all countries came to Joseph in Egypt to buy *grain,* because the famine was severe in all lands.

Genesis 42:

¹ When Jacob saw that there was grain in Egypt, Jacob said to his sons, "Why do you look at one another?" ² And he said, "Indeed I have heard that there is grain in Egypt; go down to that place and buy for us there, that we may live and not die." ³ So Joseph's ten brothers went down to buy grain in Egypt. ⁴ But Jacob did not send Joseph's brother Benjamin with his brothers, for he said, "Lest some calamity befall him." ⁵ And the sons of Israel went to buy *grain* among those who journeyed, for the famine was in the land of Canaan.

⁶ Now Joseph *was* governor over the land; and it was he who sold to all the people of the land. And Joseph's brothers came and bowed down before him with *their* faces to the earth. ⁷ Joseph saw his brothers and recognized them, but he acted as a stranger to them and spoke roughly to them. Then he said to them, "Where do you come from?" And they said, "From the land of Canaan to buy food."

⁸ So Joseph recognized his brothers, but they did not recognize him.

[9] Then Joseph remembered the dreams which he had dreamed about them, and said to them, "...You have come to see the nakedness of the land!" [10] And they said to him, "No, my lord... your servants have come to buy food. [11] We *are* all one man's sons; we *are* honest *men*... [13] Your servants *are* twelve brothers, the sons of one man in the land of Canaan; and in fact, the youngest *is* with our father today, and one *is* no more."

[14] But Joseph said to them, "It *is* as I spoke to you... [15] In this *manner* you shall be tested: By the life of Pharaoh, you shall not leave this place unless your youngest brother comes here. [16] Send one of you, and let him bring your brother; and you shall be kept in prison, that your words may be tested to see whether *there is* any truth in you..." [17] So he put them all together in prison three days.

[18] Then Joseph said to them the third day... [19] "If you *are* honest *men,* let one of your brothers be confined to your prison house; but you, go and carry grain for the famine of your houses. [20] And bring your youngest brother to me; so your words will be verified, and you shall not die."

And they did so. [21] Then they said to one another, "We *are* truly guilty concerning our brother, for we saw the anguish of his soul when he pleaded with us, and we would not hear; therefore this distress has come upon us." [22] And Reuben answered them, saying, "Did I not speak to you, saying, 'Do not sin against the boy'; and you would not listen? Therefore behold, his blood is now required of us." [23] But they did not know that Joseph understood *them,* for he spoke to them through an interpreter. [24] And he turned himself away from them and wept. Then he returned to them again, and talked with them. And he took Simeon from them and bound him before their eyes.

[25] Then Joseph gave a command to fill their sacks with grain, to restore every man's money to his sack, and to give them provisions for the journey. Thus he did for them. [26] So they loaded their donkeys with the grain and departed from there. [27] But as one *of them* opened his sack to give his donkey feed at the encampment, he saw his money; and there it was, in the mouth of his sack. [28] So he said to his brothers, "My money has been restored, and there it is, in my sack!" Then their hearts failed *them* and they were afraid, saying to one another, "What *is* this *that* God has done to us?"

[29] Then they went to Jacob their father in the land of Canaan and told him all that had happened... [35] Then it happened as they emptied their sacks... and when they and their father saw the bundles of money, they were afraid. [36] And Jacob their father said to them, "You have bereaved me: Joseph is no *more,* Simeon is no *more,* and you want to take Benjamin. All these things are against me." [37] Then Reuben spoke to his father, saying, "...[P]ut him in my hands, and I will bring him back to you."

[38] But he said, "My son shall not go down with you, for his brother is dead, and he is left alone. If any calamity should befall him along the way in which you go, then you would bring down my gray hair with sorrow to the grave."

Genesis 43:

[1] Now the famine *was* severe in the land. [2] And it came to pass, when they had eaten

up the grain which they had brought from Egypt, that their father said to them, "Go back, buy us a little food."

³ But Judah spoke to him, saying, "The man solemnly warned us, saying, 'You shall not see my face unless your brother *is* with you.' ⁴ If you send our brother with us, we will go down and buy you food. ⁵ But if you will not send *him,* we will not go down; for the man said to us, 'You shall not see my face unless your brother *is* with you.'" ⁶ And Israel said, "Why did you deal *so* wrongfully with me *as* to tell the man whether you had still *another* brother?"

⁷ But they said, "The man asked us pointedly about ourselves and our family, saying, '*Is* your father still alive? Have you *another* brother?' And we told him according to these words. Could we possibly have known that he would say, 'Bring your brother down?'"

⁸ Then Judah said to Israel his father, "Send the lad with me, and we will arise and go, that we may live and not die, both we and you *and* also our little ones. ⁹ I myself will be surety for him; from my hand you shall require him. If I do not bring him *back* to you and set him before you, then let me bear the blame forever. ¹⁰ For if we had not lingered, surely by now we would have returned this second time."

¹¹ And their father Israel said to them, "If *it must be* so, then do this: Take some of the best fruits of the land in your vessels and carry down a present for the man — a little balm and a little honey, spices and myrrh, pistachio nuts and almonds. ¹² Take double money in your hand, and take back in your hand the money that was returned in the mouth of your sacks; perhaps it was an oversight. ¹³ Take your brother also, and arise, go back to the man. ¹⁴ And may God Almighty give you mercy before the man, that he may release your other brother and Benjamin. If I am bereaved, I am bereaved!"

¹⁵ So the men took that present and Benjamin, and they took double money in their hand, and arose and went down to Egypt; and they stood before Joseph. ¹⁶ When Joseph saw Benjamin with them, he said to the steward of his house, "Take *these* men to my home... for [*they*] will dine with me." ¹⁷ Then the man did as Joseph ordered and brought the men into Joseph's house.

¹⁸ Now the men were afraid because they were brought into Joseph's house; and they said, "*It is* because of the money, which was returned in our sacks the first time, that we are brought in, so that he may make a case against us and seize us, to take us as slaves with our donkeys."

¹⁹ When they drew near to the steward of Joseph's house, they talked with him at the door of the house, ²⁰ and said, "O sir, we indeed came down the first time to buy food; ²¹ but it happened, when we came to the encampment, that we opened our sacks, and there, *each* man's money *was* in the mouth of his sack, our money in full weight; so we have brought it back in our hand. ²² And we have brought down other money in our hands to buy food. We do not know who put our money in our sacks." ²³ But he said, "Peace *be* with you, do not be afraid. Your God and the God of your father has given you treasure in your sacks; I had your money." Then he brought Simeon out to them.

^{24} So the man brought the men into Joseph's house and gave *them* water, and they washed their feet; and he gave their donkeys feed. ^{25} Then they made the present ready for Joseph's coming at noon, for they heard that they would eat bread there. ^{26} And when Joseph came home, they brought him the present, which *was* in their hand into the house, and bowed down before him to the earth. ^{27} Then he asked them about *their* well-being, and said, "*Is* your father well, the old man of whom you spoke? *Is* he still alive?"

^{28} And they answered, "Your servant our father *is* in good health; he *is* still alive." And they bowed their heads down and prostrated themselves.

^{29} Then he lifted his eyes and saw his brother Benjamin, his mother's son, and said, "*Is* this your younger brother of whom you spoke to me?" And he said, "God be gracious to you, my son." ^{30} Now his heart yearned for his brother; so Joseph made haste and sought *somewhere* to weep. And he went into *his* chamber and wept there. ^{31} Then he washed his face and came out; and he restrained himself, and said, "Serve the bread."

^{33} And they sat before him, the firstborn according to his birthright and the youngest according to his youth; and the men looked in astonishment at one another. ^{34} Then he took servings to them from before him, but Benjamin's serving was five times as much as any of theirs. So they drank and were merry with him.

Genesis 44:

^{1} And he commanded the steward of his house, saying, "Fill the men's sacks with food, as much as they can carry, and put each man's money in the mouth of his sack.

Genesis 45:

^{1} Then Joseph could not restrain himself before all those who stood by him, and he cried out, "Make everyone go out from me!" So no one stood with him while Joseph made himself known to his brothers. ^{2} And he wept aloud...

^{3} Then Joseph said to his brothers, "I *am* Joseph; does my father still live?" But his brothers could not answer him, for they were dismayed in his presence. ^{4} And Joseph said to his brothers, "Please come near to me." So they came near. Then he said: "I *am* Joseph your brother, whom you sold into Egypt. ^{5} But now, do not therefore be grieved or angry with yourselves because you sold me here; for God sent me before you to preserve life. ^{6} For these two years the famine *has been* in the land, and *there are* still five years in which *there will be* neither plowing nor harvesting. ^{7} And God sent me before you to preserve a posterity for you in the earth, and to save your lives by a great deliverance. ^{8} So now *it was* not you *who* sent me here, but God; and He has made me a father to Pharaoh, and lord of all his house, and a ruler throughout all the land of Egypt.

^{9} Hurry and go up to my father, and say to him, Thus says your son Joseph: 'God has made me lord of all Egypt; come down to me, do not tarry. ^{10} You shall dwell in the land of Goshen, and you shall be near to me, you and your children, your children's children, your flocks and your herds, and all that you have. ^{11} There I will provide for you, lest you and your household, and all that you have, come to poverty; for *there are* still five years of famine.'

¹² And behold, your eyes and the eyes of my brother Benjamin see that *it is* my mouth that speaks to you. ¹³ So you shall tell my father of all my glory in Egypt, and of all that you have seen; and you shall hurry and bring my father down here." ¹⁵ [H]e kissed all his brothers and wept over them, and after that his brothers talked with him.

¹⁶ Now the report of it was heard in Pharaoh's house, saying, "Joseph's brothers have come." So it pleased Pharaoh and his servants well. ¹⁷ And Pharaoh said to Joseph, "Say to your brothers, 'Do this: Load your animals and depart; go to the land of Canaan. ¹⁸ Bring your father and your households and come to me; I will give you the best of the land of Egypt, and you will eat the fat of the land. ¹⁹ Now you are commanded — do this: Take carts out of the land of Egypt for your little ones and your wives; bring your father and come. ²⁰ Also do not be concerned about your goods, for the best of all the land of Egypt *is* yours.'"

²¹ Then the sons of Israel did so; and Joseph gave them carts, according to the command of Pharaoh, and he gave them provisions for the journey. ²² He gave to all of them, to each man, changes of garments; but to Benjamin he gave three hundred *pieces* of silver and five changes of garments. ²³ And he sent to his father these *things:* ten donkeys loaded with the good things of Egypt, and ten female donkeys loaded with grain, bread, and food for his father for the journey. ²⁴ So he sent his brothers away, and they departed; and he said to them, "See that you do not become troubled along the way."

²⁵ Then they went up out of Egypt, and came to the land of Canaan to Jacob their father. ²⁶ And they told him, saying, "Joseph *is* still alive, and he *is* governor over all the land of Egypt." And Jacob's heart stood still, because he did not believe them. ²⁷ But when they told him all the words, which Joseph had said to them, and when he saw the carts which Joseph had sent to carry him, the spirit of Jacob their father revived. ²⁸ Then Israel said, "*It is* enough. Joseph my son *is* still alive. I will go and see him before I die."

Genesis 46:

¹ So Israel took his journey with all that he had... and offered sacrifices to... God... ² Then God spoke to Israel in the visions of the night, and said, "Jacob, Jacob!" And he said, "Here I am."

³ So He said, "I *am* God, the God of your father; do not fear to go down to Egypt, for I will make of you a great nation there. ⁴ I will go down with you to Egypt, and I will also surely bring you up *again;* and Joseph will put his hand on your eyes."

⁵ Then Jacob arose... and the sons of Israel carried their father Jacob, their little ones, and their wives, in the carts which Pharaoh had sent to carry him. ⁶ So they took their livestock and their goods, which they had acquired in the land of Canaan, and went to Egypt, Jacob and all his descendants with him. ²⁷ All the persons of the house of Jacob who went to Egypt were seventy.

²⁸ Then he sent Judah before him to Joseph, to point out before him *the way* to Goshen. And they came to the land of Goshen. ²⁹ So Joseph made ready his chariot and went up to Goshen to meet his father Israel; and he presented himself to him, and wept a good while.

³⁰ And Israel said to Joseph, "Now let me die, since I have seen your face, because you *are* still alive."

Genesis 47:

¹ Then Joseph went and told Pharaoh, and said, "My father and my brothers, their flocks and their herds and all that they possess, have come from the land of Canaan; and indeed they *are* in the land of Goshen." ² And he took five men from among his brothers and presented them to Pharaoh. ³ Then Pharaoh said to his brothers, "What *is* your occupation?"

And they said to Pharaoh, "Your servants *are* shepherds, both we *and* also our fathers... ⁴ We have come to dwell in the land, because your servants have no pasture for their flocks, for the famine *is* severe in the land of Canaan. Now therefore, please let your servants dwell in the land of Goshen."

⁵ Then Pharaoh spoke to Joseph, saying, "Your father and your brothers have come to you. ⁶ The land of Egypt *is* before you. Have your father and brothers dwell in the best of the land; let them dwell in the land of Goshen. And if you know *any* competent men among them, then make them chief herdsmen over my livestock." ⁷ Then Joseph brought in his father Jacob and set him before Pharaoh; and Jacob blessed Pharaoh.

¹¹ And Joseph situated his father and his brothers, and gave them a possession in the land of Egypt, in the best of the land... as Pharaoh had commanded. ¹² Then Joseph provided his father, his brothers, and all his father's household with bread, according to the number in *their* families.

²⁷ So Israel dwelt in the land of Egypt, in the country of Goshen; and they had possessions there and grew and multiplied exceedingly. ²⁹ When the time drew near that Israel must die, he called his son Joseph and said to him, "Please do not bury me in Egypt, ³⁰ but let me lie with my fathers; you shall carry me out of Egypt and bury me in their burial place." And he said, "I will do as you have said."

Genesis 50:

²² Joseph dwelt in Egypt, he and his father's household. ²⁴ [But he] said to his brethren, "...God will surely visit you, and bring you out of this land to the land of which He swore to Abraham, to Isaac, and to Jacob."

Islam:

^{Yusuf 12:4-6} When Yusuf (Joseph) said to his father: O my father! [S]urely I saw eleven stars and the sun and the moon — I saw them making obeisance to me. He said: O my son! [D]o not relate your vision to your brothers, lest they devise a plan against

you; surely the Shaitan (Satan) is an open enemy to man. And thus will your Lord choose you and teach you the interpretation of sayings and make His favor complete to you and to the children of Yaqoub (Jacob), as He made it complete before to your fathers, Ibrahim (Abraham) and Ishaq (Isaac).

Yusuf 12:8-10 When they said: Certainly Yusuf and his brother are dearer to our father than we, though we are a (stronger) company; most surely our father is in manifest error: Slay Yusuf or cast him (forth) into some land, so that your father's regard may be exclusively for you, and after that you may be a righteous people. A speaker from among them said: Do not slay Yusuf, and cast him down into the bottom of the pit if you must do (it), (so that) some of the travellers may pick him up.

Yusuf 12:11-14 They said: O our father! what reason have you that you do not trust in us with respect to Yusuf? And most surely we are his sincere well-wishers: Send him with us tomorrow that he may enjoy himself and sport, and surely we will guard him well. He said: Surely it grieves me that you should take him off, and I fear lest the wolf devour him while you are heedless of him. They said: Surely if the wolf should devour him notwithstanding that we are a (strong) company, we should then certainly be losers.

Yusuf 12:15 So when they had gone off with him… they… put him down at the bottom of the pit…

Yusuf 12:16-18 And they came to their father at nightfall, weeping. They said: O our father! [S]urely we went off racing and left Yusuf by our goods, so the wolf devoured him, and you will not believe us though we are truthful. And they brought his shirt with false blood upon it. He said: Nay, your souls have made the matter light for you, but patience is good and [God] is He Whose help is sought for against what you describe.

Yusuf 12:16-18 And there came travellers and they sent their water-drawer and he let down his bucket. He said: O good news! [T]his is a youth; and they concealed him as an article of merchandise, and [God] knew what they did. And they sold him for a small price, a few pieces of silver, and they showed no desire for him. And the Egyptian who bought him said to his wife: Give him an honorable abode, maybe he will be useful to us, or we may adopt him as a son. And thus did [God] establish Yusuf in the land and that [He] might teach him the interpretation of sayings; and [God] is the master of His affair, but most people do not know.

Yusuf 12:16 And when he had attained his maturity, [God] gave him wisdom and knowledge: and thus do[es] [He] reward those who do good.

Yusuf 12:23-27 And she in whose house he was sought to make himself yield (to her), and she made fast the doors and said: Come forward. He said: I seek [God's] refuge, surely my Lord made good my abode: Surely the unjust do not prosper. And certainly she made for him, and he would have made for her, were it not that he had seen the manifest evidence of his Lord; thus that [He] might turn away from him evil and indecency, surely he was one of [God's] sincere servants. And they both hastened to the door, and she rent his shirt from behind and they met her husband at the door. She said: What is the punishment of him who intends evil to your wife except imprisonment or a painful chastisement? [Yusuf] said: She sought to make me yield (to her); and a witness of her own family bore witness: If his shirt is rent from front, she speaks the truth and he is one of the liars: And if his shirt is rent from behind, she tells a lie and he is one of the truthful.

Yusuf 12:28-30 So when he saw his shirt rent from behind, he said: Surely it is a guile of you...; surely your guile is great: O Yusuf! turn aside from this; and (O my wife)! [A]sk forgiveness for your fault... And women in the city said: The chief's wife seeks her slave to yield himself (to her), surely he has affected her deeply with (his) love...

Yusuf 12:32-33 She said: This is he with respect to whom you blamed me, and certainly I sought his yielding himself (to me), but he abstained, and if he does not do what I bid him, he shall certainly be imprisoned, and he shall certainly be of those who are in a state of ignominy. He said: My Lord! the prison house is dearer to me than that to which they invite me; and if Thou turn not away their device from me, I will yearn towards them and become (one) of the ignorant.

Yusuf 12:35 Then it occurred to them after they had seen the signs that they should imprison him till a time.

Yusuf 12:43-44 And the king said: Surely I see seven fat kine which seven lean ones devoured; and seven green ears and (seven) others dry: O chiefs! [E]xplain to me my dream, if you can interpret the dream. They said: Confused dreams, and we do not know .the interpretation of dreams.

Yusuf 12:46-49 Yusuf! O truthful one! [E]xplain to us seven fat kine which seven lean ones devoured, and seven green ears and (seven) others dry, that I may go back to the people so that they may know. He said: You shall sow for seven years continuously, then what you reap leave it in its ear except a little of which you eat. Then there shall come after that seven years of hardship which shall eat away all that you have beforehand laid up in store for them, except a little of what you shall have preserved: Then there will come after that a year in which people shall have rain and in which they shall press (grapes).

Yusuf 12:54-56 And the king said: Bring him to me, I will choose him for myself. So when he had spoken with him, he said: Surely you are in our presence today an honorable, a faithful one. [Yusuf] said: Place me over the treasures of the land, surely I am a good keeper, knowing well. And thus did [I] give to Yusuf power in the land – he had mastery in it wherever he liked...

Yusuf 12:58-60 And Yusuf's brothers came and went in to him, and he knew them, while they did not recognize him. And when he furnished them with their provision, he said: Bring to me a brother of yours from your father; do you not see that I give full measure and that I am the best of hosts? But if you do not bring him to me, you shall have no measure (of corn) from me, nor shall you come near me.

Yusuf 12:58-60 They said: We will strive to make his father yield in respect of him, and we are sure to do (it). And he said to his servants: Put their money into their bags that they may recognize it when they go back to their family, so that they may come back. So when they returned to their father, they said: O our father, the measure is withheld from us, therefore send with us our brother, (so that) we may get the measure, and we will most surely guard him.

Yusuf 12:84-85 And [Yaqoub] turned away from them, and said: O my sorrow for Yusuf! and his eyes became white on account of the grief... They said: By [God]! [Y]ou will not cease to remember Yusuf until you are a prey to constant disease or you are of those who perish. ^{Yusuf 12:86-87} He said: I only complain of my grief and sorrow to [God], and I know from [Him] what you do not know. ...[D]espair not of [God's] mercy...

^{Yusuf 12:64-66} [Yaqoub] said: I cannot trust in you with respect to him, except as I trusted in you with respect to his brother before... And when they opened their goods, they found their money returned to them. They said: O our father! [W]hat (more) can we desire? This is our property returned to us, and we will bring corn for our family and guard our brother, and will have in addition the measure of a camel (load); this is an easy measure. He said: I will by no means send him with you until you give me a firm covenant in [God's] name that you will most certainly bring him back to me, unless you are completely surrounded. And when they gave him their covenant, he said: [God] is the One in Whom trust is placed as regards what we say.

^{Yusuf 12:69} And when they went in to Yusuf, he lodged his brother with himself, saying: I am your brother, therefore grieve not at what they do.

^{Yusuf 12:88-90} So when they came in to him, they said: O chief! [D]istress has afflicted us and our family and we have brought scanty money, so give us full measure and be charitable to us; surely [God] rewards the charitable. He said: Do you know how you treated Yusuf and his brother when you were ignorant? They [asked]: Are you indeed Yusuf? He said: I am Yusuf and this is my brother...

^{Yusuf 12:91} They said: ...[God has] certainly chosen you over us, and we were certainly sinners.

^{Yusuf 12:92-94} He said: (There shall be) no reproof against you... Take this my shirt and cast it on my father's face, he will (again) be able to see, and come to me with all your families. And when the caravan had departed, their father said: Most surely I perceive the greatness of Yusuf...

^{Yusuf 12:96-98} So when the bearer of good news came [Yaqoub] cast it on his face, so forthwith he regained his sight. He said: Did I not say to you that I know from [God] what you do not know? They said: O our father! [A]sk forgiveness of our faults for us, surely we were sinners. He said: I will ask for you forgiveness from my Lord; surely He is the Forgiving, the Merciful.

^{Yusuf 12:99-100} Then when they came in to Yusuf, he took his parents to lodge with him and said: Enter safe into Egypt, if [God] pleases. And he raised his parents upon the throne and they fell down in prostration before him, and he said: O my father! [T]his is the significance of my vision of old; my Lord has indeed made it to be true; and He was indeed kind to me when He brought me forth from the prison and brought you from the desert after the Shaitan had sown dissensions between me and my brothers...

^{The Believer 40:34} And certainly Yusuf came to you before with clear arguments, but you ever remained in doubt as to what he brought; until when he died, you said: [God] will never raise an apostle [like] him.

VII. The Journey

Christianity/Judaism:

Exodus 2:

[1] ... [A] man of the house of Levi went and took *as wife* a daughter of Levi. [2] So the woman conceived and bore a son. And when she saw that he *was* a beautiful *child,* she hid him three months. [3] But when she could no longer hide him, she took an ark... put the child in it, and laid *it* in the reeds by the river's bank. [4] And his sister stood afar off, to know what would be done to him.

[5] Then the daughter of Pharaoh came down to bathe at the river. And her maidens walked along the riverside; and when she saw the ark among the reeds, she sent her maid to get it. [6] And when she opened *it,* she saw the child, and behold, the baby wept. So she had compassion on him, and said, "This is one of the Hebrews' children."

[7] Then his sister said to Pharaoh's daughter, "Shall I go and call a nurse for you from the Hebrew women, that she may nurse the child for you?"

[8] And Pharaoh's daughter said to her, "Go." So the maiden went and called the child's mother. [9] Then Pharaoh's daughter said to her, "Take this child away and nurse him for me, and I will give *you* your wages." So the woman took the child and nursed him. [10] And the child grew, and she brought him to Pharaoh's daughter, and he became her son. So she called his name Moses, saying, "Because I drew him out of the water."

[16] Now the priest of Midian had seven daughters. And they came and drew water, and they filled the troughs to water their father's flock. [17] Then the shepherds came and drove them away; but Moses stood up and helped them, and watered their flock. [18] When they came to Reuel their father, he said, "How *is it that* you have come so soon today?"

[19] And they said, "An Egyptian delivered us from the hand of the shepherds, and he also drew enough water for us and watered the flock."

[20] So he said to his daughters, "And where *is* he? Why *is* it *that* you have left the man? Call him, that he may eat bread."

[21] Then Moses was content to live with the man, and he gave Zipporah his daughter to Moses. [22] And she bore *him* a son.

Exodus 3:

[1] Now Moses was tending the flock of Jethro his father-in-law, the priest of Midian. And he led the flock to the back of the desert, and came to Horeb, the mountain of God. [2] And the Angel of the LORD appeared to him in a flame of fire from the midst of a bush. So he looked, and behold, the bush was burning with fire, but the bush *was* not consumed. [3] Then Moses said, "I will now turn aside and see this great sight, why the bush does not burn."

⁴ So when the LORD saw that he turned aside to look, God called to him from the midst of the bush and said, "Moses, Moses!" And he said, "Here I am."

⁵ Then He said, "Do not draw near this place. Take your sandals off your feet, for the place where you stand *is* holy ground." ⁶ …And Moses hid his face, for he was afraid to look upon God.

⁷ And the LORD said: "I have surely seen the oppression of My people… and have heard their cry… ⁸ So I have come down to deliver them… and to bring them… to a land flowing with milk and honey.

¹³ Then Moses said to God, "Indeed, *when* I come [Your people] and say to them, 'The God of your fathers has sent me to you,' and they say to me, 'What *is* His name?' [W]hat shall I say to them?"

¹⁴ And God said to Moses, "I AM WHO I AM." And He said, "Thus you shall say… 'I AM has sent me to you.' ¹⁶ [S]ay to them, 'The LORD God… ¹⁷ will bring you up out of the affliction to a land flowing with milk and honey.'" ¹⁸ Then they will heed your voice…"

Exodus 4:

¹⁸ So Moses went and returned to Jethro his father-in-law, and said to him, "Please let me go and return to my brethren… and see whether they are still alive." And Jethro said to Moses, "Go in peace."

²⁰ Then Moses took his wife and his sons and set them on a donkey, and he returned to the land of Egypt…

²⁸ …Moses told Aaron all the words of the LORD who had sent him, and all the signs, which He had commanded him. ²⁹ Then Moses and Aaron went and gathered together all the elders… ³⁰ And Aaron spoke all the words, which the LORD had spoken to Moses. Then he did the signs in the sight of the people. ³¹ So the people believed; and when they heard that the LORD had visited… and that He had looked on their affliction, then they bowed their heads and worshiped.

Exodus 12:

¹ Now the LORD spoke to Moses and Aaron in the land of Egypt, saying, ³ "Speak to all the congregation… saying: 'On the tenth of this month every man shall take for himself a lamb, according to the house of *his* father, a lamb for a household. ⁴ And if the household is too small for the lamb, let him and his neighbor next to his house take *it* according to the number of the persons; according to each man's need you shall make your count for the lamb. ⁵ Your lamb shall be without blemish, a male of the first year. You may take *it* from the sheep or from the goats. ⁶ Now you shall keep it until the fourteenth day of the same month. Then the whole assembly of the congregation… shall kill it at twilight. ⁷ And they shall take *some* of the blood and put *it* on the two doorposts and on the lintel of the houses where they eat it. ⁸ Then they shall eat the flesh on that night; roasted in fire, with unleavened bread *and* with bitter *herbs* they shall eat it. ¹⁰ You shall let none of it remain until morning, and what remains of it until morning you shall burn with fire. ¹¹ And thus you shall eat it: *with* a belt on your waist,

your sandals on your feet, and your staff in your hand. So you shall eat it in haste. It *is* the LORD's Passover.

[13] [T]he blood shall be a sign for you on the houses where you *are.* And when I see the blood, I will pass over you..."

[31] Then [Pharaoh] called for Moses and Aaron by night, and said, "Rise, go out from among my people, both you and [your people]. And go serve the LORD as you have said. [32] Also take your flocks and your herds, as you have said, and be gone; and bless me also."

[37] Then the[y] journeyed from Rameses to Succoth, about six hundred thousand men on foot, besides children. [38] A mixed multitude went up with them also, and flocks and herds — a great deal of livestock. [39] And they baked unleavened cakes of the dough, which they had brought out of Egypt...

Exodus 13:

[17] Then it came to pass, when Pharaoh had let the people go, that God did not lead them *by* way of the land of the Philistines, although that *was* near; for God said, "Lest perhaps the people change their minds when they see war, and return to Egypt." [18] So God led the people around *by* way of the wilderness of the Red Sea. And the[y] went up in orderly ranks out of the land of Egypt.

[21] And the LORD went before them by day in a pillar of cloud to lead the way, and by night in a pillar of fire to give them light, so as to go by day and night. [22] He did not take away the pillar of cloud by day or the pillar of fire by night *from* before the people.

Exodus 14:

[1] Now the LORD spoke to Moses, saying: [3] "...Pharaoh will say... 'They *are* bewildered by the land; the wilderness has closed them in.' [4] [and] will pursue them..."

[5] Now it was told the king of Egypt that the people had fled; they said, "Why have we done this, that we have let Israel go from serving us?" [6] So he made ready his chariot and took his people with him. [7] Also, he took six hundred choice chariots, and all the chariots of Egypt with captains over every one of them. [8] ...[A]nd he pursued the[m]... [9] all the horses *and* chariots of Pharaoh, his horsemen and his army...

[10] And when Pharaoh drew near, the children of Israel lifted their eyes, and behold, the Egyptians marched after them. So they were very afraid...

[13] And Moses said to the people, "Do not be afraid. Stand still, and see the salvation of the LORD, which He will accomplish for you today..."

[15] And the LORD said to Moses, "...Tell the children of Israel to go forward. [16] But lift up your rod, and stretch out your hand over the sea and divide it. And the children of Israel shall go on dry *ground* through the midst of the sea."

¹⁹ And the Angel of God, who went before the camp of Israel, moved and went behind them; and the pillar of cloud went from before them and stood behind them. ²⁰ So it came between the camp of the Egyptians and the camp of Israel. Thus it was a cloud and darkness *to the one,* and it gave light by night *to the other,* so that the one did not come near the other all that night.

²¹ Then Moses stretched out his hand over the sea; and the LORD caused the sea to go *back* by a strong east wind all that night, and made the sea into dry *land,* and the waters were divided. ²² So the children of Israel went into the midst of the sea on the dry *ground,* and the waters *were* a wall to them on their right hand and on their left.

²⁶ Then the LORD said to Moses, "Stretch out your hand over the sea, that the waters may come back..." ²⁷ And Moses stretched out his hand over the sea... ²⁸ Then the waters returned...

³¹ Thus Israel saw the great work which the LORD had done... so the people feared the LORD, and believed the LORD and His servant Moses.

Exodus 15:

² So Moses brought Israel from the Red Sea; then they went out into the Wilderness of Shur. And they went three days in the wilderness and found no water. ²³ Now when they came to Marah, they could not drink the waters of Marah, for they *were* bitter... ²⁴ And the people complained..., saying, "What shall we drink?" ²⁵ So [Moses] cried out to the LORD, and the LORD showed him a tree. When he cast *it* into the waters, the waters were made sweet...

²⁷ Then they came to Elim, where there *were* twelve wells of water and seventy palm trees; so they camped there by the waters.

Exodus 16:

¹ And they journeyed from Elim, and all the congregation... came to the Wilderness of Sin... on the fifteenth day of the second month after they departed from the land of Egypt. ² Then the whole congregation... complained against Moses and Aaron... ³ "Oh, that we had died by the hand of the LORD in the land of Egypt, when we sat by the pots of meat *and* when we ate bread to the full! For you have brought us out into this wilderness to kill this whole assembly with hunger."

¹¹ And the LORD spoke to Moses, saying, ¹² "I have heard the complaints of the children of Israel. Speak to them, saying, 'At twilight you shall eat meat, and in the morning you shall be filled with bread.'"

¹³ So it was that quails came up at evening and covered the camp, and in the morning the dew lay all around the camp. ¹⁴ And when the layer of dew lifted, there, on the surface of the wilderness, was a small round substance, *as* fine as frost on the ground. ¹⁵ So when the children of Israel saw *it,* they said to one another, "What is it?" For they did not know what it *was.* And Moses said to them, "This *is* the bread which the LORD has given you to eat. ¹⁶ This is the thing which the LORD has commanded: 'Let

every[one] gather it according to [their] need…'"

[17] Then the children of Israel did so and gathered, some more, some less. [18] …Every [person] had gathered according to [their] need.

[31] And the house of Israel called its name Manna. And it *was* like white coriander seed, and the taste of it *was* like wafers *made* with honey.

[35] And the children of Israel ate manna forty years… until they came to the border of the land of Canaan.

Exodus 17:

[1] Then all the congregation of the children of Israel set out on their journey from the Wilderness of Sin, according to the commandment of the LORD, and camped in Rephidim; but *there was* no water for the people to drink. [2] Therefore the people contended with Moses, and said, "Give us water, that we may drink." So Moses said to them, "Why do you contend with me? Why do you tempt the LORD?"

[3] And the people thirsted there for water, and the people complained against Moses, and said, "Why *is* it you have brought us up out of Egypt, to kill us and our children and our livestock with thirst?"

[4] So Moses cried out to the LORD, saying, "What shall I do with this people? They are almost ready to stone me!"

[5] And the LORD said to Moses, "Go on before the people, and take with you some of the elders… Also take in your hand your rod… [6] Behold, I will stand before you there on the rock in Horeb; and you shall strike the rock, and water will come out of it, that the people may drink." And Moses did so in the sight of the elders…

Exodus 24:

[12] Then the LORD said to Moses, "Come up to Me on the mountain and be there; and I will give you tablets of stone, and the law and commandments which I have written, that you may teach them."

[13] So Moses arose with his assistant Joshua, and Moses went up to the mountain of God.

[16] [T]he glory of the LORD rested on Mount Sinai, and the cloud covered it six days. And on the seventh day He called to Moses out of the midst of the cloud. [17] The sight of the glory of the LORD *was* like a consuming fire on the top of the mountain in the eyes of the children of Israel. [18] So Moses went into the midst of the cloud and went up into the mountain. And Moses was on the mountain forty days and forty nights.

Exodus 32:

[1] Now when the people saw that Moses delayed coming down from the mountain, the

people gathered together to Aaron, and said to him, "Come, make us gods that shall go before us; for *as for* this Moses, the man who brought us up out of the land of Egypt, we do not know what has become of him."

² And Aaron said to them, "Break off the golden earrings which *are* in the ears of your wives, your sons, and your daughters, and bring *them* to me." ³ So all the people broke off the golden earrings which *were* in their ears, and brought *them* to Aaron. ⁴ And he received *the gold* from their hand, and he fashioned it with an engraving tool, and made a molded calf.   Then they said, "This *is* your god… that brought you out of the land of Egypt!"

⁷ And the LORD said to Moses, "Go, get down! For your people whom you brought out of the land of Egypt have corrupted *themselves*. ⁸ …They have made themselves a molded calf, and worshiped it and sacrificed to it…"

¹⁵ And Moses turned and went down from the mountain, and the two tablets of the Testimony *were* in his hand. The tablets *were* written on both sides; on the one *side* and on the other they were written. ¹⁶ Now the tablets *were* the work of God, and the writing *was* the writing of God engraved on the tablets.

¹⁹ So it was, as soon as he came near the camp, that he saw the calf *and* the dancing. So Moses' anger became hot, and he cast the tablets out of his hands and broke them at the foot of the mountain. ²⁰ Then he took the calf which they had made, burned *it* in the fire, and ground *it* to powder…

Moses Smashing the Tablets
by Rembrandt 1659

²⁶ …then Moses stood in the entrance of the camp, and said, "Whoever *is* on the LORD's side — *come* to me! ²⁹ …Consecrate yourselves today to the LORD, that He may bestow on you a blessing this day…" ³⁰ Now it came to pass on the next day that Moses said to the people, "You have committed a great sin. So now I will go up to the LORD; perhaps I can make atonement for your sin…"

Exodus 34:

¹ And the LORD said to Moses, "Cut two tablets of stone like the first *ones,* and I will write on *these* tablets the words that were on the first tablets which you broke."

⁴ So he cut two tablets of stone like the first *ones.* Then Moses rose early in the morning and went up Mount Sinai, as the LORD had commanded him; and he took in his hand the two tablets of stone.

⁵ Now the LORD descended in the cloud and stood with him there… ¹⁰ And He said: "Behold, I make a covenant…."

²⁸ So [Moses] was there with the LORD forty days and forty nights; he neither ate bread nor drank water. And [the LORD] wrote on the tablets the words of the covenant, the Ten Commandments.

Exodus 20:

¹ And God spoke all these words, [giving the **Ten Commandments**]:

² "I *am* the LORD your God, who brought you out of the land of Egypt, out of the house of bondage. ³ You shall have no other gods before Me.

⁴ You shall not make for yourself a carved image—any likeness *of anything* that *is* in heaven above, or that *is* in the earth beneath, or that *is* in the water under the earth; ⁵ you shall not bow down to them nor serve them. For I, the LORD your God…⁶ [show] mercy to… those who love Me and keep My commandments.

⁷ You shall not take the name of the LORD your God in vain…

⁸ Remember the Sabbath day, to keep it holy. ⁹ Six days you shall labor and do all your work, ¹⁰ but the seventh day *is* the Sabbath of the LORD your God. *In it* you shall do no work… ¹¹ For *in* six days the LORD made the heavens and the earth, the sea, and all that *is* in them, and rested the seventh day. Therefore the LORD blessed the Sabbath day and hallowed it.

¹² Honor your father and your mother, that your days may be long upon the land which the LORD your God is giving you.

¹³ You shall not [kill]. ¹⁴ You shall not commit adultery. ¹⁵ You shall not steal. ¹⁶ You shall not bear false witness against your neighbor. ¹⁷ You shall not covet your neighbor's house; you shall not covet your neighbor's wife… nor anything that *is* your neighbor's."

Deuteronomy 4:

³² "…[A]sk from one end of heaven to the other… ³³ Did *any* people *ever* hear the voice of God speaking out of the midst of the fire, as you have heard, and live? ³⁴ Or did God

ever try to go *and* take for Himself a nation…?

³⁵ To you it was shown, that you might know that the LORD Himself *is* God; *there is* none other besides Him. ³⁶ Out of heaven He let you hear His voice, that He might instruct you; on earth He showed you His great fire, and you heard His words out of the midst of the fire. ³⁷ And because He loved your fathers, therefore He chose their descendants after them; and He brought you out of Egypt…

³⁹ Therefore know… *it* in your heart, that the LORD Himself *is* God in heaven above and on the earth beneath; *there is* no other. ⁴⁰ You shall therefore keep His statutes and His commandments which I command you today, that it may go well with you and with your children after you, and that you may prolong *your* days in the land which the LORD your God is giving you for all time."

Exodus 33:

¹ Then the LORD said to Moses, "Depart *and* go up from here, you and the people whom you have brought out of the land of Egypt, to the land of which I swore to Abraham, Isaac, and Jacob, saying, 'To your descendants I will give it.' ² And I will send *My* Angel before you… ¹⁴ My Presence will go *with you,* and I will give you rest.

¹⁹ I will make all My goodness pass before you…I will be gracious… and I will have compassion…"

Exodus 40:

¹⁷ And it came to pass in the first month of the second year, on the first *day* of the month, *that* the tabernacle was raised up. ³⁴ Then the cloud covered the tabernacle of meeting, and the glory of the LORD filled the tabernacle. ³⁶ Whenever the cloud was taken up from above the tabernacle, the children of Israel would go onward in all their journeys. ³⁷ But if the cloud was not taken up, then they did not journey till the day that it was taken up. ³⁸ For the cloud of the LORD *was* above the tabernacle by day, and fire was over it by night, in the sight of all… throughout all their journeys.

Islam:

The Narratives 28:8-9 And Firon's (Pharaoh's) family took [Musa (Moses)] up. …Firon's wife said: A refreshment of the eye to me and to you; do not slay him; maybe he will be useful to us, or we may take him for a son…

Abraham 14:5 And certainly [the Lord] sent Musa… saying: Bring forth your people from utter darkness into light and remind them of the days of [God]; most surely there are signs in this for every patient, grateful one.

The Poets 26:18 Firon [asked]: Did we not bring you up as a child among us, and you tarried among us for (many) years of your life?

The Distinction 25:35 And certainly [God]… appointed with [Musa] his brother Haroun (Aaron) an aider.

^{Ta Ha 20:77} And certainly [God] revealed to Musa, saying: Travel by night with My servants, then make for them a dry path in the sea…

^{The Poets 26:52} …[for] surely you will be pursued.

^{The Poets 26:60-63} Then they pursued them at sunrise. So when the two hosts saw each other, the companions of Musa cried out: Most surely we are being overtaken. He said: By no means; surely my Lord is with me: He will show me a way out. Then [He] revealed to Musa: Strike the sea with your staff. So it had cloven asunder, and each part was like a huge mound.

^{The Elevated Places 7:138 and Jonah 10:90} And [God] made the children of Israel to pass through the sea…

^{The Poets 26:65} And [God] saved Musa and those with him, all of them.

^{Abraham 14:6} [He]… delivered [them] from… severe torment…

^{Ta Ha 20:80-81} O children of Israel! [I]ndeed [I] delivered you from your enemy, and [I] made a covenant with you on the blessed side of the mountain, and [I] sent to you the manna and the quails. Eat of the good things [I] have given you for sustenance, and be not inordinate with respect to them…

^{The Cow 2:60} And when Musa prayed for drink for his people, [God] said: Strike the rock with your staff So there gushed from it twelve springs… Eat and drink of the provisions of [God]…

^{The Elevated Places 7:160} And… [God] revealed to Musa when his people asked him for water: Strike the rock with your staff, so outflowed from it twelve springs; and [God] made the clouds to give shade over them and sent to them manna and quails: Eat of the good things [I] have given you.

^{The Elevated Places 7:142} And [God] appointed with Musa a time of thirty nights and completed them with ten, so the appointed time of his Lord was complete forty nights, and Musa said to his brother Haroun: Take my place among my people, and act well…

^{The Elevated Places 7:143-145} And when Musa came at [God's] appointed time and his Lord spoke to him… He said: O Musa! [S]urely I have chosen you above the people with My messages and with My words, therefore take hold of what I give to you… And [He] ordained for him in the tablets admonition of every kind and clear explanation of all things; so take hold of them with firmness and enjoin your people to take hold of what is best thereof…

^{The Cow 2:51} And when [God] appointed a time of forty nights with Musa, then you took the calf after him and you were unjust.

^{The Elevated Places 7:148-150} And Musa's people made of their ornaments a calf after him, a

(mere) body... They took it (for worship) and they were unjust. And when they repented and saw that they had gone astray, they said: If our Lord show not mercy to us and forgive us we shall certainly be of the losers. And when Musa returned to his people, wrathful, in violent grief, he said: Evil is it that you have done after me; did you turn away from the bidding of your Lord? And he threw down the tablets and seized his brother by the head, dragging him towards him. He said: Son of my mother! [S]urely the people reckoned me weak and had well-nigh slain me, therefore make not the enemies to rejoice over me and count me not among the unjust people.

The Elevated Places 7:151,153 He said: My Lord! [F]orgive me and my brother and cause us to enter into Thy mercy... And (as to) those who do evil deeds, then repent after that and believe, your Lord after that is most surely Forgiving, Merciful.

The Elevated Places 7:154 And when Musa's anger calmed down he took up the tablets, and in the writing thereof was guidance and mercy for those who fear for the sake of their Lord.

The Cow 2:52-54 Then [God] pardoned you after that so that you might give thanks. ...[He] gave Musa the Book and the distinction that you might walk aright. And when Musa said to his people: O my people! [Y]ou have surely been unjust to yourselves by taking the calf, therefore turn to your Creator (penitently)... for surely He is the Oft-returning (to mercy), the Merciful.

Marium 19:51-53 ...[S]urely [Musa] was one purified, and he was an apostle, a prophet. And [I] called to him from the blessed side of the mountain, and made him draw nigh, holding communion (with Me). And [I] gave to him out of [My] mercy his brother Haroun a prophet.

The Cattle 6:154 [God] gave the Book to Musa to complete ([His] blessings) on him who would do good (to others), and making plain all things and a guidance and a mercy, so that they should believe in the meeting of their Lord.

The Children of Israel 17:2 And [I] gave Musa the Book and made it a guidance to the children of Israel, saying: Do not take a protector besides Me.

Ta Ha 20:82 And most surely I am most Forgiving to him who repents and believes and does good, then continues to follow the right direction.

The Women 4:154 And [God] lifted the mountain (Sinai) over them... and ...made with them a firm covenant (the **Ten Commandments**):

The Children of Israel 17:23 [Y]our Lord has commanded that you shall not serve but Him...

The Pilgrimage 22:30 [A]void the uncleanness of the idols and avoid false words.

The Cow 2:224 And make not [God] because of your swearing (by Him) an obstacle to your doing good and guarding (against evil) and making peace...

The Women 4:154 Do not exceed the limits of the Sabbath...

The Children of Israel 17:23 and The Cattle 6:151 …[Do] goodness to your parents. If either or both of them reach old age with you, say not to them "Ugh" nor chide them, and speak to them a generous word. And make yourself submissively gentle to them with compassion, and say: O my Lord! [H]ave compassion on them, as they brought me up (when I was) little. …[S]how kindness to your parents.

The Cattle 6:151 [D]o not kill the soul, which [God] has forbidden… **The Children of Israel 17:32** And go not nigh to fornication (adultery); surely it is an indecency and an evil way. **The Dinner Table 5:38** And (as for) the man who steals and the woman who steals… they have earned, an exemplary punishment from [God]… **The Distinction 25:72** And they who do not bear witness to what is false, and when they pass by what is vain, they pass by nobly.

The Women 4:32 and The Rock 15:88 And do not covet that by which [God] has made some of you excel (over) others; men shall have the benefit of what they earn and women shall have the benefit of what they earn… Do not strain your eyes after what [I] have given [some]… to enjoy…

Hinduism:

Bhagavad-Gita 7:9:

"I am the life of all that lives…"

Bhagavad-Gita 4:11:

"All of them – as they surrender unto Me [and] follow My path in all respects – I reward accordingly."

Bhagavad-Gita 7:2:

"I shall now declare unto you in full this knowledge [so that]… by knowing… there shall remain nothing further to be known."

Bhagavad-Gita 8:14:

"For one who remembers Me without deviation, I am easy to obtain…"

Bhagavad-Gita 18:42:

"Peacefulness, self-control, austerity, purity, tolerance, honesty, knowledge, wisdom, and religiousness – these are the natural qualities [I desire].

Bhagavad-Gita 16:1-3:

"The Blessed Lord said: …[P]urification…, cultivation of spiritual knowledge, charity, self-control, austerity and simplicity; nonviolence, truthfulness, freedom from anger; renunciation, tranquility, aversion to faultfinding, compassion and freedom from covetousness; gentleness, modesty and… forgiveness; …freedom from envy and the passion for honor – these… qualities [I seek]."

Buddhism:

Adapted from "The Word of the Buddha, Niyamatolika." The Buddhist Publication Society. 1971:

I undertake to abstain from: 1. [H]arming living beings, 2. [S]exual misconduct, 3. [T]aking things not freely given, [and] 4. [F]alse speech.

Law of Karma: [F]or every event that occurs, there will follow another event whose existence was caused by the first, and this second event will be pleasant or unpleasant according as its cause… There is a resonating impact or consequence for every action good or bad – "*[W]hat goes around comes around*" – thus do good and "strive to develop a compassion that is undiscriminating and all-embracing."

Jainism:

[Four] Great Vows:

1. Nonviolence (Ahimsa) – not to cause harm to any living beings
2. Truthfulness (Satya) – to speak the harmless truth only
3. Non-stealing (Asteya) – not to take anything not properly given
4. Chastity (Brahmacharya) – not to indulge in sensual pleasure

The "Luminous" Religion:

Source: **Martin Palmer.** The Jesus Sutras **(Ballantine Wellspring, New York, 2001):**

Ten covenants:

1. Honor God… the Sacred One…
2. Honor and care for elderly parents.
3. Acknowledge we have been brought into existence through our parents.
4. Be kind and considerate to everything and… do no evil to anything that lives.
5. [Do not] take the life of another living being… [and] teach others to do likewise.
6. …Nobody should commit adultery, or persuade anyone else to do so.
7. [D]o not steal… Do not obtain anything by deception or force… Tell only the truth. Never try to use false means to achieve anything.
8. [N]obody should covet a living man's wife, or his lands, or his [home]…
9. [Do] not let your envy of somebody's good wife, or [child], or house or gold, lead you to bear false witness against them.
10. [O]ffer to God only that which is yours to give.

Scientology:

[T]he laws of God forbid [people] [t]o destroy [their] own kind… [and] [t]o… enslave [others]…

…[A]ll [people] of whatever race, color or creed were created with equal rights…

VIII. The Books of Samuel

Christianity/Judaism:

1 Samuel 1:

[1] Now there was a certain man... his name *was* Elkanah... [2] And he had two wives: the name of one *was* Hannah, and the name of the other Peninnah. Peninnah had children, but Hannah had no children. [3] This man went up from his city yearly to worship and sacrifice to the LORD of hosts in Shiloh... [4] And whenever the time came for Elkanah to make an offering, he would give portions to Peninnah his wife and to all her sons and daughters. [5] But to Hannah he would give a double portion, for he loved Hannah although... her womb [was closed]. [6] And her rival also provoked her severely, to make her miserable, because... her womb [was closed]. [7] So it was, year by year, when she went up to the house of the LORD, that she provoked her; therefore she wept and did not eat.

[8] Then Elkanah her husband said to her, "Hannah, why do you weep? Why do you not eat? And why is your heart grieved? *Am* I not better to you than ten sons?" [9] So Hannah arose after they had finished eating and drinking in Shiloh. Now Eli the priest was sitting on the seat by the doorpost of the tabernacle of the LORD. [10] And she *was* in bitterness of soul, and prayed to the LORD and wept in anguish. [11] Then she made a vow and said, "O LORD of hosts, if You will indeed look on the affliction of Your maidservant and remember me, and not forget Your maidservant, but will give Your maidservant a male child, then I will give him to the LORD all the days of his life..."

[15] ...Hannah... said, "... I *am* a woman of sorrowful spirit. [I] have poured out my soul before the LORD..."

[17] Then Eli answered and said, "Go in peace, and the God of Israel grant your petition which you have asked of Him."

[18] And she said, "Let your maidservant find favor in your sight." So the woman went her way and ate, and her face was no longer *sad.*

[19] Then they rose early in the morning and worshiped before the LORD, and returned and came to their house at Ramah. And Elkanah knew Hannah his wife, and the LORD remembered her. [20] So it came to pass in the process of time that Hannah conceived and bore a son, and called his name Samuel, *saying,* "Because I have asked for him from the LORD."

[24] Now when she had weaned him, she took him up with her... [26] And she said, [27] "For this child I prayed, and the LORD has granted me my petition which I asked of Him. [28] Therefore I also have lent him to the LORD; as long as he lives he shall be lent to the LORD."

1 Samuel 2:

And Hannah prayed and said:

[1] "My heart rejoices in the LORD; My horn is exalted in the LORD. I smile at my enemies, [b]ecause I rejoice in Your salvation.

[2] No one is holy like the LORD, [f]or *there is* none besides You, [n]or *is there* any rock like our God.

[3] …[T]he LORD *is* the God of knowledge; And by Him actions are weighed.

[5] …[T]he hungry have ceased to hunger. Even the barren has borne seven…

[8] He raises the poor from the dust [a]nd lifts the beggar from the ash heap, [t]o set *them* among princes [a]nd make them inherit the throne of glory.

For the pillars of the earth *are* the LORD's, [a]nd He has set the world upon them.

[9] He will guard the feet of His saints…

[10] …The LORD will judge the ends of the earth. He will give strength to His king, [a]nd exalt the horn of His anointed.

[18] …Samuel ministered before the LORD, *even as* a child… [20] And Eli would bless Elkanah and his wife, and say, "The LORD give you descendants from this woman for the loan that was given to the LORD."

[21] And the LORD visited Hannah, so that she conceived and bore three sons and two daughters. Meanwhile the child Samuel grew before the LORD.

1 Samuel 3:

[1] Now the boy Samuel ministered to the LORD before Eli. And the word of the LORD was rare in those days; *there was* no widespread revelation. [2] And it came to pass at that time, while Eli *was* lying down in his place, and when his eyes had begun to grow so dim that he could not see, [3] and before the lamp of God went out in the tabernacle of the LORD where the ark of God *was,* and while Samuel was lying down, [4] that the LORD called Samuel. And he answered, "Here I am!" [5] So he ran to Eli and said, "Here I am, for you called me."

And he said, "I did not call; lie down again." And he went and lay down. [6] Then the LORD called yet again, "Samuel!"

So Samuel arose and went to Eli, and said, "Here I am, for you called me." He answered, "I did not call, my son; lie down again."

[8] And the LORD called Samuel again the third time. So he arose and went to Eli, and said, "Here I am, for you did call me."

Then Eli perceived that the LORD had called the boy. [9] Therefore Eli said to Samuel, "Go, lie down; and it shall be, if He calls you, that you must say, 'Speak, LORD, for Your servant hears.'" So Samuel went and lay down in his place.

[10] Now the LORD came and stood and called as at other times, "Samuel! Samuel!" And Samuel answered, "Speak, for Your servant hears."

[11] Then the LORD [spoke] to Samuel…

[16] Then Eli called Samuel and said, "Samuel, my son!" He answered, "Here I am."

[17] And he said, "What *is* the word that *the LORD* spoke to you? Please do not hide *it* from me… [18] Then Samuel told him everything, and hid nothing from him. And he said, "It *is* the LORD. Let Him do what seems good to Him."

[19] So Samuel grew, and the LORD was with him and let none of his words fall to the ground. [20] And all… knew that Samuel *had been* established as a prophet of the LORD.

1 Samuel 4:

[1] And the word of Samuel came to all Israel.

1 Samuel 7:

[3] …Samuel spoke to all the house of Israel, saying, "If you return to the LORD with all your hearts… and prepare your hearts for the LORD, and serve Him only; He will deliver you…" [4] So the children of Israel… served the LORD only.

[5] And Samuel said, "Gather all Israel… and I will pray to the LORD for you." [6] So they gathered together… drew water, and poured *it* out before the LORD. And they fasted that day, and said, "We have sinned against the LORD." And Samuel judged the children of Israel…

[7] …And when the children of Israel… were afraid… [8] [they] said to Samuel, "Do not cease to cry out to the LORD our God for us, that He may save us…"

[9] And… Samuel cried out to the LORD for Israel, and the LORD answered him.

[15] And Samuel judged Israel all the days of his life...

1 Samuel 8:

[1] Now it came to pass when Samuel was old that he made his sons judges over Israel. [4] Then all the elders of Israel gathered together and came to Samuel… [5] and said to him, "Look, you are old and your sons do not walk in your ways. [6] Give us a king to judge us."

So Samuel prayed to the LORD. [7] And the LORD said to Samuel, "Heed the voice of the people in all that they say to you… [22] and make them a king."

1 Samuel 9:

[15] Now the LORD had told Samuel in his ear the day before Saul came, saying, [16] "Tomorrow about this time I will send you a man from the land of Benjamin, and you shall anoint him commander over My people… because their cry has come to Me."

[17] So when Samuel saw Saul, the LORD said to him, "There he is, the man of whom I spoke to you. This one shall reign over My people." [18] Then Saul drew near to Samuel…

[27] …Samuel said to Saul, "…[S]tand here awhile, that I may announce to you the word of God."

1 Samuel 10:

[1] Then Samuel took a flask of oil and poured *it* on his head, and kissed him… and said: [6] "[T]he Spirit of the LORD will come upon you, and you will… be turned into another man… [7] for God *is* with you."

[9] So it was, when he had turned his back to go from Samuel, that God gave him another heart…. [10] When [Saul] came there to the hill, there was a group of prophets to meet him; then the Spirit of God came upon him, and he prophesied among them.

[17] Then Samuel called the people together… [18] and said to the children of Israel, [19] "Now therefore, present yourselves before the LORD by your tribes and by your clans." [20] And when Samuel had caused all the tribes of Israel to come near… [21] Saul the son of Kish was chosen. [24] And Samuel said to all the people, "Do you see him whom the LORD has chosen, that *there is* no one like him among all the people?" So all the people shouted and said, "Long live the king!"

1 Samuel 11:

[15] So all the people… made Saul king before the LORD… and all… rejoiced greatly.

1 Samuel 12:

[1] Now Samuel said to all… "Indeed I have heeded your voice in all that you said to me, and have made a king over you. [2] And now here is the king… [3] Whose ox have I taken, or whose donkey have I taken, or whom have I cheated? Whom have I oppressed, or from whose hand have I received *any* bribe with which to blind my eyes? I will restore *it* to you."

[4] And they said, "You have not cheated us or oppressed us, nor have you taken anything from any man's hand."

[6] Then Samuel said to the people, "*It is* the LORD who raised up Moses and Aaron, and who brought your fathers up from the land of Egypt. [7] Now therefore, stand still, that I may reason with you before the LORD concerning all the righteous acts of the LORD which He did to you and your fathers: [8] When Jacob had gone into Egypt, and your fathers cried out to the LORD, then the LORD sent Moses and Aaron, who brought your fathers out of Egypt and made them dwell in this place.

[10] Then they cried out to the LORD, and said, 'We have sinned, because we have forsaken the LORD… but now deliver us… and we will serve You.'

[13] "Now therefore, here is the king whom you have chosen *and* whom you have desired. And take note, the LORD has set a king over you. [14] If you fear the LORD and serve Him

and obey His voice, and do not rebel against the commandment of the LORD, then both you and the king who reigns over you will continue following the LORD your God.

[16] "Now therefore, stand and see this great thing which the LORD will do before your eyes: [17] *Is* today not the wheat harvest? I will call to the LORD, and He will send thunder and rain…"

[18] So Samuel called to the LORD, and the LORD sent thunder and rain that day; and all the people greatly feared the LORD and Samuel.

[19] And all the people said to Samuel, "Pray for your servants to the LORD your God, that we may not die; for we have… sin[ned]."

[20] Then Samuel said to the people, "Do not fear… but serve the LORD with all your heart [22] [f]or the LORD will not forsake His people, for His great name's sake, because it has pleased the LORD to make you His people. [24] Only fear the LORD, and serve Him in truth with all your heart; for consider what great things He has done for you."

1 Samuel 13:

[1] Saul reigned one year; and when he had reigned two years over Israel, [13] …Samuel said, "…You have not kept the commandment of the LORD your God, which He commanded you. For now the LORD would have established your kingdom over Israel forever. [14] But now your kingdom shall not continue. The LORD has sought for Himself a man after His own heart, and the LORD has commanded him *to be* commander over His people, because you have not kept what the LORD commanded you."

1 Samuel 16:

[1] Now the LORD said to Samuel, "How long will you mourn for Saul, seeing I have rejected him from reigning over Israel? Fill your horn with oil, and go; I am sending you to Jesse the Bethlehemite. For I have provided Myself a king among his sons."

[4] So Samuel did what the LORD said, and went to Bethlehem. And the elders of the town trembled at his coming, and said, "Do you come peaceably?" [5] And he said, "Peaceably; I have come…" Then he consecrated Jesse and his sons… [6] So it was, when they came, that he looked at Eliab and said, "Surely the LORD's anointed *is* before Him!"

[7] But the LORD said to Samuel, "Do not look at his appearance or at his physical stature, because I have refused him. For *the LORD does* not *see* as man sees; for man looks at the outward appearance, but the LORD looks at the heart."

[8] So Jesse called Abinadab, and made him pass before Samuel. And he said, "Neither has the LORD chosen this one." [9] Then Jesse made Shammah pass by. And he said, "Neither has the LORD chosen this one." [10] Thus Jesse made seven of his sons pass before Samuel. And Samuel said to Jesse, "The LORD has not chosen these." [11] And Samuel said to Jesse, "Are all the young men here?" Then he said, "There remains yet the youngest, and there he is, keeping the sheep."

And Samuel said to Jesse, "Send and bring him. For we will not sit down till he comes here." [12] ...And the LORD said, "Arise, anoint him; for this *is* the one!" [13] Then Samuel took the horn of oil and anointed him in the midst of his brothers; and the Spirit of the LORD came upon David from that day forward.

[14] But the Spirit of the LORD departed from Saul, and a distressing spirit... troubled him. [15] And Saul's servants said to him, "Surely, a distressing spirit... is troubling you. [16] Let our master now command your servants, *who are* before you, to seek out a man *who is* a skillful player on the harp. And it shall be that he will play it with his hand when the distressing spirit... is upon you, and you shall be well." [17] So Saul said to his servants, "Provide me now a man who can play well, and bring *him* to me."

[18] Then one of the servants answered and said, "Look, I have seen a son of Jesse the Bethlehemite, *who is* skillful in playing, a mighty man of valor..., prudent in speech, and a handsome person; and the LORD *is* with him."

[19] Therefore Saul sent messengers to Jesse, and said, "Send me your son David, who *is* with the sheep." [20] And Jesse took a donkey *loaded with* bread, a skin of wine, and a young goat, and sent *them* by his son David to Saul. [21] So David came to Saul and stood before him. And he loved him greatly, and he became his armorbearer. [22] Then Saul sent to Jesse, saying, "Please let David stand before me, for he has found favor in my sight." [23] And so it was, whenever the spirit... was upon Saul, that David would take a harp and play *it* with his hand. Then Saul would become refreshed and well, and the distressing spirit would depart from him.

1 Samuel 18:

[20] Now Michal, Saul's daughter, loved David. And they told Saul, and the thing pleased him. [27] therefore... Saul gave him Michal his daughter as a wife.

[28] Thus Saul saw and knew that the LORD *was* with David, and *that* Michal, Saul's daughter, loved him; [29] and Saul was still more afraid of David. So Saul became David's enemy continually.

1 Samuel 19:

[1] Now Saul spoke to Jonathan his son and to all his servants, that they should kill David; but Jonathan, Saul's son, delighted greatly in David. [2] So Jonathan told David, saying, "My father Saul seeks to kill you. Therefore please be on your guard until morning, and stay in a secret *place* and hide. [3] And I will go out and stand beside my father in the field where you *are,* and I will speak with my father about you. Then what I observe, I will tell you."

[4] Thus Jonathan spoke well of David to Saul his father, and said to him, "Let not the king sin against his servant, against David, because he has not sinned against you, and because his works *have been* very good toward you. [5] ...Why... will you sin against innocent blood, to kill David without a cause?"

[6] So Saul heeded the voice of Jonathan, and Saul swore, "*As* the LORD lives, he shall not be killed." [7] Then Jonathan called David, and Jonathan told him all these things. So Jonathan brought David to Saul, and he was in his presence as in times past.

⁹ Now the distressing spirit… came upon Saul as he sat in his house with his spear in his hand. And David was playing *music* with *his* hand. ¹⁰ Then Saul sought to pin David to the wall with the spear, but he slipped away from Saul's presence; and he drove the spear into the wall. So David fled and escaped that night.

¹¹ Saul also sent messengers to David's house to watch him and to kill him in the morning. And Michal, David's wife, told him, saying, "If you do not save your life tonight, tomorrow you will be killed." ¹² So Michal let David down through a window. And he went and fled and escaped.

²⁰ Then Saul sent messengers to take David. And when they saw the group of prophets prophesying, and Samuel standing *as* leader over them, the Spirit of God came upon the messengers of Saul, and they also prophesied. ²¹ And when Saul was told, he sent other messengers, and they prophesied likewise. Then Saul sent messengers again the third time, and they prophesied also. ²² Then he also went…²³ …Then the Spirit of God *was* upon him also, and he went on and prophesied …

1 Samuel 20:

¹ Then David fled [again asking,] "What have I done? What *is* my iniquity, and what *is* my sin before [Saul], that he seeks my life?"

1 Samuel 21:

¹ Now David came to… Ahimelech the priest. And Ahimelech was afraid when he met David, and said to him, "Why *are* you alone, and no one is with you?"

² So David said to Ahimelech… "The king has ordered me on some business, and said to me, 'Do not let anyone know anything about the business on which I send you, or what I have commanded you.' And I have directed *my* young men to such and such a place. ³ Now therefore, what have you on hand? Give *me* five *loaves of* bread in my hand, or whatever can be found."

⁴ And the priest answered David and said, "*There is* no common bread on hand; but there is holy bread, if the young men have at least kept themselves from women." ⁵ Then David answered the priest, and said to him, "Truly, women *have been* kept from us about three days since I came out. And the vessels of the young men are holy, and *the bread is* in effect common, even though it was consecrated in the vessel this day."

⁶ So the priest gave him holy *bread;* for there was no bread there but the showbread which had been taken from before the LORD, in order to put hot bread *in its place* on the day when it was taken away.

¹⁰ Then David arose and [left]…

1 Samuel 24:

¹ Now it happened ² Saul took three thousand chosen men from all Israel, and went to seek David and his men… ³ So he came to the sheepfolds by the road, where there *was*

a cave; and Saul went in to attend to his needs. (David and his men were staying in the recesses of the cave).

[4] Then the men of David said to him, "This is the day of which the LORD said to you, 'Behold, I will deliver your enemy into your hand, that you may do to him as it seems good to you.'" And David arose and secretly cut off a corner of Saul's robe.

[5] Now it happened afterward that David's heart troubled him because he had cut Saul's robe. [6] And he said to his men, "The LORD forbid that I should do this thing to my master, the LORD's anointed, to stretch out my hand against him, seeing he *is* the anointed of the LORD." [7] So David restrained his servants with *these* words, and did not allow them to rise against Saul. And Saul got up from the cave and went on *his* way.

[8] David also arose afterward, went out of the cave, and called out to Saul, saying, "My lord the king!" And when Saul looked behind him, David stooped with his face to the earth, and bowed down. [9] And David said to Saul: "Why do you listen to the words of men who say, 'Indeed David seeks your harm'? [10] Look, this day your eyes have seen that the LORD delivered you today into my hand in the cave, and *someone* urged *me* to kill you. But [I] spared you, and I said, 'I will not stretch out my hand against my lord, for he *is* the LORD's anointed.' [11] Moreover, my father, see! Yes, see the corner of your robe in my hand! For in that I cut off the corner of your robe, and did not kill you, know and see that *there is* neither evil nor rebellion in my hand, and I have not sinned against you. Yet you hunt my life to take it. [12] …But my hand shall not be against you. [13] As the proverb of the ancients says, 'Wickedness proceeds from the wicked.' But my hand shall not be against you. [14] After whom has the king of Israel come out? Whom do you pursue? A dead dog? A flea? [15] Therefore let the LORD be judge…and deliver me out of your hand."

[16] So it was, when David had finished speaking these words to Saul, that Saul said, "*Is* this your voice, my son David?" And Saul lifted up his voice and wept. [17] Then he said to David: "You *are* more righteous than I; for you have rewarded me with good, whereas I have rewarded you with evil. [18] And you have shown this day how you have dealt well with me; for when the LORD delivered me into your hand, you did not kill me. [19] …Therefore may the LORD reward you with good for what you have done to me this day. [20] And now I know indeed that you shall surely be king, and that the kingdom of Israel shall be established in your hand.

1 Samuel 25:

[2] A certain man in Maon, who had property… at Carmel, was very wealthy. He had a thousand goats and three thousand sheep, which he was shearing in Carmel. [3] His name was Nabal and his wife's name was Abigail. She was an intelligent and beautiful woman, but her husband was surly and mean in his dealings…

[4] While David was in the wilderness, he heard that Nabal was shearing sheep. [5] So he sent ten young men and said to them, "Go up to Nabal at Carmel and greet him in my name. [6] Say to him: 'Long life to you! Good health to you and your household! And good health to all that is yours!

[7] "'Now I hear that it is sheep-shearing time. When your shepherds were with us, we did not mistreat them, and the whole time they were at Carmel nothing of theirs was

missing. [8] …Therefore be favorable toward my men, since we come at a festive time. Please give your servants and your son David whatever you can find for them.'"

[9] When David's men arrived, they gave Nabal this message in David's name. Then they waited.

[10] Nabal answered David's servants, "Who is this David? Who is this son of Jesse? Many servants are breaking away from their masters these days. [11] Why should I take my bread and water, and the meat I have slaughtered for my shearers, and give it to men coming from who knows where?"

[12] David's men turned around and went back. When they arrived, they reported every word.

[14] One of the servants told Abigail, Nabal's wife, "David sent messengers from the wilderness to give our master his greetings, but he hurled insults at them. [15] Yet these men were very good to us. They did not mistreat us, and the whole time we were out in the fields near them nothing was missing. [16] Night and day they were a wall around us the whole time we were herding our sheep near them. [17] Now think it over and see what you can do, because disaster is hanging over our master and his whole household…"

[18] Abigail acted quickly. She took two hundred loaves of bread, two skins of wine, five dressed sheep, [60 pounds/27 kilograms] of roasted grain, a hundred cakes of raisins and two hundred cakes of pressed figs, and loaded them on donkeys. [19] Then she told her servants, "Go on ahead; I'll follow you." But she did not tell her husband Nabal.

[20] As she came riding her donkey into a mountain ravine, there were David and his men descending toward her, and she met them.

[23] When Abigail saw David, she quickly got off her donkey and bowed down before David with her face to the ground. [24] She fell at his feet and said: "Pardon your servant, my lord, and let me speak to you; hear what your servant has to say. [25] Please pay no attention, my lord… Nabal. He is just like his name — his name means Fool, and folly goes with him. And as for me, your servant, I did not see the men my lord sent. [26] And now, my lord, as surely as the LORD your God lives and as you live… [27] let this gift, which your servant has brought to my lord, be given to the men who follow you.

[28] "Please forgive your servant's presumption. The LORD your God will certainly make a lasting dynasty for my lord… [29] Even though someone is pursuing you to take your life, the life of my lord will be bound securely in the bundle of the living by the LORD your God… [30] When the LORD has fulfilled for my lord every good thing [H]e promised concerning him and has appointed him ruler over Israel, [31] my lord will not have on his conscience the staggering burden of needless bloodshed… And when the LORD your God has brought my lord success, remember your servant."

[32] David said to Abigail, "Praise be to the LORD… [W]ho has sent you today to meet me. [33] May you be blessed for your good judgment and for keeping me from bloodshed this day… [34]

[35] Then David accepted from her hand what she had brought him and said, "Go home in

peace. I have heard your words and granted your request."

1 Samuel 26:

[2] ...Saul went... with three thousand select... troops, to search... for David. [3] ...When [David] saw that Saul had followed him... [4] he sent out scouts [and] [5] went to the place where Saul had camped. He saw where Saul and Abner son of Ner, the commander of the army, had lain down. Saul was lying inside the camp, with the army encamped around him.

[6] David then asked Ahimelek and Abishai, "Who will go down into the camp with me to Saul?"

 "I'll go with you," said Abishai.

[7] So David and Abishai went to the army by night, and there was Saul, lying asleep inside the camp with his spear stuck in the ground near his head. Abner and the soldiers were lying around him.

[8] Abishai said to David, "Today God has delivered your enemy into your hands. Now let me pin him to the ground with one thrust of the spear; I won't strike him twice."

[9] But David said to Abishai, "Don't destroy him! Who can lay a hand on the LORD's anointed and be guiltless? [11] ...[T]he LORD forbid that I should lay a hand on [His] anointed..."

[12] So David took the spear and water jug near Saul's head, and they left. No one saw or knew about it, nor did anyone wake up.

[13] Then David crossed over to the other side and stood on top of the hill some distance away; there was a wide space between them. [14] He called out to the army and to Abner son of Ner, "Aren't you going to answer me, Abner?"

Abner replied, "Who are you who calls to the king?"

[15] David said, "Why didn't you guard your lord the king? [16] What you have done is not good... Look around you. Where are the king's spear and water jug that were near his head?"

[17] Saul recognized David's voice and said, "Is that your voice, David my son?"

David replied, "Yes it is, my lord the king." [18] And he added, "Why is my lord pursuing his servant? What have I done, and what wrong am I guilty of?"

[21] Then Saul said, "I have sinned. Come back, David my son. Because you considered my life precious today, I will not try to harm you again. Surely I have acted like a fool and have been terribly wrong."

[22] "Here is the king's spear," David answered. "Let one of your young men come over and get it. [23] The LORD rewards everyone for their righteousness and faithfulness. The

LORD delivered you into my hands today, but I would not lay a hand on the LORD's anointed. ²⁴ As surely as I valued your life today, so may the LORD value my life and deliver me from all trouble."

²⁵ Then Saul said to David, "May you be blessed, David my son; you will do great things and surely triumph."

So David went on his way, and Saul returned home.

1 Samuel 27:

¹ But David thought to himself, "One of these days I will be destroyed by the hand of Saul. The best thing I can do is to escape to the land of the Philistines. Then Saul will give up searching for me anywhere in Israel, and I will slip out of his hand."

² So... ³ David and his men settled in Gath [with their families]... ⁴ When Saul was told that David had fled to Gath, he no longer searched for him.

⁷ David lived in Philistine territory a year and four months.

2 Samuel 1:

¹ After the death of Saul, David returned…

¹⁷ David took up this lament concerning Saul… ²⁴ "Daughters of Israel, weep for Saul, who clothed you in scarlet and finery, who adorned your garments with ornaments of gold.

2 Samuel 2:

¹ In the course of time, David inquired of the LORD. "Shall I go up to one of the towns of Judah?" he asked.   The LORD said, "Go up." David asked, "Where shall I go?" "To Hebron," the LORD answered.

² So David went up there… ³ David also took the men who were with him, each with his family, and they settled in Hebron and its towns. ⁴ Then the men of Judah came to Hebron, and there they anointed David king over the tribe of Judah.

When David was told that it was the men from Jabesh Gilead who had buried Saul, ⁵ he sent messengers to them to say to them, "The LORD bless you for showing this kindness to Saul your master by burying him. ⁶ May the LORD now show you kindness and faithfulness, and I too will show you the same favor because you have done this…"

2 Samuel 5:

¹ All the tribes of Israel came to David at Hebron and said, "We are your own flesh and blood. ² …And the LORD said… 'You will shepherd [M]y people… and you will become their ruler.'"

³ When all the elders of Israel had come to King David at Hebron, the king made a

covenant with them at Hebron before the LORD, and they anointed David king over Israel.

⁴ David was thirty years old when he became king, and he reigned forty years. ⁵ In Hebron he reigned over Judah seven years and six months, and in Jerusalem he reigned over all Israel and Judah thirty-three years.

2 Samuel 8:

¹⁵ David reigned over all Israel, doing what was just and right for all his people.

2 Samuel 23:

³ ...God... spoke...:   'When one rules... in righteousness, when he rules in the fear of God, ⁴ he is like the light of morning at sunrise on a cloudless morning, like the brightness after rain that brings grass from the earth.'

2 Samuel 7:

¹ After the king was settled in his palace and the LORD had given him rest... ² [David] said to Nathan the prophet, "Here I am, living in a house of cedar, while the ark of God remains in a tent."

³ Nathan replied to the king, "Whatever you have in mind, go ahead and do it, for the LORD is with you."

⁴ But that night the word of the LORD came to Nathan, saying: ⁸ "Now then, tell my servant David, 'This is what the LORD Almighty says: I took you from the pasture, from tending the flock, and appointed you ruler over my people... ⁹ I have been with you wherever you have gone... Now I will make your name great, like the names of the greatest men on earth. ¹⁰ And I will provide a place for [M]y people... and will plant them so that they can have a home of their own... ¹¹ I will also give you rest...   The LORD declares to you that the LORD [H]imself will establish a house for you: ¹² When your days are over and you rest with your ancestors, I will raise up your offspring to succeed you, your own flesh and blood, and I will establish his kingdom. ¹³ He is the one who will build a house for my Name, and I will establish the throne of his kingdom forever. ¹⁴ I will be his father, and he will be [M]y son. ¹⁵ ...[M]y love will never be taken away from him... ¹⁶ Your house and your kingdom will endure forever before [M]e; your throne will be established forever.'"

¹⁷ Nathan reported to David all the words of this entire revelation.

¹⁸ Then King David went in and sat before the LORD, and he said: "Who am I, Sovereign LORD, and what is my family, that [Y]ou have brought me this far? ¹⁹ And as if this were not enough in [Y]our sight, Sovereign LORD, [Y]ou have also spoken about the future of the house of [Y]our servant — and this decree, Sovereign LORD, is for a mere human!

²⁰ What more can David say to [Y]ou? For [Y]ou know [Y]our servant, Sovereign LORD. ²¹ For the sake of [Y]our word and according to [Y]our will, [Y]ou have done this great thing and made it known to [Y]our servant.

²² How great [Y]ou are, Sovereign LORD! There is no one like [Y]ou, and there is no God but [Y]ou… ²⁵ And now, LORD God, keep forever the promise [Y]ou have made concerning [Y]our servant and his house. Do as [Y]ou promised, ²⁶ so that [Y]our name will be great forever…"

²⁷ LORD Almighty, God of Israel, [Y]ou have revealed this to [Y]our servant, saying, 'I will build a house for you.' So [Y]our servant has found courage to pray this prayer to [Y]ou. ²⁸ Sovereign LORD, [Y]ou are God! Your covenant is trustworthy, and [Y]ou have promised these good things to [Y]our servant. ²⁹ Now be pleased to bless the house of [Y]our servant, that it may continue forever in [Y]our sight; for [Y]ou, Sovereign LORD, have spoken, and with [Y]our blessing the house of [Y]our servant will be blessed forever."

2 Samuel 11:

² One evening David got up from his bed and walked around on the roof of the palace. From the roof he saw a woman bathing. The woman was very beautiful, ³ and David sent someone to find out about her. The man said, "She is Bathsheba… the wife of Uriah…" ⁴ Then David sent messengers to get her. She came to him, and he slept with her. Then she went back home. ⁵ The woman conceived…

2 Samuel 12:

¹ The LORD sent Nathan to David. When he came to him, he said, "There were two men in a certain town, one rich and the other poor. ² The rich man had a very large number of sheep and cattle, ³ but the poor man had nothing except one little ewe lamb he had bought. He raised it, and it grew up with him and his children. It shared his food, drank from his cup and even slept in his arms. It was like a daughter to him.

⁴ Now a traveler came to the rich man, but the rich man refrained from taking one of his own sheep or cattle to prepare a meal for the traveler who had come to him. Instead, he took the ewe lamb that belonged to the poor man and prepared it for the one who had come to him."

⁵ David burned with anger against the man and said to Nathan, "As surely as the LORD lives… ⁶ [h]e must pay for that lamb four times over, because he did such a thing and had no pity."

⁷ Then Nathan said to David, "You are the man! This is what the LORD… says: 'I anointed you king over Israel, and I delivered you from the hand of Saul… ⁹ Why did you despise the word of the LORD by doing what is evil in his eyes?"

¹³ Then David said to Nathan, "I have sinned against the LORD."

Nathan replied, "The LORD has taken away your sin…"

2 Samuel 22:

¹ David sang to the LORD the words of this song when the LORD delivered him from the hand of all his enemies and from the hand of Saul. ² He said: "The LORD is my rock, my

fortress and my deliverer; ³ my God is my rock, in whom I take refuge, my shield and the horn of my salvation. He is my stronghold, my refuge and my savior — from violent people [Y]ou save me.

⁴ "I called to the LORD, [W]ho is worthy of praise, and have been saved from my enemies. ⁵ The waves of death swirled about me; the torrents of destruction overwhelmed me. ⁶ The cords of the grave coiled around me; the snares of death confronted me. ⁷ In my distress I called to the LORD; I called out to my God. From [H]is temple [H]e heard my voice; my cry came to [H]is ears.

⁸ The earth trembled and quaked, the foundations of the heavens shook... ¹⁰ He parted the heavens and came down; dark clouds were under [H]is feet.

¹¹ He mounted the cherubim and flew; [H]e soared on the wings of the wind. ¹² He made darkness [H]is canopy around [H]im — the dark rain clouds of the sky. ¹³ Out of the brightness of [H]is presence bolts of lightning blazed forth. ¹⁴ The LORD thundered from heaven; the voice of the Most High resounded.

¹⁶ The valleys of the sea were exposed and the foundations of the earth laid bare at the rebuke of the LORD... ¹⁷ He reached down from on high and took hold of me; [H]e drew me out of deep waters. ¹⁸ He rescued me from my powerful enemy, from my foes, who were too strong for me. ¹⁹ ...[T]he LORD was my support.

²⁰ He brought me out into a spacious place; [H]e rescued me because [H]e delighted in me. ²³ All [H]is laws are before me; ²⁵ The LORD has rewarded me...

²⁶ To the faithful [Y]ou show [Y]ourself faithful, to the blameless [Y]ou show [Y]ourself blameless, ²⁷ to the pure [Y]ou show [Y]ourself pure... ²⁸ You save the humble... ²⁹ You, LORD, are my lamp; the LORD turns my darkness into light.

³¹ As for God, [H]is way is perfect: The LORD's word is flawless; [H]e shields all who take refuge in [H]im. ³² For who is God besides the LORD? And who is the Rock except our God? ³³ It is God [W]ho arms me with strength and keeps my way secure. ³⁴ He makes my feet like the feet of a deer; [H]e causes me to stand on the heights.

³⁶ You make your saving help my shield; [Y]our help has made me great. ³⁷ You provide a broad path for my feet, so that my ankles do not give way. ⁴⁴ You have delivered me...; [Y]ou have preserved me...

⁴⁷ The LORD lives! Praise be to my Rock! Exalted be my God, the Rock, my Savior! ⁴⁸ He is the God... ⁴⁹ who sets me free... ⁵⁰ Therefore I will praise [Y]ou, LORD, among the nations; I will sing the praises of [Y]our name. ⁵¹ "He... shows unfailing kindness to [H]is anointed... and his descendants forever."

1 Chronicles 16:

⁸ "Oh, give thanks to the LORD! Call upon His name; Make known His deeds among the peoples! ⁹ Sing to Him, sing psalms to Him; Talk of all His wondrous works! ¹⁰ Glory in His holy name; Let the hearts of those rejoice who seek the LORD! ¹¹ Seek the LORD

and His strength; Seek His face evermore!

¹² Remember His marvelous works which He has done, His wonders, and the judgments of His mouth, ¹³ O… [y]ou children… His chosen ones!

¹⁴ He *is* the LORD our God; His judgments *are* in all the earth. ¹⁵ Remember His covenant forever, [t]he word which He commanded, for a thousand generations…

²³ Sing to the LORD, all the earth; Proclaim the good news of His salvation from day to day. ²⁴ Declare His glory among the nations, His wonders among all peoples. ²⁵ For the LORD *is* great and greatly to be praised; ²⁷ Honor and majesty *are* before Him; Strength and gladness are in His place.

²⁸ Give to the LORD, O families of the peoples, [g]ive to the LORD glory and strength. ²⁹ Give to the LORD the glory *due* His name; …Oh, worship the LORD in the beauty of holiness!

³⁰ Tremble before Him, all the earth… ³¹ Let the heavens rejoice, and let the earth be glad; And let them say among the nations, 'The LORD reigns.'

³² Let the sea roar, and all its fullness; Let the field rejoice, and all that *is* in it. ³³ Then the trees of the woods shall rejoice before the LORD… ³⁴ Oh, give thanks to the LORD, for *He is* good! For His mercy *endures* forever.

³⁵ And say, 'Save us, O God of our salvation; Gather us together, and deliver us… [t]o give thanks to Your holy name, [t]o triumph in Your praise.'

³⁶ Blessed *be* the LORD God… [f]rom everlasting to everlasting!" And all the people said, "Amen!" and praised the LORD.

1 Chronicles 29:

¹⁸ O LORD God of Abraham, Isaac, and Israel, our fathers… ¹⁹ give my son Solomon a loyal heart to keep Your commandments and Your testimonies and Your statutes, to do all *these things,* and to build the temple for which I have made provision."

Islam:

The Cow 2:246-247 Have you not considered the chiefs of the children of Israel after Musa (Moses), when they said to a prophet (Samuel) of theirs: Raise up for us a king… And their prophet said to them: Surely [God] has raised Talut (Saul) to be a king over you. They said: How can he hold kingship over us while we have a greater right to kingship than he, and he has not been granted an abundance of wealth? He said: Surely [God] has chosen him in preference to you, and He has increased him abundantly in knowledge and physique, and [God] grants His kingdom to whom He pleases…

The Cow 2:251 And… [God] gave [Dawood (David)] kingdom and wisdom, and taught him of what He pleased. And were it not for [God]…the earth would certainly be in a state of disorder; but [God] is Gracious to the creatures.

The Women 4:163 Surely… We gave to Dawood.

The Children of Israel 17:55 And your Lord best knows those who are in the heavens and the earth; and certainly [I] have made some of the prophets to excel [over] others, and to Dawood [I] gave a scripture.

The Saba 34:10-11 And certainly [I] gave to Dawood excellence…: O mountains! [S]ing praises with him, and the birds; and [I] made the iron pliant to him, [s]aying: …do good; surely I am Seeing what you do.

Suad 38:17-20 Bear patiently what they say, and remember [My] servant Dawood, the possessor of power; surely he was frequent [in] returning (to God). Surely [I] made the mountains to sing the glory (of God) in unison with him at the evening and the sunrise, [a]nd the birds gathered together; all joined in singing with him. And [I] strengthened his kingdom and [I] gave him wisdom and a clear judgment

.
Suad 38:21-23 And has there come to you the story of the litigants, when they made an entry into the private chamber by ascending over the walls? When they entered in upon Dawood and he was frightened at them, they said: Fear not; two litigants, of whom one has acted wrongfully towards the other, therefore decide between us with justice, and do not act unjustly, and guide us to the right way. Surely this is my brother; he has ninety-nine ewes and I have a single ewe; but he said: Make it over to me, and he has prevailed against me in discourse.

Suad 38:24-26 He said: Surely he has been unjust to you in demanding your ewe (to add) to his own ewes; and most surely most of the partners act wrongfully towards one another, save those who believe and do good, and very few are they; and Dawood was sure that [I] had tried him, so he sought the protection of his Lord and he fell down bowing and turned time after time (to Him). Therefore [I] rectified for him this, and most surely he had a nearness to [Me] and an excellent resort. O Dawood ! [S]urely [I] have made you a ruler in the land; so judge between men with justice and do not follow desire, lest it should lead you astray from the path of God…

The Prophets 21:79 [A]nd [I] made the mountains, and the birds to celebrate [My] praise with Dawood.

The Ant 27:15 And certainly [I] gave knowledge to Dawood and Sulaiman (Solomon), and they both said: Praise be to [God], Who has made us to excel many of His believing servants.

Suad 38:30 And [I] gave to Dawood Sulaiman, most excellent the servant! Surely he was frequent in returning (to God).

The Ant 27:15 And Sulaiman was Dawood's heir, and he said: O men! [W]e have been taught the language of birds, and we have been given all things; most surely this is manifest grace.

IX. First Book of Kings

Christianity/Judaism:

1 Kings 1:

[34] "There let Zadok the priest and Nathan the prophet anoint him king over Israel; and blow the horn, and say, '*Long* live King Solomon!' [35] Then you shall come up after him, and he shall come and sit on my throne, and he shall be king in my place. For I have appointed him to be ruler over Israel and Judah."

[36] Benaiah the son of Jehoiada answered the king and said, "Amen! May the LORD God of my lord the king say so *too*. [37] As the LORD has been with my lord the king, even so may He be with Solomon, and make his throne greater than the throne of my lord King David."

[38] So Zadok the priest, Nathan the prophet, Benaiah…, the Cherethites, and the Pelethites went down and had Solomon ride on King David's mule, and took him to Gihon. [39] Then Zadok the priest took a horn of oil from the tabernacle and anointed Solomon. And they blew the horn, and all the people said, *"Long* live King Solomon!" [40] And all the people went up after him; and the people played the flutes and rejoiced with great joy…

[47] And moreover the king's servants have gone to bless… King David, saying, "May God make the name of Solomon better than your name, and may He make his throne greater than your throne." Then the king bowed himself on the bed. [48] Also the king said thus, "Blessed *be* the LORD God… [W]ho has given *one* to sit on my throne this day, while my eyes see *it!*"

1 Kings 3:

[1] Now Solomon made a treaty with Pharaoh king of Egypt, and married Pharaoh's daughter; then he brought her to the City of David until he had finished building his own house, and the house of the LORD, and the wall all around Jerusalem. [3] And Solomon loved the LORD…

[5] …[T]he LORD appeared to Solomon in a dream by night; and God said, "Ask! What shall I give you?"

[6] And Solomon said: "You have shown great mercy to Your servant David my father, because he walked before You in truth, in righteousness, and in uprightness of heart with You; You have continued this great kindness for him, and You have given him a son to sit on his throne, as *it is* this day. [7] Now, O LORD my God, You have made Your servant king… but I *am* a little child; I do not know *how* to go out or come in. [8] And Your servant *is* in the midst of Your people whom You have chosen, a great people, too numerous to be numbered or counted. [9] Therefore give to Your servant an understanding heart to judge Your people, that I may discern between good and evil. For who is able to judge this great people of Yours?"

¹⁰ The speech pleased the Lord, that Solomon had asked this thing. ¹¹ Then God said to him: "Because you have asked this thing, and have not asked long life for yourself, nor have asked riches for yourself, nor have asked the life of your enemies, but have asked for yourself understanding to discern justice, ¹² behold, I have done according to your words; see, I have given you a wise and understanding heart, so that there has not been anyone like you before you, nor shall any like you arise after you. ¹³ And I have also given you what you have not asked: both riches and honor, so that there shall not be anyone like you among the kings all your days. ¹⁴ So if you walk in My ways, to keep My statutes and My commandments, as your father David walked, then I will lengthen your days."

¹⁵ Then Solomon awoke; and indeed it had been a dream. And he came to Jerusalem and stood before the ark of the covenant of the LORD, offered up burnt offerings, offered peace offerings, and made a feast for all his servants.

¹⁶ Now two women… came to the king, and stood before him. ¹⁷ And one woman said, "O my lord, this woman and I dwell in the same house; and I gave birth while she *was* in the house. ¹⁸ Then it happened, the third day after I had given birth, that this woman also gave birth. And we *were* together; no one *was* with us in the house, except the two of us in the house. ¹⁹ And this woman's son died in the night, because she lay on him. ²⁰ So she arose in the middle of the night and took my son from my side, while your maidservant slept, and laid him in her bosom, and laid her dead child in my bosom.

²² Then the other woman said, "No! [T]he living one *is* my son, and the dead one *is* your son."

And the first woman said, "No! [T]he dead one *is* your son, and the living one *is* my son." Thus they spoke before the king.

²⁴ …[T]he king said, "Bring me a sword." So they brought a sword before the king. ²⁵ And the king said, "Divide the living child in two, and give half to one, and half to the other." ²⁶ Then the woman whose son *was* living spoke to the king, for she yearned with compassion for her son; and she said, "O my lord, give her the living child, and by no means kill him!"

But the other said, "Let him be neither mine nor yours, *but* divide *him*."

²⁷ So the king answered and said, "Give the first woman the living child, and by no means kill him; she *is* his mother."

²⁸ And all… heard of the judgment, which the king had rendered; and… they saw that the wisdom of God *was* in him to administer justice.

1 Kings 4:

¹ So King Solomon was king over all Israel.

²⁰ Judah and Israel *were* as numerous as the sand by the sea in multitude, eating and drinking and rejoicing. ²¹ So Solomon reigned over all kingdoms from the River *to* the land of the Philistines, as far as the border of Egypt. *They* brought tribute and served Solomon all the days of his life.

²⁴ ...[H]e had peace on every side all around him. ²⁵ And Judah and Israel dwelt safely, each man under his vine and his fig tree, from Dan as far as Beersheba, all the days of Solomon.

²⁹ And God gave Solomon wisdom and exceedingly great understanding, and largeness of heart like the sand on the seashore. ³⁰ Thus Solomon's wisdom excelled the wisdom of all the men of the East and all the wisdom of Egypt. ³¹ For he was wiser than all men... and his fame was in all the surrounding nations. ³² He spoke three thousand proverbs, and his songs were one thousand and five. ³³ Also he spoke of trees, from the cedar tree of Lebanon even to the hyssop that springs out of the wall; he spoke also of animals, of birds, of creeping things, and of fish. ³⁴ And men of all nations, from all the kings of the earth who had heard of his wisdom, came to hear the wisdom of Solomon.

1 Kings 5:

¹ Now Hiram king of Tyre sent his servants to Solomon, because he heard that they had anointed him king in place of his father, for Hiram had always loved David. ² Then Solomon sent to Hiram, saying: ⁴ [T]he LORD my God has given me rest on every side; *there is* neither adversary nor evil occurrence.

⁵ And behold, I propose to build a house for the name of the LORD my God, as the LORD spoke to my father David, saying, "Your son, whom I will set on your throne in your place, he shall build the house for My name."

⁶ Now therefore, command that they cut down cedars for me from Lebanon; and my servants will be with your servants, and I will pay you wages for your servants according to whatever you say. For you know *there is* none among us who has skill to cut timber like the Sidonians.

⁷ So it was, when Hiram heard the words of Solomon, that he rejoiced greatly and said, Blessed *be* the LORD this day, for He has given David a wise son over this great people!

⁸ Then Hiram sent to Solomon, saying: I have considered *the message,* which you sent me, *and* I will do all you desire concerning the cedar and cypress logs. ⁹ My servants shall bring *them* down from Lebanon to the sea; I will float them in rafts by sea to the place you indicate to me, and will have them broken apart there; then you can take *them* away. And you shall fulfill my desire by giving food for my household. ¹⁰ Then Hiram gave Solomon cedar and cypress logs *according to* all his desire. ¹¹ And Solomon gave Hiram... wheat... and... pressed oil. Thus Solomon gave to Hiram year by year.

¹² So the LORD gave Solomon wisdom, as He had promised him; and there was peace between Hiram and Solomon, and the two of them made a treaty together.

¹³ Then King Solomon raised up a labor force out of all Israel; and the labor force was thirty thousand men. ¹⁴ And he sent them to Lebanon, ten thousand a month in shifts: they were one month in Lebanon *and* two months at home... ¹⁵ Solomon had seventy thousand who carried burdens, and eighty thousand who quarried *stone* in the mountains...¹⁷ And the king commanded them to quarry large stones, costly stones, *and*

hewn stones, to lay the foundation of the temple. [18] So Solomon's builders, Hiram's builders, and the Gebalites quarried *them;* and they prepared timber and stones to build the temple.

1 Kings 6:

[1] And it came to pass… in the fourth year of Solomon's reign over Israel he began to build the house of the LORD.

[11] Then the word of the LORD came to Solomon, saying: [12] "*Concerning* this temple which you are building, if you walk in My statutes, execute My judgments, keep all My commandments, and walk in them, then I will perform My word with you, which I spoke to your father David. [13] And I will dwell among the children of Israel, and will not forsake My people…"

[14] So Solomon built the temple and finished it. [38] And in the eleventh year… the house was finished in all its details and according to all its plans…

1 Kings 8:

[1] Now Solomon assembled the elders of Israel and all the heads of the tribes, the chief fathers of the children of Israel, to King Solomon in Jerusalem, that they might bring up the ark of the covenant of the LORD from the City of David, which *is* Zion. [3] So all the elders of Israel came, and the priests took up the ark. [4] Then they brought up the ark of the LORD, the tabernacle of meeting, and all the holy furnishings that *were* in the tabernacle. The priests and the Levites brought them up. [9] Nothing *was* in the ark except the two tablets of stone which Moses put there at Horeb, when the LORD made *a covenant* with the children of Israel, when they came out of the land of Egypt. [10] And it came to pass, when the priests came out of the holy *place,* that the cloud filled the house of the LORD, [11] so that the priests could not continue ministering because of the cloud; for the glory of the LORD filled the house of the LORD. [12] Then Solomon spoke: "The LORD said He would dwell in the dark cloud. [13] I have surely built You an exalted house, [a] place for you to dwell in forever."

[14] Then the king turned around and blessed the whole assembly of Israel… [15] And he said: "Blessed *be* the LORD God… [20] So the LORD has fulfilled His word which He spoke; and I have filled the position of my father David, and sit on the throne of Israel, as the LORD promised; and I have built a temple for the name of the LORD God… [21] And there I have made a place for the ark, in which *is* the covenant of the LORD…"

[22] Then Solomon stood before the altar of the LORD in the presence of all the assembly… and spread out his hands toward heaven; [23] and he said: "LORD God… *there is* no God in heaven above or on earth below like You, who keep *Your* covenant and mercy with Your servants who walk before You with all their hearts. [24] You have kept what You promised…

[27] "But will God indeed dwell on the earth? Behold, heaven and the heaven of heavens cannot contain You. How much less this temple which I have built! [28] Yet regard the prayer of Your servant and his supplication, O LORD my God, and listen to the cry and the prayer which Your servant is praying before You today: [29] that Your eyes may be

open toward this temple night and day, toward the place of which You said, 'My name shall be there,' that You may hear the prayer which Your servant makes toward this place. [30] And may You hear the supplication of Your servant and of Your people… when they pray toward this place. Hear in heaven Your dwelling place; and when You hear, forgive."

[54] And so it was, when Solomon had finished praying all this prayer and supplication to the LORD, that he arose from before the altar of the LORD, from kneeling on his knees with his hands spread up to heaven. [55] Then he stood and blessed all the assembly…

1 Kings 9:

[1] And it came to pass, when Solomon had finished building the house of the LORD… [2] that the LORD appeared to Solomon the second time… [3] And the LORD said to him: "I have heard your prayer and your supplication that you have made before Me; I have consecrated this house which you have built to put My name there forever, and My eyes and My heart will be there perpetually. [4] Now if you walk before Me as your father David walked, in integrity of heart and in uprightness, to do according to all that I have commanded you, *and* if you keep My statutes and My judgments, [5] then I will establish the throne of your kingdom over Israel forever, as I promised David your father, saying, 'You shall not fail to have a man on the throne of Israel.'

2 Chronicles 8:

[1] It came to pass at the end of twenty years, when Solomon had built the house of the LORD and his own house, [2] that the cities which Hiram had given to Solomon, Solomon built them; and he settled the children of Israel there.

1 Kings 10:

[1] Now when the queen of Sheba heard of the fame of Solomon concerning the name of the LORD, she came to test him with hard questions. [2] She came to Jerusalem with a very great retinue, with camels that bore spices, very much gold, and precious stones; and when she came to Solomon, she spoke with him about all that was in her heart. [3] So Solomon answered all her questions; there was nothing so difficult for the king that he could not explain *it* to her. [4] And when the queen of Sheba had seen all the wisdom of Solomon, the house that he had built, [5] the food on his table… the service of his waiters and their apparel, his cupbearers, and his entryway by which he went up to the house of the LORD, there was no more spirit in her.

[6] Then she said to the king: "It was a true report which I heard in my own land about your words and your wisdom. [7] However I did not believe the words until I came and saw with my own eyes; and indeed the half was not told me. Your wisdom and prosperity exceed the fame of which I heard. [8] Happy *are* your [people]… who stand continually before you *and* hear your wisdom! [9] Blessed be the LORD your God, [W]ho delighted in you, setting you on the throne of Israel… to do justice and righteousness."

[10] Then she gave the king one hundred and twenty talents of gold, spices in great quantity, and precious stones. There never again came such abundance of spices as the queen of Sheba gave to King Solomon. [11] Also, the ships of Hiram, which brought gold

from Ophir, brought great quantities of almug wood and precious stones from Ophir. ¹² And the king made steps of the almug wood for the house of the LORD and for the king's house, also harps and stringed instruments for singers. There never again came such almug wood, nor has the like been seen to this day.

¹³ Now King Solomon gave the queen of Sheba all she desired, whatever she asked, besides what Solomon had given her according to the royal generosity. So she turned and went to her own country...

²¹ ...King Solomon surpassed all the kings of the earth in riches and wisdom. ²⁴ Now all the earth sought the presence of Solomon to hear his wisdom, which God had put in his heart.

Solomon and the Queen of Sheba
By Piero della Francesca c. 1452-1466

1 Kings 11:

⁴² And the period that Solomon reigned in Jerusalem over all Israel *was* forty years.

1 Kings 17:

¹ And Elijah... said to Ahab, "*As* the LORD God of Israel lives, before whom I stand, there shall not be dew nor rain these years, except at my word."

² Then the word of the LORD came to him, saying, ³ "Get away from here and turn eastward, and hide by the Brook Cherith, which flows into the Jordan. ⁴ And it will be *that* you shall drink from the brook, and I have commanded the ravens to feed you there." ⁵ So he went and did according to the word of the LORD, for he went and stayed by the Brook Cherith, which flows into the Jordan. ⁶ The ravens brought him bread and meat in the morning, and bread and meat in the evening; and he drank from the brook. ⁷ And it happened after a while that the brook dried up, because there had been no rain in the land.

[8] Then the word of the LORD came to him, saying, [9] "Arise, go to Zarephath… and dwell there. See, I have commanded a widow there to provide for you." [10] So he arose and went to Zarephath. And when he came to the gate of the city, indeed a widow *was* there gathering sticks. And he called to her and said, "Please bring me a little water in a cup, that I may drink." [11] And as she was going to get *it,* he called to her and said, "Please bring me a morsel of bread in your hand."

[12] So she said, "As the LORD your God lives, I do not have bread, only a handful of flour in a bin, and a little oil in a jar; and see, I *am* gathering a couple of sticks that I may go in and prepare it for myself and my son, that we may eat it, and die." [13] And Elijah said to her, "Do not fear; go *and* do as you have said, but make me a small cake from it first, and bring *it* to me; and afterward make *some* for yourself and your son. [14] For thus says the LORD…: 'The bin of flour shall not be used up, nor shall the jar of oil run dry, until the day the LORD sends rain on the earth.'"

[15] So she went away and did according to the word of Elijah; and she and he and her household ate for *many* days. [16] The bin of flour was not used up, nor did the jar of oil run dry, according to the word of the LORD, which He spoke by Elijah.

[17] Now it happened after these things *that* the son of the woman who owned the house became sick. And his sickness was so serious that there was no breath left in him. [19] …[H]e said to her, "Give me your son." So he took him out of her arms and carried him to the upper room where he was staying, and laid him on his own bed. [21] And he stretched himself out on the child three times, and cried out to the LORD and said, "O LORD my God, I pray, let this child's soul come back to him." [22] Then the LORD heard the voice of Elijah; and the soul of the child came back to him, and he revived. [23] And Elijah took the child and brought him down from the upper room into the house, and gave him to his mother. And Elijah said, "See, your son lives!" [24] Then the woman said to Elijah, "Now by this I know that you *are* a man of God, *and* that the word of the LORD in your mouth *is* the truth."

1 Kings 18:

[1] And it came to pass *after* many days that the word of the LORD came to Elijah, in the third year, saying, "Go, present yourself to Ahab, and I will send rain on the earth." [2] So Elijah went to present himself to Ahab.

[17] Then it happened, when Ahab saw Elijah, that Ahab said to him, "*Is that* you, O troubler of Israel?"

[18] And he answered, "I have not troubled Israel, but you and your father's house *have,* in that you have forsaken the commandments of the LORD and have followed the Baals. [19] Now therefore, send *and* gather all Israel to me on Mount Carmel, the four hundred and fifty prophets of Baal, and the four hundred prophets of Asherah, who eat at Jezebel's table."

[20] So Ahab sent for all the children of Israel, and gathered the prophets together on Mount Carmel. [21] And Elijah came to all the people, and said, "How long will you falter between two opinions? If the LORD *is* God, follow Him; but if Baal, follow him." But the people answered him not a word. [22] Then Elijah said to the people, "I alone am left a

prophet of the LORD; but Baal's prophets *are* four hundred and fifty men. ²³ Therefore let them give us two bulls; and let them choose one bull for themselves, cut it in pieces, and lay *it* on the wood, but put no fire *under it;* and I will prepare the other bull, and lay *it* on the wood, but put no fire *under it.* ²⁴ Then you call on the name of your gods, and I will call on the name of the LORD; and the God who answers by fire, He is God." So all the people answered and said, "It is well spoken."

²⁵ Now Elijah said to the prophets of Baal, "Choose one bull for yourselves and prepare *it* first, for you *are* many; and call on the name of your god, but put no fire *under it.*" ²⁶ So they took the bull which was given them, and they prepared *it,* and called on the name of Baal from morning... till noon, saying, "O Baal, hear us!" But *there was* no voice; no one answered. Then they leaped about the altar, which they had made. ²⁷ And so it was, at noon, that Elijah mocked them and said, "Cry aloud, for he *is* a god; either he is meditating, or he is busy, or he is on a journey, *or* perhaps he is sleeping and must be awakened." ²⁸ So they cried aloud... ²⁹ And when midday was past, they prophesied until the *time* of the offering of the *evening* sacrifice. But *there was* no voice; no one answered, no one paid attention.

³⁰ Then Elijah said to all the people, "Come near to me." So all the people came near to him. And he repaired the altar of the LORD *that was* broken down. ³¹ And Elijah took twelve stones, according to the number of the tribes of the sons of Jacob... ³² Then with the stones he built an altar in the name of the LORD... ³³ And he put the wood in order, cut the bull in pieces, and laid *it* on the wood, and said, "Fill four waterpots with water, and pour *it* on the burnt sacrifice and on the wood." ³⁴ Then he said, "Do *it* a second time," and they did *it* a second time; and he said, "Do *it* a third time," and they did *it* a third time. ³⁵ So the water ran all around the altar; and he also filled the trench with water.

³⁶ And it came to pass, at *the time of* the offering of the *evening* sacrifice, that Elijah the prophet came near and said, "LORD God... let it be known this day that You *are* God... and I *am* Your servant, and *that* I have done all these things at Your word. ³⁷ Hear me, O LORD, hear me, that this people may know that You *are* the LORD God, and *that* You have turned their hearts back *to You* again."

³⁸ Then the fire of the LORD fell and consumed the burnt sacrifice, and the wood and the stones and the dust, and it licked up the water that *was* in the trench. ³⁹ Now when all the people saw *it,* they fell on their faces; and they said, "The LORD, He *is* God! The LORD, He *is* God!"

⁴¹ Then Elijah said to Ahab, "Go up, eat and drink; for *there is* the sound of abundance of rain." ⁴² So Ahab went up to eat and drink...

⁴⁵ Now it happened in the meantime that the sky became black with clouds and wind, and there was a heavy rain.

1 Kings 19:

¹ And Ahab told Jezebel all that Elijah had done... ² Then Jezebel [threatened to kill] Elijah...³ ...[Elijah then] arose and ran for his life...⁴ [H]e... went a day's journey into the wilderness, and came and sat down under a broom tree. And he prayed that he might die, and said, "It is enough! Now, LORD, take my life..."

5 Then as he lay and slept under a broom tree, suddenly an angel touched him, and said to him, "Arise *and* eat." 6 Then he looked, and there by his head *was* a cake baked on coals, and a jar of water. So he ate and drank, and lay down again. 7 And the angel of the LORD came back the second time, and touched him, and said, "Arise *and* eat, because the journey *is* too great for you." 8 So he arose, and ate and drank; and he went in the strength of that food forty days and forty nights as far as Horeb, the mountain of God.

9 And there he went into a cave, and spent the night in that place; and behold, the word of the LORD *came* to him, and He said to him, "What are you doing here, Elijah?" 10 So he said, "I have been very zealous for the LORD God of hosts; for the [people] have forsaken Your covenant, torn down Your altars...I alone am left; and they seek to take my life."

11 Then He said, "Go out, and stand on the mountain before the LORD." And behold, the LORD passed by, and a great and strong wind tore into the mountains and broke the rocks in pieces before the LORD, *but* the LORD *was* not in the wind; and after the wind an earthquake, *but* the LORD *was* not in the earthquake; 12 and after the earthquake a fire, *but* the LORD *was* not in the fire; and after the fire a still small voice. 13 So it was, when Elijah heard *it,* that he wrapped his face in his mantle and went out and stood in the entrance of the cave. Suddenly a voice *came* to him, and said, "What are you doing here, Elijah?"

14 And he said, "I have been very zealous for the LORD God of hosts; because the [people] have forsaken Your covenant, torn down Your altars...I alone am left; and they seek to take my life."

15 Then the LORD said to him: "Go, return on your way to the Wilderness of Damascus; and when you arrive, anoint Hazael *as* king over Syria. 16 Also you shall anoint Jehu the son of Nimshi *as* king over Israel. And Elisha the son of Shaphat of Abel Meholah you shall anoint *as* prophet in your place..."

19 So he departed from there, and found Elisha the son of Shaphat, who *was* plowing *with* twelve yoke *of oxen* before him... Then Elijah passed by him and threw his mantle on him. 20 And he left the oxen and ran after Elijah, and said, "Please let me kiss my father and my mother, and *then* I will follow you."

21 So *Elisha...* arose and followed Elijah, and became his servant.

Islam:

The Ant 27:15-16 And certainly [I] gave knowledge to Dawood (David) and Sulaiman (Solomon), and they both said: Praise be to God, Who has made us to excel... And Sulaiman was Dawood's heir, and he said: O men! [W]e have been taught the language of birds, and we have been given all things; most surely this is manifest grace.

The Prophets 21:78-79,81 And Dawood and Sulaiman when they gave judgment concerning the field when the people's sheep pastured therein by night, and [I was a] bearer of witness to their judgment. So [I] made Sulaiman to understand it... And ([I] made subservient) to Sulaiman the wind blowing violent, pursuing its course by his command to the land which [I] had blessed, and [I am a] knower of all things.

The Saba 34:12 And ([I] made) the wind (subservient) to Sulaiman...

The Cattle 6:84 And [I] gave to... Sulaiman... thus do [I] reward those who do good.

The Ant 27:28-31 Take this my letter and hand it over to them, then turn away from them and see what (answer) they return. [Balqis (Sheba)] said: O chief! [S]urely an honorable letter has been delivered to me. Surely it is from Sulaiman, and surely it is in the name of [God], the Beneficent, the Merciful; [s]aying: exalt not yourselves against me and come to me in submission.

The Ant 27:42-44 So when [Balqis] came, it was said: Is your throne like this? She said: It is as it were the same, and we were given the knowledge before it, and we were submissive.

And what she worshipped besides [God] prevented her, surely she was of an unbelieving people. It was said to her: Enter the palace; but when she saw it she deemed it to be a great expanse of water... He said: Surely it is a palace made smooth with glass. She said: My Lord! [S]urely I have been unjust to myself, and I submit with Sulaiman to [God], the Lord of the worlds.

The Suad 38:34-35 And certainly [I] tried Sulaiman, and [I] put on his throne a (mere) body, so he turned (to [God]). [Sulaiman] said: My Lord! [D]o Thou forgive me and grant me a kingdom which is not fit for anyone after me...

The Cattle 6:85 And Zakariya (Zechariah) and Yahya (John) and Isa (Jesus) and Ilyas (Elijah); every one was of the good...

The Rangers 37:124 And Ilyas was most surely of the apostles. When he said to his people: Do you not guard (against evil)?

The Rangers 37:125-127 What! [D]o you call upon Ba'l and forsake the best of the creators, ... your Lord and the Lord of your fathers of yore? But they called him a liar...

The Rangers 37:129-132 And [I] perpetuated to him (praise) among the later generations. Peace be on Ilyas. Even thus do [I] reward the doers of good. Surely he was one of [My] believing servants.

Judaism (Talmud):

[Babylonian Talmud. Baba Metzia 114b]:

The Leaves of Paradise:

Rabbah b. Abbuha met Elijah standing in a non-Jewish cemetery... Rabbah said to him:

"Are you not... a descendant of the Temple priests? Why then do you stand here, in a cemetery where contact with the dead will make you impure and unfit for service in the Temple?"

Elijah replied, "It seems as though the learned sage has not studied the laws of purity. For there it has been taught... that the graves of non-Jews do not make one unfit..."

Rabbah replied: "Alas, I cannot even make the time to properly study the most useful parts of the Mishnah that teach me about holidays and everyday life; how could I then study... the Mishnah including the very difficult... division about 'Purities?'"

"And why is it that you can not study more?" asked Elijah.

"I am too hard pressed to make a living," Rabbah answered.

Elijah then led him into Paradise and said to him: "Remove your outer robe, spread it out and gather some of these leaves." So he gathered the leaves of Paradise and carried them off. As he was coming out, he heard a voice: "Who would use up his portion in the world to come as Rabbah... has done?" When Rabbah heard that, he quickly shook the leaves out of his robe and left Paradise, returning to the cemetery where he had been before. Yet, even so, since he carried the leaves of Paradise in his robe, it had absorbed their fragrance and so he sold it for twelve thousand denars, which he distributed among his children.

X. Second Book of Kings

Christianity/Judaism:

2 Kings 2:

[1] And it came to pass, when the LORD was about to take up Elijah into heaven by a whirlwind, that Elijah went with Elisha from Gilgal. [2] Then Elijah said to Elisha, "Stay here, please, for the LORD has sent me on to Bethel." But Elisha said, "*As* the LORD lives, and *as* your soul lives, I will not leave you!" So they went down to Bethel.

[3] Now the sons of the prophets who *were* at Bethel came out to Elisha, and said to him, "Do you know that the LORD will take away your master from over you today?" And he said, "Yes, I know; keep silent!"

[4] Then Elijah said to him, "Elisha, stay here, please, for the LORD has sent me on to Jericho." But he said, "*As* the LORD lives, and *as* your soul lives, I will not leave you!" So they came to Jericho.

[5] Now the sons of the prophets who *were* at Jericho came to Elisha and said to him, "Do you know that the LORD will take away your master from over you today?" So he answered, "Yes, I know; keep silent!"

[6] Then Elijah said to him, "Stay here, please, for the LORD has sent me on to the Jordan." But he said, "*As* the LORD lives, and *as* your soul lives, I will not leave you!" So the two of them went on. [7] And fifty men of the sons of the prophets went and stood facing *them* at a distance, while the two of them stood by the Jordan. [8] Now Elijah took his mantle, rolled *it* up, and struck the water; and it was divided this way and that, so that the two of them crossed over on dry ground.

[9] And so it was, when they had crossed over, that Elijah said to Elisha, "Ask! What may I do for you, before I am taken away from you?" Elisha said, "Please let a double portion of your spirit be upon me."

[10] So he said, "You have asked a hard thing. *Nevertheless,* if you see me *when I am* taken from you, it shall be so for you; but if not, it shall not be *so.*" [11] Then it happened, as they continued on and talked, that suddenly a chariot of fire *appeared* with horses of fire, and separated the two of them; and Elijah went up by a whirlwind into heaven. [12] And Elisha saw *it,* and he cried out, "My father, my father, the chariot... and its horsemen!" So he saw him no more. And he took hold of his own clothes and tore them into two pieces. [13] He also took up the mantle of Elijah that had fallen from him, and went back and stood by the bank of the Jordan. [14] Then he took the mantle of Elijah that had fallen from him, and struck the water, and said, "Where *is* the LORD God of Elijah?" And when he also had struck the water, it was divided this way and that; and Elisha crossed over.

[15] Now when the sons of the prophets who *were* from Jericho saw him, they said, "The spirit of Elijah rests on Elisha." And they came to meet him, and bowed to the ground before him.

¹⁹ Then the men of the city said to Elisha, "Please notice, the situation of this city *is* pleasant, as my lord sees; but the water *is* bad, and the ground barren." ²⁰ And he said, "Bring me a new bowl, and put salt in it." So they brought *it* to him. ²¹ Then he went out to the source of the water, and cast in the salt there, and said, "Thus says the LORD: 'I have healed this water...'" ²² So the water [was] healed... according to the word of Elisha which he spoke.

²⁵ Then he went from there to Mount Carmel, and from there he returned to Samaria.

2 Kings 4:

¹ A certain woman of the wives of the sons of the prophets cried out to Elisha, saying, "Your servant my husband is dead, and you know that your servant feared the LORD. And the creditor is coming to take my two sons to be his slaves."

² So Elisha said to her, "What shall I do for you? Tell me, what do you have in the house?" And she said, "Your maidservant has nothing in the house but a jar of oil." ³ Then he said, "Go, borrow vessels from everywhere, from all your neighbors — empty vessels; do not gather just a few. ⁴ And when you have come in, you shall shut the door behind you and your sons; then pour it into all those vessels, and set aside the full ones."

⁵ So she went from him and shut the door behind her and her sons, who brought *the vessels* to her; and she poured *it* out. ⁶ Now it came to pass, when the vessels were full, that she said to her son, "Bring me another vessel."

And he said to her, "*There is* not another vessel." So the oil ceased. ⁷ Then she came and told the man of God. And he said, "Go, sell the oil and pay your debt; and you *and* your sons live on the rest."

⁸ Now it happened one day that Elisha went to Shunem, where there *was* a notable woman, and she persuaded him to eat some food. So it was, as often as he passed by, he would turn in there to eat some food. ⁹ And she said to her husband, "Look now, I know that this *is* a holy man of God, who passes by us regularly. ¹⁰ Please, let us make a small upper room on the wall; and let us put a bed for him there, and a table and a chair and a lampstand; so it will be, whenever he comes to us, he can turn in there." ¹¹ And it happened one day that he came there, and he turned in to the upper room and lay down there. ¹² Then he said to Gehazi..., "Call this Shunammite woman." When he had called her, she stood before him. ¹³ And he said... "Look, you have been concerned for us with all this care. What *can I* do for you? Do you want me to speak on your behalf to the king?"

She answered, "I dwell among my own people." ¹⁴ So he said, "What then *is* to be done for her?" And Gehazi answered, "Actually, she has no son, and her husband is old."

¹⁵ So he said, "Call her." When he had called her, she stood in the doorway. ¹⁶ Then he said, "About this time next year you shall embrace a son." And she said, "No, my lord. Man of God, do not lie to your maidservant!"

¹⁷ But the woman conceived, and bore a son when the appointed time had come, of which Elisha had told her. ¹⁸ And the child grew. Now it happened one day that he went out to his father, to the reapers. ¹⁹ And he said to his father, "My head, my head!"

So he said to a servant, "Carry him to his mother." ²⁰ When he had taken him and brought him to his mother, he sat on her knees till noon, and *then* died. ²¹ And she went up and laid him on the bed of the man of God, shut *the door* upon him, and went out.

²⁷ Now when she came to the man of God at the hill, she caught him by the feet, but Gehazi came near to push her away. But the man of God said, "Let her alone; for her soul *is* in deep distress, and the LORD has hidden *it* from me, and has not told me." ²⁸ So she said, "Did I ask a son of my lord? Did I not say, 'Do not deceive me?'"

³² When Elisha came into the house, there was the child, lying dead on his bed. ³³ He went in therefore, shut the door behind the two of them, and prayed to the LORD. ³⁴ And he went up and lay on the child, and put his mouth on his mouth, his eyes on his eyes, and his hands on his hands; and he stretched himself out on the child, and the flesh of the child became warm. ³⁵ He returned and walked back and forth in the house, and again went up and stretched himself out on him; then the child sneezed seven times, and the child opened his eyes. ³⁶ And he called Gehazi and said, "Call this Shunammite woman." So he called her. And when she came in to him, he said, "Pick up your son." ³⁷ So she went in, fell at his feet, and bowed to the ground; then she picked up her son and went out.

⁴² Then a man came from Baal Shalisha, and brought the man of God bread of the firstfruits, twenty loaves of barley bread, and newly ripened grain in his knapsack. And [Elisha] said, "Give *it* to the people that they may eat."

⁴³ But his servant said, "What? Shall I set this before one hundred men?" He said again, "Give it to the people, that they may eat; for thus says the LORD: 'They shall eat and have *some* left over.'" ⁴⁴ So he set *it* before them; and they ate and had *some* left over, according to the word of the LORD.

2 Kings 5:

¹ Now Naaman was commander of the army of the king of Aram. He was a great man in the sight of his master and highly regarded…but he had leprosy.

² [A] young girl from Israel, [who] served Naaman's wife [said]… ³, "If only [he] would see the prophet who is in Samaria! He would cure him of his leprosy."

⁴ Naaman went to his master and told him what the girl from Israel had said. ⁵ "By all means, go," the king of Aram replied. "I will send a letter to the king of Israel." So Naaman left, taking with him ten talents of silver, six thousand shekels of gold and ten sets of clothing. ⁶ The letter that he took to the king of Israel read: "With this letter I am sending my servant Naaman to you so that you may cure him of his leprosy."

⁷ As soon as the king of Israel read the letter, he tore his robes and said, "Am I God? Can I kill and bring back to life? Why does this fellow send someone to me to be cured of his leprosy?"

[8] When Elisha the man of God heard that the king of Israel had torn his robes, he sent him this message: "Why have you torn your robes? Have the man come to me and he will know that there is a prophet in Israel." [9] So Naaman went with his horses and chariots and stopped at the door of Elisha's house. [10] Elisha sent a messenger to say to him, "Go, wash yourself seven times in the Jordan, and your flesh will be restored and you will be cleansed."

[11] But Naaman went away angry and said, "I thought that he would surely come out to me and stand and call on the name of the LORD his God, wave his hand over the spot and cure me of my leprosy. [12] Are not... the rivers of Damascus, better than all the waters of Israel? Couldn't I wash in them and be cleansed?" So he turned and went off in a rage.

[13] Naaman's servants went to him and said, "My father, if the prophet had told you to do some great thing, would you not have done it? How much more, then, when he tells you, 'Wash and be cleansed!'" [14] So he went down and dipped himself in the Jordan seven times, as the man of God had told him, and his flesh was restored and became clean like that of a young boy.

[15] Then Naaman and all his attendants went back to the man of God. He stood before him and said, "Now I know that there is no God [but your God]. So please accept a gift from your servant."

[16] The prophet answered, "As surely as the LORD lives, whom I serve, I will not accept a thing." And even though Naaman urged him, he refused. [19] "Go in peace," Elisha said.

2 Kings 6:

[1] The company of the prophets said to Elisha, "Look, the place where we meet with you is too small for us. [2] Let us go to the Jordan, where each of us can get a pole; and let us build a place there for us to meet." And he said, "Go."

[3] Then one of them said, "Won't you please come with your servants?" "I will," Elisha replied. [4] And he went with them. They went to the Jordan and began to cut down trees. [5] As one of them was cutting down a tree, the iron axhead fell into the water. "Oh no, my lord!" he cried out. "It was borrowed!"

[6] The man of God asked, "Where did it fall?" When he showed him the place, Elisha cut a stick and threw it there, and made the iron float. [7] "Lift it out," he said. Then the man reached out his hand and took it.

2 Kings 18:

[1] In the third year of Hoshea son of Elah king of Israel, Hezekiah son of Ahaz king of Judah began to reign. [2] He was twenty-five years old when he became king, and he reigned in Jerusalem twenty-nine years. His mother's name was Abijah daughter of Zechariah. [3] He did what was right in the eyes of the LORD, just as his father David had done. [4]

[5] Hezekiah trusted in the LORD, the God of Israel. There was no one like him among all

the kings of Judah, either before him or after him. [6] He held fast to the LORD and did not stop following [H]im; he kept the commands the LORD had given Moses. [7] And the LORD was with him; he was successful in whatever he undertook.

2 Chronicles 31:

[20] ...Hezekiah did throughout Judah... what was good and right and faithful before the LORD his God. [21] In everything that he undertook... he sought his God and worked wholeheartedly. And so he prospered.

2 Chronicles 29:

[3] In the first month of the first year of his reign, he opened the doors of the temple of the LORD and repaired them. [4] He brought in the priests and the Levites, assembled them in the square on the east side [5] and said: "Listen to me, Levites! Consecrate yourselves now and consecrate the temple of the LORD, the God of your ancestors. Remove all defilement from the sanctuary. [6] Our parents were unfaithful; they did evil in the eyes of the LORD our God and forsook him. They turned their faces away from the LORD's dwelling place and turned their backs on him. [10] Now I intend to make a covenant with the LORD... [11] [D]o not be negligent now, for the LORD has chosen you to stand before [H]im and serve [H]im, to minister before [H]im and to burn incense."

[12] Then these Levites [did]... [15] as the king had ordered, following the word of the LORD. [35] ...So the service of the temple of the LORD was reestablished.

2 Chronicles 30:

[21] The Israelites who were present in Jerusalem celebrated the Festival of Unleavened Bread for seven days with great rejoicing, while the Levites and priests praised the LORD every day with resounding instruments dedicated to the LORD.

[26] There was great joy in Jerusalem, for since the days of Solomon son of David king of Israel there had been nothing like this in Jerusalem. [27] The priests and the Levites stood to bless the people, and God heard them, for their prayer reached heaven, [H]is holy dwelling place.

2 Kings 18:

[13] In the fourteenth year of King Hezekiah's reign, Sennacherib king of Assyria attacked all the fortified cities of Judah and captured them. [14] So Hezekiah king of Judah sent this message to the king of Assyria at Lachish: "I have done wrong. Withdraw from me, and I will pay whatever you demand of me." The king of Assyria exacted from Hezekiah king of Judah three hundred talents of silver and thirty talents of gold. [15] So Hezekiah gave him all the silver that was found in the temple of the LORD and in the treasuries of the royal palace.

[16] At this time Hezekiah king of Judah stripped off the gold with which he had covered the doors and doorposts of the temple of the LORD, and gave it to the king of Assyria.

[17] The king of Assyria sent his supreme commander, his chief officer and his field

commander with a large army ...to King Hezekiah... They came up to Jerusalem and stopped at the aqueduct... ¹⁸ They called for the king; and Eliakim son of Hilkiah the palace administrator, Shebna the secretary, and Joah son of Asaph the recorder went out to them.

"This is what the great king, the king of Assyria, says: On what are you basing this confidence of yours? ²⁰ You say you have the counsel and the might for war — but you speak only empty words. On whom are you depending...? ²² But if you say to me, 'We are depending on the LORD our God' —isn't [H]e the one whose high places and altars Hezekiah removed, saying to Judah and Jerusalem, 'You must worship before this altar in Jerusalem?'

²³ Come now, make a bargain with my master, the king of Assyria...: I will give you two thousand horses — if you can put riders on them! ²⁴ How can you repulse one officer of the least of my master's officials, even though you are depending on Egypt for chariots and horsemen?"

²⁶ Then Eliakim son of Hilkiah, and Shebna and Joah said to the field commander, "Please speak to your servants in Aramaic, since we understand it. Don't speak to us in Hebrew in the hearing of the people on the wall."

²⁷ But the commander replied, "Was it only to your master and you that my master sent me to say these things, and not to the people sitting on the wall — who, like you, will have to eat their own excrement and drink their own urine?"

²⁸ Then the commander stood and called out in Hebrew, "Hear the word of the great king, the king of Assyria! ²⁹ This is what the king says: Do not let Hezekiah deceive you. He cannot deliver you from my hand. ³⁰ Do not let Hezekiah persuade you to trust in the LORD when he says, 'The LORD will surely deliver us...'

³¹ ...This is what the king of Assyria says: Make peace with me and come out to me. Then each of you will eat fruit from your own vine and fig tree and drink water from your own cistern, ³² until I come and take you to a land like your own — a land of grain and new wine, a land of bread and vineyards, a land of olive trees and honey. Choose life and not death!"

2 Kings 19:

¹ When King Hezekiah heard this, he tore his clothes and put on sackcloth and went into the temple of the LORD. ² He sent Eliakim the palace administrator, Shebna the secretary and the leading priests, all wearing sackcloth, to the prophet Isaiah son of Amoz.

⁵ When King Hezekiah's officials came to Isaiah, ⁶ Isaiah said to them, "Tell your master, 'This is what the LORD says: Do not be afraid of what you have heard...'"

¹⁴ Hezekiah... went up to the temple... ¹⁵ [a]nd prayed to the LORD: "LORD... enthroned between the cherubim, [Y]ou alone are God over all the kingdoms of the earth. You have made heaven and earth. ¹⁹ ...[D]eliver us from [Sennacherib's] hand, so that all the kingdoms of the earth may know that you alone, LORD, are God."

20 Then Isaiah... sent a message to Hezekiah: "This is what the LORD... says: I have heard your prayer concerning Sennacherib king of Assyria... **32** He will not enter this city or shoot an arrow here. He will not come before it with shield or build a siege ramp against it. **33** ...[H]e will not enter this city, declares the LORD."

35 [N]ext morning... **36** Sennacherib king of Assyria broke camp and withdrew.

2 Kings 20:

1 In those days Hezekiah became ill and was at the point of death. The prophet Isaiah son of Amoz went to him and said, "This is what the LORD says: Put your house in order, because you are going to die; you will not recover."

2 Hezekiah turned his face to the wall and prayed to the LORD, **3** "Remember, LORD, how I have walked before you faithfully and with wholehearted devotion and have done what is good in your eyes." And Hezekiah wept bitterly.

4 Before Isaiah had left the middle court, the word of the LORD came to him: **5** "Go back and tell Hezekiah, the ruler of my people, 'This is what the LORD, the God of your father David, says: I have heard your prayer and seen your tears; I will heal you... **6** I will add fifteen years to your life...'"

King Hezekiah by Unknown,
17th Century

2 Kings 22:

1 Josiah was eight years old when he became king, and he reigned in Jerusalem thirty-one years. His mother's name was Jedidah daughter of Adaiah; she was from Bozkath. **2** He did what was right in the eyes of the LORD and followed completely the ways of his father David, not turning aside to the right or to the left.

8 Hilkiah the high priest said to Shaphan the secretary, "I have found the Book of the Law in the temple of the LORD." He gave it to Shaphan, who read it.

[11] When the king heard the words of the Book of the Law, he tore his robes. [12] He gave these orders to Hilkiah the priest, Ahikam son of Shaphan, Akbor son of Micaiah, Shaphan the secretary and Asaiah the king's attendant: [13] "Go and inquire of the LORD for me and for the people and for all Judah about what is written in this book that has been found…"

[14] [They] went to speak to the prophet Huldah… [15] She said to them, [16] "This is what the LORD says: [19] "Because your heart was responsive and you humbled yourself before the LORD when you heard what I have spoken against this place and its people… and because you tore your robes and wept in my presence[20] …I will gather you to your ancestors, and you will be buried in peace."   So they took her answer back to the king.

2 Kings 23:

[1] Then the king called together all the elders of Judah and Jerusalem. [2] He went up to the temple of the LORD with the people of Judah, the inhabitants of Jerusalem, the priests and the prophets — all the people from the least to the greatest. He read in their hearing all the words of the Book of the Covenant, which had been found in the temple of the LORD. [3] The king stood by the pillar and renewed the covenant in the presence of the LORD — to follow the LORD and keep [H]is commands, statutes and decrees with all his heart and all his soul… Then all the people pledged themselves to the covenant.

2 Chronicles 34:

[33] …As long [Josiah] lived, [the Israelites] did not fail to follow the LORD…

2 Kings 23:

[25] Neither before nor after Josiah was there a king like him who turned to the LORD as he did — with all his heart and with all his soul and with all his strength, in accordance with all the Law of Moses.

Islam:

The Cattle 6:86-87 …Ismail (Ishmael) and Al-Yasha (Elisha) and Yunus (Jonah) and Lut (Lot); and every one [I] made to excel (in) the worlds: And from among their fathers and their descendants and their brethren, and [I] chose them and guided them into the right way.

The Suad 38:48 And remember Ismail (Ishmael) and Al-Yasha (Elisha) and Zulkifl (Isaiah); and they were all of the best.

The Prophets 21:85-86 And Ismail and Idris (Enoch) and Zulkifl; all were of the patient ones; And [I] caused them to enter into [My] mercy, surely they were of the good ones.

XI. Chronicles

Christianity/Judaism:

2 Chronicles 17:

[1] Then Jehoshaphat… reigned… [3] Now the LORD was with Jehoshaphat, because he walked in the… ways of his father David; he did not seek the Baals, [4] but sought the God of his father, and walked in His commandments… [5] Therefore the LORD established the kingdom in his hand; and all Judah gave presents to Jehoshaphat, and he had riches and honor in abundance. [6] And his heart took delight in the ways of the LORD…

[8] And… *he sent* Levites: Shemaiah, Nethaniah, Zebadiah, Asahel, Shemiramoth, Jehonathan, Adonijah, Tobijah, and Tobadonijah — and with them Elishama and Jehoram, the priests. [9] So they taught in Judah, and *had* the Book of the Law of the LORD with them; they went throughout all the cities of Judah and taught the people. [10] And the fear of the LORD fell on all the kingdoms of the lands that *were* around Judah… [T]hey did not make war.

2 Chronicles 18:

[1] Jehoshaphat had riches and honor in abundance; and by marriage he allied himself with Ahab (King of Israel).

[6] …Jehoshaphat said, "*Is there* not still a prophet of the LORD here, that we may inquire of Him?"

[7] So the king of Israel said to Jehoshaphat, "*There is* still one man by whom we may inquire of the LORD; but I hate him, because he never prophesies good concerning me, but always evil. He *is* Micaiah the son of Imla."

And Jehoshaphat said, "Let not the king say such things!"

[8] Then the king of Israel called one *of his* officers and said, "Bring Micaiah… quickly!" [9] The king of Israel and Jehoshaphat king of Judah, clothed in *their* robes, sat each on his throne… and all the prophets prophesied before them.

[13] And Micaiah said, "*As* the LORD lives, whatever my God says, that I will speak." [16] Then he said, "I saw all Israel scattered on the mountains, as sheep that have no shepherd. And the LORD said, 'These have no master. Let each return to his house in peace.'"

2 Chronicles 19:

[1] Then Jehoshaphat the king of Judah returned safely to his house in Jerusalem.

[4] So Jehoshaphat dwelt at Jerusalem; and he went out again among the people… and brought them back to the LORD God of their fathers. [5] Then he set judges in the land throughout all the… cities of Judah, city by city, [6] and said to the judges, "Take heed to what you are doing, for you do not judge for man but for the LORD, who *is* with you in

the judgment. ⁷ Now therefore, let the fear of the LORD be upon you; take care and do *it,* for *there is* no iniquity with the LORD our God, no partiality, nor taking of bribes." ⁸ Moreover in Jerusalem, for the judgment of the LORD… Jehoshaphat appointed some of the Levites and priests, and some of the chief fathers of Israel, when they returned to Jerusalem. ⁹ And he commanded them, saying, "Thus you shall act in the fear of the LORD, faithfully and with a loyal heart… ¹¹ And take notice: Amariah the chief priest *is* over you in all matters of the LORD; and Zebadiah the son of Ishmael, the ruler of the house of Judah, for all the king's matters; also the Levites *will be* officials before you. Behave courageously, and the LORD will be with the good."

2 Chronicles 20:

² Some people came and told Jehoshaphat, "A vast army is coming against you from Edom, from the other side of the Dead Sea… ³ Alarmed, Jehoshaphat resolved to inquire of the LORD, and he proclaimed a fast for all Judah. ⁴ The people of Judah came together to seek help from the LORD; indeed, they came from every town in Judah to seek him.

⁵ Then Jehoshaphat stood up in the assembly of Judah and Jerusalem at the temple of the LORD in the front of the new courtyard ⁶ and said: "LORD… are you not the God who is in heaven? You rule over all the kingdoms of the nations. Power and might are in [Y]our hand, and no one can withstand [Y]ou… ⁹ If calamity comes upon us, whether the sword of judgment, or plague or famine, we will stand in [Y]our presence before this temple that bears [Y]our Name and will cry out to [Y]ou in our distress, and [Y]ou will hear us and save us. ¹² [W]e have no power to face this vast army… We do not know what to do, but our eyes are on [Y]ou."

¹³ All the men of Judah, with their wives and children and little ones, stood there before the LORD.

¹⁴ Then the Spirit of the LORD came on Jahaziel son of Zechariah… as he stood in the assembly. ¹⁵ He said: "Listen, King Jehoshaphat and all who live in Judah and Jerusalem! This is what the LORD says to you: 'Do not be afraid or discouraged… ¹⁷ [T]he LORD will be with you.'"

¹⁸ Jehoshaphat bowed down with his face to the ground, and all the people of Judah and Jerusalem fell down in worship before the LORD. ¹⁹ Then some Levites… stood up and praised the LORD… with a very loud voice.

²⁰ Early in the morning… Jehoshaphat stood and said, "Listen to me, Judah and people of Jerusalem! Have faith in the LORD your God…" ²¹ After consulting the people, Jehoshaphat appointed men to sing to the LORD and to praise [H]im for the splendor of [H]is holiness… saying: "Give thanks to the LORD, for [H]is love endures forever."

²⁷ [A]ll the men of Judah and Jerusalem returned joyfully to Jerusalem… ²⁸ They entered Jerusalem and went to the temple of the LORD with harps and lyres and trumpets.

³⁰ [T]he kingdom of Jehoshaphat was at peace, for his God had given him rest on every side.

31 So Jehoshaphat reigned over Judah. He was thirty-five years old when he became king of Judah, and he reigned in Jerusalem twenty-five years… **32** He… did what was right in the eyes of the LORD.

2 Chronicles 25:

1 Amaziah was twenty-five years old when he became king, and he reigned in Jerusalem twenty-nine years… **2** He did what was right in the eyes of the LORD, but not wholeheartedly…

2 Chronicles 26:

3 Uzziah was sixteen years old when he became king, and he reigned in Jerusalem fifty-two years. His mother's name was Jekoliah; she was from Jerusalem. **4** He did what was right in the eyes of the LORD… **5** He sought God during the days of Zechariah, who instructed him in the fear of God. As long as he sought the LORD, God gave him success.

2 Chronicles 27:

1 Jotham was twenty-five years old when he became king, and he reigned in Jerusalem sixteen years… **2** He did what was right in the eyes of the LORD, just as his father Uzziah had done… **3** Jotham rebuilt the Upper Gate of the temple of the LORD and did extensive work on the wall at the hill of Ophel. **4** He built towns in the hill country of Judah and… towers in the wooded areas.

6 Jotham grew powerful because he walked steadfastly before the LORD his God.

XII. The Book of Ezra

Christianity/Judaism:

Ezra 1:

[1] Now in the first year of Cyrus king of Persia... he made a proclamation throughout all his kingdom, and also *put it* in writing, saying, [2] Thus says Cyrus king of Persia: "All the kingdoms of the earth the LORD God of heaven has given me. And He has commanded me to build Him a house at Jerusalem which *is* in Judah. [3] Who *is* among you of all His people? May his God be with him, and let him go up to Jerusalem which *is* in Judah, and build the house of the LORD..."

[5] Then the heads of the fathers' *houses* of Judah and Benjamin, and the priests and the Levites, with all whose spirits God had moved, arose to go up and build the house of the LORD... [6] And all those who *were* around them encouraged them with articles of silver and gold, with goods and livestock, and with precious things, besides all *that* was willingly offered.

[7] King Cyrus also brought out the articles of the house of the LORD, which [had been] taken from Jerusalem... [8] and Cyrus king of Persia... counted them out to Sheshbazzar the prince of Judah. [11] All the articles of gold and silver *were* five thousand four hundred. All *these* Sheshbazzar took with the captives who were brought from Babylon to Jerusalem.

Ezra 3:

[1] And when the seventh month had come, and the children of Israel *were* in the cities, the people gathered together as one... [in] Jerusalem.

[10] When the builders laid the foundation of the temple of the LORD, the priests stood in their apparel with trumpets, and the Levites... with cymbals, to praise the LORD, according to the ordinance of David king of Israel. [11] And they sang responsively, praising and giving thanks to the LORD: "For *He* is good [f]or His mercy *endures* forever..."

Then all the people shouted with a great shout, when they praised the LORD, because the foundation of the house of the LORD was laid.

[12] [M]any... who had seen the first temple, wept with a loud voice when the foundation of this temple was laid before their eyes. [M]any [also] shouted aloud for joy, [13] ...and the sound was heard afar off.

Ezra 5:

[6] [Tattenai], governor of *the region* beyond the River, and Shethar-Boznai, and his companions, the Persians who *were in the region* beyond the River, [wrote] to Darius the king:

[8] Let it be known to the king that we went into the province of Judea, to the temple of the

great God, which is being built with heavy stones, and timber is being laid in the walls; and this work goes on diligently and prospers in their hands.

⁹ Then we asked those elders, *and* spoke thus to them: "Who commanded you to build this temple and to finish these walls?" ¹⁰ We also asked them their names to inform you, that we might write the names of the men who *were* chief among them.

¹¹ And thus they returned us an answer, saying: "We are the servants of the God of heaven and earth, and we are rebuilding the temple that was built many years ago, which a great king of Israel built and completed... ¹³ King Cyrus issued a decree to build this house of God..."

¹⁷ Now therefore, if *it seems* good to the king, let a search be made in the king's treasure house, which *is* there in Babylon, whether it is *so* that a decree was issued by King Cyrus to build this house of God at Jerusalem, and let the king send us his pleasure concerning this *matter.*

Ezra 6:

¹ Then King Darius issued a decree, and a search was made in the archives, where the treasures were stored in Babylon. ² And at Achmetha, in the palace that *is* in the province of Media, a scroll was found, and in it a record *was* written thus:

³ In the first year of King Cyrus, King Cyrus issued a decree *concerning* the house of God at Jerusalem: "Let the house be rebuilt and let the foundations of it be firmly laid... ⁴ Let the expenses be paid from the king's treasury. ⁵ Also let the gold and silver articles of the house of God, [taken] from the temple which *is* in Jerusalem... be restored and taken back to the temple which *is* in Jerusalem, *each* to its place; and deposit *them* in the house of God —

⁶ Now *therefore,* Tattenai... and your companions... who *are* beyond the River, keep yourselves far from there. ⁷ Let the work of this house of God alone; let [them] build this house of God on its site."

¹³ Then Tattenai ... and [his] companions diligently did according to what King Darius had sent. ¹⁴ So the elders... built, and they prospered through the prophesying of Haggai the prophet and Zechariah the son of Iddo. And they built and finished *it,* according to the commandment of... God... and according to the command of Cyrus, Darius, and Artaxerxes king of Persia. ¹⁵ Now the temple was finished... in the sixth year of the reign of King Darius. ¹⁶ Then the children of Israel, the priests and the Levites and the rest of the descendants of the captivity, celebrated the dedication of this house of God with joy.
¹⁷

¹⁹ And the descendants of the captivity kept the Passover... ²¹ [and] the children of Israel who had returned from the captivity ate together...²² [a]nd they kept the Feast of Unleavened Bread seven days with joy; for the LORD made them joyful...

Ezra 7:

¹ Now after these things, in the reign of Artaxerxes king of Persia, Ezra... came up from Babylon; and he *was* a skilled scribe in the Law of Moses, which the LORD... had given.

The king granted him all his request[s]... [8] And Ezra came to Jerusalem... [10] [f]or [he] had prepared his heart to seek the Law of the LORD, and to do *it,* and to teach statutes and ordinances...

[11] This *is* a copy of the letter that King Artaxerxes gave Ezra the priest, the scribe, expert in the words of the commandments of the LORD, and of His statutes:

[12] "Artaxerxes, king of kings, [t]o Ezra the priest, a scribe of the Law of the God of heaven: [13] I issue a decree that all those of the people of Israel and the priests and Levites in my realm, who volunteer to go up to Jerusalem, may go with you. [14] And whereas you are being sent by the king and his seven counselors to inquire concerning Judah and Jerusalem, with regard to the Law of your God which *is* in your hand...

[21] I, Artaxerxes the king, issue a decree to all the treasurers who *are in the region* beyond the River, that whatever Ezra the priest, the scribe of the Law of the God of heaven, may require of you, let it be done diligently... [23] Whatever is commanded by the God of heaven, let it diligently be done for the house of the God of heaven.

[25] And you, Ezra, according to your God-given wisdom, set magistrates and judges who may judge all the people who *are in the region* beyond the River, all such as know the laws of your God; and teach those who do not know *them.*"

[27] "Blessed *be* the LORD God of our fathers, who has put *such a thing* as this in the king's heart, to beautify the house of the LORD which *is* in Jerusalem, [28] and has extended mercy to me before the king and his counselors, and before all the king's mighty princes. So I was encouraged, as the hand of the LORD my God *was* upon me; and I gathered leading men of Israel to go up with me," [Ezra declared].

Islam:

The Cow 2:259 Or the like of [Uzair] (Ezra) who passed by a town, and it had fallen down upon its roofs; he said: When will [God] give it life after its death? ... so when it became clear to [Uzair], he said: I know that [God] has power over all things.

The Immunity 9:30 And the Jews say: Uzair is [a child] of [God]...

The Cave 18:83-84 And they ask you about Zulqarnain (Cyrus, king of Persia). Say: I will recite to you an account of him. Surely [I] established him in the land and granted him means of access to every thing.

The Cave 18:85-87, 98 So he followed a course. Until when he reached the place where the sun set, he found it going down into a black sea, and found by it a people. [I] said: O Zulqarnain! ... [D]o them a benefit. [Zulqarnain] said: And as for him who believes and does good, he shall have goodly reward... This is a mercy from my Lord...and the promise of my Lord is ever true.

XIII. The Book of Nehemiah

Christianity/Judaism:

Nehemiah 1:

¹ The words of Nehemiah the son of Hachaliah. It came to pass… ² … I asked… concerning the [people] who had escaped, who had survived the captivity, and concerning Jerusalem. ³ And [I was told], "The survivors who are left from the captivity in the province *are* there in great distress and reproach. The wall of Jerusalem *is* also broken down, and its gates are burned with fire."

⁴ So it was, when I heard these words, that I sat down and wept, and mourned *for many* days; I was fasting and praying before the God of heaven.

Nehemiah 2:

¹ And it came to pass… in the twentieth year of King Artaxerxes, *when* wine *was* before him, that I took the wine and gave it to the king. Now I had never been sad in his presence before. ² Therefore the king said to me, "Why *is* your face sad, since you *are* not sick? This *is* nothing but sorrow of heart." So I became dreadfully afraid, ³ and said to the king, "May the king live forever! Why should my face not be sad, when the city, the place of my fathers' tombs, *lies* waste, and its gates are burned with fire?"

⁴ Then the king said to me, "What do you request?" So I prayed to the God of heaven. ⁵ And I said to the king, "If it pleases the king, and if your servant has found favor in your sight, I ask that you send me to Judah, to the city of my fathers' tombs, that I may rebuild it."

⁶ Then the king said to me… "How long will your journey be? And when will you return?" So it pleased the king to send me; and I set him a time. ¹¹ So I came to Jerusalem and was there [in] three days. ¹³ And I went out by night… and viewed the walls of Jerusalem which were broken down and its gates which were burned with fire.

¹⁷ Then I said to [everyone], "You see the distress that we *are* in: Jerusalem *lies* in ruins, and its gates have been burned with fire. Come and let us build the wall of Jerusalem, that we may no longer be a reproach." ¹⁸ And I told them of the hand of my God which had been good upon me, and also of the king's words that he had spoken to me. So they said, "Let us rise up and build." Then they set their hands to *this* good *work.*

Nehemiah 6:

⁵ So the wall was finished… ¹⁶ And it happened, when all our enemies heard *of it,* and all the nations around us saw *these things,* that they were very disheartened in their own eyes; for they perceived that this work was done by our God.

Nehemiah 8:

⁶ And Ezra blessed the LORD, the great God. Then all the people answered, "Amen, Amen!" while lifting up their hands. And they bowed their heads and worshiped the LORD with *their* faces to the ground.

⁹ And Nehemiah, who *was* the governor, Ezra the priest *and* scribe, and the Levites who taught the people said… "This day *is* holy to the LORD your God; do not mourn nor weep." For all the people wept, when they heard the words of the Law. ¹⁰ Then he said to them, "Go your way, eat the fat, drink the sweet, and send portions to those for whom nothing is prepared; for *this* day *is* holy to our Lord. Do not sorrow, for the joy of the LORD is your strength."

¹² And all the people went their way to eat and drink, to send portions and rejoice greatly, because they understood the words that were declared to them.

Nehemiah 5:

¹⁴ Moreover, from the time that I was appointed to be their governor in the land of Judah, from the twentieth year until the thirty-second year of King Artaxerxes… neither I nor my brothers ate the governor's provisions. ¹⁸ …I did not demand the governor's provisions, because the bondage was heavy on this people.

¹⁹ Remember me, my God, for good, *according to* all that I have done for this people.

Nehemiah 9:

⁵ "Stand up *and* bless the LORD your God [f]orever and ever! Blessed be Your glorious name, [w]hich is exalted above all blessing and praise! ⁶ You alone *are* the LORD; You made the heavens, even the highest heavens with all their starry host, The earth and everything on it, The seas and all that is in them, [a]nd You preserve them all. The host of heaven worships You.

⁷ You *are* the LORD God, Who chose Abram, And brought him out of Ur of the Chaldeans, [a]nd gave him the name Abraham; ⁸ You found his heart faithful before You, [a]nd made a covenant with him… You have performed Your words, [f]or You *are* righteous.

⁹ You saw the affliction of our fathers in Egypt, [a]nd heard their cry by the Red Sea. ¹¹ And You divided the sea before them, [s]o that they went through the midst of the sea on the dry land; ¹² Moreover You led them by day with a cloudy pillar, [a]nd by night with a pillar of fire, [t]o give them light on the road [w]hich they should travel.

¹³ You came down also on Mount Sinai, [a]nd spoke with them from heaven, [a]nd gave them just ordinances and true laws, [g]ood statutes and commandments.

¹⁵ You gave them bread from heaven for their hunger, [a]nd brought them water out of the rock for their thirst, ¹⁷ …You *are* God, [r]eady to pardon, [g]racious and merciful, [s]low to anger, [a]bundant in kindness…

³² Now therefore, our God, [t]he great, the mighty, and awesome God, Who keeps covenant and mercy: Do not let all the trouble seem small before You [t]hat has come upon us… ³⁸ And because of all this, [w]e make a sure *covenant* and write *it;* [o]ur leaders… *and* our priests seal *it.*"

XIV. The Book of Esther

Christianity/Judaism:

Esther 2:

[2] …[T]he king's servants… said: "Let beautiful young virgins be sought for the king; [3] and let the king appoint officers in all the provinces of his kingdom, that they may gather all the beautiful young virgins to Shushan the citadel, into the women's quarters, under the custody of Hegai the king's eunuch, custodian of the women… [4] Then let the young woman who pleases the king be queen…" This thing pleased the king, and he did so.

[5] In Shushan the citadel there was a certain Jew whose name *was* Mordecai… [7] And *Mordecai* had brought up Hadassah, that *is,* Esther, his uncle's daughter, for she had neither father nor mother. The young woman *was* lovely and beautiful. When her father and mother died, Mordecai took her as his own daughter.

[8] So it was, when the king's command and decree were heard, and when many young women were gathered… that Esther also was taken to the king's palace…

[15] Now when the turn came for Esther… to go in to the king, she… obtained favor in the sight of all who saw her. [16] So Esther was taken to King Ahasuerus, into his royal palace… [17] The king loved Esther more than all the *other* women, and she obtained grace and favor in his sight more than all the virgins; so he set the royal crown upon her head and made her queen… [18] Then the king made a great feast, the Feast of Esther, for all his officials and servants; and he proclaimed a holiday in the provinces and gave gifts according to the generosity of a king.

Esther 3:

[1] After these things King Ahasuerus promoted Haman… and set his seat above all the princes who *were* with him. [2]

[5] When Haman saw that Mordecai did not bow or pay him homage, [he] was filled with wrath. [6] But he disdained to lay hands on Mordecai alone… Instead, Haman sought to destroy all the Jews who *were* throughout the whole kingdom of Ahasuerus…

Esther 4:

[1] When Mordecai learned [of the plot], he tore his clothes and put on sackcloth and ashes, and went out into the midst of the city. He cried out with a loud and bitter cry. [2] He went as far as the front of the king's gate, for no one *might* enter the king's gate clothed with sackcloth. [3] And in every province… *there was* great mourning among the Jews, with fasting, weeping, and wailing; and many lay in sackcloth and ashes.

[4] [Esther] was deeply distressed… [S]he sent garments to clothe Mordecai and take his sackcloth away from him, but he would not accept *them.*

[15] Then Esther [instructed]: [16] "Go, gather all the Jews who are present in Shushan, and

fast for me; neither eat nor drink for three days, night or day. My maids and I will fast likewise. And so I will go to the king, which *is* against the law; and if I perish, I perish!"

[11] All the king's servants and the people of the king's provinces kn[e]w that any man or woman who [went] into the inner court to the king, who ha[d] not been called... [would be] put... to death, except [if] the king h[eld] out the golden scepter, that he may live. [Esther had] not been called to go in to the king these thirty days.

[17] ...Mordecai went his way and did according to all that Esther commanded him.

Esther 5:

[1] Now it happened on the third day that Esther put on *her* royal *robes* and stood in the inner court of the king's palace, across from the king's house, while the king sat on his royal throne in the royal house, facing the entrance of the house. [2] So it was, when the king saw Queen Esther standing in the court, *that* she found favor in his sight, and the king held out to Esther the golden scepter that *was* in his hand. Then Esther went near and touched the top of the scepter.

[3] And the king said to her, "What do you wish, Queen Esther? What *is* your request? It shall be given to you — up to half the kingdom!"

Esther 7:

[3] Then Queen Esther answered and said, "If I have found favor in your sight, O king, and if it pleases the king, let my life be given me at my petition, and my people at my request. [4] For we have been sold, my people and I, to be destroyed, to be killed, and to be annihilated..."

Esther 8:

[7] Then King Ahasuerus said to Queen Esther and Mordecai the Jew, [8] "You yourselves write *a decree* concerning the Jews, as you please, in the king's name, and seal *it* with the king's signet ring; for whatever is written in the king's name and sealed with the king's signet ring no one can revoke."

[9] So the king's scribes were called... and it was written, according to all that Mordecai commanded... [10] And he wrote in the name of King Ahasuerus, sealed *it* with the king's signet ring, and sent letters by couriers on horseback, riding on royal horses bred from swift steeds.

[15] So Mordecai went out from the presence of the king in royal apparel of blue and white, with a great crown of gold and a garment of fine linen and purple; and the city of Shushan rejoiced and was glad. [16] The Jews had light and gladness, joy and honor. [17] And in every province and city, wherever the king's command and decree came, the Jews had joy and gladness, a feast and a holiday...

Judaism (Talmud):

[Babylonian Talmud. Midrash Tehilim Buber, 22:16]:

"Master of the universe, you have given me (Esther) three commandments – *niddah* (purity), *challah* (eating of loaves of bread to commemorate the manna that God had provided), and lighting candles – ...I have not broken one of them."

XV. The Book of Job

Christianity/Judaism:

Job 1:

¹ In the land of Uz there lived a man whose name was Job. This man was blameless and upright; he feared God and shunned evil. ¹³ One day when Job's sons and daughters were feasting and drinking wine at the oldest brother's house, ¹⁴ a messenger came to Job and said, "The oxen [that] were plowing and the donkeys [that] were grazing nearby [were stolen]."

¹⁶ While he was still speaking, another messenger came and said, "[F]ire… fell from the heavens and burned up the sheep…" ¹⁷ While he was still speaking, another messenger came and said, "The Chaldeans formed three raiding parties and swept down on your camels and made off with them…"

¹⁸ While he was still speaking, yet another messenger came and said, "Your sons and daughters were feasting and drinking wine at the oldest brother's house, ¹⁹ when suddenly a mighty wind swept in from the desert and struck the four corners of the house. It collapsed on them and they are dead…" ²⁰ At this, Job got up and tore his robe and shaved his head. Then he fell to the ground in worship ²¹ and said: "Naked I came from my mother's womb, and naked I will depart… [M]ay the name of the LORD be praised."

Job 2:

⁷ [Then] Job [was afflicted] with painful sores from the soles of his feet to the crown of his head. ⁹ His wife said to him, "Are you still maintaining your integrity?" ¹⁰ He replied, "…Shall we accept good from God, and not trouble?"

¹¹ When Job's three friends, Eliphaz the Temanite, Bildad the Shuhite and Zophar the Naamathite, heard about all the troubles that had come upon him, they set out from their homes and met together by agreement to go and sympathize with him and comfort him. ¹² When they saw him from a distance, they could hardly recognize him; they began to weep aloud, and they tore their robes and sprinkled dust on their heads. ¹³ Then they sat on the ground with him for seven days and seven nights. No one said a word to him, because they saw how great his suffering was.

Job 3:

¹ After this, Job… cursed the day of his birth. ¹¹ "Why did I not perish at birth, and die as I came from the womb?"

Job 4:

¹ Then Eliphaz the Temanite replied: ⁶ "Should not your piety be your confidence and your blameless ways your hope? ⁷ …Who, being innocent, has ever perished? ¹⁰ The lions may roar and growl, yet the teeth of the great lions are broken."

Job 6:

¹ Then Job replied: ⁸ "Oh, that I might have my request, that God would grant what I hope for, ⁹ that God would be willing to crush me, to let loose [H]is hand and cut off my life! ¹⁰ Then I would still have this consolation – my joy in unrelenting pain – that I had not denied the words of the Holy One."

Job 8:

¹ Then Bildad the Shuhite replied: ²⁰ "Surely God does not reject one who is blameless or strengthen the hands of evildoers. ²¹ He will yet fill your mouth with laughter and your lips with shouts of joy."

Job 9:

¹ Then Job replied: ² "Indeed, I know that this is true… ⁴ [God's] wisdom is profound, [H]is power is vast… ⁵ He moves mountains without their knowing it … ⁷ He speaks to the sun and it does not shine… ⁸ He alone stretches out the heavens and treads on the waves of the sea. ¹⁰ He performs wonders that cannot be fathomed, miracles that cannot be counted. ¹⁴ How then can I dispute with [H]im? How can I find words to argue with [H]im? ²¹ Although I am blameless, I have no concern for myself…"

Job 10:

¹⁹ "If only I had never come into being, or had been carried straight from the womb to the grave!"

Job 11:

¹ Then Zophar the Naamathite replied: ⁷ "Can you fathom the mysteries of God? Can you probe the limits of the Almighty? ⁸ They are higher than the heavens above — what can you do? They are deeper than the depths below — what can you know? ⁹ Their measure is longer than the earth and wider than the sea.

¹³ …[I]f you devote your heart to [H]im and stretch out your hands to [H]im, ¹⁵ …you will stand firm and without fear. ¹⁶ You will surely forget your trouble, recalling it only as waters gone by. ¹⁷ Life will be brighter than noonday, and darkness will become like morning. ¹⁸ You will be secure, because there is hope…"

Job 12:

¹ Then Job replied:

Job 14:

⁷ "… [T]here is hope for a tree: If it is cut down, it will sprout again, and its new shoots will not fail. ⁵ [But][a] person's days are determined; [Y]ou have decreed the number of his months and have set limits he cannot exceed. ¹³ If only [Y]ou would hide me in the grave and conceal me till [Y]our anger has passed! If only [Y]ou would set me a time and then remember me! ¹⁴ If someone dies, will they live again? All the days of my hard service I will wait for my renewal to come. ¹⁵ You will call and I will answer you…"

Job 15:

¹ Then Eliphaz the Temanite replied: ¹¹ "Are God's consolations not enough for you [?] ¹² Why has your heart carried you away... ¹³ so that you vent your rage against God and pour out such words from your mouth?"

Job 16:

¹ Then Job replied: ² "[Y]ou are miserable comforters, all of you! ⁴ I also could speak like you, if you were in my place; ⁵ But my mouth would encourage you; comfort from my lips would bring you relief. ¹⁵ I have sewed sackcloth over my skin and buried my brow in the dust. ¹⁶ My face is red with weeping, dark shadows ring my eyes; ¹⁷ yet my hands have been free of violence and my prayer is pure.

¹⁸ Earth, do not cover my blood; may my cry never be laid to rest! ¹⁹ Even now my witness is in heaven; my advocate is on high. ²⁰ My intercessor is my friend as my eyes pour out tears to God..."

Job 17:

¹ "My spirit is broken, my days are cut short, the grave awaits me. ¹⁵ where then is my hope – who can see any hope for me?"

Job 18:

¹ Then Bildad the Shuhite replied: ² "When will you end these speeches? Be sensible, and then we can talk..."

Job 19:

¹ Then Job replied: ² "How long will you torment me and crush me with words? ²¹ Have pity on me, my friends, have pity..."

Job 20:

¹ Then Zophar the Naamathite replied: ² "My troubled thoughts prompt me to answer because I am greatly disturbed. ³ I hear a rebuke that dishonors me, and my understanding inspires me to reply. ⁵ [Know] the joy of the godless lasts but a moment."

Job 21:

¹ Then Job replied: ⁴ "Why should I not be impatient? ²⁷ I know full well what you are thinking... ³⁴ So how can you console me...?"

Job 22:

¹ Then Eliphaz the Temanite replied: ¹² "Is not God in the heights of heaven? And see how lofty are the highest stars! ¹³ Does [H]e judge through... darkness?

²¹ ...[B]e at peace with [H]im; in this way prosperity will come to you. ²³ ...[Y]ou will be restored: ²⁶ Surely then you will find delight in the Almighty and will lift up your face to God. ²⁷ You will pray to him, and [H]e will hear you, and you will fulfill your vows. ²⁸

…[L]ight will shine on your ways. ³⁰ He will deliver even one who is not innocent…"

Job 23:

¹ Then Job replied: ³ "If only I knew where to find [H]im; if only I could go to [H]is dwelling! ⁸ But if I go to the east, [H]e is not there; if I go to the west, I do not find [H]im. ⁹ When [H]e is at work in the north, I do not see [H]im; when [H]e turns to the south, I catch no glimpse of [H]im.

⁷ There the upright can establish their innocence before [H]im, and there I would be delivered forever… ¹¹ …I have kept to [H]is way without turning aside. ¹² I have not departed from the commands of [H]is lips; I have treasured the words of [H]is mouth more than my daily bread."

Job 25:

¹ Then Bildad the Shuhite replied: ² "Dominion and awe belong to God; [H]e establishes order in the heights of heaven. ³ …On whom does [H]is light not rise?"

Job 26:

¹ Then Job replied: ⁷ "He spreads out the northern skies over empty space; [H]e suspends the earth over nothing. ⁸ He wraps up the waters in [H]is clouds, yet the clouds do not burst under their weight. ⁹ He covers the face of the full moon, spreading [H]is clouds over it. ¹⁰ He marks out the horizon on the face of the waters for a boundary between light and darkness. ¹³ By [H]is breath the skies became fair; ¹⁴ And these are but the outer fringe of [H]is works; how faint the whisper we hear of [H]im! Who then can understand the thunder of [H]is power?"

Job 27:

² "As surely as God lives… ³ as long as I have life within me, the breath of God in my nostrils, ⁴ my lips will not say anything wicked, and my tongue will not utter lies. ⁶ I will maintain my innocence and never let go of it…"

Job 38:

¹ Then the LORD spoke to Job… He said: ² "Who [speaks] without knowledge?"

Job 40:

² "Will the one who contends with the Almighty correct [H]im? Let him who accuses God answer [H]im!" ³ Then Job answered the LORD: ⁴ "I am unworthy — how can I reply to [Y]ou? I put my hand over my mouth. ⁵ I spoke… but I have no answer — "

Job 42:

² "I know that [Y]ou can do all things; no purpose of [Y]ours can be thwarted. ³ You asked, 'Who [speaks] without knowledge?' Surely I spoke of things I did not understand, things too wonderful for me to know. ⁵ My ears had heard of [Y]ou but now my eyes have seen [Y]ou. ⁶ Therefore I despise myself and repent in dust and ashes."

Job 40:

[5] "...I will say no more."

Job 42:

[10] After[wards]... the LORD... gave [Job] twice as much as he had before. [12] ...He had fourteen thousand sheep, six thousand camels, a thousand yoke of oxen and a thousand donkeys. [13] And he also had seven sons and three daughters. [15] Nowhere in all the land [was] there found women as beautiful as Job's daughters, and their father granted them an inheritance along with their brothers.

Job 28:

[12] [W]here can wisdom be found? Where does understanding dwell? [13] No mortal comprehends its worth; it cannot be found in the land of the living. [14] The deep says, "It is not in me;" the sea says, "It is not with me." [15] It cannot be bought with the finest gold, nor can its price be weighed out in silver. [20] Where then does wisdom come from? Where does understanding dwell? [23] God understands the way to it and [H]e alone knows where it dwells, [28] And [H]e said to the human race, "The fear of the Lord — that is wisdom, and to shun evil is understanding."

Islam:

The Prophets 21:83-84 And Ayub (Job), when he cried to his Lord, (saying): Harm has afflicted me, and Thou art the most Merciful of the merciful. ...[I] responded to him and took off what harm he had, and [I] gave him his family and the like of them with them: a mercy from [Me] and a reminder to the worshippers.

Suad 38:41-43 And remember [My] servant Ayub, when he called upon his Lord: The Shaitan (Satan) has afflicted me with toil and torment. ...[I said]: [H]ere is a cool washing-place and a drink. And [I] gave him his family and the like of them with them, as a mercy from [Me], and as a reminder to those possessed of understanding.

Suad 38:44 [When Job was concerned about the oath he took since he did not want to hurt his wife when he punished her with a hundred strokes (for saying, "Curse God and die!" [Job 2:9]) if his affliction was lifted, the Lord said]: [T]ake in your hand a [thin] green branch and [strike] her [softly] with it [so as] not break your oath; surely [I] found him patient; most excellent the servant! Surely he was frequent in returning (to [God]).

XVI. Psalms

Christianity/Judaism:

Book I:

Psalm 1:

[1] Blessed is the one… [2] whose delight is in the law of the LORD, and who meditates on [H]is law day and night. [3] That person is like a tree planted by streams of water, which yields its fruit in season and whose leaf does not wither — whatever they do prospers.

[4] Not so the wicked! They are like chaff that the wind blows away. [5] Therefore the wicked will not stand in the judgment, nor sinners in the assembly of the righteous. [6] For the LORD watches over the way of the righteous, but the way of the wicked leads to destruction.

Psalm 2:

[1] Why do the nations conspire and the peoples plot in vain? [2] The kings of the earth rise up and the rulers band together against the LORD and against his anointed, saying, [3] "Let us break their chains and throw off their shackles."

[7] I will proclaim the LORD's decree: He said to me, "You are my [child]; today I have become your father. [8] Ask [M]e, and I will make the nations your inheritance, the ends of the earth your possession. [10] Therefore, you kings, be wise; be warned, you rulers of the earth. [11] Serve the LORD… and celebrate [H]is rule. [12] …Blessed are all who take refuge in [H]im.

Psalm 3:

[1] LORD, how many are my foes! How many rise up against me! [2] Many are saying of me, "God will not deliver him."

[3] But you, LORD, are a shield around me, my glory, the One who lifts my head high.

[4] I call out to the LORD, and [H]e answers me from [H]is holy mountain.

[5] I lie down and sleep; I wake again, because the LORD sustains me. [6] I will not fear though tens of thousands assail me on every side.

[7] Arise, LORD! Deliver me, my God! [8] From the LORD comes deliverance. May [Y]our blessing be on [Y]our people.

Psalm 4:

[1] Answer me when I call to [Y]ou, my righteous God. Give me relief from my distress; have mercy on me and hear my prayer.

[3] Know that the LORD has set apart his faithful servant for [H]imself; the LORD hears

when I call to [H]im.

[4] Tremble and do not sin; when you are on your beds, search your hearts and be silent.
[5] ...[T]rust in the LORD.

[6] Let the light of [Y]our face shine on us. [7] Fill my heart with joy...

[8] In peace I will lie down and sleep, for [Y]ou alone, LORD, make me dwell in safety.

Psalm 5:

[1] Listen to my words, LORD, consider my lament. [2] Hear my cry for help, my King and my God, for to [Y]ou I pray.

[3] In the morning, LORD, [Y]ou hear my voice; in the morning I lay my requests before [Y]ou and wait expectantly. [4] For [Y]ou are not a God who is pleased with wickedness...

[8] Lead me, LORD, in your righteousness... — make [Y]our way straight before me.

[11] ...[L]et all who take refuge in [Y]ou be glad; let them ever sing for joy. Spread [Y]our protection over them, that those who love [Y]our name may rejoice in [Y]ou.

[12] Surely, LORD, you bless the righteous; [Y]ou surround them with [Y]our favor as with a shield.

Psalm 6:

[2] Have mercy on me, LORD, for I am faint; heal me, LORD, for my bones are in agony. [3] My soul is in deep anguish. How long, LORD, how long?

[4] Turn, LORD, and deliver me; save me because of [Y]our unfailing love.

[5] Among the dead no one proclaims [Y]our name. Who praises you from the grave?

[6] I am worn out from my groaning. All night long I flood my bed with weeping and drench my couch with tears. [7] My eyes grow weak with sorrow; they fail because of all my foes.

[8] ...[T]he LORD has heard my weeping. [9] The LORD has heard my cry for mercy; the LORD accepts my prayer.

Psalm 7:

[1] LORD my God, I take refuge in [Y]ou; save and deliver me from all who pursue me,
[2] or they will tear me apart like a lion and rip me to pieces with no one to rescue me.

[7] Let the assembled peoples gather around [Y]ou, while [Y]ou sit enthroned over them on high. [8] Let the LORD judge the peoples. Vindicate me, LORD, according to my righteousness, according to my integrity, O Most High.

[9] Bring to an end the violence of the wicked and make the righteous secure — [Y]ou, the righteous God who probes minds and hearts.

[10] My shield is God Most High, [W]ho saves the upright in heart. [11] God is a righteous judge...

[17] I will give thanks to the LORD because of [H]is righteousness; I will sing the praises of the name of the LORD Most High.

Psalm 8:

[1] LORD, our Lord, how majestic is [Y]our name in all the earth! You have set [Y]our glory in the heavens. [2] Through the praise of children and infants [Y]ou have established a stronghold...

[3] When I consider [Y]our heavens, the work of [Y]our fingers, the moon and the stars, which [Y]ou have set in place, [4] what is mankind that [Y]ou are mindful of them, human beings that [Y]ou care for them? [5] You have made them a little lower than the angels and crowned them with glory and honor. [9] LORD, our Lord, how majestic is [Y]our name in all the earth!

Psalm 9:

[1] I will give thanks to [Y]ou, LORD, with all my heart; I will tell of all [Y]our wonderful deeds. [2] I will be glad and rejoice in [Y]ou; I will sing the praises of [Y]our name, O Most High.

[3] My enemies turn back... [4] For [Y]ou have upheld my right and my cause, sitting enthroned as the righteous judge.

[7] The LORD reigns forever; [H]e has established [H]is throne for judgment. [8] He rules the world in righteousness and judges the peoples with equity.

[9] The LORD is a refuge for the oppressed, a stronghold in times of trouble. [10] Those who know [Y]our name trust in [Y]ou, for [Y]ou, LORD, have never forsaken those who seek [Y]ou.

[11] Sing the praises of the LORD... proclaim among the nations what [H]e has done. [12] For... [H]e does not ignore the cries of the afflicted.

[13] LORD, see how my enemies persecute me! Have mercy and lift me up from the gates of death, [14] that I may declare [Y]our praises... and... rejoice in [Y]our salvation.

[16] The LORD is known by [H]is acts of justice; the wicked are ensnared by the work of their hands. [18] ...God will never forget the needy; the hope of the afflicted will never perish. [19] Arise, LORD... let the nations be judged in [Y]our presence.

Psalm 10:

[1] Why, LORD, do [Y]ou stand far off? Why do [Y]ou hide yourself in times of trouble?

[2] In his arrogance the wicked man hunts down the weak, who are caught in the schemes he devises. [3] He boasts about the cravings of his heart; he blesses the greedy and reviles the LORD. [4] In his pride the wicked man does not seek [H]im; in all his thoughts there is no room for God.

[5] His ways are always prosperous; [Y]our laws are rejected by him; he sneers at all his enemies. [6] He says to himself, "Nothing will ever shake me." He swears, "No one will ever do me harm." [7] His mouth is full of lies and threats; trouble and evil are under his tongue.

[8] He lies in wait near the villages; from ambush he murders the innocent. His eyes watch in secret for his victims; [9] like a lion in cover he lies in wait. He lies in wait to catch the helpless; he catches the helpless and drags them off in his net.

[10] His victims are crushed, they collapse; they fall under his strength. [11] He says to himself, "God will never notice; [H]e covers his face and never sees."

[12] Arise, LORD! Do not forget the helpless. [13] Why does the wicked man revile God? Why does he say to himself, "He won't call me to account?"

[14] But [Y]ou, God, see the trouble of the afflicted; [Y]ou consider their grief and take it in hand. The victims commit themselves to [Y]ou; [Y]ou are the helper of the fatherless.

[16] The LORD is King for ever and ever…

[17] You, LORD, hear the desire of the afflicted; [Y]ou encourage them, and [Y]ou listen to their cry, [18] defending the fatherless and the oppressed, so that mere earthly mortals will never again strike terror.

Psalm 11:

[1] In the LORD I take refuge… [7] For the LORD is righteous, [H]e loves justice; the upright will see [H]is face.

Psalm 12:

[5] "Because the poor are plundered and the needy groan, I will now arise," says the LORD. "I will protect them from those who malign them."

[6] And the words of the LORD are flawless, like silver purified in a crucible, like gold refined seven times. [7] You, LORD, will keep the needy safe and will protect us forever from the wicked…

Psalm 13:

[1] How long, LORD? Will [Y]ou forget me forever? How long will [Y]ou hide [Y]our face from me? [2] How long must I wrestle with my thoughts and day after day have sorrow in my heart? How long will my enemy triumph over me?

[3] Look on me and answer, LORD my God. Give light to my eyes, or I will sleep in death,

4 and my enemy will say, "I have overcome him," and my foes will rejoice when I fall.

5 But I trust in [Y]our unfailing love; my heart rejoices in [Y]our salvation. 6 I will sing the LORD's praise, for [H]e has been good to me.

Psalm 14:

5 …God is present in the company of the righteous. 6 …the LORD is their refuge.

Psalm 15:

1 LORD, who may dwell in [Y]our sacred tent? Who may live on [Y]our holy mountain?

2 The one whose walk is blameless, who does what is righteous, who speaks the truth from their heart; 3 whose tongue utters no slander, who does no wrong to a neighbor, and casts no slur on others; 4 who… honors those who fear the LORD; who keeps an oath even when it hurts, and does not change their mind; 5 who lends money to the poor without interest; who does not accept a bribe against the innocent. Whoever does these things will never be shaken.

Psalm 16:

1 Keep me safe, my God, for in [Y]ou I take refuge.   2 I say to the LORD, "You are my Lord; apart from [Y]ou I have no good thing."

5 LORD, [Y]ou alone are my portion and my cup; [Y]ou make my lot secure. 6 The boundary lines have fallen for me in pleasant places; surely I have a delightful inheritance.   7 I will praise the LORD, [W]ho counsels me; even at night my heart instructs me. 8 I keep my eyes always on the LORD. With [H]im at my right hand, I will not be shaken.

9 Therefore my heart is glad and my tongue rejoices; my body also will rest secure, 10 because [Y]ou will not abandon me to the realm of the dead, nor will [Y]ou let [Y]our faithful one see decay.

11 You make known to me the path of life; [Y]ou will fill me with joy in [Y]our presence, with eternal pleasures at [Y]our right hand.

Psalm 17:

1 Hear me, LORD, my plea is just; listen to my cry. Hear my prayer — it does not rise from deceitful lips. 2 Let my vindication come from [Y]ou; may [Y]our eyes see what is right.

3 Though [Y]ou probe my heart, though [Y]ou examine me at night and test me, [Y]ou will find that I have planned no evil; my mouth has not transgressed. 4 Though people tried to bribe me, I have kept myself from the ways of the violent through what [Y]our lips have commanded. 5 My steps have held to [Y]our paths; my feet have not stumbled.

6 I call on [Y]ou, my God, for [Y]ou will answer me; turn [Y]our ear to me and hear my prayer. 7 Show me the wonders of [Y]our great love, [Y]ou who save by [Y]our right

hand those who take refuge in [Y]ou from their foes. [8] Keep me as the apple of [Y]our eye; hide me in the shadow of [Y]our wings [9] from the wicked who are out to destroy me, from my mortal enemies who surround me.

[10] They close up their callous hearts, and their mouths speak with arrogance. [11] They have tracked me down, they now surround me, with eyes alert, to throw me to the ground. [12] They are like a lion hungry for prey, like a fierce lion crouching in cover.

[13] Rise up, LORD... [14] By [Y]our hand save me... [15] ...I will be vindicated and will see [Y]our face; when I awake, I will be satisfied with seeing [Y]our likeness.

Psalm 18:

[1] I love [Y]ou, LORD, my strength. [2] The LORD is my rock, my fortress and my deliverer; my God is my rock, in [W]hom I take refuge, my shield and the horn of my salvation, my stronghold.

[3] I called to the LORD, [W]ho is worthy of praise, and I have been saved from my enemies. [4] The cords of death entangled me; the torrents of destruction overwhelmed me. [5] The cords of the grave coiled around me; the snares of death confronted me.

[6] In my distress I called to the LORD; I cried to my God for help. ...[H]e heard my voice... [16] He reached down from on high and took hold of me; [H]e drew me out of deep waters. [17] He rescued me from my powerful enemy, from my foes, who were too strong for me. [18] They confronted me in the day of my disaster, but the LORD was my support. [19] He brought me out into a spacious place; [H]e rescued me because [H]e delighted in me.

[20] The LORD has dealt with me according to my righteousness; according to the cleanness of my hands [H]e has rewarded me. [21] For I have kept the ways of the LORD; I am not guilty of turning from my God. [22] All [H]is laws are before me; I have not turned away from [H]is decrees. [23] I have been blameless before [H]im and have kept myself from sin.

[24] The LORD has rewarded me according to my righteousness, according to the cleanness of my hands in [H]is sight.

[25] To the faithful [Y]ou show [Y]ourself faithful, to the blameless [Y]ou show [Y]ourself blameless, [26] to the pure [Y]ou show [Y]ourself pure... [27] You save the humble... [28] You, LORD, keep my lamp burning; my God turns my darkness into light.

[30] As for God, [H]is way is perfect: The LORD's word is flawless; [H]e shields all who take refuge in [H]im.

[31] For who is God besides the LORD? And who is the Rock except our God? [32] It is God who arms me with strength and keeps my way secure. [35] You make [Y]our saving help my shield, and [Y]our right hand sustains me; [Y]our help has made me great.

[46] The LORD lives! Praise be to my Rock! Exalted be God my Savior! [47] He is the

God... ⁴⁸ who saves me from my enemies. ⁴⁹ Therefore I will praise [Y]ou, LORD, among the nations; I will sing the praises of [Y]our name.

⁵⁰ ...[H]e shows unfailing love to [H]is anointed... and to [their] descendants forever.

Psalm 19:

¹ The heavens declare the glory of God; the skies proclaim the work of [H]is hands. ² Day after day they pour forth speech; night after night they reveal knowledge. ⁴ [T]heir voice goes out into all the earth, their words to the ends of the world. In the heavens God has pitched a tent for the sun. ⁵ It is like a bridegroom coming out of his chamber, like a champion rejoicing to run his course. ⁶ It rises at one end of the heavens and makes its circuit to the other; nothing is deprived of its warmth.

⁷ The law of the LORD is perfect, refreshing the soul. The statutes of the LORD are trustworthy, making wise the simple. ⁸ The precepts of the LORD are right, giving joy to the heart. The commands of the LORD are radiant, giving light to the eyes. ⁹ The fear of the LORD is pure, enduring forever. The decrees of the LORD are firm, and all of them are righteous.

¹⁰ They are more precious than gold, [much more than] pure gold; they are sweeter than honey, than honey from the honeycomb. ¹¹ ...[I]n keeping them there is great reward.

Psalm 20:

¹ May the LORD answer you when you are in distress; may the name of...God... protect you. ² May [H]e send you help... and grant you support... ⁴ May [H]e give you the desire of your heart and make all your plans succeed. ⁵ May we shout for joy over your victory and lift up our banners in the name of our God. May the LORD grant all your requests.

⁶ ...The LORD gives victory to [H]is anointed. He answers [them] from [H]is heavenly sanctuary... ⁷ Some trust in chariots and some in horses, but we trust in the name of the LORD our God. ⁹ LORD... [a]nswer us when we call!

Psalm 21:

¹ The king rejoices in [Y]our strength, LORD. How great is his joy in the victories [Y]ou give! ² You have granted him his heart's desire and have not withheld the request of his lips. ³ You came to greet him with rich blessings and placed a crown of pure gold on his head. ⁴ He asked [Y]ou for life, and [Y]ou gave it to him — length of days, for ever and ever.

⁶ Surely [Y]ou have granted him unending blessings and made him glad with the joy of [Y]our presence. ⁷ For the king trusts in the LORD; through the unfailing love of the Most High he will not be shaken. ¹³ Be exalted... LORD; we will sing and praise [Y]our might.

Psalm 22:

¹ My God, my God, why have [Y]ou forsaken me? Why are [Y]ou so far from saving me, so far from my cries of anguish? ² My God, I cry out by day, but [Y]ou do not answer, by night, but I find no rest.

³ Yet [Y]ou are enthroned as the Holy One… ⁴ In [Y]ou our ancestors put their trust; they trusted and [Y]ou delivered them. ⁵ To [Y]ou they cried out and were saved; in [Y]ou they trusted and were not put to shame.

⁶ But I am a worm and not a man, scorned by everyone, despised by the people. ⁷ All who see me mock me; they hurl insults, shaking their heads. ⁸ "He trusts in the LORD," they say, "[L]et the LORD rescue him. Let [H]im deliver him, since [H]e delights in him."

⁹ Yet [Y]ou brought me out of the womb; [Y]ou made me trust in [Y]ou, even at my mother's breast. ¹⁰ From birth I was cast on [Y]ou; from my mother's womb [Y]ou have been my God.

¹¹ Do not be far from me, for trouble is near and there is no one to help. ¹² Many bulls surround me; strong bulls… encircle me. ¹³ Roaring lions that tear their prey open their mouths wide against me. ¹⁴ I am poured out like water, and all my bones are out of joint. My heart has turned to wax; it has melted within me.

¹⁵ My mouth is dried up like a potsherd, and my tongue sticks to the roof of my mouth; [Y]ou lay me in the dust of death. ¹⁶ Dogs surround me, a pack of villains encircles me; they pierce my hands and my feet. ¹⁷ All my bones are on display; [P]eople stare and gloat over me. ¹⁸ They divide my clothes among them and cast lots for my garment.

¹⁹ But [Y]ou, LORD, do not be far from me. You are my strength; come quickly to help me. ²⁰ Deliver me from the sword, my precious life from the power of the dogs. ²¹ Rescue me from the mouth of the lions; save me from the horns of the wild oxen.

²² I will declare [Y]our name to my people; in the assembly I will praise [Y]ou. ²³ You who fear the LORD, praise [H]im! All… honor [H]im! Revere [H]im…²⁴ For [H]e has not despised or scorned the suffering of the afflicted one; [H]e has not hidden [H]is face from him but has listened to his cry for help.

²⁶ The poor will eat and be satisfied; those who seek the LORD will praise [H]im — may your hearts live forever! ²⁷ All the ends of the earth will remember and turn to the LORD, and all the families of the nations will bow down before [H]im, ²⁸ for dominion belongs to the LORD and [H]e rules over the nations.

²⁹ All the rich of the earth will feast and worship; all who go down to the dust will kneel before [H]im — those who cannot keep themselves alive. ³⁰ Posterity will serve [H]im; future generations will be told about the Lord. ³¹ They will proclaim [H]is righteousness, declaring to a people yet unborn: He has done it!

Psalm 23:

¹ The LORD *is* my shepherd; I shall not want. ² He makes me to lie down in green pastures; He leads me beside the still waters. ³ He restores my soul; He leads me in the paths of righteousness [f]or His name's sake.

⁴ …[T]hough I walk through the valley of the shadow of death, I will fear no evil; For You *are* with me; Your rod and Your staff, they comfort me. ⁵ You prepare a table before me

in the presence of my enemies; You anoint my head with oil; My cup runs over. [6] Surely goodness and mercy shall follow me [a]ll the days of my life; And I will dwell in the house of the LORD [f]orever.

Psalm 24:

[1] The earth is the LORD's, and everything in it, the world, and all who live in it; [2] for [H]e founded it on the seas and established it on the waters. [3] Who may ascend the mountain of the LORD? Who may stand in [H]is holy place? [4] The one who has clean hands and a pure heart... [5] They will receive blessing from the LORD and vindication from God their Savior.

[7] Lift up your heads, you gates; be lifted up, you ancient doors that the King of glory may come in. [8] Who is this King of glory? The LORD strong and mighty... [9] Lift up your heads, you gates; lift them up, you ancient doors that the King of glory may come in. [10] Who is he, this King of glory? The LORD Almighty — [H]e is the King of glory.

Psalm 25:

[1] In [Y]ou, LORD my God, I put my trust. [2] I trust in [Y]ou; do not let me be put to shame, nor let my enemies triumph over me. [3] No one who hopes in [Y]ou will ever be put to shame... [4] Show me [Y]our ways, LORD, teach me [Y]our paths. [5] Guide me in [Y]our truth and teach me, for [Y]ou are God my Savior, and my hope is in [Y]ou all day long.

[6] Remember, LORD, [Y]our great mercy and love, for they are from of old. [7] Do not remember the sins of my youth and my rebellious ways; according to [Y]our love remember me, for [Y]ou, LORD, are good. [8] Good and upright is the LORD; therefore [H]e instructs sinners in [H]is ways. [9] He guides the humble in what is right and teaches them [H]is way. [10] All the ways of the LORD are loving and faithful toward those who keep... [H]is covenant. [11] For the sake of [Y]our name, LORD, forgive my iniquity, though it is great.

[12] Who, then, are those who fear the LORD? He will instruct them in the ways they should choose. [13] They will spend their days in prosperity, and their descendants will inherit the land. [14] The LORD confides in those who fear [H]im; [H]e makes [H]is covenant known to them. [15] My eyes are ever on the LORD, for only [H]e will release my feet from the snare.

[16] Turn to me and be gracious to me, for I am lonely and afflicted. [17] Relieve the troubles of my heart and free me from my anguish. [18] Look on my affliction and my distress and take away all my sins. [20] Guard my life and rescue me; do not let me be put to shame, for I take refuge in [Y]ou. [21] May integrity and uprightness protect me, because my hope, LORD, is in [Y]ou.

Psalm 26:

[1] Vindicate me, LORD, for I have led a blameless life; I have trusted in the LORD and have not faltered. [2] Test me, LORD, and try me, examine my heart and my mind; [3] for I have always been mindful of [Y]our unfailing love and have lived in reliance on [Y]our faithfulness.

[6] I... go about [Y]our altar, LORD, [7] proclaiming aloud [Y]our praise and telling of all [Y]our wonderful deeds. [8] LORD, I love the house where [Y]ou live, the place where [Y]our glory dwells. [9] Do not take away my soul... [11] I lead a blameless life; deliver me and be merciful to me. [12] ...I will praise the LORD.

Psalm 27:

[1] The LORD is my light and my salvation — whom shall I fear? The LORD is the stronghold of my life — of whom shall I be afraid?

[2] When the wicked advance against me to devour me, it is my enemies and my foes who will stumble and fall. [3] Though an army besiege me, my heart will not fear; though war break out against me, even then I will be confident.

[4] One thing I ask from the LORD, this only do I seek: that I may dwell in the house of the LORD all the days of my life... [5] For in the day of trouble [H]e will keep me safe in [H]is dwelling; [H]e will hide me in the shelter of [H]is sacred tent and set me high upon a rock.

[7] Hear my voice when I call, LORD; be merciful to me and answer me. [8] My heart says of [Y]ou, "Seek [H]is face!" Your face, LORD, I will seek. [9] Do not hide [Y]our face from me, do not turn [Y]our servant away in anger; [Y]ou have been my helper. Do not reject me or forsake me, God my Savior. [10] Though my father and mother forsake me, the LORD will receive me.

[11] Teach me [Y]our way, LORD; lead me in a straight path... [13] I remain confident of this: I will see the goodness of the LORD in the land of the living. [14] Wait for the LORD; be strong and take heart and wait for the LORD.

Psalm 28:

[1] To [Y]ou, LORD, I call; [Y]ou are my Rock, do not turn a deaf ear to me. For if [Y]ou remain silent, I will be like those who go down to the pit. [2] Hear my cry for mercy as I call to [Y]ou for help, as I lift up my hands toward [Y]our Most Holy Place...

[6] Praise be to the LORD, for [H]e has heard my cry for mercy. [7] The LORD is my strength and my shield; my heart trusts in [H]im, and [H]e helps me. My heart leaps for joy, and with my song I praise [H]im. [8] The LORD is the strength of [H]is people, a fortress of salvation for [H]is anointed one[s]. [9] Save [Y]our people and bless [Y]our inheritance; be their shepherd and carry them forever.

Psalm 29:

[1] Ascribe to the LORD, you heavenly beings, ascribe to the LORD glory and strength. [2] Ascribe to the LORD the glory due [H]is name; worship the LORD in the splendor of [H]is holiness.

[3] The voice of the LORD is over the waters; the God of glory thunders, the LORD thunders over the mighty waters. [4] The voice of the LORD is powerful; the voice

of the LORD is majestic. [9] ...[I]n [H]is temple all cry, "Glory!" [10] The... LORD is enthroned as King forever. [11] The LORD gives strength to [H]is people; the LORD blesses [H]is people with peace.

Psalm 30:

[1] I will exalt you, LORD, for [Y]ou lifted me out of the depths and did not let my enemies gloat over me. [2] LORD my God, I called to [Y]ou for help, and [Y]ou healed me. [3] You, LORD, brought me up from the realm of the dead; [Y]ou spared me from going down to the pit.

[4] Sing the praises of the LORD, you his faithful people; praise [H]is holy name. [5] For [H]is anger lasts only a moment, but [H]is favor lasts a lifetime; weeping may stay for the night, but rejoicing comes in the morning.

[7] LORD, when [Y]ou favored me, [Y]ou made my royal mountain stand firm; but when [Y]ou hid your face, I was dismayed. [8] To [Y]ou, LORD, I called; to the Lord I cried for mercy: [9] "What is gained if I am silenced, if I go down to the pit? Will the dust praise [Y]ou? Will it proclaim [Y]our faithfulness? [10] Hear, LORD, and be merciful to me; LORD, be my help."

[11] You turned my wailing into dancing; [Y]ou removed my sackcloth and clothed me with joy, [12] that my heart may sing [Y]our praises and not be silent. LORD my God, I will praise [Y]ou forever.

Psalm 31:

[1] In [Y]ou, LORD, I have taken refuge; let me never be put to shame; deliver me in [Y]our righteousness. [2] Turn [Y]our ear to me, come quickly to my rescue; be my rock of refuge, a strong fortress to save me.

[3] Since [Y]ou are my rock and my fortress, for the sake of [Y]our name lead and guide me. [4] Keep me free from the trap that is set for me, for [Y]ou are my refuge. [5] Into [Y]our hands I commit my spirit; deliver me, LORD, my faithful God. [6] ...I trust in the LORD. [7] I will be glad and rejoice in [Y]our love, for [Y]ou saw my affliction and knew the anguish of my soul. [8] You have not given me into the hands of the enemy but have set my feet in a spacious place.

[9] Be merciful to me, LORD, for I am in distress; my eyes grow weak with sorrow, my soul and body with grief. [10] My life is consumed by anguish and my years by groaning; my strength fails because of my affliction, and my bones grow weak. [11] Because of all my enemies, I am the utter contempt of my neighbors and an object of dread to my closest friends — those who see me on the street flee from me. [12] I am forgotten as though I were dead; I have become like broken pottery.

[13] For I hear many whispering... They conspire against me and plot to take my life. [14] But I trust in [Y]ou, LORD; I say, "You are my God." [15] ...[D]eliver me from the hands of my enemies, from those who pursue me. [16] Let [Y]our face shine on [Y]our servant; save me in [Y]our unfailing love.

¹⁷ Let me not be put to shame, LORD, for I have cried out to [Y]ou... ¹⁹ How abundant are the good things that [Y]ou have stored up for those who fear [Y]ou, that [Y]ou bestow in the sight of all, on those who take refuge in [Y]ou. ²⁰ In the shelter of [Y]our presence [Y]ou hide them...; [Y]ou keep them safe in [Y]our dwelling...

²¹ Praise be to the LORD, for [H]e showed me the wonders of [H]is love when I was in a city under siege. ²² In my alarm I said, "I am cut off from [Y]our sight!" Yet [Y]ou heard my cry for mercy when I called to [Y]ou for help.

²³ Love the LORD, all [H]is faithful people! The LORD preserves those who are true to [H]im... ²⁴ Be strong and take heart, all you who hope in the LORD.

Psalm 32:

¹ Blessed is the one whose transgressions are forgiven, whose sins are covered. ² Blessed is the one whose sin the LORD does not count against them and in whose spirit is no deceit.

³ When I kept silent, my bones wasted away through my groaning all day long. ⁴ For day and night [Y]our hand was heavy on me; my strength was sapped as in the heat of summer. ⁵ Then I acknowledged my sin to [Y]ou and did not cover up my iniquity. I said, "I will confess my transgressions to the LORD." And [Y]ou forgave the guilt of my sin. ⁶ Therefore let all the faithful pray to [Y]ou while [Y]ou may be found; surely the rising of the mighty waters will not reach them.

⁷ You are my hiding place; [Y]ou will protect me from trouble and surround me with songs of deliverance. ¹⁰ Many are the woes of the wicked, but the LORD's unfailing love surrounds the one who trusts in [H]im. ¹¹ Rejoice in the LORD and be glad, you righteous; sing, all you who are upright in heart!

Psalm 33:

¹ Sing joyfully to the LORD, you righteous; it is fitting for the upright to praise [H]im. ² Praise the LORD with the harp; make music to [H]im on the ten-stringed lyre. ³ Sing to [H]im a new song; play skillfully, and shout for joy. ⁴ For the word of the LORD is right and true; [H]e is faithful in all [H]e does.

⁵ The LORD loves righteousness and justice; the earth is full of [H]is unfailing love. ⁶ By the word of the LORD the heavens were made, their starry host by the breath of [H]is mouth.

⁸ Let all the earth fear the LORD; let all the people of the world revere [H]im. ⁹ For [H]e spoke, and it came to be; [H]e commanded, and it stood firm. ¹¹ ...[T]he plans of the LORD stand firm forever, the purposes of [H]is heart through all generations.

¹² Blessed [are they] whose God is the LORD, the people [H]e chose for [H]is inheritance.

¹³ From heaven the LORD looks down and sees all mankind; ¹⁴ from [H]is dwelling place [H]e watches all who live on earth — ¹⁵ [H]e who forms the hearts of all, who considers

everything they do.

¹⁶ No king is saved by the size of his army; no warrior escapes by his great strength. ¹⁷ A horse is a vain hope for deliverance; despite all its great strength it cannot save. ¹⁸ But the eyes of the LORD are on those who fear [H]im, on those whose hope is in [H]is unfailing love, ¹⁹ to deliver them from death and keep them alive in famine.

²⁰ We wait in hope for the LORD; [H]e is our help and our shield. ²¹ In [H]im our hearts rejoice, for we trust in [H]is holy name. ²² May [Y]our unfailing love be with us, LORD, even as we put our hope in [Y]ou.

Psalm 34:

¹ I will extol the LORD at all times; [H]is praise will always be on my lips. ² I will glory in the LORD; let the afflicted hear and rejoice. ³ Glorify the LORD with me; let us exalt [H]is name together. ⁴ I sought the LORD, and [H]e answered me; [H]e delivered me from all my fears.

⁵ Those who look to [H]im are radiant; their faces are never covered with shame. ⁸ Taste and see that the LORD is good; blessed is the one who takes refuge in [H]im.

⁹ Fear the LORD, you [H]is holy people, for those who fear [H]im lack nothing. ¹⁰ The lions may grow weak and hungry, but those who seek the LORD lack no good thing.

¹² Whoever of you loves life and desires to see many good days, ¹³ keep your tongue from evil and your lips from telling lies. ¹⁴ Turn from evil and do good; seek peace and pursue it. ¹⁵ The eyes of the LORD are on the righteous, and [H]is ears are attentive to their cry… ¹⁷ The righteous cry out, and the LORD hears them; [H]e delivers them from all their troubles.

¹⁸ The LORD is close to the brokenhearted and saves those who are crushed in spirit.

¹⁹ The righteous person may have many troubles, but the LORD delivers him from them all; ²⁰ [H]e protects all his bones, not one of them will be broken. ²² The LORD will rescue [H]is servants; no one who takes refuge in [H]im will be condemned.

Psalm 35:

⁹ …[M]y soul will rejoice in the LORD and delight in [H]is salvation. ¹⁰ My whole being will exclaim, "Who is like [Y]ou, LORD?

¹³ …When my prayers returned to me unanswered, ¹⁴ I went about mourning as though for my friend or brother. I bowed my head in grief as though weeping for my mother. ¹⁵ …They slandered me without ceasing. ¹⁶ …[T]hey maliciously mocked; they gnashed their teeth at me. ¹⁷ How long, Lord, will [Y]ou look on? Rescue me from their ravages, my precious life from these lions.

²² LORD… do not be silent. Do not be far from me, Lord. ²³ Awake, and rise to my defense! Contend for me, my God and Lord. ²⁴ Vindicate me in [Y]our righteousness, LORD my God; do not let them gloat over me. ¹⁸ I will give [Y]ou thanks…; among the throngs I will praise [Y]ou. ²⁸ My tongue will proclaim [Y]our righteousness, [Y]our

praises all day long.

Psalm 36:

[5] Your love, LORD, reaches to the heavens, [Y]our faithfulness to the skies. [6] Your righteousness is like the highest mountains, [Y]our justice like the great deep. You, LORD, preserve both people and animals.

[7] How priceless is [Y]our unfailing love, O God! People take refuge in the shadow of [Y]our wings. [8] They feast on the abundance of [Y]our house; [Y]ou give them drink from [Y]our river of delights. [9] For with [Y]ou is the fountain of life; in [Y]our light we see light.

[10] Continue [Y]our love to those who know [Y]ou, [Y]our righteousness to the upright in heart.

Psalm 37:

[3] Trust in the LORD and do good; dwell in the land and enjoy safe pasture. [4] Take delight in the LORD, and [H]e will give you the desires of your heart. [5] Commit your way to the LORD; trust in [H]im and [H]e will do this: [6] He will make your righteous reward shine like the dawn, your vindication like the noonday sun.

[7] Be still before the LORD and wait patiently for [H]im... [8] Refrain from anger and turn from wrath; ...it leads only to evil. [9] For... those who hope in the LORD will inherit the land. [11] ...[T]he meek will inherit the land and enjoy peace and prosperity. [17] ...[T]he LORD upholds the righteous.

[18] The blameless spend their days under the LORD's care, and their inheritance will endure forever. [19] In times of disaster they will not wither; in days of famine they will enjoy plenty.

[23] The LORD makes firm the steps of the one who delights in [H]im; [24] though he may stumble, he will not fall, for the LORD upholds him with [H]is hand.

[25] I was young and now I am old, yet I have never seen the righteous forsaken... [26] They are always generous and lend freely; their children will be a blessing.

[27] Turn from evil and do good; then you will dwell in the land forever. [28] For the LORD loves the just and will not forsake [H]is faithful ones. [29] The righteous will inherit the land and dwell in it forever.

[30] The mouths of the righteous utter wisdom, and their tongues speak what is just. [31] The law of their God is in their hearts; their feet do not slip. [33] ...[T]he LORD will not leave them in the power of the wicked or let them be condemned...

[34] Hope in the LORD and keep [H]is way. [7] Consider the blameless, observe the upright; a future awaits those who seek peace.

[39] The salvation of the righteous comes from the LORD; [H]e is their stronghold in time of trouble. [40] The LORD helps them and delivers them; [H]e delivers them from the wicked

and saves them, because they take refuge in [H]im.

Psalm 38:

[1] LORD, do not rebuke me...   [4] My guilt has overwhelmed me like a burden too heavy to bear.   [6] I am bowed down and brought very low; all day long I go about mourning.   [7] My back is filled with searing pain; there is no health in my body.   [8] I am feeble and utterly crushed; I groan in anguish of heart.   [10] My heart pounds, my strength fails me; even the light has gone from my eyes.

[13] I am like the deaf, who cannot hear, like the mute, who cannot speak;   [15] LORD, I wait for [Y]ou; [Y]ou will answer, Lord my God.   [16] For I said, "Do not let them gloat or exalt themselves over me when my feet slip."

[17] ...I am about to fall, and my pain is ever with me.   [18] I confess my iniquity; I am troubled by my sin...   [20] though I seek only to do what is good.   [21] LORD, do not forsake me; do not be far from me, my God.   [22] Come quickly to help me, my Lord and my Savior.

Psalm 39:

[1] I said, "I will watch my ways and keep my tongue from sin..."   [2] So I remained utterly silent, not even saying anything good. But my anguish increased;   [3] my heart grew hot within me. While I meditated, the fire burned; then I spoke with my tongue:

[4] "Show me, LORD, my life's end and the number of my days; let me know how fleeting my life is.   [5] You have made my days a mere handbreadth; the span of my years is as nothing before [Y]ou. Everyone is but a breath, even those who seem secure.

[7] But now, Lord, what do I look for? My hope is in [Y]ou.   [8] Save me from all my transgressions...   [12] Hear my prayer, LORD, listen to my cry for help; do not be deaf to my weeping...   [13] that I may enjoy life again before I depart and am no more."

Psalm 40:

[1] I waited patiently for the LORD; [H]e turned to me and heard my cry.   [2] He lifted me out of the slimy pit, out of the mud and mire; [H]e set my feet on a rock and gave me a firm place to stand.

[3] He put a new song in my mouth, a hymn of praise to our God. Many will see and fear the LORD and put their trust in [H]im.   [4] Blessed is the one who trusts in the LORD...

[5] Many, LORD my God, are the wonders [Y]ou have done, the things [Y]ou planned for us. None can compare with [Y]ou; were I to speak and tell of [Y]our deeds, they would be too many to declare.

[6] Sacrifice and offering you did not desire — but my ears [Y]ou have opened — burnt offerings and sin offerings you did not require.   [7] Then I said, "Here I am, I have come — [8] I desire to do [Y]our will, my God; [Y]our law is within my heart."

⁹ I proclaim your saving acts... ¹⁰ I do not hide [Y]our righteousness in my heart; I speak of [Y]our faithfulness and [Y]our saving help.   I do not conceal [Y]our love and [Y]our faithfulness…

¹¹ Do not withhold [Y]our mercy from me, LORD; may [Y]our love and faithfulness always protect me. ¹² For troubles without number surround me; my sins have overtaken me, and I cannot see. They are more than the hairs of my head, and my heart fails within me.

¹³ Be pleased to save me, LORD; come quickly, LORD, to help me. ¹⁶ …[M]ay all who seek [Y]ou rejoice and be glad in [Y]ou; may those who long for [Y]our saving help always say, "The LORD is great!"

¹⁷ But as for me, I am poor and needy; may the Lord think of me. You are my help and my deliverer; [Y]ou are my God, do not delay.

Psalm 41:

¹ Blessed are those who have regard for the weak; the LORD delivers them in times of trouble. ² The LORD protects and preserves them — they are counted among the blessed in the land — [H]e does not give them over to the desire of their foes.

³ The LORD sustains them on their sickbed and restores them from their bed of illness. ⁴ I said, "Have mercy on me, LORD; heal me, for I have sinned against [Y]ou." ¹⁰ …[M]ay [Y]ou have mercy on me, LORD; raise me up…

¹² Because of my integrity [Y]ou uphold me and set me in [Y]our presence forever. ¹³ Praise be to the LORD… from everlasting to everlasting. Amen and Amen.

Book II:

Psalm 42:

¹ As the deer pants for streams of water, so my soul pants for [Y]ou, my God. ² My soul thirsts for God, for the living God. When can I go and meet with God?

³ My tears have been my food day and night, while people say to me all day long, "Where is your God?" ⁴ These things I remember as I pour out my soul: [H]ow I used to go to the house of God under the protection of the Mighty One with shouts of joy and praise among the festive throng.

⁵ Why, my soul, are you downcast? Why so disturbed within me? Put your hope in God, for I will yet praise [H]im, my Savior and my God. ⁶ My soul is downcast within me; therefore I will remember [Y]ou…

⁷ Deep calls to deep in the roar of [Y]our waterfalls; all [Y]our waves and breakers have swept over me.

⁸ By day the LORD directs [H]is love, at night [H]is song is with me — a prayer to the God of my life. ⁹ I say to God my Rock, "Why have you forgotten me? Why must I go

about mourning, oppressed by the enemy?"

[10] My bones suffer mortal agony as my foes taunt me, saying to me all day long, "Where is your God?" [11] Why, my soul, are you downcast? Why so disturbed within me? Put your hope in God, for I will yet praise [H]im, my Savior and my God.

Psalm 43:

[1] Vindicate me, my God, and plead my cause… Rescue me from those who are deceitful and wicked. [2] You are God my stronghold. Why have [Y]ou rejected me? Why must I go about mourning, oppressed by the enemy?

[3] Send me [Y]our light and [Y]our faithful care, let them lead me; let them bring me to [Y]our holy mountain, to the place where [Y]ou dwell. [4] Then I will go to the altar of God, to God, my joy and my delight. I will praise [Y]ou with the lyre, O God, my God.

[5] Why, my soul, are you downcast? Why so disturbed within me? Put your hope in God, for I will yet praise [H]im, my Savior and my God.

Psalm 44:

[4] You are my King and my God… [8] [W]e will praise [Y]our name forever.

[23] Awake, Lord! Why do you sleep? Rouse yourself! [24] Why do [Y]ou hide [Y]our face…? [25] We are brought down to the dust; our bodies cling to the ground. [26] Rise up and help us; rescue us because of [Y]our unfailing love.

Psalm 45:

[6] Your throne, O God, will last for ever and ever; a scepter of justice will be the scepter of [Y]our kingdom.

Psalm 46:

[1] God is our refuge and strength, an ever-present help in trouble. [2] Therefore we will not fear, though the earth give way and the mountains fall into the heart of the sea, [3] though its waters roar and foam and the mountains quake with their surging.

[4] There is a river whose streams make glad the city of God, the holy place where the Most High dwells. [5] God is within her, she will not fall; God will help her at break of day.

[7] The LORD Almighty is with us; …God …is our fortress.

[8] Come and see what the LORD has done… [9] He makes wars cease to the ends of the earth. He breaks the bow and shatters the spear; [H]e burns the shields… [10] He says, "Be still, and know that I am God; I will be exalted among the nations, I will be exalted in the earth." [11] The LORD Almighty is with us; …God …is our fortress.

Psalm 47:

[1] Clap your hands, all you nations; shout to God with cries of joy. [2] For the LORD Most

High is awesome, the great King over all the earth.

5 God has ascended amid shouts of joy, the LORD amid the sounding of trumpets. 6 Sing praises to God, sing praises; sing praises to our King, sing praises. 7 For God is the King of all the earth; sing to [H]im a psalm of praise. 8 God reigns over the nations; God is seated on [H]is holy throne…; [H]e is greatly exalted.

Psalm 48:

1 Great is the LORD, and most worthy of praise, in the city of our God, [H]is holy mountain. 2 Beautiful in its loftiness, the joy of the whole earth… is… the city of the Great King.

3 God is in [Jerusalem's] citadels; [H]e has shown [H]imself to be her fortress. 9 Within [Y]our temple, O God, we meditate on [Y]our unfailing love. 10 Like [Y]our name, O God, [Y]our praise reaches to the ends of the earth; [Y]our right hand is filled with righteousness. 11 [We] rejoice, the villages… are glad because of [Y]our judgments.

12 Walk about… go around her, count her towers, 13 consider well her ramparts, view her citadels, that you may tell of them to the next generation. 14 For this God is our God for ever and ever; [H]e will be our guide even to the end.

Psalm 49:

1 Hear this, all you peoples; listen, all who live in this world, 2 both low and high, rich and poor alike: 3 My mouth will speak words of wisdom; the meditation of my heart will give you understanding.

7 No one can redeem the life of another or give to God a ransom for them — 9 so that they should live on forever and not see decay. 10 For all can see that the wise die, that the foolish and the senseless also perish, leaving their wealth to others. 11 Their tombs will remain their houses forever, their dwellings for endless generations, though they had named lands after themselves.

13 This is the fate of those who trust in themselves… 15 …[But] God will redeem me from the realm of the dead; [H]e will surely take me to [H]imself.

Psalm 50:

1 The Mighty One, God, the LORD, speaks and summons the earth from the rising of the sun to where it sets. 2 …[P]erfect in beauty, God shines forth. 3 Our God comes and will not be silent… 4 He summons the heavens above, and the earth, that [H]e may judge [H]is people: 5 "Gather to [M]e this consecrated people, who made a covenant with [M]e…" 6 And the heavens proclaim [H]is righteousness, for [H]e is a God of justice.

7 "Listen, my people, and I will speak; I am God, your God. 8 I bring no charges against you… 9 I have no need of a bull from your stall or of goats from your pens, 10 for every animal of the forest is [M]ine, and the cattle on a thousand hills. 11 I know every bird in the mountains, and the insects in the fields are [M]ine. 12 [T]he world is [M]ine, and all that is in it. 15 …[C]all on [M]e in the day of trouble; I will deliver you, and you will honor

[M]e.

²² Consider this, you who forget God... ²³ Those who... honor [M]e, and to the blameless I will show [M]y salvation."

Psalm 51:

¹ Have mercy on me, O God, according to [Y]our unfailing love; according to [Y]our great compassion blot out my transgressions. ² Wash away all my iniquity and cleanse me from my sin.

³ For I know my transgressions, and my sin is always before me. ⁴ Against [Y]ou, [Y]ou only, have I sinned and done what is evil in [Y]our sight; so [Y]ou are right in [Y]our verdict and justified when [Y]ou judge. ⁵ Surely I was sinful at birth, sinful from the time my mother conceived me. ⁶ Yet [Y]ou desired faithfulness even in the womb; [Y]ou taught me wisdom in that secret place.

⁷ Cleanse me with hyssop, and I will be clean; wash me, and I will be whiter than snow. ⁸ Let me hear joy and gladness... ⁹ Hide [Y]our face from my sins and blot out all my iniquity.

¹⁰ Create in me a pure heart, O God, and renew a steadfast spirit within me. ¹¹ Do not cast me from [Y]our presence or take [Y]our Holy Spirit from me. ¹² Restore to me the joy of [Y]our salvation and grant me a willing spirit, to sustain me. ¹³ Then I will teach transgressors [Y]our ways, so that sinners will turn back to [Y]ou.

¹⁴ Deliver me from... guilt, O God, [Y]ou who are God my Savior, and my tongue will sing of [Y]our righteousness. ¹⁵ Open my lips, Lord, and my mouth will declare [Y]our praise. ¹⁶ You do not delight in sacrifice, or I would bring it; [Y]ou do not take pleasure in burnt offerings. ¹⁷ My sacrifice, O God, is a broken spirit; a broken and contrite heart [Y]ou, God, will not despise.

Psalm 52:

⁸ ...I am like an olive tree flourishing in the house of God; I trust in God's unfailing love for ever and ever. ⁹ For what [Y]ou have done I will always praise [Y]ou in the presence of [Y]our faithful people. And I will hope in [Y]our name, for [Y]our name is good.

Psalm 53:

¹ The fool says in his heart, "There is no God." ⁴ Do [they] know nothing?

Psalm 54:

¹ Save me, O God, by [Y]our name; vindicate me by [Y]our might. ² Hear my prayer, O God; listen to the words of my mouth.

³ Arrogant foes are attacking me; ruthless people are trying to kill me — people without regard for God.

⁴ Surely God is my help; the Lord is the one [W]ho sustains me. ⁶ ...I will praise [Y]our name, LORD, for it is good. ⁷ You have delivered me from all my troubles...

Psalm 55:

¹ Listen to my prayer, O God, do not ignore my plea; ² hear me and answer me. My thoughts trouble me and I am distraught ³ because of what my enemy is saying, because of the threats of the wicked; for they bring down suffering on me and assail me in their anger.

⁴ My heart is in anguish within me; the terrors of death have fallen on me. ⁵ Fear and trembling have beset me; horror has overwhelmed me. ⁶ I said, "Oh, that I had the wings of a dove! I would fly away and be at rest. ⁷ I would flee far away and stay in the desert; ⁸ I would hurry to my place of shelter, far from the tempest and storm."

¹¹ Destructive forces are at work in the city; threats and lies never leave its streets. ¹⁶ ...I call to God, and the LORD saves me.

¹⁷ Evening, morning and noon I cry out in distress, and [H]e hears my voice. ¹⁸ He rescues me unharmed... ²² Cast your cares on the LORD and [H]e will sustain you; [H]e will never let the righteous be shaken. ²³ ...I trust in [Y]ou.

Psalm 56:

¹ Be merciful to me, my God, for my enemies are in hot pursuit; all day long they press their attack. ² My adversaries pursue me all day long...

³ When I am afraid, I put my trust in [Y]ou. ⁴ In God, [W]hose word I praise — in God I trust and am not afraid. What can mere mortals do to me?

⁵ All day long they twist my words; all their schemes are for my ruin. ⁶ They conspire, they lurk, they watch my steps, hoping to take my life. ¹⁰ In God, [W]hose word I praise, in the LORD, [W]hose word I praise — ¹¹ in God I trust and am not afraid. What can man do to me?

¹² I am under vows to [Y]ou, my God; I will present my thank offerings to [Y]ou. ¹³ For [Y]ou have delivered me from death and my feet from stumbling, that I may walk before God in the light of life.

Psalm 57:

¹ Have mercy on me, my God, have mercy on me, for in [Y]ou I take refuge. I will take refuge in the shadow of [Y]our wings until the disaster has passed. ² I cry out to God Most High, to God, [W]ho vindicates me. ³ He sends from heaven and saves me... God sends forth [H]is love and [H]is faithfulness.

⁴ I am in the midst of lions; I am forced to dwell among ravenous beasts — men whose teeth are spears and arrows, whose tongues are sharp swords. ⁵ Be exalted, O God,

above the heavens; let [Y]our glory be over all the earth.

[6] They spread a net for my feet — I was bowed down in distress. They dug a pit in my path — but they have fallen into it themselves. [7] My heart, O God, is steadfast, my heart is steadfast; I will sing and make music. [8] Awake, my soul! Awake, harp and lyre! [9] I will praise [Y]ou, Lord, among the nations; I will sing of [Y]ou among the peoples. [10] For great is [Y]our love, reaching to the heavens; [Y]our faithfulness reaches to the skies. [11] Be exalted, O God, above the heavens; let [Y]our glory be over all the earth.

Psalm 58:

[11] "Surely the righteous… are rewarded; surely there is a God [W]ho judges the earth."

Psalm 59:

[1] Deliver me from my enemies, O God; be my fortress against those who are attacking me. [2] Deliver me from evildoers and save me from those who are after my blood. [3] See how they lie in wait for me! Fierce men conspire against me for no offense or sin of mine, LORD. [4] I have done no wrong, yet they are ready to attack me. Arise to help me; look on my plight! [5] You, LORD God Almighty… rouse yourself…

[6] They return at evening, snarling like dogs, and prowl about the city. [7] See what they spew from their mouths — the words from their lips are sharp as swords, and they think, "Who can hear us?" [9] You are my strength, I watch for [Y]ou; [Y]ou, God, are my fortress, [10] my God on whom I can rely.

[14] They return at evening, snarling like dogs, and prowl about the city. [15] They wander about for food and howl if not satisfied. [16] But I will sing of [Y]our strength, in the morning I will sing of [Y]our love; for [Y]ou are my fortress, my refuge in times of trouble. [17] You are my strength, I sing praise to [Y]ou; [Y]ou, God, are my fortress, my God on [W]hom I can rely.

Psalm 60:

[4] …[F]or those who fear [Y]ou, [Y]ou have raised a banner to be unfurled against the bow. [5] Save us and help us with [Y]our right hand, that those [Y]ou love may be delivered. [11] Give us aid against the enemy, for human help is worthless. [12] With God we will gain… victory…

Psalm 61:

[1] Hear my cry, O God; listen to my prayer. [2] From the ends of the earth I call to [Y]ou, I call as my heart grows faint; lead me to the rock that is higher than I. [3] For [Y]ou have been my refuge, a strong tower against the foe.

[4] I long to dwell in [Y]our tent forever and take refuge in the shelter of [Y]our wings. [5] For [Y]ou, God, have heard my vows; [Y]ou have given me the heritage of those who fear [Y]our name.

[6] Increase the days of [my] life, [my] years for many generations. [7] May [I] be… in God's

presence forever; appoint [Y]our love and faithfulness to protect [me]. [8] Then I will ever sing in praise of [Y]our name and fulfill my vows day after day.

Psalm 62:

[1] Truly my soul finds rest in God; my salvation comes from [H]im. [2] Truly [H]e is my rock and my salvation; [H]e is my fortress, I will never be shaken.

[5] Yes, my soul, find rest in God; my hope comes from [H]im. [6] Truly [H]e is my rock and my salvation; [H]e is my fortress, I will not be shaken. [7] My salvation and my honor depend on God; [H]e is my mighty rock, my refuge. [8] Trust in [H]im at all times, you people; pour out your hearts to [H]im, for God is our refuge.

[10] Do not... put vain hope in [material] goods; though your riches increase, do not set your heart on them. [11] One thing God has spoken, two things I have heard: "Power belongs to [Y]ou, God, [12] and with [Y]ou, Lord, is unfailing love" and "You reward everyone according to what they have done."

Psalm 63:

[1] You, God, are my God, earnestly I seek [Y]ou; I thirst for [Y]ou, my whole being longs for [Y]ou, in a dry and parched land where there is no water.

[3] Because [Y]our love is better than life, my lips will glorify [Y]ou. [4] I will praise [Y]ou as long as I live, and in [Y]our name I will lift up my hands. [5] I will be fully satisfied as with the richest of foods; with singing lips my mouth will praise [Y]ou.

[6] On my bed I remember [Y]ou; I think of [Y]ou through the watches of the night. [7] Because [Y]ou are my help, I sing in the shadow of your wings. [8] I cling to [Y]ou; [Y]our right hand upholds me.

Psalm 64:

[1] Hear me, my God... [P]rotect my life from the threat of the enemy. [2] Hide me from the conspiracy of the wicked, from the plots of evildoers. [3] They sharpen their tongues like swords and aim cruel words like deadly arrows. [4] They shoot from ambush at the innocent; they shoot suddenly, without fear. [5] They encourage each other in evil plans, they talk about hiding their snares; they say, "Who will see it?" [6] They plot injustice and say, "We have devised a perfect plan!"

[7] But... [8] [they will see] ruin; [9] All people... will proclaim the works of God and ponder what [H]e has done. [10] The righteous will rejoice in the LORD and take refuge in [H]im; all the upright in heart will glory in [H]im!

Psalm 65:

[1] Praise awaits [Y]ou, our God... to [Y]ou our vows will be fulfilled. [2] You who answer prayer, to [Y]ou all people will come. [3] When we were overwhelmed by sins, [Y]ou forgave our transgressions. [4] Blessed are [we]... We are filled with... good things...

⁵ You answer us with awesome and righteous deeds, God our Savior, the hope of all the ends of the earth and of the farthest seas, ⁶ [W]ho formed the mountains by [Y]our power, having armed [Y]ourself with strength, ⁷ [W]ho stilled the roaring of the seas, the roaring of their waves, and the turmoil of the nations.

⁸ The whole earth is filled with awe at [Y]our wonders; where morning dawns, where evening fades, [Y]ou call forth songs of joy.

⁹ You care for the land and water it; [Y]ou enrich it abundantly. The streams of God are filled with water to provide the people with grain, for so [Y]ou have ordained it. ¹⁰ You drench its furrows and level its ridges; [Y]ou soften it with showers and bless its crops. ¹¹ You crown the year with [Y]our bounty, and [Y]our carts overflow with abundance.

¹² The grasslands of the wilderness overflow; the hills are clothed with gladness. ¹³ The meadows are covered with flocks and the valleys are mantled with grain; they shout for joy and sing.

Psalm 66:

¹ Shout for joy to God, all the earth! ² Sing the glory of [H]is name; make [H]is praise glorious. ³ Say to God, "How awesome are [Y]our deeds! So great is [Y]our power… ⁴ All the earth bows down to [Y]ou; they sing praise to [Y]ou, they sing the praises of [Y]our name."

⁵ Come and see what God has done, [H]is awesome deeds for mankind! ⁶ He turned the sea into dry land, they passed through the waters on foot — come, let us rejoice in [H]im.

⁷ He rules forever by [H]is power, [H]is eyes watch the nations… ⁸ Praise… God — all peoples, let the sound of [H]is praise be heard; ⁹ [H]e has preserved our lives and kept our feet from slipping. ¹² You… brought us to a place of abundance.

¹⁶ Come and hear, all you who fear God; let me tell you what [H]e has done for me. ¹⁷ I cried out to [H]im with my mouth; [H]is praise was on my tongue. ¹⁸ If I had cherished sin in my heart, the Lord would not have listened; ¹⁹ but God has surely listened and has heard my prayer. ²⁰ Praise be to God, [W]ho has not rejected my prayer or withheld [H]is love from me!

Psalm 67:

¹ May God be gracious to us and bless us and make [H]is face shine on us — ² so that [Y]our ways may be known on earth, [Y]our salvation among all nations. ³ May the peoples praise [Y]ou, God; may all the peoples praise [Y]ou. ⁴ May the nations be glad and sing for joy, for [Y]ou rule the peoples with equity and guide the nations of the earth.

⁵ May the peoples praise [Y]ou, God; may all the peoples praise [Y]ou. ⁶ The land yields its harvest; God… blesses us. ⁷ May God bless us still, so that all the ends of the earth will fear [H]im.

Psalm 68:

¹ May God arise...³ ...[M]ay the righteous be glad and rejoice before God; may they be happy and joyful. ⁴ Sing to God, sing in praise of [H]is name, extol [H]im who rides on the clouds; rejoice before [H]im — [H]is name is the LORD. ⁵ A father to the fatherless, a defender of widows, is God in [H]is holy dwelling. ⁶ God sets the lonely in families, [H]e leads out the prisoners with singing...

⁷ When [Y]ou, God, went out before [Y]our people, when [Y]ou marched through the wilderness, ⁸ the earth shook, the heavens poured down rain... ⁹ You gave abundant showers, O God; [Y]ou refreshed [Y]our weary inheritance. ¹⁰ ...[F]rom [Y]our bounty, God, [Y]ou provided for the poor.

¹⁹ Praise be to the Lord, to God our Savior, [W]ho daily bears our burdens. ²⁰ Our God is a God [W]ho saves; from the Sovereign LORD comes escape from death.

²⁴ Your procession, God, has come into view, the procession of my God and King into the sanctuary. ²⁵ In front are the singers, after them the musicians; with them are the young women playing the timbrels. ²⁶ Praise God in the great congregation; praise the LORD...

³² Sing to God, you kingdoms of the earth, sing praise to the Lord, ³³ to [H]im [W]ho rides across the highest heavens, the ancient heavens, [W]ho thunders with mighty voice. ³⁴ Proclaim the power of God... [W]hose power is in the heavens. ³⁵ You, God, are awesome... [You] give power and strength to [Your] people. Praise be to God!

Psalm 69:

¹ Save me, O God, for the waters have come up to my neck. ² I sink in the miry depths, where there is no foothold. I have come into the deep waters; the floods engulf me. ³ I am worn out calling for help; my throat is parched. My eyes fail, looking for my God.

⁴ Those who hate me without reason outnumber the hairs of my head; many are my enemies without cause, those who seek to destroy me... ⁵ You, God, know my folly; my guilt is not hidden from you. ⁶ Lord, the LORD Almighty, may those who hope in [Y]ou not be disgraced... [M]ay those who seek [Y]ou not be put to shame...

¹³ ...I pray to you, LORD, in the time of [Y]our favor; in [Y]our great love, O God, answer me with [Y]our sure salvation. ¹⁴ Rescue me from the mire, do not let me sink; deliver me from those who hate me, from the deep waters. ¹⁵ Do not let the floodwaters engulf me or the depths swallow me up or the pit close its mouth over me.

¹⁶ Answer me, LORD, out of the goodness of [Y]our love; in [Y]our great mercy turn to me. ¹⁷ Do not hide [Y]our face from [Y]our servant; answer me quickly, for I am in trouble. ¹⁸ Come near and rescue me; deliver me because of my foes. ¹⁹ You know how I am scorned, disgraced and shamed; all my enemies are before [Y]ou.

²⁰ Scorn has broken my heart and has left me helpless; I looked for sympathy, but there was none, for comforters, but I found none. ²¹ They put gall in my food and gave me vinegar for my thirst. ²⁹ ...[F]or me, afflicted and in pain — may [Y]our salvation, God,

protect me.

30 I will praise God's name in song and glorify [H]im with thanksgiving. 32 The poor will see and be glad — you who seek God, may your hearts live! 33 The LORD hears the needy and does not despise [H]is captive people. 34 Let heaven and earth praise [H]im, the seas and all that move in them, 35 for God will save… 36 those who love [H]is name…

Psalm 70:

1 Hasten, O God, to save me; come quickly, LORD, to help me. 4 …[M]ay all who seek [Y]ou rejoice and be glad in [Y]ou; may those who long for [Y]our saving help always say, "The LORD is great!"

5 But as for me, I am poor and needy; come quickly to me, O God. You are my help and my deliverer; LORD, do not delay.

Psalm 71:

1 In [Y]ou, LORD, I have taken refuge; let me never be put to shame. 2 In [Y]our righteousness rescue me and deliver me; turn [Y]our ear to me and save me. 3 Be my rock of refuge, to which I can always go; give the command to save me, for [Y]ou are my rock and my fortress.

4 Deliver me, my God, from the hand of the wicked, from the grasp of those who are evil and cruel. 5 For [Y]ou have been my hope, Sovereign LORD, my confidence since my youth. 6 From birth I have relied on [Y]ou; [Y]ou brought me forth from my mother's womb. I will ever praise [Y]ou.

7 …[Y]ou are my strong refuge. 8 My mouth is filled with [Y]our praise, declaring [Y]our splendor all day long. 9 Do not cast me away when I am old; do not forsake me when my strength is gone. 10 For my enemies speak against me; those who wait to kill me conspire together. 11 They say, "God has forsaken him; pursue him and seize him, for no one will rescue him."

12 Do not be far from me, my God; come quickly, God, to help me. 14 …I will always have hope; I will praise [Y]ou more and more. 15 My mouth will tell of [Y]our righteous deeds, of [Y]our saving acts all day long… 16 I will come and proclaim [Y]our mighty acts, Sovereign LORD; I will proclaim [Y]our righteous deeds, [Y]ours alone. 17 Since my youth, God, [Y]ou have taught me, and to this day I declare [Y]our marvelous deeds.

18 Even when I am old and gray do not forsake me, my God, till I declare [Y]our power to the next generation, [Y]our mighty acts to all who are to come. 19 Your righteousness, God, reaches to the heavens, [Y]ou who have done great things. Who is like [Y]ou, God? 20 …[Y]ou will restore my life again; …[Y]ou will again bring me up. 21 You will increase my honor and comfort me once more.

22 I will praise you with the harp for [Y]our faithfulness, my God; I will sing praise to [Y]ou with the lyre… 23 My lips will shout for joy when I sing praise to [Y]ou — I whom [Y]ou have delivered. 24 My tongue will tell of [Y]our righteous acts all day long…

Psalm 72:

[12] [H]e will deliver the needy who cry out, the afflicted who have no one to help. [13] He will take pity on the weak and the needy... [14] He will rescue them from oppression and violence, for precious is their blood in [H]is sight.

[18] Praise be to the LORD God... [W]ho alone does marvelous deeds. [19] Praise be to [H]is glorious name forever; may the whole earth be filled with [H]is glory. Amen and Amen.

Book III:

Psalm 73:

[1] Surely God is good to... those who are pure in heart.

[2] But as for me, my feet had almost slipped; I had nearly lost my foothold. [21] When my heart was grieved and my spirit embittered, [22] I was senseless and ignorant... [23] Yet I am always with [Y]ou; [Y]ou hold me by my right hand. [24] You guide me with [Y]our counsel, and afterward [Y]ou will take me into glory. [25] Whom have I in heaven but [Y]ou? And earth has nothing I desire besides [Y]ou.

[26] My flesh and my heart may fail, but God is the strength of my heart and my portion forever. [28] ...[I]t is good to be near God. I have made the Sovereign LORD my refuge; I will tell of all [Y]our deeds.

Psalm 74:

[12] ...God is my King from long ago; [H]e brings salvation on the earth.

[13] It was [Y]ou who split open the sea by your power... [15] It was [Y]ou who opened up springs and streams... [16] The day is [Y]ours, and [Y]ours also the night; [Y]ou established the sun and moon. [17] It was [Y]ou who set all the boundaries of the earth; [Y]ou made both summer and winter.

[19] Do not hand over the life of [Y]our dove to wild beasts; do not forget the lives of [Y]our afflicted people... [21] [M]ay the poor and needy praise [Y]our name. [22] Rise up, O God, and defend [Y]our cause...

Psalm 75:

[1] We praise [Y]ou, God, we praise [Y]ou, for [Y]our Name is near; people tell of [Y]our wonderful deeds.

[2] You say, "I choose the appointed time; it is I who judge with equity. [3] When the earth and all its people quake, it is I who hold its pillars firm. [6] No one from the east or the west or from the desert can exalt themselves. [7] It is God [W]ho judges... [9] ...I will sing praise to God... [for] [10] the righteous will be lifted up.

Psalm 76:

[1] God is renowned... [H]is name is great. [4] You are radiant with light, more majestic

than mountains rich with game. ⁷ It is [Y]ou alone who are to be feared... ⁸ From heaven [Y]ou pronounced judgment, and the land feared and was quiet — ⁹ when [Y]ou, God, rose up to judge, to save all the afflicted of the land.

¹¹ Make vows to the LORD your God and fulfill them; let all the… lands bring [Him] gifts…

Psalm 77:

¹ I cried out to God for help; I cried out to God to hear me. ² When I was in distress, I sought the Lord; at night I stretched out untiring hands, and I would not be comforted. ³ I remembered [Y]ou, God, and I groaned; I meditated, and my spirit grew faint. ⁴ You kept my eyes from closing; I was too troubled to speak.

⁵ I thought about the former days, the years of long ago; ⁶ I remembered my songs in the night. My heart meditated and my spirit asked: ⁷ "Will the Lord… never show [H]is favor again? ⁸ Has [H]is unfailing love vanished forever?" ¹⁰ Then I thought, ¹¹ "…I will remember the deeds of the LORD; yes, I will remember [Y]our miracles of long ago. ¹² I will consider all [Y]our works and meditate on all [Y]our mighty deeds." ¹³ Your ways, God, are holy… ¹⁴ You are the God who performs miracles; [Y]ou display [Y]our power among the peoples. ¹⁵ With [Y]our mighty arm [Y]ou redeemed [Y]our people…

¹⁶ The waters saw [Y]ou… and writhed; the very depths were convulsed. ¹⁷ The clouds poured down water, the heavens resounded with thunder… ¹⁸ Your thunder was heard in the whirlwind, [Y]our lightning lit up the world; the earth trembled and quaked. ¹⁹ Your path led through the sea, [Y]our way through the mighty waters, though [Y]our footprints were not seen. ²⁰ You led [Y]our people like a flock…

Psalm 79:

⁹ Help us, God our Savior, for the glory of [Y]our name; deliver us and forgive our sins for [Y]our name's sake. ¹⁰ …[M]ake [it] known among the nations… ¹³ Then we [Y]our people, the sheep of [Y]our pasture, will praise [Y]ou forever; from generation to generation we will proclaim [Y]our praise.

Psalm 80:

¹ Hear us… You who sit enthroned between the cherubim, shine forth… ² Awaken [Y]our might; come and save us. ³ Restore us, O God; make [Y]our face shine on us, that we may be saved.

⁷ Restore us, God Almighty; make [Y]our face shine on us, that we may be saved. ¹⁴ Return to us, God Almighty! Look down from heaven and see! Watch over this vine, ¹⁵ the root [Y]our right hand has planted, the son [Y]ou have raised up for [Y]ourself.

¹⁷ Let [Y]our hand rest on the man at [Y]our right hand, the son of man [Y]ou have raised up for [Y]ourself. ¹⁸ Then we will not turn away from [Y]ou; revive us, and we will call on [Y]our name. ¹⁹ Restore us, LORD God Almighty; make [Y]our face shine on us, that we may be saved.

Psalm 81:

¹ Sing for joy to God our strength; shout aloud… ² Begin the music, strike the timbrel,

play the melodious harp and lyre.

[6] "I removed the burden from their shoulders; their hands were set free from the basket. [7] In your distress you called and I rescued you... [10] I am the LORD your God... Open wide your mouth and I will fill it. [13] If my people would only listen to me, if [they] would only follow my ways... [16] [they] would be fed with the finest of wheat; with honey from the rock I would satisfy you."

Psalm 82:

[1] God presides in the great assembly; [H]e renders judgment... [3] Defend the weak and the fatherless; uphold the cause of the poor and the oppressed. [4] Rescue the weak and the needy; deliver them from the hand of the wicked. [8] Rise up, O God, judge the earth, for all the nations are [Y]our inheritance.

Psalm 83:

[1] O God, do not remain silent; do not turn a deaf ear, do not stand aloof, O God. [2] See how [Y]our enemies growl, how [Y]our foes rear their heads. [3] With cunning they conspire against [Y]our people; they plot against those [Y]ou cherish. [4] "Come," they say, "let us destroy them..."

[5] With one mind they plot together; they form an alliance against [Y]ou... [18] Let them know that [Y]ou, [W]hose name is the LORD — that [Y]ou alone are the Most High over all the earth.

Psalm 84:

[1] How lovely is [Y]our dwelling place, LORD Almighty! [2] My soul yearns, even faints, for the courts of the LORD; my heart and my flesh cry out for the living God.

[3] Even the sparrow has found a home, and the swallow a nest for herself, where she may have her young — a place near [Y]our altar, LORD Almighty, my King and my God.

[4] Blessed are those who dwell in [Y]our house; they are ever praising [Y]ou. [5] Blessed are those whose strength is in [Y]ou... [8] Hear my prayer, LORD God Almighty; [9] Look... with favor on [us]...

[10] Better is one day in [Y]our courts than a thousand elsewhere... [11] For the LORD God is a sun and shield; the LORD bestows favor and honor; no good thing does [H]e withhold from those whose walk is blameless. [12] LORD Almighty, blessed is the one who trusts in [Y]ou.

Psalm 85:

[1] You, LORD, showed favor... [2] You forgave the iniquity of [Y]our people and covered all their sins. [7] Show us [Y]our unfailing love, LORD, and grant us [Y]our salvation.

[8] I will listen to what God the LORD says; [H]e promises peace to [H]is people, [H]is faithful servants... [9] Surely [H]is salvation is near those who fear [H]im that his glory may

dwell…

10 Love and faithfulness meet together; righteousness and peace kiss each other. **11** Faithfulness springs forth from the earth, and righteousness looks down from heaven. **12** The LORD will indeed give what is good… **13** Righteousness goes before [H]im…

Psalm 86:

1 Hear me, LORD, and answer me, for I am poor and needy. **2** Guard my life, for I am faithful to [Y]ou; save [Y]our servant who trusts in [Y]ou. You are my God; **3** have mercy on me, Lord, for I call to [Y]ou all day long. **4** Bring joy to [Y]our servant, Lord, for I put my trust in [Y]ou.

5 You, Lord, are forgiving and good, abounding in love to all who call to [Y]ou. **6** Hear my prayer, LORD; listen to my cry for mercy. **7** When I am in distress, I call to [Y]ou, because [Y]ou answer me.

8 …[T]here is none like [Y]ou, Lord; no deeds can compare with [Y]ours. **9** All the nations [Y]ou have made will come and worship before [Y]ou, Lord; they will bring glory to [Y]our name. **10** For [Y]ou are great and do marvelous deeds; [Y]ou alone are God.

11 Teach me [Y]our way, LORD, that I may rely on [Y]our faithfulness; give me an undivided heart, that I may fear [Y]our name.

12 I will praise [Y]ou, Lord my God, with all my heart; I will glorify [Y]our name forever. **13** For great is [Y]our love toward me; [Y]ou have delivered me from the depths, from the realm of the dead.

15 …[Y]ou, Lord, are a compassionate and gracious God, slow to anger, abounding in love and faithfulness. **16** Turn to me and have mercy on me; show [Y]our strength [on] behalf of [Y]our servant; save me, because I serve [Y]ou… **17** Give me a sign of [Y]our goodness… for [Y]ou, LORD, have helped me and comforted me.

Psalm 88:

1 LORD, [Y]ou are the God [W]ho saves me; day and night I cry out to [Y]ou. **2** May my prayer come before [Y]ou; turn [Y]our ear to my cry.

3 I am overwhelmed with troubles and my life draws near to death. **4** I am counted among those who go down to the pit; I am like one without strength. **5** I am set apart with the dead… **8** I am confined and cannot escape; **9** my eyes are dim with grief. I call to [Y]ou, LORD, every day; I spread out my hands to [Y]ou.

10 Do [Y]ou show [Y]our wonders to the dead? Do their spirits rise up and praise [Y]ou? **11** Is your love declared in the grave…? **12** Are [Y]our wonders known in the place of darkness, or [Y]our righteous deeds in the land of oblivion?

13 …I cry to [Y]ou for help, LORD; in the morning my prayer comes before [Y]ou. **14** Why, LORD, do [Y]ou… hide [Y]our face from me?

Psalm 89:

[1] I will sing of the LORD's great love forever; with my mouth I will make [Y]our faithfulness known through all generations. [2] I will declare that [Y]our love stands firm forever, that [Y]ou have established [Y]our faithfulness in heaven itself.

[5] The heavens praise [Y]our wonders, LORD, [Y]our faithfulness too…[6] For who in the skies above can compare with the LORD? Who is like the LORD among the heavenly beings? [8] Who is like [Y]ou, LORD God Almighty? You, LORD, are mighty, and [Y]our faithfulness surrounds [Y]ou.

[9] You rule over the surging sea; when its waves mount up, [Y]ou still them. [11] The heavens are [Y]ours, and [Y]ours also the earth; [Y]ou founded the world and all that is in it. [12] You created the north and the south; [13] Your arm is endowed with power; [Y]our hand is strong, [Y]our right hand exalted.

[14] Righteousness and justice are the foundation of [Y]our throne; love and faithfulness go before [Y]ou. [15] Blessed are those who… walk in the light of [Y]our presence, LORD. [16] They rejoice in [Y]our name all day long; they celebrate [Y]our righteousness. [17] For [Y]ou are their glory and strength…

[52] Praise be to the LORD forever! Amen and Amen.

Book IV:

Psalm 90:

[1] Lord, [Y]ou have been our dwelling place throughout all generations. [2] Before the mountains were born or [Y]ou brought forth the whole world, from everlasting to everlasting [Y]ou are God.

[3] You turn people back to dust, saying, "Return to dust, you mortals." [4] A thousand years in [Y]our sight are like a day that has just gone by, or like a watch in the night. [5] Yet [Y]ou sweep people away in the sleep of death — they are like the new grass of the morning: [6] In the morning it springs up new, but by evening it is dry and withered.

[13] Relent, LORD! How long will it be? Have compassion on [Y]our servants. [14] Satisfy us in the morning with [Y]our unfailing love that we may sing for joy and be glad all our days. [16] May [Y]our deeds be shown to your servants, [Y]our splendor to their children. [17] May the favor of the Lord our God rest on us; establish the work of our hands for us…

Psalm 91:

[1] Whoever dwells in the shelter of the Most High will rest in the shadow of the Almighty. [2] I will say of the LORD, "He is my refuge and my fortress, my God, in whom I trust."

[3] Surely [H]e will save you from the fowler's snare and from the deadly pestilence. [4] He will cover you with [H]is feathers, and under [H]is wings you will find refuge; [H]is faithfulness will be your shield and rampart. [5] You will not fear the terror of night, nor the arrow that flies by day, [6] nor the pestilence that stalks in the darkness, nor the plague

that destroys at midday.

⁹ If you say, "The LORD is my refuge," and you make the Most High your dwelling, ¹⁰ no harm will overtake you, no disaster will come near [to you]. ¹¹ For [H]e will command [H]is angels… to guard you in all your ways; ¹² they will lift you up in their hands, so that you will not strike your foot against a stone.

¹³ You will tread on the lion and the cobra; you will trample the great lion and the serpent. ¹⁴ "Because he loves [M]e," says the LORD, "I will rescue him; I will protect him, for he acknowledges [M]y name. ¹⁵ He will call on [M]e, and I will answer him; I will be with him in trouble, I will deliver him and honor him. ¹⁶ With long life I will satisfy him and show him [M]y salvation."

Psalm 92:

¹ It is good to praise the LORD and make music to [Y]our name, O Most High, ² proclaiming [Y]our love in the morning and [Y]our faithfulness at night, ³ to the music of the ten-stringed lyre and the melody of the harp.

⁴ For [Y]ou make me glad by [Y]our deeds, LORD; I sing for joy at what [Y]our hands have done. ⁵ How great are [Y]our works, LORD, how profound [Y]our thoughts! ⁸ …[Y]ou, LORD, are forever exalted.

¹² The righteous will flourish like a palm tree… ¹³ planted in the house of the LORD… ¹⁴ They will still bear fruit in old age, they will stay fresh and green, ¹⁵ proclaiming, "The LORD is upright; [H]e is my Rock…"

Psalm 93:

¹ The LORD reigns, [H]e is robed in majesty; the LORD is robed in majesty and armed with strength; indeed, the world is established, firm and secure. ² Your throne was established long ago; [Y]ou are from all eternity.

³ The seas have lifted up, LORD, the seas have lifted up their voice; the seas have lifted up their pounding waves. ⁴ Mightier than the thunder of the great waters, mightier than the breakers of the sea — the LORD on high is mighty. ⁵ Your statutes, LORD, stand firm; holiness adorns [Y]our house for endless days.

Psalm 95:

¹ Come, let us sing for joy to the LORD; let us shout aloud to the Rock of our salvation. ² Let us come before [H]im with thanksgiving and extol [H]im with music and song. ³ For the LORD is the great God… ⁴ In [H]is hand are the depths of the earth, and the mountain peaks belong to [H]im. ⁵ The sea is [H]is, for [H]e made it, and [H]is hands formed the dry land.

⁶ Come, let us bow down in worship, let us kneel before the LORD our Maker; ⁷ for [H]e is our God and we are the people of his pasture, the flock under [H]is care. Today, if only you would hear [H]is voice, ⁸ "Do not harden your hearts…"

Psalm 96:

[1] Sing to the LORD a new song; sing to the LORD, all the earth. [2] Sing to the LORD, praise [H]is name; proclaim [H]is salvation day after day. [3] Declare [H]is glory among the nations, [H]is marvelous deeds among all peoples. [4] For great is the LORD and most worthy of praise...[6] Splendor and majesty are before [H]im; strength and glory are in [H]is sanctuary.

[9] Worship the LORD in the splendor of [H]is holiness; tremble before [H]im, all the earth. [10] Say among the nations, "The LORD reigns." The world is firmly established, it cannot be moved; [H]e will judge the peoples with equity.

[11] Let the heavens rejoice, let the earth be glad; let the sea resound, and all that is in it. [12] Let the fields be jubilant, and everything in them; let all the trees of the forest sing for joy. [13] Let all creation rejoice before the LORD, for [H]e comes... to judge the earth. He will judge the world in righteousness and the peoples in [H]is faithfulness.

Psalm 97:

[1] The LORD reigns, let the earth be glad; let the distant shores rejoice. [2] Clouds and thick darkness surround [H]im; righteousness and justice are the foundation of [H]is throne.

[6] The heavens proclaim [H]is righteousness, and all peoples see [H]is glory. [9] For [Y]ou, LORD, are the Most High over all the earth; [Y]ou are exalted...[10] Let those who love the LORD hate evil, for [H]e guards the lives of his faithful ones and delivers them from the hand of the wicked.

[11] Light shines on the righteous and joy on the upright in heart. [12] Rejoice in the LORD, you who are righteous, and praise [H]is holy name.

Psalm 98:

[1] Sing to the LORD a new song, for [H]e has done marvelous things; [H]is right hand and [H]is holy arm have worked salvation for [H]im. [2] The LORD has made [H]is salvation known and revealed [H]is righteousness to the nations. [3] ...[A]ll the ends of the earth have seen the salvation of... God.

[4] Shout for joy to the LORD, all the earth, burst into jubilant song with music; [5] make music to the LORD with the harp, with the harp and the sound of singing, [6] with trumpets and the blast of the ram's horn — shout for joy before the LORD, the King.

[7] Let the sea resound, and everything in it, the world, and all who live in it. [8] Let the rivers clap their hands, let the mountains sing together for joy; [9] let them sing before the LORD, for [H]e comes to judge the earth. He will judge the world in righteousness and the peoples with equity.

Psalm 99:

[1] The LORD reigns, let the nations tremble; [H]e sits enthroned between the cherubim,

let the earth shake. ² Great is the LORD... [H]e is exalted over all the nations. ³ Let them praise [Y]our great and awesome name — [H]e is holy.

Psalm 100:

¹ Shout for joy to the LORD, all the earth. ² Worship the LORD with gladness; come before [H]im with joyful songs. ³ Know that the LORD is God. It is [H]e who made us, and we are [H]is; we are [H]is people, the sheep of [H]is pasture.

⁴ Enter [H]is gates with thanksgiving and [H]is courts with praise; give thanks to [H]im and praise [H]is name. ⁵ For the LORD is good and [H]is love endures forever; [H]is faithfulness continues through all generations.

Psalm 101:

¹ I will sing of [Y]our love and justice; to [Y]ou, LORD, I will sing praise. ² I will be careful to lead a blameless life — when will [Y]ou come to me? I will conduct the affairs of my house with a blameless heart.

⁶ My eyes will be on the faithful in the land, that they may dwell with [M]e; the one whose walk is blameless will minister to [M]e.

Psalm 102:

¹ Hear my prayer, LORD; let my cry for help come to [Y]ou. ² Do not hide [Y]our face from me when I am in distress. Turn [Y]our ear to me; when I call, answer me quickly. ³ For my days vanish like smoke; my bones burn like glowing embers. ⁴ My heart is blighted and withered like grass; I forget to eat my food.

⁵ In my distress I groan aloud and am reduced to skin and bones. ⁶ I am like a desert owl, like an owl among the ruins. ⁷ I lie awake; I have become like a bird alone on a roof. ⁸ All day long my enemies taunt me; those who rail against me use my name as a curse. ⁹ For I eat ashes as my food and mingle my drink with tears... ¹¹ My days are like the evening shadow; I wither away like grass.

¹² But you, LORD, sit enthroned forever; [Y]our renown endures through all generations. ¹³ You will arise and have compassion... ¹⁶ For the LORD will... appear in [H]is glory. ¹⁷ He will respond to the prayer of the destitute; [H]e will not despise their plea.

¹⁸ Let this be written for a future generation, that a people not yet created may praise the LORD: ¹⁹ "The LORD looked down from [H]is sanctuary on high, from heaven [H]e viewed the earth, ²⁰ to hear the groans of the prisoners and release those condemned to death. ²⁸ The children of [Y]our servants will live in [Y]our presence; their descendants will be established before [Y]ou."

Psalm 103:

¹ Praise the LORD, my soul; all my inmost being, praise [H]is holy name. ² Praise the LORD, my soul, and forget not all [H]is benefits — ³ [W]ho forgives all your sins and heals all your diseases, ⁴ [W]ho redeems your life from the pit and crowns you with love and compassion, ⁵ [W]ho satisfies your desires with good things so that your youth is

126

renewed like the eagle's.

⁶ The LORD works righteousness and justice for all the oppressed. ⁸ The LORD is compassionate and gracious, slow to anger, abounding in love. ¹⁰ [H]e does not treat us as our sins deserve or repay us according to our iniquities. ¹¹ For as high as the heavens are above the earth, so great is [H]is love for those who fear [H]im; ¹² as far as the east is from the west, so far has [H]e removed our transgressions from us.

¹³ As a father has compassion on his children, so the LORD has compassion on those who fear [H]im; ¹⁴ for [H]e knows how we are formed, [H]e remembers that we are dust. ¹⁵ The life of mortals is like grass, they flourish like a flower of the field; ¹⁶ the wind blows over it and it is gone, and its place remembers it no more.

¹⁷ But from everlasting to everlasting the LORD's love is with those who fear [H]im, and [H]is righteousness with their children's children — ¹⁸ with those who keep [H]is covenant and remember to obey [H]is precepts. ¹⁹ The LORD has established [H]is throne in heaven, and [H]is kingdom rules over all.

²⁰ Praise the LORD, you [H]is angels, you mighty ones who do [H]is bidding, who obey [H]is word. ²¹ Praise the LORD, all [H]is heavenly hosts, you [H]is servants who do [H]is will. ²² Praise the LORD, all [H]is works… Praise the LORD, my soul.

Psalm 104:

¹ Praise the LORD, my soul. LORD my God, [Y]ou are very great; [Y]ou are clothed with splendor and majesty. ² The LORD wraps [H]imself in light as with a garment… He makes the clouds his chariot and rides on the wings of the wind. ⁴ He makes winds [H]is messengers, flames of fire [H]is servants.

⁵ He set the earth on its foundations; it can never be moved. ⁶ You covered it with the watery depths as with a garment; the waters stood above the mountains. ⁷ But at [Y]our rebuke the waters fled, at the sound of [Y]our thunder they took to flight; ⁸ they flowed over the mountains, they went down into the valleys, to the place [Y]ou assigned for them. ⁹ You set a boundary they cannot cross; never again will they cover the earth.

¹⁰ He makes springs pour water into the ravines; it flows between the mountains. ¹¹ They give water to all the beasts of the field; the wild donkeys quench their thirst. ¹² The birds of the sky nest by the waters; they sing among the branches. ¹³ He waters the mountains from [H]is upper chambers; the land is satisfied by the fruit of [H]is work.

¹⁴ He makes grass grow for the cattle, and plants for people to cultivate — bringing forth food from the earth: ¹⁵ wine that gladdens human hearts, oil to make their faces shine, and bread that sustains their hearts. ¹⁶ The trees of the LORD are well watered… ¹⁷ There the birds make their nests; the stork has its home in the junipers. ¹⁸ The high mountains belong to the wild goats; the crags are a refuge for the hyrax.

¹⁹ He made the moon to mark the seasons, and the sun knows when to go down. ²⁰ You bring darkness, it becomes night, and all the beasts of the forest prowl. ²¹ The lions roar for their prey and seek their food from God. ²² The sun rises, and they steal away; they return and lie down in their dens. ²³ Then people go out to their work, to their labor until

evening.

[24] How many are [Y]our works, LORD! In wisdom [Y]ou made them all; the earth is full of [Y]our creatures. [25] There is the sea, vast and spacious, teeming with creatures beyond number — living things both large and small.

[27] All creatures look to [Y]ou to give them their food at the proper time. [28] When [Y]ou give it to them, they gather it up; when [Y]ou open [Y]our hand, they are satisfied with good things… [30] When [Y]ou send [Y]our Spirit, they are created, and [Y]ou renew the face of the ground.

[31] May the glory of the LORD endure forever; may the LORD rejoice in [H]is works… [33] I will sing to the LORD all my life; I will sing praise to my God as long as I live. [34] May my meditation be pleasing to [H]im, as I rejoice in the LORD. [35] …Praise the LORD, my soul. Praise the LORD.

Psalm 105:

[1] Give praise to the LORD, proclaim [H]is name; make known among the nations what [H]e has done. [2] Sing to [H]im, sing praise to [H]im; tell of all [H]is wonderful acts. [3] Glory in [H]is holy name; let the hearts of those who seek the LORD rejoice.

[4] Look to the LORD and [H]is strength; seek [H]is face always. [5] Remember the wonders [H]e has done, [H]is miracles, and the judgments [H]e pronounced… [8] He remembers [H]is covenant forever…

[14] He allowed no one to oppress [the righteous]; [15] "Do not touch [M]y anointed ones; do [M]y prophets no harm." [45] Praise the LORD.

Psalm 106:

[1] Praise the LORD. Give thanks to the LORD, for [H]e is good; [H]is love endures forever. [3] Blessed are those who act justly, who always do what is right.

[4] Remember me, LORD, when you show favor to [Y]our people, come to my aid when [Y]ou save them, [5] that I may enjoy the prosperity of [Y]our chosen ones, that I may share in the joy of [Y]our nation and join [Y]our inheritance in giving praise.

[47] Save us, LORD our God, and gather us from the nations, that we may give thanks to [Y]our holy name and glory in [Y]our praise. [48] Praise be to the LORD… from everlasting to everlasting. Let all the people say, "Amen!" Praise the LORD.

Book V:

Psalm 107:

[1] Give thanks to the LORD, for [H]e is good; [H]is love endures forever.

[2] Let the redeemed of the LORD tell their story — those [H]e redeemed from the hand of the foe, [3] those [H]e gathered from the lands, from east and west, from north and south. [4] Some wandered in desert wastelands… [5] They were hungry and thirsty, and their lives

ebbed away. [6] Then they cried out to the LORD in their trouble, and [H]e delivered them from their distress.

[8] Let them give thanks to the LORD for [H]is unfailing love and [H]is wonderful deeds... [9] for [H]e satisfies the thirsty and fills the hungry with good things.

[19] ...[T]hey cried to the LORD in their trouble, and [H]e saved them from their distress. [20] He sent out his word and healed them; [H]e rescued them from the grave. [21] Let them give thanks to the LORD for [H]is unfailing love and [H]is wonderful deeds... [22] Let them... tell of [H]is works with songs of joy.

[35] He turned the desert into pools of water and the parched ground into flowing springs; [37] They sowed fields and planted vineyards that yielded a fruitful harvest; [38] [H]e blessed them, and their numbers greatly increased, and [H]e did not let their herds diminish.

[41] ...[H]e lifted the needy out of their affliction and increased their families like flocks. [42] The upright see and rejoice... [43] Let the one who is wise... ponder the loving deeds of the LORD.

Psalm 108:

[1] My heart, O God, is steadfast; I will sing and make music with all my soul. [2] Awake, harp and lyre! [3] I will praise [Y]ou, LORD, among the nations; I will sing of [Y]ou among the peoples. [4] For great is [Y]our love, higher than the heavens; [Y]our faithfulness reaches to the skies. [5] Be exalted, O God, above the heavens; let [Y]our glory be over all the earth.

[6] Save us and help us with [Y]our right hand, that those [Y]ou love may be delivered.

Psalm 110:

[4] The LORD has sworn and will not change [H]is mind: "You are a priest forever, in the order of Melchizedek." [5] The Lord is at your right hand... [6] He will judge the nations...

Psalm 111:

[1] Praise the LORD, I will extol the LORD with all my heart... [2] Great are the works of the LORD; they are pondered by all who delight in them. [3] Glorious and majestic are [H]is deeds, and [H]is righteousness endures forever. [4] ...[T]he LORD is gracious and compassionate. [5] He provides food for those who fear [H]im; [H]e remembers [H]is covenant forever.

[7] The works of [H]is hands are faithful and just; all [H]is precepts are trustworthy. [8] They are established for ever and ever, enacted in faithfulness and uprightness. [9] He provided redemption for [H]is people; [H]e ordained [H]is covenant forever — holy and awesome is [H]is name.

[10] The fear of the LORD is the beginning of wisdom; all who follow [H]is precepts have good understanding. To [H]im belongs eternal praise.

Psalm 112:

[1] Praise the LORD. Blessed are those who fear the LORD, who find great delight in [H]is commands. [2] Their children will be mighty in the land; the generation of the upright will be blessed.

[3] Wealth and riches are in their houses, and their righteousness endures forever. [4] Even in darkness light dawns for the upright, for those who are gracious and compassionate and righteous. [5] Good will come to those who are generous and lend freely, who conduct their affairs with justice.

[6] Surely the righteous will never be shaken; they will be remembered forever. [7] They will have no fear of bad news; their hearts are steadfast, trusting in the LORD. [8] Their hearts are secure, they will have no fear; [9] [t]hey have freely scattered their gifts to the poor… [8] [I]n the end they will look in triumph… [9] their righteousness endures forever…

Psalm 113:

[1] Praise the LORD. Praise the LORD, you [H]is servants; praise the name of the LORD. [2] Let the name of the LORD be praised, both now and forevermore. [3] From the rising of the sun to the place where it sets, the name of the LORD is to be praised.

[4] The LORD is exalted over all the nations, [H]is glory above the heavens. [7] He raises the poor from the dust and lifts the needy from the ash heap; [9] He settles the childless woman in her home as a happy mother of children. Praise the LORD.

Psalm 115:

[1] Not to us, LORD, not to us but to [Y]our name be the glory, because of [Y]our love and faithfulness.

[12] The LORD remembers us and will bless us: [13] [H]e will bless those who fear the LORD — small and great alike. [14] May the LORD cause you to flourish, both you and your children. [15] May you be blessed by the LORD, the Maker of heaven and earth.

[16] The highest heavens belong to the LORD, but the earth [H]e has given to mankind. [17] It is not the dead who praise the LORD… [18] it is we who extol the LORD, both now and forevermore. Praise the LORD.

Psalm 116:

[1] I love the LORD, for [H]e heard my voice; [H]e heard my cry for mercy. [2] Because [H]e turned [H]is ear to me, I will call on [H]im as long as I live.

[3] The cords of death entangled me, the anguish of the grave came over me; I was overcome by distress and sorrow. [4] Then I called on the name of the LORD: "LORD, save me!"

[5] The LORD is gracious and righteous; our God is full of compassion. [6] The LORD protects the unwary; when I was brought low, [H]e saved me.

[8] For [Y]ou, LORD, have delivered me from death, my eyes from tears, my feet from

stumbling, that I may walk before the LORD in the land of the living.

[12] What shall I return to the LORD for all [H]is goodness to me?   [14] I will fulfill my vows to the LORD in the presence of all [H]is people.

[15] Precious in the sight of the LORD is the death of [H]is faithful servants. [16] Truly I am [Y]our servant, LORD; I serve [Y]ou…; [Y]ou have freed me from my chains. [18] I will fulfill my vows to the LORD in the presence of all [H]is people… [19] Praise the LORD.

Psalm 117:

[1] Praise the LORD, all you nations; extol [H]im, all you peoples.   [2] For great is [H]is love toward us, and the faithfulness of the LORD endures forever. Praise the LORD.

Psalm 118:

[1] Give thanks to the LORD, for [H]e is good; [H]is love endures forever.

[5] When hard pressed, I cried to the LORD; [H]e brought me into a spacious place. [6] The LORD is with me; I will not be afraid. What can mere mortals do to me? [7] The LORD is with me; [H]e is my helper…

[8] It is better to take refuge in the LORD than to trust in humans. [9] It is better to take refuge in the LORD than to trust in princes. [13] I was… about to fall, but the LORD helped me. [14] The LORD is my strength and my defense; [H]e has become my salvation.

[15] Shouts of joy and victory resound in the tents of the righteous: "The LORD's right hand has done mighty things! [16] The LORD's right hand is lifted high; the LORD's right hand has done mighty things!" [17] I will not die but live, and will proclaim what the LORD has done. [21] I will give [Y]ou thanks, for [Y]ou answered me; [Y]ou have become my salvation.

[22] The stone the builders rejected has become the cornerstone; [23] the LORD has done this, and it is marvelous in our eyes. [24] The LORD has done it this very day; let us rejoice today and be glad. [26] Blessed is he who comes in the name of the LORD.

[27] The LORD is God, and [H]e has made [H]is light shine on us. [28] You are my God, and I will praise [Y]ou; [Y]ou are my God, and I will exalt [Y]ou. [29] Give thanks to the LORD, for [H]e is good; [H]is love endures forever.

Psalm 119:

[1] Blessed are those whose ways are blameless, who walk according to the law of the LORD. [2] Blessed are those who keep [H]is statutes and seek [H]im with all their heart — [3] they do no wrong but follow [H]is ways.

[4] You have laid down precepts that are to be fully obeyed. [5] Oh, that my ways were steadfast in obeying [Y]our decrees! [6] Then I would not be put to shame when I consider all [Y]our commands. [7] I will praise [Y]ou with an upright heart as I learn [Y]our righteous laws. [8] I will obey [Y]our decrees; do not utterly forsake me.

[9] How can a young person stay on the path of purity? By living according to [Y]our word. [10] I seek [Y]ou with all my heart; do not let me stray from [Y]our commands.

¹¹ I have hidden [Y]our word in my heart that I might not sin against [Y]ou. ¹² Praise be to [Y]ou, LORD; teach me [Y]our decrees.

¹³ With my lips I recount all the laws that come from [Y]our mouth. ¹⁴ I rejoice in following [Y]our statutes as one rejoices in great riches. ¹⁵ I meditate on [Y]our precepts and consider [Y]our ways. ¹⁶ I delight in [Y]our decrees; I will not neglect [Y]our word.

¹⁷ Be good to [Y]our servant while I live, that I may obey [Y]our word. ¹⁸ Open my eyes that I may see wonderful things in [Y]our law. ¹⁹ I am a stranger on earth; do not hide [Y]our commands from me. ²⁰ My soul is consumed with longing for [Y]our laws at all times. ²⁴ Your statutes are my delight; they are my counselors.

²⁵ I am laid low in the dust; preserve my life according to [Y]our word. ²⁶ I gave an account of my ways and [Y]ou answered me; teach me [Y]our decrees. ²⁷ Cause me to understand the way of [Y]our precepts, that I may meditate on [Y]our wonderful deeds.

²⁸ My soul is weary with sorrow; strengthen me according to [Y]our word. ²⁹ ...[B]e gracious to me and teach me [Y]our law. ³⁰ I have chosen the way of faithfulness; I have set my heart on [Y]our laws. ³¹ I hold fast to [Y]our statutes, LORD; do not let me be put to shame. ³² I run in the path of [Y]our commands, for [Y]ou have broadened my understanding.

³³ Teach me, LORD, the way of [Y]our decrees, that I may follow it to the end. ³⁴ Give me understanding, so that I may keep [Y]our law and obey it with all my heart. ³⁵ Direct me in the path of [Y]our commands, for there I find delight.

³⁶ Turn my heart toward [Y]our statutes and not toward selfish gain. ³⁷ Turn my eyes away from worthless things; preserve my life according to [Y]our word. ³⁸ Fulfill [Y]our promise to [Y]our servant, so that [Y]ou may be feared. ³⁹ Take away the disgrace I dread, for [Y]our laws are good. ⁴⁰ How I long for [Y]our precepts! In [Y]our righteousness preserve my life.

⁴¹ May [Y]our unfailing love come to me, LORD, [Y]our salvation, according to [Y]our promise; ⁴² then I can answer anyone who taunts me, for I trust in [Y]our word. ⁴³ Never take [Y]our word of truth from my mouth, for I have put my hope in [Y]our laws. ⁴⁴ I will always obey [Y]our law, for ever and ever.

⁴⁵ I will walk about in freedom, for I have sought out [Y]our precepts. ⁴⁶ I will speak of [Y]our statutes before kings and will not be put to shame, ⁴⁷ for I delight in [Y]our commands because I love them. ⁴⁸ I reach out for [Y]our commands, which I love, that I may meditate on [Y]our decrees.

⁴⁹ Remember [Y]our word to [Y]our servant, for [Y]ou have given me hope. ⁵⁰ My comfort in my suffering is this: Your promise preserves my life. ⁵¹ The arrogant mock me unmercifully, but I do not turn from [Y]our law. ⁵² I remember, LORD, [Y]our ancient laws, and I find comfort in them. ⁵⁴ Your decrees are the theme of my song wherever I lodge. ⁵⁵ In the night, LORD, I remember [Y]our name, that I may keep [Y]our law. ⁵⁶ This has been my practice: I obey [Y]our precepts.

⁵⁷ You are my portion, LORD; I have promised to obey [Y]our words. ⁵⁸ I have sought

[Y]our face with all my heart; be gracious to me according to [Y]our promise. ⁵⁹ I have considered my ways and have turned my steps to [Y]our statutes. ⁶⁰ I will hasten and not delay to obey [Y]our commands.

⁶¹ Though the wicked bind me with ropes, I will not forget [Y]our law. ⁶² At midnight I rise to give [Y]ou thanks for [Y]our righteous laws. ⁶³ I am a friend to all who fear [Y]ou, to all who follow [Y]our precepts. ⁶⁴ The earth is filled with [Y]our love, LORD; teach me [Y]our decrees.

⁶⁵ Do good to [Y]our servant according to [Y]our word, LORD. ⁶⁶ Teach me knowledge and good judgment, for I trust [Y]our commands. ⁶⁷ Before I was afflicted I went astray, but now I obey [Y]our word. ⁶⁸ You are good, and what [Y]ou do is good; teach me [Y]our decrees. ⁶⁹ Though the arrogant have smeared me with lies, I keep [Y]our precepts with all my heart. ⁷⁰ ...I delight in [Y]our law. ⁷² The law from [Y]our mouth is more precious to me than thousands of pieces of silver and gold.

⁷³ Your hands made me and formed me; give me understanding to learn [Y]our commands. ⁷⁴ May those who fear [Y]ou rejoice when they see me, for I have put my hope in [Y]our word. ⁷⁵ I know, LORD, that [Y]our laws are righteous...⁷⁶ May [Y]our unfailing love be my comfort, according to [Y]our promise to [Y]our servant. ⁷⁷ Let [Y]our compassion come to me that I may live, for [Y]our law is my delight. ⁸⁰ May I wholeheartedly follow [Y]our decrees, that I may not be put to shame.

⁸¹ My soul faints with longing for [Y]our salvation, but I have put my hope in [Y]our word. ⁸² My eyes fail, looking for [Y]our promise; I say, "When will [Y]ou comfort me?" ⁸³ Though I am like a wineskin in the smoke, I do not forget [Y]our decrees. ⁸⁴ How long must [Y]our servant wait? ⁸⁶ All [Y]our commands are trustworthy; help me, for I am being persecuted without cause. ⁸⁸ In [Y]our unfailing love preserve my life, that I may obey the statutes of [Y]our mouth.

⁸⁹ Your word, LORD, is eternal; it stands firm in the heavens. ⁹⁰ Your faithfulness continues through all generations; [Y]ou established the earth, and it endures. ⁹¹ Your laws endure to this day, for all things serve [Y]ou. ⁹² If [Y]our law had not been my delight, I would have perished in my affliction. ⁹³ I will never forget [Y]our precepts, for by them [Y]ou have preserved my life. ⁹⁴ Save me, for I am [Y]ours; I have sought out [Y]our precepts. ⁹⁵ The wicked are waiting to destroy me, but I will ponder [Y]our statutes. ⁹⁶ To all perfection I see a limit, but [Y]our commands are boundless.

⁹⁷ Oh, how I love [Y]our law! I meditate on it all day long. ⁹⁸ Your commands are always with me and make me wiser than my enemies. ⁹⁹ I have more insight than all my teachers, for I meditate on [Y]our statutes. ¹⁰⁰ I have more understanding than the elders, for I obey [Y]our precepts. ¹⁰¹ I have kept my feet from every evil path so that I might obey [Y]our word. ¹⁰² I have not departed from [Y]our laws, for [Y]ou [Y]ourself have taught me. ¹⁰³ How sweet are [Y]our words to my taste, sweeter than honey to my mouth! ¹⁰⁴ I gain understanding from [Y]our precepts; therefore I hate every wrong path.

¹⁰⁵ Your word is a lamp for my feet, a light on my path. ¹⁰⁶ I have taken an oath and confirmed it, that I will follow [Y]our righteous laws. ¹⁰⁷ I have suffered much; preserve my life, LORD, according to [Y]our word. ¹⁰⁸ Accept, LORD, the willing praise of my mouth, and teach me [Y]our laws. ¹⁰⁹ Though I constantly take my life in my hands, I will not forget [Y]our law. ¹¹⁰ The wicked have set a snare for me, but I have not strayed from [Y]our precepts. ¹¹¹ Your statutes are my heritage forever; they are the joy of my

heart. ¹¹² My heart is set on keeping [Y]our decrees to the very end.

¹¹³ ...I love [Y]our law. ¹¹⁴ You are my refuge and my shield; I have put my hope in [Y]our word. ¹¹⁵ Away from me, you evildoers, that I may keep the commands of my God! ¹¹⁶ Sustain me, my God, according to [Y]our promise, and I will live; do not let my hopes be dashed. ¹¹⁷ Uphold me, and I will be delivered; I will always have regard for [Y]our decrees. ¹¹⁹ ...I love [Y]our statutes. ¹²⁰ My flesh trembles in fear of [Y]ou; I stand in awe of [Y]our laws.

¹²¹ I have done what is righteous and just; do not leave me to my oppressors. ¹²² Ensure [Y]our servant's well-being; do not let the arrogant oppress me. ¹²⁴ Deal with [Y]our servant according to [Y]our love and teach me [Y]our decrees. ¹²⁵ I am [Y]our servant; give me discernment that I may understand [Y]our statutes.

¹²⁹ Your statutes are wonderful; therefore I obey them. ¹³⁰ The unfolding of your words gives light; it gives understanding to the simple. ¹³¹ I open my mouth and pant, longing for [Y]our commands. ¹³² Turn to me and have mercy on me, as [Y]ou always do to those who love [Y]our name. ¹³³ Direct my footsteps according to [Y]our word; let no sin rule over me. ¹³⁴ Redeem me from human oppression, that I may obey [Y]our precepts. ¹³⁵ Make [Y]our face shine on [Y]our servant and teach me [Y]our decrees.

¹³⁷ You are righteous, LORD, and [Y]our laws are right. ¹³⁸ The statutes [Y]ou have laid down are righteous; they are fully trustworthy. ¹³⁹ My zeal wears me out... ¹⁴⁰ Your promises have been thoroughly tested, and [Y]our servant loves them. ¹⁴¹ Though I am lowly and despised, I do not forget [Y]our precepts. ¹⁴² Your righteousness is everlasting and [Y]our law is true. ¹⁴³ Trouble and distress have come upon me, but [Y]our commands give me delight. ¹⁴⁴ Your statutes are always righteous; give me understanding that I may live.

¹⁴⁵ I call with all my heart; answer me, LORD, and I will obey [Y]our decrees. ¹⁴⁶ I call out to [Y]ou; save me and I will keep [Y]our statutes. ¹⁴⁷ I rise before dawn and cry for help; I have put my hope in [Y]our word. ¹⁴⁸ My eyes stay open through the watches of the night, that I may meditate on [Y]our promises. ¹⁴⁹ Hear my voice in accordance with [Y]our love; preserve my life, LORD, according to [Y]our laws. ¹⁵⁰ Those who devise wicked schemes are near, but they are far from [Y]our law. ¹⁵¹ Yet [Y]ou are near, LORD, and all [Y]our commands are true. ¹⁵² Long ago I learned from [Y]our statutes that [Y]ou established them to last forever.

¹⁵³ Look on my suffering and deliver me, for I have not forgotten [Y]our law. ¹⁵⁴ Defend my cause and redeem me; preserve my life according to [Y]our promise. ¹⁵⁶ Your compassion, LORD, is great; preserve my life according to [Y]our laws. ¹⁵⁷ Many are the foes who persecute me, but I have not turned from [Y]our statutes. ¹⁵⁹ See how I love [Y]our precepts; preserve my life, LORD, in accordance with [Y]our love. ¹⁶⁰ All [Y]our words are true; all [Y]our righteous laws are eternal.

¹⁶¹ Rulers persecute me without cause, but my heart trembles at [Y]our word. ¹⁶² I rejoice in [Y]our promise like one who finds great spoil. ¹⁶³ ...I love [Y]our law. ¹⁶⁴ Seven times a day I praise [Y]ou for [Y]our righteous laws. ¹⁶⁵ Great peace have those who love [Y]our law, and nothing can make them stumble. ¹⁶⁶ I wait for [Y]our salvation, LORD, and I follow [Y]our commands. ¹⁶⁷ I obey [Y]our statutes, for I love them greatly. ¹⁶⁸ I obey [Y]our precepts and [Y]our statutes, for all my ways are known to [Y]ou.

[169] May my cry come before [Y]ou, LORD; give me understanding according to [Y]our word. [170] May my supplication come before [Y]ou; deliver me according to [Y]our promise. [171] May my lips overflow with praise, for [Y]ou teach me [Y]our decrees. [172] May my tongue sing of [Y]our word, for all [Y]our commands are righteous. [173] May [Y]our hand be ready to help me, for I have chosen [Y]our precepts. [174] I long for [Y]our salvation, LORD, and [Y]our law gives me delight. [175] Let me live that I may praise [Y]ou, and may [Y]our laws sustain me. [176] I have strayed like a lost sheep. Seek [Y]our servant, for I have not forgotten [Y]our commands.

Psalm 120:

[7] I am for peace…

Psalm 121:

[1] I lift up my eyes to the mountains — where does my help come from? [2] My help comes from the LORD, the Maker of heaven and earth. [3] He will not let your foot slip — [H]e who watches over you will not slumber… [5] The LORD watches over you — the LORD is your shade at your right hand; [6] the sun will not harm you by day, nor the moon by night.

[7] The LORD will keep you from all harm — [H]e will watch over your life; [8] the LORD will watch over your coming and going both now and forevermore.

Psalm 122:

[1] I rejoiced with those who said to me, "Let us go to the house of the LORD. [6] May those who love [Y]ou be secure. [7] May there be peace within [Y]our walls and security within [Y]our citadels."

Psalm 123:

[1] I lift up my eyes to [Y]ou, to [Y]ou who sit enthroned in heaven. [2] As the eyes of slaves look to the hand of their master… so our eyes look to the LORD our God, till [H]e shows us [H]is mercy. [3] Have mercy on us, LORD, have mercy on us, for we have endured no end of contempt. [4] We have endured no end of ridicule from the arrogant, of contempt from the proud.

Psalm 124:

[6] Praise be to the LORD, [W]ho has not let us be torn by their teeth. [7] We have escaped like a bird from the fowler's snare; the snare has been broken, and we have escaped. [8] Our help is in the name of the LORD, the Maker of heaven and earth.

Psalm 125:

[1] Those who trust in the LORD… cannot be shaken… [t]hey endure forever. [2] …[T]he LORD surrounds [H]is people both now and forevermore. [4] LORD, do good to those who are good, to those who are upright in heart.

Psalm 126:

[1] When the LORD restored [us]; we were like those who dreamed. [2] Our mouths were

filled with laughter, our tongues with songs of joy. Then it was said among the nations, "The LORD has done great things..." ³ ...[W]e are filled with joy.

⁴ Restore our fortunes, LORD... ⁵ Those who sow with tears will reap with songs of joy. ⁶ Those who go out weeping, carrying seed to sow, will return with songs of joy, carrying sheaves with them.

Psalm 127:

¹ Unless the LORD builds the house, the builders labor in vain.   Unless the LORD watches over the city, the guards stand watch in vain. ² In vain you rise early and stay up late, toiling for food to eat — for [H]e grants sleep to those [H]e loves.

³ Children are a heritage from the LORD, offspring a reward from [H]im.

Psalm 128:

¹ Blessed are all who fear the LORD, who walk in obedience to [H]im. ² You will eat the fruit of your labor; blessings and prosperity will be yours. ³ Your wife will be like a fruitful vine within your house; your children will be like olive shoots around your table. ⁴ Yes, this will be the blessing for the man who fears the LORD. ⁵ May the LORD bless you... [M]ay you see... prosperity... all the days of your life. ⁶ May you live to see your children's children...

Psalm 129:

² "[T]hey have greatly oppressed me from my youth, but they have not gained the victory over me. ⁴ ...[T]he LORD is righteous; [H]e has cut me free from the cords of the wicked."

Psalm 130:

¹ Out of the depths I cry to [Y]ou, LORD; ² Lord, hear my voice. Let [Y]our ears be attentive to my cry for mercy. ³ If [Y]ou, LORD, kept a record of sins, Lord, who could stand? ⁴ But with [Y]ou there is forgiveness, so that we can, with reverence, serve [Y]ou.

⁵ I wait for the LORD, my whole being waits, and in [H]is word I put my hope. ⁶ I wait for the Lord more than watchmen wait for the morning... ⁷ ...[P]ut your hope in the LORD, for with the LORD is unfailing love and with [H]im is full redemption. ⁸ He himself will redeem... all [your] sins.

Psalm 131:

³ ...[P]ut your hope in the LORD both now and forevermore.

Psalm 132:

⁸ "...Arise, LORD, and come to [Y]our resting place, [Y]ou and the ark of [Y]our might. ⁹ May [Y]our priests be clothed with [Y]our righteousness; may [Y]our faithful people sing for joy."

Psalm 133:

¹ How good and pleasant it is when God's people live together in unity! ² It is like precious oil poured on the head... ³ It is as if... dew were falling... For... the LORD bestows [H]is blessing, even life forevermore.

Psalm 134:

¹ Praise the LORD, all you... who minister by night in the house of the LORD. ² Lift up your hands in the sanctuary and praise the LORD. ³ May the LORD bless you... [H]e who is the Maker of heaven and earth.

Psalm 135:

¹ Praise the LORD. Praise the name of the LORD; praise [H]im... ² you who minister in the house of the LORD, in the courts of the house of our God.

³ Praise the LORD, for the LORD is good; sing praise to [H]is name, for that is pleasant. ⁵ I know that the LORD is great... ⁶ The LORD does whatever pleases [H]im, in the heavens and on the earth, in the seas and all their depths. ⁷ He makes clouds rise from the ends of the earth; [H]e sends lightning with the rain and brings out the wind from [H]is storehouses.

¹³ Your name, LORD, endures forever, [Y]our renown, LORD, through all generations. ¹⁴ For the LORD will... have compassion on [H]is servants. ¹⁹ All... praise the LORD...

Psalm 136:

¹ Give thanks to the LORD, for [H]e is good. *His love endures forever.* ⁴ [T]o [H]im who alone does great wonders, *His love endures forever.* ⁵ [W]ho by [H]is understanding made the heavens, *His love endures forever.* ⁶ [W]ho spread out the earth upon the waters, *His love endures forever.* ⁷ [W]ho made the great lights — *His love endures forever.* ⁸ the sun to govern the day, *His love endures forever.* ⁹ the moon and stars to govern the night; *His love endures forever.*

²⁵ He gives food to every creature. *His love endures forever.* ²⁶ Give thanks to the God of heaven. *His love endures forever.*

Psalm 138:

¹ I will praise [Y]ou, LORD, with all my heart; ...I will sing [Y]our praise. ² I will bow down toward [Y]our holy temple and will praise [Y]our name for [Y]our unfailing love and [Y]our faithfulness...³ When I called, [Y]ou answered me...

⁴ May all the kings of the earth praise [Y]ou, LORD... ⁵ May they sing of the ways of the LORD, for the glory of the LORD is great.

⁶ Though the LORD is exalted, [H]e looks kindly on the lowly... ⁷ Though I walk in the midst of trouble, [Y]ou preserve my life. You stretch out [Y]our hand... [W]ith [Y]our right hand [Y]ou save me. ⁸ ...[Y]our love, LORD, endures forever — do not abandon

the works of [Y]our hands.

Psalm 139:

[1] You have searched me, LORD, and [Y]ou know me. [2] You know when I sit and when I rise; [Y]ou perceive my thoughts from afar. [3] You discern my going out and my lying down; [Y]ou are familiar with all my ways. [4] Before a word is on my tongue [Y]ou, LORD, know it completely... [6] Such knowledge is too wonderful for me, too lofty for me to attain.

[7] Where can I go from [Y]our Spirit? Where can I flee from [Y]our presence? [8] If I go up to the heavens, [Y]ou are there; if I make my bed in the depths, [Y]ou are there. [9] If I rise on the wings of the dawn, if I settle on the far side of the sea, [10] even there [Y]our hand will guide me... [11] If I say, "Surely the darkness will hide me and the light become night around me," [12] even the darkness will not be dark to [Y]ou; the night will shine like the day, for darkness is as light to [Y]ou.

[13] For [Y]ou created my inmost being; [Y]ou knit me together in my mother's womb. [14] I praise [Y]ou because I am fearfully and wonderfully made; [Y]our works are wonderful...

[15] My frame was not hidden from [Y]ou when I was made in the secret place, when I was woven together in the depths of the earth. [16] Your eyes saw my unformed body; all the days ordained for me were written in [Y]our book before one of them came to be. [17] How precious to me are [Y]our thoughts, God! How vast is the sum of them!

[18] Were I to count them, they would outnumber the grains of sand — when I awake, I am still with [Y]ou. [24] ...[L]ead me in the way everlasting.

Psalm 140:

[1] Rescue me, LORD, from evildoers; protect me from the violent, [2] who devise evil plans in their hearts...[3] They make their tongues as sharp as a serpent's; the poison of vipers is on their lips.

[4] Keep me safe, LORD, from the hands of the wicked; protect me from the violent, who devise ways to trip my feet. [5] The arrogant have hidden a snare for me; they have spread out the cords of their net and have set traps for me along my path.

[6] I say to the LORD, "You are my God." Hear, LORD, my cry for mercy. [12] I know that the LORD secures justice for the poor and upholds the cause of the needy. [13] Surely the righteous will praise [Y]our name, and the upright will live in [Y]our presence.

Psalm 141:

[1] I call to [Y]ou, LORD, come quickly to me; hear me when I call to [Y]ou. [2] May my prayer be set before [Y]ou like incense...

[3] Set a guard over my mouth, LORD; keep watch over the door of my lips. [4] Do not let my heart be drawn to what is evil so that I take part in wicked deeds... [8] ...[M]y eyes are fixed on [Y]ou, Sovereign LORD; in [Y]ou I take refuge — do not give me over to death. [9] Keep me safe from the traps set by evildoers, from the

snares they have laid for me.

Psalm 142:

[1] I cry aloud to the LORD; I lift up my voice to the LORD for mercy. [2] I pour out before [H]im my complaint; before [H]im I tell my trouble.

[3] When my spirit grows faint within me, it is [Y]ou who watch over my way. In the path where I walk people have hidden a snare for me. [4] Look and see, there is no one at my right hand; no one is concerned for me. I have no refuge; no one cares for my life. [5] I cry to [Y]ou, LORD; I say, "You are my refuge, my portion in the land of the living."

[6] Listen to my cry, for I am in desperate need; rescue me from those who pursue me, for they are too strong for me. [7] Set me free from my prison, that I may praise [Y]our name. Then the righteous will gather about me because of [Y]our goodness to me.

Psalm 143:

[1] LORD, hear my prayer, listen to my cry for mercy; in [Y]our faithfulness and righteousness come to my relief. [2] Do not bring [Y]our servant into judgment, for no one living is righteous before [Y]ou.

[3] The enemy pursues me, he crushes me to the ground; he makes me dwell in the darkness like those long dead. [4] So my spirit grows faint within me; my heart within me is dismayed. [5] ...[C]onsider what [Y]our hands have done. [6] I spread out my hands to [Y]ou; I thirst for [Y]ou like a parched land.

[7] Answer me quickly, LORD; my spirit fails. Do not hide [Y]our face from me or I will be like those who go down to the pit. [8] Let the morning bring me word of [Y]our unfailing love, for I have put my trust in [Y]ou. Show me the way I should go, for to [Y]ou I entrust my life. [9] Rescue me from my enemies, LORD, for I hide myself in [Y]ou. [10] Teach me to do [Y]our will, for [Y]ou are my God; may [Y]our good Spirit lead me on level ground.

[11] For [Y]our name's sake, LORD, preserve my life; in [Y]our righteousness, bring me out of trouble [12] ...for I am [Y]our servant.

Psalm 144:

[1] Praise be to the LORD my Rock... [2] He is my loving God and my fortress, my stronghold and my deliverer... in [W]hom I take refuge...

[3] LORD, what are human beings that [Y]ou care for them, mere mortals that [Y]ou think of them? [4] They are like a breath; their days are like a fleeting shadow.

[7] Reach down [Y]our hand from on high; deliver me and rescue me from the mighty waters, from the hands of [evildoers]. [9] I will sing a new song to [Y]ou, my God; on the ten-stringed lyre I will make music to [Y]ou... [15] Blessed is the people... whose God is the LORD.

Psalm 145:

[1] I will exalt [Y]ou, my God the King; I will praise [Y]our name for ever and ever. [2] Every

day I will praise [Y]ou and extol [Y]our name for ever and ever.

[3] Great is the LORD and most worthy of praise; [H]is greatness no one can fathom. [4] One generation commends [Y]our works to another; they tell of [Y]our mighty acts. [5] They speak of the glorious splendor of [Y]our majesty — and I will meditate on your wonderful works. [6] They tell of the power of [Y]our awesome works — and I will proclaim [Y]our great deeds. [7] They celebrate [Y]our abundant goodness and joyfully sing of [Y]our righteousness.

[8] The LORD is gracious and compassionate, slow to anger and rich in love. [9] The LORD is good to all; [H]e has compassion on all [H]e has made. [10] All [Y]our works praise [Y]ou, LORD; [Y]our faithful people extol [Y]ou. [11] They tell of the glory of [Y]our kingdom and speak of [Y]our might, [12] so that all people may know of [Y]our mighty acts and the glorious splendor of [Y]our kingdom. [13] Your kingdom is an everlasting kingdom, and [Y]our dominion endures through all generations.

The LORD is trustworthy in all [H]e promises and faithful in all [H]e does. [14] The LORD upholds all who fall and lifts up all who are bowed down. [15] The eyes of all look to [Y]ou, and [Y]ou give them their food at the proper time. [16] You open [Y]our hand and satisfy the desires of every living thing.

[17] The LORD is righteous in all [H]is ways and faithful in all [H]e does. [18] The LORD is near to all who call on [H]im, to all who call on [H]im in truth. [19] He fulfills the desires of those who fear [H]im; [H]e hears their cry and saves them. [20] The LORD watches over all who love [H]im… [21] My mouth will speak in praise of the LORD. Let every creature praise [H]is holy name for ever and ever.

Psalm 146:

[1] Praise the LORD. Praise the LORD, my soul. [2] I will praise the LORD all my life; I will sing praise to my God as long as I live. [3] Do not put your trust in princes, in human beings, who cannot save… [5] Blessed are those whose… hope is in the LORD their God.

[6] He is the Maker of heaven and earth, the sea, and everything in them — [H]e remains faithful forever. [7] He upholds the cause of the oppressed and gives food to the hungry. The LORD sets prisoners free, [8] the LORD gives sight to the blind, the LORD lifts up those who are bowed down, the LORD loves the righteous. [9] The LORD watches over the foreigner and sustains the fatherless and the widow… [10] The LORD reigns forever… for all generations. Praise the LORD.

Psalm 147:

[1] Praise the LORD. How good it is to sing praises to… God, how pleasant and fitting to praise [H]im! [3] He heals the brokenhearted and binds up their wounds. [4] He determines the number of the stars and calls them each by name. [5] Great is [the] Lord and mighty in power; [H]is understanding has no limit. [6] The LORD sustains the humble…

[7] Sing to the LORD with grateful praise; make music to… God on the harp. [8] He covers the sky with clouds; [H]e supplies the earth with rain and makes grass grow on the hills. [9] He provides food for the cattle and for the young ravens when they call.

[11] [T]he LORD delights in those who fear [H]im, who put their hope in [H]is unfailing love.

¹² Extol the LORD… [P]raise… God… ¹³ He… blesses [the] people… ¹⁴ He grants peace… and satisfies you with the finest of wheat.

¹⁵ He sends [H]is command to the earth; [H]is word runs swiftly. ¹⁶ He spreads the snow like wool and scatters the frost like ashes. ¹⁷ He hurls down [H]is hail like pebbles. Who can withstand [H]is icy blast? ¹⁸ He sends [H]is word and melts them; [H]e stirs up his breezes, and the waters flow.

¹⁹ He has revealed [H]is word… [and] [H]is laws and decrees… Praise the LORD.

Psalm 148:

¹ Praise the LORD. Praise the LORD from the heavens; praise [H]im in the heights above. ² Praise [H]im, all [H]is angels; praise [H]im, all [H]is heavenly hosts. ³ Praise [H]im, sun and moon; praise [H]im, all you shining stars. ⁴ Praise [H]im, you highest heavens and you waters above the skies.

⁵ Let them praise the name of the LORD, for at [H]is command they were created, ⁶ and [H]e established them for ever and ever — [H]e issued a decree that will never pass away.

⁷ Praise the LORD from the earth, you great sea creatures and all ocean depths, ⁸ lightning and hail, snow and clouds, stormy winds that do [H]is bidding, ⁹ you mountains and all hills, fruit trees and all cedars, ¹⁰ wild animals and all cattle, small creatures and flying birds, ¹¹ kings of the earth and all nations, you princes and all rulers on earth, ¹² young men and women, old men and children.

¹³ Let them ¹⁴ the people close to [H]is heart ¹³ praise the name of the LORD, for [H]is name alone is exalted; [H]is splendor is above the earth and the heavens. ¹⁴ Praise the LORD.

Psalm 149:

¹ Praise the LORD. Sing to the LORD a new song, [H]is praise in the assembly of [H]is faithful people. ² Let [all] rejoice in their Maker; …[and] be glad in their King. ³ Let them praise [H]is name with dancing and make music to [H]im with timbrel and harp. ⁴ For the LORD takes delight in [H]is people; [H]e crowns the humble with victory. ⁵ Let [H]is faithful people rejoice in this honor and sing for joy on their beds.

⁶ May the praise of God be in their mouths… Praise the LORD.

Psalm 150:

¹ Praise the LORD. Praise God in [H]is sanctuary; praise [H]im in [H]is mighty heavens. ² Praise [H]im for [H]is acts of power; praise [H]im for [H]is surpassing greatness. ³ Praise [H]im with the sounding of the trumpet, praise [H]im with the harp and lyre, ⁴ praise [H]im with timbrel and dancing, praise [H]im with the strings and pipe, ⁵ praise [H]im with the clash of cymbals, praise [H]im with resounding cymbals.

[6] Let everything that has breath praise the LORD. Praise the LORD.

Islam:

The Cow 2:153 O you who believe! [S]eek assistance through patience and prayer; surely [God] is with the patient.

Source: As-Shafia. Al-Kamilah Al-Sajjadiyya: The Psalms of Islam.

Supplication 1:

[1] Praise belongs to God, the First, without a first before Him, the Last, without a last behind Him. [3] He originated the creatures through His power with an origination, He devised them in accordance with His will with a devising. [4] Then He made them walk on the path of His desire [and] sent them out on the way of His love.

[6] ...[F]or each... He strikes a fixed term in life, for each He sets up a determined end; Then, when [they] take [their] final step and embrace the reckoning of [their] span, God seizes [them] to the abundant reward... to which He has called [them]... *That He may... repay those who do good with goodness...*

[8] Praise belongs to God, for, had He withheld from His servants the knowledge to praise Him for the uninterrupted kindnesses with which He has tried them and the manifest favors which He has lavished upon them, they would have moved about in His kindnesses without praising Him, and spread themselves out in His provision without thanking Him. [9] Had such been the case, they would have left the bounds of humanity for that of beastliness: *They are but as the cattle...*

[10] Praise belongs to God, for the true knowledge of Himself He has given to us, the thanksgiving He has inspired us to offer Him, the doors to knowing His Lordship He has opened for us, the sincerity towards Him in professing His Unity to which He has led us... [11] a praise through which we may be given long life among those of His creatures who praise Him, and overtake those who have gone ahead toward His good pleasure and pardon; [12] a praise through which He will illuminate for us the shadows of the interworld [and] ease for us the path of the Resurrection... the day *when every soul will be repaid for what it has earned...*

[17] Praise belongs to God, who chose for us the good qualities of creation [and] granted us the agreeable things of provision... [19] Praise belongs to God, who locked for us the gate of need except toward Him. So how can we praise Him? When can we thank Him? Indeed, when?

[20] Praise belongs to God, [W]ho... freed us from need through His bounty, and gave us possessions through His kindness. [22] Praise belongs to God, [W]ho showed us the way to repentance, which we would not have won save through His bounty. Had we nothing to count as His bounty but this... His beneficence toward us [would have been] great, His bounty upon us immense. [23] ...He has lifted up from us *what we have not the strength to bear,* charged us only to our capacity, [and] imposed upon us nothing but ease...

[25] And praise belongs to God with all the praises of His angels closest to Him, His

creatures most noble in His eyes, and His praisers most pleasing to Him; [26] a praise that may surpass other praises as our Lord surpasses all His creatures. [27] Then to Him belongs praise, in place of His every favor upon us and upon all His servants, past and still remaining, to the number of all things His knowledge encompasses, and in place of each of His favors, their number doubling and redoubling always and forever, to the Day of Resurrection; [28] a praise whose bound has no utmost end, whose number has no reckoning, whose limit cannot be reached, whose period cannot be cut off; [29] a praise which will become a link to His... pardon... a means to His forgiveness, a path to His Garden... an aid to obeying Him, a barrier against disobeying Him, a help in fulfilling... His duties; [30] a praise that will make us felicitous... and bring us into the ranks of [His] [saints]!

Supplication 6:

[1] Praise belongs to God, [W]ho created night and day through His strength, [2] set them apart through His power, [3] and appointed for each a determined limit and a drawn-out period. [4] He makes each of the two enter into its companion, and makes its companion enter into it, as an ordainment from Him for His servants... [5] He created for them the night, *that they might rest in it...for...* refreshment and strength... [6] He created for them *the daytime, giving sight, that they might seek* within it of His *bounty,* find the means to His provision, and roam freely in His earth, searching for that through which to attain the immediate in their life in this world and to achieve the deferred in their life to come.

[8] O God, to [You] belongs praise for the sky [You] [have] split into dawn for us, giving us to enjoy thereby the brightness of daytime, showing us sought-after nourishments, and protecting us from the striking of blights.

[11] We own nothing of the affair except what [You] [have] decreed and nothing of the good except what [You] [have] given. [12] This is a fresh, new day... If we do good, it will take leave from us with praise... [13] O God... preserve us... [from] committing... sin, whether small or great! [14] Make our good deeds... plentiful....

[15] O God... fill our pages for us with our good deeds and degrade us not before them with our [sins]! [16] O God, appoint for us in each of the day's hours a share from [Your] servants, a portion of giving thanks to [You], and a truthful witness among [Your] angels!

[17] O God... safeguard us from before us and behind us, from our right hands and our left hands and from all our directions, a safeguarding that will preserve [us] from disobeying [You], guide [us] to obeying [You], and be employed for [Your] love!

[18] O God... give us success in this day of ours, this night of ours, and in all our days, to employ the good, stay away from the evil, give thanks for favors... guide the misguided, assist the weak, and reach out to the troubled!

[21] O God... I bear witness that [You] [are] God, other than whom there is no god, [u]pholding justice, [e]quitable in judgement, *[c]lement to the servants, Master of the kingdom,* [and] [c]ompassionate to the creatures... [24] [You] [are] [a]ll-kind with immensity, the Forgiver of the great, and [You] [are] more merciful than every possessor of mercy!

Supplication 8:

[10] O God... through [Your] mercy, give to me refuge from all [sins]... O Most Merciful of

143

the merciful!

Supplication 19:

[1] O God, water us with rain, unfold upon us [Your] mercy… so that [Your] goodly earth may grow on all horizons! [2] Show kindness to [Your] servants through the ripening of the fruit [and] through the blossoming of the flowers…

[6] O God, make not the cloud's shadow over us a burning wind, allow not its coldness to be cutting, let not its pouring down upon us be a stoning, and make not its waters for us bitter! [7] O God, bless… and provide us with the blessings of the heavens and the earth! *[You] [are] powerful over everything!*

Supplication 38:

[1] O God, I ask pardon from [You] for the person wronged in my presence whom I did not help, the favor conferred upon me for which I returned no thanks, the [sinner] who asked pardon from me and whom I did not pardon, the needy person who asked from me and whom I preferred not over myself… and [for] every sin which presented itself to me and which I failed to avoid. [2] I ask pardon, my God, for all of these and their likes, with an asking of pardon in remorse…

[3] So bless [me] and make my remorse for the slips into which I have fallen and my determination to refrain from the evil deeds which present themselves to me a repentance which will make [Your] love for me obligatory O lover of those who repent!

Supplication 47:

[1] *Praise belongs to God, Lord of the worlds!* [2] O God, to [You] belongs praise! Originator of the heavens and the earth! Possessor of majesty and munificence! Lord of lords! Object of worship of every worshiper! Creator of every creature! *There is nothing like Him,* knowledge of nothing escapes Him, He *encompasses everything,* and He is *watchful over everything.*

[3] [You] [are] God, there is no god but [You], the Unique, the Alone, the Single, the Isolated. [4] [You] [are] God… the Generous, the Generously Bestowing, the All-mighty, the Mightily Exalted, the Magnificent, the Magnificently Magnified. [5] [You] [are] God… the All-high, the Sublimely High, the Strong in prowess. [6] [You] [are] God… the All-merciful, the All-compassionate, the All-knowing, the All-wise. [7] [You] [are] God… the All-hearing, the All-seeing, the Eternal, the All-aware. [8] [You] [are] God… the Generous, the Most Generous, the Everlasting, the Most Everlasting. [9] [You] [are] God… the First before every one, the Last after every number. [10] [You] [are] God… the Close in His highness, the High in His closeness.

[11] [You] [are] God… Possessor of radiance and glory, magnificence and praise. [12] [You] [are] God… [You] [have] brought forth the things without root, formed what [You] [have] formed without exemplar, and originated the originated things without limitation. [13] It is [You] [W]ho [have]… governed everything below [Yourself] with a governing. [15] It is [You] [W]ho willed, and what [You] willed was unfailing, [W]ho decreed, and what [You] decreed was just, [W]ho decided, and what [You] decided was fair. [16] It is [You] [W]hom place does not contain, before [W]hose authority no authority stands up… [17] It is [You] [W]ho [has] counted everything in numbers [and] appointed for everything a term… [19] It is [You] [W]ho [has] no bounds… [20] It is [You]… [W]ho [has] no equal…

144

²¹ It is [You] [W]ho [are] He [W]ho began, devised, brought forth, originated, and made well all that He made. ²² Glory be to [You]! How majestic is [Your] station! How high [Your] place among the places! ²³ Glory be to [You]! The Gentle - how gentle [You] [are]! The Clement - how clement [You] [are]! The Wise - how knowing [You] [are]! ²⁴ Glory be to [You]! The King - how invincible [You] [are]! The Munificent - how full of plenty [You] [are]! The Elevated - how elevated [You] [are]! Possessor of radiance and glory, magnificence and praise! ²⁵ Glory be to [You]! [You] [have] stretched forth [Your] hand with good things, and from [Your] guidance has come to be known...

²⁶ Glory be to [You]! Whatever passes in [Your] knowledge is subjected to [You], all below [Your] Throne are humbled before [Your] mightiness, and every one of [Your] creatures follows [You] in submission. ²⁷ Glory be to [You]! [You] [are] not... deceived, nor circumvented. ²⁸ Glory be to [You]! [Your] path is smooth ground, [Your] command right guidance, and [You] [are] a living, eternal refuge. ²⁹ Glory be to [You]! [Your] word is decisive, [Your] decree unfailing, [Your] will resolute.

³¹ Glory be to [You]! Outdazzling in signs, Creator of the heavens... ³² To [You] belongs praise, a praise that will be permanent with [Your] permanence! ³³ To [You] belongs praise, a praise everlasting through [Your] favor! ³⁴ To [You] belongs praise, a praise that will parallel [Your] benefaction! ³⁵ To [You] belongs praise... ³⁷ a praise which is suitable for none but [You] and through which nearness is sought to none but [You]; ³⁹ a praise which will multiply through recurrence of times...; ⁴⁰ a praise which the guardians will not be able to number...; ⁴⁴ a praise with whose like no creature has praised [You] and whose excellence none knows but [You]; ⁴⁵ a praise in which [they] who [strive] to multiply... will be helped...; ⁴⁷ a praise than which no praise is nearer to [Your] word and than which none is greater from any who praise [You]; ⁴⁹ a praise that will befit the generosity of [Your] face and meet the might of [Your] majesty! ⁵⁰ My Lord, bless... the distinguished, the chosen, the honored, the brought [near], with the most excellent of [Your] blessings, benedict [them] with the most complete of [Your] benedictions, and have mercy upon [us] with the most enjoyable of [Your] mercies!

⁶⁶ O God, [each day] [You] spread [Your] mercy, [show] kindness through [Your] pardon, and [make] plentiful [Your] giving, and by it [You] [have] been bounteous toward [Your] servants. ⁶⁷ I am [Your] servant whom [You] favored before creating [me] and after creating [me]. ⁶⁹ Here I am... before [You], despised, lowly, humble, abject, fearful, confessing the dreadful sins with which I am burdened and the great offenses that I have committed, seeking sanctuary in [Your] forgiveness, asking shelter in [Your] mercy... ⁷⁰ So act... kindly toward me... ⁷¹ Appoint for me in this day an allotment through which I may attain a share of [Your] good pleasure...

⁸⁶ Shield me in this day of mine, by that through which [You] [shield] [they] who pray fervently to [You]... and [they] who seek refuge in [Your] forgiveness while repenting! ⁸⁷ Attend to me with that through which [You] [attend] to the people of obedience toward [You]... ⁸⁹ Take me not to task... ⁹³ Give me refuge... ⁹⁴ Make easy for me the road of good deeds toward [You]... ⁹⁸ Deliver me from the floods of trial, save me from the gullets of affliction, and grant me sanctuary...

⁹⁹ Come between me and the enemy who misguides me, the caprice, which ruins me, and the failing which overcomes me! ¹⁰⁰ Turn not away from me... ¹⁰¹ Let me not lose heart... lest I be overcome by despair of [Your] mercy! ¹⁰³ Send me not from [Your] hand... ¹⁰⁴ Cast me not [from You]... Rather take my hand [and save me]...

[107] Impart to my heart restraint... [108] [and] that which... makes [You] pleased with me! [112] Give me purification... dress me in the dress of [Your] well-being, cloak me in the cloak of [Your] release, wrap me in [Your] ample favors, and clothe me in [Your] bounty and [Your] graciousness! [113] ...[H]elp me toward righteous intention, pleasing words, and approved works, and entrust me not to my force and my strength in place of [Your] force and [Your] strength!

[114] ...[M]ake me not forget remembering [You]... and inspire me to laud what [You] [have] done for me and confess to what [You] [have] conferred upon me! [116] Abandon me not with my neediness for [You]... for I am submitted to [You]. I know that... [You] [are]... most accustomed to beneficence... closer to pardoning than to punishing, and... nearer to covering over than to making notorious! [117] Let me live an agreeable life that will tie together what I want and reach what I love while I not bring what [You] [dislike] and not commit what [You] [have] prohibited...

[118] Abase me before [Yourself]... and raise me among [Your] servants, [and] increase me in neediness and poverty toward [You]! [119] Give me refuge from the gloating of enemies, the arrival of affliction... and suffering! Shield me... [and] [120] ...deliver me from [evil], for I seek [Your] shelter... [121] Couple for me the beginnings of [Your] kindnesses with their ends and the ancient of [Your] benefits with the freshly risen!

[124] Leave me not blindly wandering in my insolence... [125] Let me find the coolness of [Your] pardon and the sweetness of [Your] mercy, [Your] repose, [Your] ease, and the garden of [Your] bliss! [126] Make... me yearn for the meeting with [You], and allow me to repent with an unswerving repentance along with which [You] [let] no sins remain, small or large, and [leave] no wrongs, open or secret! [127] ...[B]end my heart toward the humble, be toward me as [You] [are] toward the righteous [and] adorn me with the adornment of the god-fearing... [128] Complete the lavishness of [Your] favor upon me, clothe me in its repeated generosities, fill my hand with [Your] benefits... and wrap me in [Your] noble presents...

[129] Appoint for me a resting place with [You] where I may seek haven in serenity, and a resort to which I may revert and rest my eyes, weigh not against me my [sins]... [A]ppoint for me a way in the truth from every mercy, make plentiful for me the portions of gifts from [Your] granting of awards, and fill out for me the shares of beneficence from [Your] bestowal of bounty! [130] Make my heart trust in what is with [You]... and combine within me independence, continence, ease, release, health, plenty, tranquility, and well-being! [132] ...Defend me... [and] [o]pen toward me the gates of [Your] repentance, [Your] mercy, [Your] clemency, and [Your] boundless provision! Surely I am one of those who beseech [You]! ...[C]omplete [Your] favor toward me! Surely [You] [are] the best of those who show favor! [133] ...[May Your] [p]eace be upon [us]... always and forever!

Supplication 55:

[1] Glory be to [You], O God, and I beg [Your] loving care! [2] Glory be to [You], O God, and high [are] [You] exalted! [3] Glory be to [You], O God, and might is [Your] loincloth! [4] Glory be to [You], O God, and mightiness is [Your] cloak! [5] Glory be to [You], O God, and magnificence is [Your] authority! [6] Glory be to [You], All-Mighty! How mighty [You] [are]! [7] Glory be to [You]! [You] [are] glorified in the highest! [10] Glory be to [You], present in every assembly!

[11] Glory be to [You], object of great hopes! [14] Glory be to [You]! [You] [know] the weight

of the heavens! ¹⁵ Glory be to [You]! [You] [know] the weight of the earths! ¹⁶ Glory be to [You]! [You] [know] [You] [know] the weight of the sun and the moon! ¹⁷ Glory be to [You]! [You] [know] the weight of the darkness and the light! ¹⁸ Glory be to [You]! [You] [know] the weight of the shadow and the air! ¹⁹ Glory be to [You]! [You] [know] the weight of the wind, how many times it is greater than the weight of a dust mote! ²⁰ Glory be to [You], All-holy, All-holy, All-holy! ²³ Glory be to God, the All-high, the All-Mighty!

Supplication 59:

¹ My God, let not my enemy gloat over me… ² My God… [r]espond to my supplication and the supplication of him who devotes his supplication sincerely to [You], for my power has become frail, my stratagems few, my situation severe… so nothing remains for me but hope in [You]!

³ My God… remembrance of [Your] acts of kindliness comforts me and hope in [You] showing favor and [Your] bounty strengthens me… ⁴ And [You], my God, [are] my place of flight, my asylum, my protector, my defender, ⁵ the loving toward me, the compassionate, and the guarantor of my provision.

⁹ Have mercy upon my frailty and the paucity of my stratagems, remove my distress, grant my supplication, ease me from my stumble, and show kindness to me in that and to everyone who supplicates [You]! ¹⁰ So bless… [Your] servant, and… help me. [S]urely [You] [are] the help of him who has no help and the stronghold of him who has no stronghold… I am… distressed… ¹¹ So respond to me, remove my concern, relieve my gloom, return my state to the best it has been, and repay me not according to what I deserve, but according to [Your] mercy which *embraces all things…* Bless… hear, and respond, O All-mighty!

Supplication 60:

¹ My God… ² give me… relief by means of the power through which [You] [bring] the dead lands to life and [revive] the spirits of the servants! Raise me up… provide for me, and release me from every blight!

³ My Lord… I know…there is no wrong in [Your] decree, and no hurry in [Your] vengeance… [You] [are] exalted… high indeed above all…

⁴ My Lord, respite me, comfort me, release me from my stumble… [You] ha[ve] seen my frailty, and the paucity of my stratagems. So give me patience, for I, my Lord, am weak, and I plead to [You], my Lord! ⁵ 'I seek refuge in [You]…' so give me refuge! ⁶ I seek sanctuary in [You] from every affliction, so grant me sanctuary! ⁷ I cover myself through [You], so cover me, my Master… ⁸ [You] [are] the All-mighty, mightier than every mighty thing! ⁹ Through [You]… I cover myself. ¹⁰ O God… [b]less…the good, the pure!

Supplication 69:

¹ My God, offenses have clothed me in the garment of my lowliness, separation from [You] has wrapped me in the clothing of my misery! My dreadful [sins] have deadened my heart, so bring it to life by a repentance from [You]! O my hope and my aim! O my wish and my want! By [Your] might, I find no one but [You] to forgive my sins and I see none but [You] to mend my brokenness! I have subjected myself to [You] in repeated

turning, I have humbled myself to [You]... If [You] [cast] me out from [Your] door, in whom shall I take shelter? If [You] [repel] me from [Your] side, in whom shall I seek refuge? O my grief at my ignominy and disgrace! O my sorrow at my evil works and what I have committed!

2 I ask [You], O Forgiver of great sins, O Mender of broken bones, to overlook my ruinous misdeeds and cover my disgraceful secret thoughts! At the witnessing place of the Resurrection, empty me not of the coolness of [Your] pardon and forgiveness, and strip me not of [Your] beautiful forbearance and covering!

3 My God, let the cloud of [Your] mercy cast its shadow upon my sins and send the billow of [You] clemency flowing over my faults! 5 My God, if remorse for sins is a repentance, I – by [Your] might – am one of the remorseful! If praying forgiveness for offenses is an alleviation, I am one of those who pray forgiveness! To [You] I return that [You] may be well pleased!

6 My God... turn toward me, through [Your] clemency... pardon me, and through [Your] knowledge of me, be gentle toward me! 7 My God, [You] ar[e] He who [has] opened a door to [Your] pardon and named it 'repentance', for [You] said, *Repent to God with unswerving repentance.*

8 ...O Responder to the distressed! O Remover of injury! O Knower of everything secret! O Beautiful through covering over! I seek [Your] munificence and [Your] generosity to intercede with [You], I seek [Your] side and [Your] showing mercy to mediate with [You], so grant my supplication, disappoint not my hope in [You], accept my repentance, and hide my offense[s], through [Your] kindness and mercy, O Most Merciful of the merciful!

Supplication 71:

1 My God... [will] [You] chastise me after my faith in [You], drive me far away after my love for [You], deprive me while I hope for [Your] mercy and forgiveness, forsake me while I seek sanctuary in [Your] pardon? How could [Your] generous face disappoint me?

5 My God, give me sanctuary... O All-loving, O All-kind! O Compassionate, O Merciful! O All-forgiver, O All-covering! Deliver me through [Your] mercy...

Supplication 75:

1 O God, inspire us to obey [You], turn us aside from disobeying [You]... set us down in the midst of [Your] Gardens, dispel... the clouds of misgiving, uncover... the wrappings of doubt and the veil, make falsehood vanish... and fix the truth in our... thoughts...

2 O God, carry us in the ships of [Your] deliverance, give us to enjoy the pleasure of whispered prayer to [You], make us drink at the pools of [Your] love, let us taste the sweetness of [Your] affection and nearness... and purify our intentions in devoting works to [You], for we exist through [You] and belong to [You], and we have no one to mediate with [You] but [You]!

3 My God, place me among the chosen, the good. Join me to the righteous, the pious..., the workers of the abiding acts of righteousness...*[You] [are] powerful over everything* and disposed to respond! By [Your] mercy, O Most Merciful of the merciful!

Supplication 76:

[1] Glory be to [You]! How plain the truth for him whom [You] [have] guided on his way! [2] My God, so make us travel on the roads that arrive at [You] and set us into motion on the paths nearest to reaching [You]! Make near for us the far, and make easy for us the hard and difficult! Join us to [Your] servants, those who hurry to [You] swiftly, knock constantly at [Your] door, and worship [You] by night and by day...

[You] [have] purified their drinking places... granted their requests, accomplished their wishes through [Your] bounty, filled their minds with [Your] love, and quenched their thirst with [Your] pure drink... O He who comes toward those who come toward Him and grants gifts and bestows bounty upon them through tenderness! He is compassionate and clement and loving and tender... I ask [You] to place me among those of them who have the fullest share from [You], the highest station with [You], the most plentiful portion of [Your] love, and the most excellent allotment of [Your] knowledge, for my aspiration has been cut off from everything but [You] and my desire has turned toward [You] alone.

...[T]o [You] alone belongs my waking and my sleeplessness. Meeting [You] is the gladness of my eye, joining [You] the wish of my soul. Toward [You] is my yearning, in love for [You] my passionate longing, in inclining toward [You] my fervent craving... In whispered prayer to [You] I find my repose and my ease.

With [You] lies the remedy of my illness, the cure for my burning thirst, the coolness of my ardor, the removal of my distress. Be my intimate in my loneliness, the releaser of my stumble, the forgiver of my slip, the accepter of my repentance, the responder to my supplication, the patron of preserving me from sin, the one who frees me from my neediness! Cut me not off from [You] and keep me not far from [You]! O my bliss and my garden! O my this world and my hereafter! O Most Merciful of the merciful!

Supplication 77:

[1] My God, who can have tasted the sweetness of [Your] love, then wanted another in place of [You]? Who can have become intimate with [Your] nearness, then sought removal from [You]?

Bahaism:

Source: Bahá'u'lláh:

"Be generous in prosperity, and thankful in adversity. Be worthy of the trust of [your] neighbor, and look upon him with a bright and friendly face. Be a treasure to the poor, an admonisher to the rich, an answerer to the cry of the needy, a preserver of the sanctity of [your] pledge. Be fair in [your] judgment, and guarded in [your] speech. Be unjust to no [person], and show all meekness to all [people]. Be as a lamp unto them that walk in darkness, a joy to the sorrowful, a sea for the thirsty, a haven for the distressed, an upholder and defender of the victim of oppression. Let integrity and uprightness distinguish all [your] acts. Be a home for the stranger, a balm to the suffering, and a tower of strength for the fugitive. Be eyes to the blind, and a guiding light unto the feet of the erring. Be an ornament to the countenance of truth, a crown to the brow of fidelity, a pillar of the temple of righteousness, a breath of life to the body of mankind, an ensign of the hosts of justice, a luminary above the horizon of virtue, a dew to the soil of the human heart, an ark on the ocean of knowledge, a sun in the heaven of bounty, a gem on the diadem of wisdom, a shining light in the firmament of [your] generation, a fruit upon the tree of humility."

"[You] are the fruits of one tree, and the leaves of one branch. Deal... with [one] another with the utmost love and harmony, with friendliness and fellowship... [for] Humanity is One Family: The earth is but one country, and mankind its citizens."

"It is incumbent upon all the peoples of the world to reconcile their differences, and, with perfect unity and peace, abide beneath the shadow of the Tree of [God's] care and loving-kindness... Set your faces towards unity, and let the radiance of its light shine upon you."

"Quench... the lamp of error, and kindle within your hearts the everlasting torch of divine guidance."

"...[P]eople need no weapons... Their hosts are the hosts of goodly deeds, and their arms the arms of upright conduct, and their commander the fear of God."

Buddhism:

Source: Shinran Shonin. Project Gutenberg EBook of Buddhist Psalms. 2004. With modifications to illumninate the unity of faiths.

[1] Seek refuge in the [Lord] [f]or the light of His [w]isdom is infinite. In all the worlds there is nothing upon which His light shines not.

[3] Take refuge in the [Lord]... His deliverance is boundless. [4] ...His glory is all-embracing [and] [10] shine[s] for ever and ever... [11] The glory of [God] is boundless... [13] Sun and moon are lost in the ocean of His splendor.

[22] In [paradise] is none... who ha[s] trusted in his own deeds for salvation. [25] Seek refuge in Almighty [God]. By [Him] was [p]aradise created. ...[T]here is [none] that may compare with [Him].

[36] [S]eek refuge in the [Lord] [f]or He is faithful... [and] merciful... [100] [God] watches over [His people] throughout the day and night, as the shadow follows its substance... [102] guarding [them] throughout the days and nights.

[39] Bring homage to [the Lord]. As the pure wind blows over the trees glorious with jewels, [i]t draw[s] from them a noble music with five-fold strains of harmony.

[42] ...By His sacred teaching He lead[s] all having life into the way of light. [44] ...[W]hen sorrow and sighing are fled away, [paradise] shall rejoice with joy and singing. [48] Let [those] that [have] faith praise the virtue of [God].

[85] Having great pity, our eternal Father light[s] the dark night of ignorance... enlighten[ing] all the worlds with [His] immeasurable glory. [181] [He] ha[s] instructed mankind in every sort of righteous deed... [203] For it is by the marvelous mercy of our Lord that we may cast aside the anguish of... death, in the shining hope of... [e]ternal [life].

150

[97] To [those] that recite [God's] Holy Name shall be good unending...

[129] Whoso believe[s]... shall verily be at one with the [Lord], even as the turbid stream is clear and pure within the ocean depth when they have flowed together. [234] Whoso believe[s] [in the Lord] shall attain [p]erfect [w]isdom, by the virtue of [His] light which embrace[s] him and shall never forsake him.

[327] I seek my refuge in [God] [though my] heart [has] not been [t]ruly sincere[;] [d]eceit and untruth are in my flesh, and in my soul is no clear shining. [331] If it were not for [God's] mercy... [h]ow should I cross the Ocean of Misery? [332] If I sought not refuge in the gift of our Father, I should die the death of the shameless. [334] [But] whoso seek[s] refuge with Him shall be certainly born into [paradise].

Hinduism:

Source: Sri Sivananda. Bliss Divine. Divine Life Society. 2009:

Truth is the seat of God... Truth is the basic law of life... Truth is the law of freedom... Truth is infinite. Truth alone endures, while everything else perishes... God is Truth. [He] is Absolute Truth.

Truth can be compared to a road of pasture, while falsehood can be compared to a bush of thorns... Truth... is the path of righteousness. ... Let truth and purity... guide your conduct and mo[ld] your character.

All is well with him whose heart is turned towards [truth]... The mover towards... truth is mighty, lives long, knows everything, and is ever delighted; for he is nearing the Almighty.

Source: Tirukkural 25:241-242:

Among the wealthy, compassionate men claim the richest wealth... Find and follow the good path and be ruled by compassion. For if the various ways are examined, compassion will prove the means to liberation.

Source: Brihadarankyaka Upanishada:

...[W]here there is unity... that is the world of [God].

Source: Taittiriya Upanishad:

May the Lord of day grant us peace. May the Lord of night grant us peace. May the Lord of sight grant us peace. May the Lord of might grant us peace. May the Lord of speech grant us peace. May the Lord of space grant us peace.

I bow down to [God], source of all power. I will speak the truth and follow the law. Guard me [God]... against all harm.

Source: Shvetashvatara Upanishad:

He is the source of all powers of life. He is the lord of all... Who dwells forever in the cosmic womb. May [H]e purify [us]. O Lord, in [W]hom alone we can find peace, [m]ay we see [Y]our [D]ivine [S]elf and be freed from [impurity]… and fear.

Source: Arun Shanbhag. _Prarthana: A Book of Hindu Psalms._ Arun Shanbhag. Arlington, MA. 2007:

Rig Veda:

[2:1:8] …[A]ll things belong to [Y]ou… [2:2:1] …[E]xalt [God] [W]ho knows all life; worship [H]im with oblation and the song of praise…

Bhagavad-Gita, Chapter XII:

For those who set their hearts on me [a]nd worship [M]e with unfailing devotion and faith, [t]he way of love leads sure and swift to [M]e…

Jainism:

Acaranga Sutra:

Nothing which breathes, which exists, which lives, or which has essence or potential of life, should be destroyed… or harmed, or denied of its essence or potential.

Suman Suttam Verse 150:

Killing a living being is killing one's own self; showing compassion to a living being is showing compassion to oneself. He who desires his own good, should avoid causing any harm to a living being.

Sikhism:

Sri Guru Granth Sahib:

[God] dwells deep within the nucleus of all beings. God is invisible; (also visible) wherever I look, there I see Him… Wherever I look, there I see My Lord… All… creation, and all languages meditate on Him, forever and ever.

How can I describe the Greatness of Your Name? O [Lord], if I had hundreds of thousands of stacks of paper, and if ink were never to fail me, and if my pen were able to move like the wind, and if I were to read and recite and embrace love for [You] – even so, I could not estimate Your Value. How can I describe the Greatness of Your Name?

The dogs of greed are with me. In the early morning, they continually bark at the wind. Falsehood is my dagger; through deception, I eat the carcasses of the dead. I live as a wild hunter, O Creator! I have not followed good advice, nor have I done good deeds. I am deformed and horribly disfigured. Your Name alone, Lord, saves the world. This is my hope; this is my support.

Without the Lord, my soul is scorched and burnt… [P]lease instill within me the yearning for You… [T]he Lord Himself has stood by my side… I seek Your Sanctuary; …shower Your Mercy upon me, and protect me. [God] is the Purifier of sinners…

[The Lord is] my shelter… He is always close at hand… Please bless me with Your

Mercy and save this sinking stone... Take pity on me, O... Lord... You are my Support and my Protection... Your Treasures are overflowing...

The [Lord's] bride... is in love with [God]. She continually enjoys and ravishes her Beloved, with true love and affection. She is such a loveable, beautiful and noble woman... [S]he decorates herself with the Love and the Fear of God... [She] sings Your Praises. You have freed us from bondage. Lord, everyone bows in reverence to You. You have saved us from our sinful ways. Lord, You are the Honor of the dishonored. Lord, You are the Strongest of the strong... She who adorns herself with the Love and the Fear of God... obtains the Mansion of the Lord's Presence as her home. Night and day, day and night, she constantly ravishes and enjoys her Beloved. She is dyed in the permanent color of His Love... [She] finds intuitive peace and poise in the Mansion of the Lord's Presence.

The Lord of the Universe, the Support of the earth, [is] Merciful; the rain is falling everywhere. He is Merciful to the meek, always Kind and Gentle; the Creator has brought cooling relief. He cherishes all His beings and creatures, as the mother cares for her children. The Destroyer of pain, the Ocean of Peace, the Lord... gives sustenance to all. The Merciful Lord is totally pervading and permeating the water and the land... He saves all. God Himself protects all; He drives out all sorrow and suffering...

I seek Your Sanctuary, O my Lord, Merciful to the meek, Ocean of Peace... Sustainer of the world. Shower Your Mercy upon [me] that [I] may sing Your Glorious Praises; preserve my honor... All my troubles and sufferings have run away. The music of intuitive peace, poise and tranquility wells up within...

We are His, and from Him, we receive our rewards. Showering His Mercy upon us, God has united us with Him... The rain has fallen... All beings and creatures dwell in peace. Suffering has been dispelled, and true happiness has dawned... The One, to [W]hom we belong, cherishes and nurtures us. The... Lord God [is] our Protector... [The] Lord... has heard my prayer; my efforts have been rewarded. He is the Giver of all souls. He blesses us with His... Grace. The beings in the water, on the land and in the sky are all satisfied... I am imbued with the Love of the... Lord... You are my God, my Lord... Body and soul and all riches are Yours. Yours is the Power, O Lord... Forever and ever, You are the Giver of Peace... O God, from You I receive... Whatever You give me, brings me happiness.

I shall never again suffer sorrow. The... Lord God has unleashed the rain clouds. Over the sea and over the land - over all the earth's surface, in all directions, He has brought the rain. Peace has come, and the thirst of all has been quenched; there is joy and ecstasy everywhere. He is the Giver of Peace, the Destroyer of pain. He gives and forgives all beings. He Himself nurtures and cherishes His Creation.... Seeking His Sanctuary, salvation is obtained. With each and every breath, I [praise His] Name...

The "Luminous" Religion:

Source: **Martin Palmer.** **The Jesus Sutras** **(Ballantine Wellspring, New York, 2001):**

...Through faith they find Happiness. It's like the spring rain that refreshes everything – If you have roots, you will flourish...

…Anyone, even if they only have a little love [c]an walk the Bright Path, and they will suffer no harm… This is the way that leads to Peace and Happiness. And they can come to this even from the darkest of darks.

The laws of compassion save us all, echoing through the world like a tolling, golden bell. …[Y]ou (God) bring us back to our original nature, and the souls that are saved are countless. [Your] Divine compassion lifts them up from the dust, redeeming them from the saddened realm… [W]e draw close to… the One [W]ho creates salvation…

To be pure and still means to be open to purity and stillness — as a result you can intuit the truth… Detach yourself from what disturbs and distracts you, [a]nd be as pure as one who breathes in purity and emptiness… This… is the gateway to… Peace and Happiness.

…[R]enounce desire, have neither male nor female slaves, see all people as equal, and do not hoard material goods… Always do good and keep your heart pure… Be watchful every day of slipping. Remember all life depends on God… All existence is an act of grace… [Revere] God.

God is always beside the believer.

The truth is like looking at the white of the moon in water. If the water is cloudy, you can't see it clearly. It's like burning straw in a fire – If the straw is wet, the fire can't burn brightly. Spiritual life can be hidden and dampened like this.

North American Indian:

Cherokee Prayer:

O Great Spirit (God) help me always to speak the truth quietly, to listen with an open mind… and to remember the peace that may be found in silence.

Lakota Prayer:

O Great Spirit (God) Whose voice I hear in the winds, and whose breath gives life to all the world, hear me. I am small and weak. I need your strength and wisdom. Let me walk in beauty and make my eyes behold the red and purple sunset. Make my hands respect the things You have made and my ears sharp to hear Your voice. Make me wise so that I may understand the things You have taught… Let me learn the lessons You have hidden… Make me always ready to come to You with clean hands and straight eyes so when life fades, as with the fading sunset, my spirit may come to You without shame.

Lakota Prayer:

…[T]each me how to trust my heart, my mind, my intuition, my inner knowing, the senses of my body, the blessings of my spirit. Teach me to trust these things so that I may… love beyond my fear, and… [w]alk [in Your ways] with the passing of each glorious [s]un.

XVII. Proverbs/Ecclesiastes:

Christianity/Judaism:

Proverbs 1:

[7] The fear of the LORD is the beginning of knowledge…

[8] Listen… to your father's instruction and do not forsake your mother's teaching. [9] They are a garland to grace your head and a chain to adorn your neck. [10] …[I]f sin[ners] entice you, do not give in to them.

[20] Out in the open wisdom calls aloud, she raises her voice in the public square; [21] on top of the wall she cries out, at the city gate she makes her speech: [23] Repent! Then I will pour out my thoughts to you, I will make known to you my teachings [33] [for] whoever listens to me will live in safety and be at ease, without fear of harm.

Proverbs 2:

[1] …[I]f you accept my words and store up my commands within you, [2] turning your ear to wisdom and applying your heart to understanding — [3] indeed, if you call out for insight and cry aloud for understanding, [4] and if you look for it as for silver and search for it as for hidden treasure, [5] then you will understand the fear of the LORD and find the knowledge of God. [6] For the LORD gives wisdom; from [H]is mouth come knowledge and understanding. [7] He holds success in store for the upright, [H]e is a shield to those whose walk is blameless, [8] for [H]e guards the course of the just and protects the way of [H]is faithful ones. [20] Thus you will walk in the ways of the good and keep to the paths of the righteous.

[21] …[T]he upright will live in the land, and the blameless will remain in it…

Proverbs 3:

[1] …[D]o not forget my teaching, but keep my commands in your heart, [2] for they will prolong your life many years and bring you peace and prosperity. [3] Let love and faithfulness never leave you; bind them around your neck, write them on the tablet of your heart.

[5] Trust in the LORD with all your heart and lean not on your own understanding; [6] in all your ways submit to [H]im, and [H]e will make your paths straight. [7] Do not be wise in your own eyes; fear the LORD and shun evil. [8] This will bring health… and nourishment…

[9] Honor the LORD with your wealth, with the firstfruits of all your crops; [10] then your barns will be filled to overflowing, and your vats will brim over with new wine. [11] …[D]o not despise the LORD's discipline, and do not resent [H]is rebuke, [12] because the LORD disciplines those [H]e loves, as a father the [child] he delights in.

[13] Blessed are those who find wisdom, those who gain understanding, [14] for she is more profitable than silver and yields better returns than gold. [15] She is more precious than rubies; nothing you desire can compare with her. [16] Long life is in her right hand; in her left hand are riches and honor. [17] Her ways are pleasant ways, and all her paths are

peace. [18] She is a tree of life to those who take hold of her; those who hold her fast will be blessed.

[19] By wisdom the LORD laid the earth's foundations, by understanding [H]e set the heavens in place; [20] by [H]is knowledge the watery depths were divided, and the clouds let drop the dew.

[21] …[D]o not let wisdom and understanding out of your sight, preserve sound judgment and discretion; [22] they will be life for you, an ornament to grace your neck. [23] Then you will go on your way in safety, and your foot will not stumble. [24] When you lie down, you will not be afraid; when you lie down, your sleep will be sweet… [26] for the LORD will be at your side and will keep your foot from being snared.

[27] Do not withhold good from those to whom it is due, when it is in your power to act. [28] Do not say to your neighbor, "Come back tomorrow and I'll give it to you" — when you already have it with you. [29] Do not plot harm against your neighbor, who lives trustfully near you. [30] Do not accuse anyone for no reason — when they have done you no harm. [31] Do not envy the violent or choose any of their ways. [32] For the LORD… takes the upright into [H]is confidence. [33] …[H]e blesses the home of the righteous [and] [34] …shows favor to the humble and oppressed. [35] The wise inherit honor, but fools get only shame.

Proverbs 4:

[1] Listen… to a father's instruction; pay attention and gain understanding. [2] I give you sound learning, so do not forsake my teaching.

[5] "Get wisdom, get understanding… [6] Do not forsake wisdom, and she will protect you; love her, and she will watch over you. [8] Cherish her, and she will exalt you; embrace her, and she will honor you. [9] She will give you a garland to grace your head and present you with a glorious crown."

[10] Listen… accept what I say, and the years of your life will be many. [11] I instruct you in the way of wisdom and lead you along straight paths. [12] When you walk, your steps will not be hampered; when you run, you will not stumble. [13] Hold on to instruction, do not let it go; guard it well, for it is your life.

[14] Do not set foot on the path of the wicked or walk in the way of evildoers. [15] Avoid it, do not travel on it; turn from it and go on your way [for] [18] [t]he path of the righteous is like the morning sun, shining ever brighter till the full light of day. [19] But the way of the wicked is like deep darkness; they do not know what makes them stumble.

[23] Above all else, guard your heart, for everything you do flows from it. [24] Keep your mouth free of perversity; keep corrupt talk far from your lips. [25] Let your eyes look straight ahead; fix your gaze directly before you. [26] Give careful thought to the paths for your feet and be steadfast in all your ways. [27] Do not turn to the right or the left; keep your foot from evil.

Proverbs 8:

[1] Does not wisdom call out? Does not understanding raise her voice? [2] At the highest point along the way, where the paths meet, she takes her stand; [3] beside the gate leading into the city, at the entrance, she cries aloud: [4] "To you, O people, I call out; I

raise my voice to all mankind. ⁶ Listen… I open my lips to speak what is right. ⁷ My mouth speaks what is true… ¹⁰ Choose my instruction instead of silver, knowledge rather than choice gold, ¹¹ for wisdom is more precious than rubies, and nothing you desire can compare with her.

¹² I, wisdom, dwell together with prudence; I possess knowledge and discretion. ¹⁴ Counsel and sound judgment are mine; I have insight, I have power. ¹⁷ I love those who love me, and those who seek me find me. ²⁰ I walk in the way of righteousness, along the paths of justice, ²¹ bestowing a rich inheritance on those who love me and making their treasuries full.

²² The LORD brought me forth as the first of [H]is works, before [H]is deeds of old; ²³ I was formed long ages ago, at the very beginning, when the world came to be. ²⁴ When there were no watery depths, I was given birth, when there were no springs overflowing with water; ²⁵ before the mountains were settled in place, before the hills, I was given birth, ²⁶ before [H]e made the world or its fields or any of the dust of the earth. ²⁷ I was there when [H]e set the heavens in place, when [H]e marked out the horizon on the face of the deep, ²⁸ when [H]e established the clouds above and fixed securely the fountains of the deep, ²⁹ when [H]e gave the sea its boundary so the waters would not overstep [H]is command, and when [H]e marked out the foundations of the earth. ³⁰ Then I was constantly at [H]is side. I was filled with delight day after day, rejoicing always in [H]is presence, ³¹ rejoicing in [H]is whole world and delighting in mankind.

³² Now then, my children, listen to me; blessed are those who keep my ways. ³³ Listen to my instruction and be wise… ³⁴ Blessed are those who listen to me, watching daily at my doors, waiting at my doorway. ³⁵ For those who find me find life and receive favor from the LORD. ¹³ [Know] "[t]o fear the LORD is to hate evil…"

Proverbs 9:

¹ Wisdom has built her house; she has set up its seven pillars. ² She has prepared her meat and mixed her wine; she has also set her table. ³ She… calls from the highest point of the city, ⁴ "Let all who are simple come to my house!" To those who have no sense she says, ⁵ "Come, eat my food and drink the wine I have mixed. ⁶ Leave your simple ways and you will live; walk in the way of insight."

¹⁰ The fear of the LORD is the beginning of wisdom, and knowledge of the Holy One is understanding. ¹¹ For through wisdom your days will be many, and years will be added to your life. ¹² If you are wise, your wisdom will reward you…

Proverbs 10:

¹ [W]ise [children] bring joy to [their] father, but foolish [children] bring grief to [their] mother.

² Ill-gotten treasures have no lasting value, but righteousness delivers from death.

³ The LORD does not let the righteous go hungry… ⁴ Lazy hands make for poverty, but diligent hands bring wealth.

⁶ Blessings crown the head of the righteous… ⁷ The name of the righteous is used in blessings… ⁸ The wise in heart accept commands, but a chattering fool comes to ruin.

[12] Hatred stirs up conflict, but love covers over all wrongs.

[9] Whoever walks in integrity walks securely...

[14] The wise store up knowledge... [16] The wages of the righteous is life... [17] Whoever heeds discipline shows the way to life...

[13] Wisdom is found on the lips of the discerning... [11] The mouth of the righteous is a fountain of life... [19] ...[T]he prudent hold their tongues. [20] The tongue of the righteous is choice silver... [21] The lips of the righteous nourish many... [31] From the mouth of the righteous comes the fruit of wisdom... [32] The lips of the righteous know what finds favor...

[22] The blessing of the LORD brings wealth... [23] A... person of understanding delights in wisdom. [24] What the wicked dread will overtake them; what the righteous desire will be granted. [28] The prospect of the righteous is joy...

[25] When the storm has swept by... the righteous stand firm forever. [30] The righteous will never be uprooted...

[27] The fear of the LORD adds length to life... [29] The way of the LORD is a refuge for the blameless...

Proverbs 11:

[1] The LORD [finds favor with] accurate weights... [3] The integrity of the upright guides them... [10] When the righteous prosper, the city rejoices... [11] Through the blessing of the upright a city is exalted...

[16] A kindhearted [person] gains honor...[17] Those who are kind benefit themselves... [24] One person gives freely, yet gains even more; another withholds unduly, but comes to poverty. [25] A generous person will prosper; whoever refreshes others will be refreshed.

[2] When pride comes, then comes disgrace, but with humility comes wisdom. [5] The righteousness of the blameless makes their paths straight, but the wicked are brought down by their own wickedness.

[28] Those who trust in their riches will fall, but the righteous will thrive like a green leaf.

[4] ...[R]ighteousness delivers from death. [6] The righteousness of the upright delivers them... [18] ...[T]he one who sows righteousness reaps a sure reward. [19] Truly the righteous attain life... [30] The fruit of the righteous is a tree of life...

[20] The LORD... delights in those whose ways are blameless. [23] The desire of the righteous ends only in good... [27] Whoever seeks good finds favor...

Proverbs 12:

[1] Whoever loves discipline loves knowledge... [4] A wife of noble character is her husband's crown... [20] ...[T]hose who promote peace have joy.

[18] The words of the reckless pierce like swords, but the tongue of the wise brings healing. [19] Truthful lips endure forever...

[5] The plans of the righteous are just... [6] The... speech of the upright rescues them. [7]

The... house of the righteous stands firm. ³ ...[T]he righteous cannot be uprooted. ¹² The... root of the righteous endures.
²² The LORD... delights in people who are trustworthy. ² Good people obtain favor from the LORD... ²¹ No harm overtakes the righteous... ²⁸ In the way of righteousness there is life; along that path is immortality.

¹⁰ The righteous care for the needs of their animals...

Proverbs 13:

²⁰ Walk with the wise and become wise, for a companion of fools suffers harm.

¹⁸ Whoever disregards discipline comes to poverty and shame, but whoever heeds correction is honored. ⁴ ...[T]he diligent are fully satisfied. ²¹ Trouble pursues the sinner, but the righteous are rewarded with good things. ²² A good person leaves an inheritance for their children's children, but a sinner's wealth is stored up for the righteous. ²⁵ The righteous eat to their hearts' content...

⁵ The righteous hate what is false, but the wicked... bring shame on themselves. ⁶ Righteousness guards the person of integrity... ³ Those who guard their lips preserve their lives... ⁹ The light of the righteous shines brightly but the lamp of the wicked is snuffed out.

Proverbs 14:

³¹ Whoever... is kind to the needy honors God. ² Whoever fears the LORD walks uprightly... ¹⁶ The wise fear the LORD and shun evil... ²⁶ Whoever fears the LORD has a secure fortress, and for their children it will be a refuge. ²⁷ The fear of the LORD is a fountain of life, turning a person from the snares of death. ³² ...[E]ven in death the righteous seek refuge in God.

⁵ An honest witness does not deceive... ⁶ The mocker seeks wisdom and finds none, but knowledge comes easily to the discerning. ³³ Wisdom reposes in the heart of the discerning... ³⁰ A heart at peace gives life to the body, but envy rots the bones.

⁹ [G]oodwill is found among the upright. ²¹ ...[B]lessed is the one who is kind to the needy.

¹⁸ The... prudent are crowned with knowledge. ⁸ The wisdom of the prudent is to give thought to their ways... ¹⁵ The simple believe anything, but the prudent give thought to their steps. ²⁹ Whoever is patient has great understanding... ¹⁷ A quick-tempered person does foolish things... ²² ...[T]hose who plan what is good find love and faithfulness.

Proverbs 15:

¹ A gentle answer turns away wrath, but a harsh word stirs up anger. ² The tongue of the wise adorns knowledge, but the mouth of the fool gushes folly. ⁴ The soothing tongue is a tree of life, but a perverse tongue crushes the spirit. ⁷ The lips of the wise spread knowledge...

⁸ ...[T]he prayer of the upright pleases [the LORD]. ⁹ ...[H]e loves those who pursue righteousness. ⁶ The house of the righteous contains great treasure...

³³ Wisdom's instruction is to fear the LORD, and humility comes before honor. ¹⁶ Better

a little with the fear of the LORD than great wealth with turmoil.

²⁵ The LORD... sets the widow's boundary stones in place. ²⁶ ...[G]racious words are pure in [H]is sight. ²⁹ The LORD... hears the prayer of the righteous. ²⁴ The path of life leads upward for the prudent to keep them from going down to the realm of the dead.

Proverbs 16:

¹ ...[F]rom the LORD comes the proper answer of the tongue. ⁹ In their hearts humans plan their course, but the LORD establishes their steps. ³ Commit to the LORD whatever you do, and [H]e will establish your plans. ⁴ The LORD works out everything to its proper end...

⁶ Through love and faithfulness sin is atoned for; through the fear of the LORD evil is avoided. ⁸ Better a little with righteousness than much gain with injustice. ¹⁶ How much better to get wisdom than gold, to get insight rather than silver!

¹¹ Honest scales and balances belong to the LORD; all the weights in the bag are of his making. ¹⁷ The highway of the upright avoids evil; those who guard their ways preserve their lives.

²² Prudence is a fountain of life... ²³ The hearts of the wise make their mouths prudent... ²⁴ Gracious words are a honeycomb, sweet to the soul and healing to the bones. ³¹ Gray hair is a crown of splendor; it is attained in the way of righteousness.

²⁰ ...[B]lessed is the one who trusts in the LORD.

Proverbs 17:

¹⁶ Why should fools have money in hand to buy wisdom, when they are not able to understand it?

¹ Better a dry crust with peace and quiet than a house full of feasting, with strife. ⁵ Whoever mocks the poor shows contempt for their Maker... ¹⁹ Whoever loves a quarrel loves sin...

⁶ Children's children are a crown to the aged, and parents are the pride of their children.

⁹ Whoever would foster love covers over an offense... ²² A cheerful heart is good medicine, but a crushed spirit dries up the bones. ¹⁷ A friend loves at all times, and a [sibling] is born for a time of adversity.

²⁴ A discerning person keeps wisdom in view, but a fool's eyes wander to the ends of the earth.

²⁷ The one who has knowledge uses words with restraint, and whoever has understanding is even-tempered. ²⁸ Even fools are thought wise if they keep silent, and discerning if they hold their tongues.

Proverbs 18:

¹ An unfriendly person pursues selfish ends and against all sound judgment starts quarrels. ¹⁹ A [sibling] wronged is more unyielding than a fortified city; disputes are like the barred gates of a citadel.

² Fools find no pleasure in understanding but delight in airing their own opinions. ³ When wickedness comes, so does contempt, and with shame comes reproach. ¹⁴ The human spirit can endure in sickness, but a crushed spirit who can bear?

⁴ The words of the mouth are deep waters, but the fountain of wisdom is a rushing stream. ²⁰ From the fruit of their mouth a person's stomach is filled; with the harvest of their lips they are satisfied. ²¹ The tongue has the power of life and death, and those who love it will eat its fruit.

¹⁵ The heart of the discerning acquires knowledge, for the ears of the wise seek it out.

¹⁰ The name of the LORD is a fortified tower; the righteous run to it and are safe. ¹¹ The wealth of the rich is their fortified city; they imagine it a wall too high to scale.

Proverbs 19:

¹ Better the poor whose walk is blameless than a fool whose lips are perverse. ² Desire without knowledge is not good — how much more will hasty feet miss the way! ³ A person's own folly leads to their ruin…

²¹ Many are the plans in a person's heart, but it is the LORD's purpose that prevails.

¹⁴ Houses and wealth are inherited from parents, but a prudent [spouse] is from the LORD.

²⁰ Listen to advice and accept discipline, and at the end you will be counted among the wise. ⁸ The one who gets wisdom loves life; the one who cherishes understanding will soon prosper. ¹¹ A person's wisdom yields patience; it is to one's glory to overlook an offense. ¹⁷ Whoever is kind to the poor lends to the LORD, and [H]e will reward them for what they have done.

²³ The fear of the LORD leads to life; then one rests content, untouched by trouble. ¹⁶ Whoever keeps commandments keeps their life…

Proverbs 20:

³ It is to one's honor to avoid strife, but every fool is quick to quarrel.

¹² Ears that hear and eyes that see — the LORD has made them both. ²⁴ A person's steps are directed by the LORD. How then can anyone understand their own way? ⁷ The righteous lead blameless lives; blessed are their children after them.

⁵ The purposes of a person's heart are deep waters, but one who has insight draws them out. ⁶ Many claim to have unfailing love, but a faithful person who can find? ⁹ Who can say, "I have kept my heart pure; I am clean and without sin?" ¹⁵ Gold there is, and rubies in abundance, but lips that speak knowledge are a rare jewel.

²⁷ The human spirit is the lamp of the LORD that sheds light on one's inmost being. ²⁸ Love and faithfulness keep [one] safe; through love [one] is made secure.

Proverbs 21:

¹ In the LORD's hand… is a stream of water that he channels toward all who please [H]im. ³¹ …[V]ictory rests with the LORD.

 A person may think their own ways are right, but the LORD weighs the heart. ¹⁵ When justice is done, it brings joy to the righteous…

²⁶ …[T]he righteous give without sparing. ³ To do what is right and just is more acceptable to the LORD than sacrifice. ²¹ Whoever pursues righteousness and love finds life, prosperity and honor. ²³ Those who guard their mouths and their tongues keep themselves from calamity.

⁷ The violence of the wicked will drag them away, for they refuse to do what is right. ⁸ The way of the guilty is devious, but the conduct of the innocent is upright.

Proverbs 22:

¹ A good name is more desirable than great riches; to be esteemed is better than silver or gold. ⁴ Humility is the fear of the LORD; its wages are riches and honor and life. ⁹ The generous will themselves be blessed, for they share their food with the poor. ¹¹ One who loves a pure heart and who speaks with grace will have [God] for a friend.

² Rich and poor have this in common: The LORD is the Maker of them all.

¹⁷ Pay attention and turn your ear to the sayings of the wise; apply your heart to what I teach, ¹⁸ for it is pleasing when you keep them in your heart and have all of them ready on your lips. ¹⁹ [Let] your trust… be in the LORD…²¹ …[B]e honest and… speak the truth…

²² Do not exploit the poor because they are poor and do not crush the needy in court, ²³ for the LORD will take up their case…

Proverbs 23:

⁴ Do not wear yourself out to get rich; do not trust your own cleverness. ⁵ Cast but a glance at riches, and they are gone, for they will surely sprout wings and fly off to the sky like an eagle.

¹² Apply your heart to instruction and your ears to words of knowledge. ¹⁷ Do not let your heart envy sinners, but always be zealous for the fear of the LORD. ¹⁸ There is surely a future hope for you, and your hope will not be cut off.

¹⁹ Listen… and be wise, and set your heart on the right path… ²² Listen to your father… and do not despise your mother when she is old. ²³ Buy the truth and do not sell it — wisdom, instruction and insight as well. ²⁴ The father of a righteous child has great joy…²⁵ May your father and mother rejoice… [and] be joyful!

Proverbs 24:

³ By wisdom a house is built, and through understanding it is established; ⁴ through knowledge its rooms are filled with rare and beautiful treasures.

¹⁰ If you falter in a time of trouble, how small is your strength! ¹¹ Rescue those being led away to death; hold back those staggering toward slaughter. ¹² If you say, "But we knew nothing about this," does not [H]e who weighs the heart perceive it? Does not [H]e who guards your life know it? Will [H]e not repay everyone according to what they have done?

¹⁴ …Know …that wisdom is like honey… If you find it, there is a future hope for you, and

your hope will not be cut off.

¹⁷ Do not gloat when your enemy falls; when they stumble, do not let your heart rejoice…

²⁶ An honest answer is like a kiss on the lips.

²⁸ Do not testify against your neighbor without cause — would you use your lips to mislead? ²⁹ Do not say, "I'll do to them as they have done to me; I'll pay them back for what they did."

Proverbs 25:

⁶ Do not exalt yourself in the king's presence, and do not claim a place among his great men; ⁷ it is better for him to say to you, "Come up here," than for him to humiliate you before his nobles.

¹¹ Like apples of gold in settings of silver is a ruling rightly given. ¹² Like an earring of gold or an ornament of fine gold is the rebuke of a wise judge to a listening ear.

¹⁵ Through patience a ruler can be persuaded…

¹⁸ Like a club or a sword or a sharp arrow is one who gives false testimony against a neighbor. ¹⁹ Like a broken tooth or a lame foot is reliance on the unfaithful in a time of trouble. ²⁰ Like one who takes away a garment on a cold day, or like vinegar poured on a wound, is one who sings songs to a heavy heart.

²¹ If your enemy is hungry, give him food to eat; if he is thirsty, give him water to drink. ²² In doing this… the LORD will reward you.

²⁵ Like cold water to a weary soul is good news from a distant land. ²⁶ Like a muddied spring or a polluted well are the righteous who give way to the wicked. ²⁸ Like a city whose walls are broken through is a person who lacks self-control.

Proverbs 26:

¹ Like snow in summer or rain in harvest, honor is not fitting for a fool. ⁹ Like a thorn bush in a drunkard's hand is a proverb in the mouth of a fool.

²⁰ Without wood a fire goes out; without a gossip a quarrel dies down. ²¹ As charcoal to embers and as wood to fire, so is a quarrelsome person for kindling strife.

²⁷ Whoever digs a pit will fall into it; if someone rolls a stone, it will roll back on them.

Proverbs 27:

¹ Do not boast about tomorrow, for you do not know what a day may bring.

² Let someone else praise you, and not your own mouth; an outsider, and not your own lips.

³ Stone is heavy and sand a burden, but a fool's provocation is heavier than both. ⁴ Anger is cruel and fury overwhelming, but who can stand before jealousy?

9 Perfume and incense bring joy to the heart, and the pleasantness of a friend springs from their heartfelt advice.

19 As water reflects the face, so one's life reflects the heart.

Proverbs 28:

1 …[T]he righteous are as bold as a lion. **12** When the righteous triumph, there is great elation… **18** The one whose walk is blameless is kept safe… **20** A faithful person will be richly blessed…

26 Those who trust in themselves are fools, but those who walk in wisdom are kept safe. **5** Evildoers do not understand what is right, but those who seek the LORD understand it fully.

13 Whoever conceals their sins does not prosper, but the one who confesses and renounces them finds mercy. **14** Blessed is the one who always trembles before God, but whoever hardens their heart falls into trouble.

Proverbs 29:

2 When the righteous thrive, the people rejoice… **11** …[T]he wise bring calm in the end. **18** …[B]lessed is the one who heeds wisdom's instruction. **25** …[W]hoever trusts in the LORD is kept safe. **26** …[I]t is from the LORD that one gets justice.

20 Do you see someone who speaks in haste? There is more hope for a fool than for them. **23** Pride brings a person low, but the lowly in spirit gain honor.

10 The bloodthirsty hate a person of integrity and seek to kill the upright. **6** Evildoers are snared by their own sin, but the righteous shout for joy and are glad.

Proverbs 30:

1 "I am weary, God, but I can prevail. **2** Surely I am only a brute, not a man; I do not have human understanding. **3** I have not learned wisdom, nor have I attained to the knowledge of the Holy One. **4** Who has gone up to heaven and come down? Whose hands have gathered up the wind? Who has wrapped up the waters in a cloak? Who has established all the ends of the earth? What is [H]is name, and what is the name of [H]is son? Surely you know!

5 Every word of God is flawless; [H]e is a shield to those who take refuge in [H]im. **6** Do not add to [H]is words…

7 Two things I ask of [Y]ou, LORD; do not refuse me before I die: **8** Keep falsehood and lies far from me; give me neither poverty nor riches, but give me only my daily bread. **9** Otherwise, I may have too much… and say, 'Who is the LORD?' Or I may become poor and steal, and so dishonor the name of my God."

Proverbs 31:

8 Speak up for those who cannot speak for themselves, for the rights of all who are destitute. **9** Speak up and judge fairly; defend the rights of the poor and needy.

Ecclesiastes 2:

26 To the person who pleases [H]im, God gives wisdom, knowledge and happiness…

Ecclesiastes 3:

1 There is a time for everything, and a season for every activity under the heavens:

2 [A] time to be born and a time to die, a time to plant and a time to uproot, 3 …a time to tear down and a time to build, 4 a time to weep and a time to laugh, a time to mourn and a time to dance, 5 a time to scatter stones and a time to gather them, a time to embrace and a time to refrain from embracing, 6 a time to search and a time to give up, a time to keep and a time to throw away… 7 a time to mend, a time to be silent and a time to speak, 8 a time to love… 3 a time to heal… 8 and a time for peace.

9 What do workers gain from their toil? 10 I have seen the burden God has laid on the human race. 11 He has made everything beautiful in its time. He has also set eternity in the human heart; yet no one can fathom what God has done from beginning to end. 14 I know that everything God does will endure forever; nothing can be added to it and nothing taken from it…

Ecclesiastes 5:

2 Do not be quick with your mouth, do not be hasty in your heart to utter anything before God. God is in heaven and you are on earth, so let your words be few. 4 When you make a vow to God, do not delay to fulfill it… 5 It is better not to make a vow than to make one and not fulfill it. 6 Do not let your mouth lead you into sin…

10 Whoever loves money never has enough; whoever loves wealth is never satisfied with their income… 12 The sleep of a laborer is sweet, whether they eat little or much, but as for the rich, their abundance permits them no sleep. 15 Everyone comes naked from their mother's womb, and as everyone comes, so they depart. They take nothing…

Ecclesiastes 7:

1 A good name is better than fine perfume, and the day of death better than the day of birth. 2 It is better to go to a house of mourning than to go to a house of feasting…

3 Frustration is better than laughter, because a sad face is good for the heart. 4 The heart of the wise is in the house of mourning, but the heart of fools is in the house of pleasure. 5 It is better to heed the rebuke of a wise person than to listen to the song of fools. 6 Like the crackling of thorns under the pot, so is the laughter of fools.

8 The end of a matter is better than its beginning, and patience is better than pride. 9 Do not be quickly provoked in your spirit, for anger resides in the lap of fools.

11 Wisdom, like an inheritance, is a good thing and benefits those who see the sun. 12 Wisdom is a shelter… [It] preserves those who have it.

13 Consider what God has done: Who can straighten what [H]e has made crooked? 14 When times are good, be happy; but when times are bad, consider this: God has made the one as well as the other…

20 Indeed, there is no one on earth… who does what is right and never sins. 21 Do not

pay attention to every word people say… [22] for you know in your heart that many times you yourself have cursed others.

[29] [Thus] "God created mankind upright, but they have gone in search of many schemes."

Ecclesiastes 9:

[7] The quiet words of the wise are more to be heeded than the shouts of a ruler of fools. [18] Wisdom is better than weapons of war…

Ecclesiastes 12:

[13] …Fear God and keep [H]is commandments, for this is the duty of all mankind. [14] For God will bring every deed into judgment, including every hidden thing, whether it is good or evil.

Tobit 4:

[15] Never do to anyone else anything that you would not want someone to do to you.

Papyrus Berolinensis 22220 ("Gospel of the Savior"):

[62] No portion is greater than your own, nor is any glory more exalted than yours.

Mary Magdalene 4:

[22] All nature, all formations, all creatures exist… with one another…

[24] He who has ears to hear, let him hear. [29] He who has a mind to understand, let him understand.

[31] …Be of good courage, and if you are discouraged be encouraged…

Islam:

The Cow 2:20, 152-153 …[God] has power over all things. …[R]emember Me, I will remember you. …[God] is with the patient.

The Cow 2:156 …Surely we are [God's] and to Him we shall surely return.

The Spider 29:57 Every soul must taste of death, then to [the Lord] you shall be brought back. The Beneficent 55:27 And there will endure for ever the person of your Lord, the Lord of glory and honor. The Beneficent 55:60 Is the reward of goodness aught but goodness?

The Children of Israel 17:15 Whoever goes aright, for his own soul does he go aright… The Companions 39:10 [F]or those who do good in this world is good…

The Chambers 49:13 …[S]urely the most honorable of you with [God] is the one among you most careful (of his duty)… Qaf 50:16 …[I] [am] nearer to him than his life-vein.

The Book of Imran 3:195 I will not lose sight of the labor of any of you who labors in My way, be it man or woman; each of you is equal to the other.

The Cow 2:256 There is no compulsion in religion… The Cow 2:286 [God] does not impose upon any soul a duty but to the extent of its ability…

The Book of Imran 3:103 And hold fast by the covenant of [God] all together and be not disunited, and remember the favor of [God] on you… The Chambers 49:10 The believers are but brethren, therefore make peace between your brethren and be careful of (your duty to) [God] that mercy may be had on you.

The Star 53:38-42 …[N]o bearer of burden shall bear the burden of another – And that man shall have nothing but what he strives for – And that his striving shall soon be seen – Then shall he be rewarded for it with the fullest reward – And that to your Lord is the goal…

The Scatterers 51:15-16 Surely those who guard (against evil) shall be in gardens and fountains. Taking what their Lord gives them; surely they were before that, the doers of good.

The Dinner Table 5:32 [W]hoever slays a soul… it is as though he slew all men; and whoever keeps it alive, it is as though he kept alive all men…

Judaism:

Source: Mishnah, Abot 1:2:

The world stands upon three things: upon the Law, upon worship and upon showing kindness.

Source: Talmud *Shabbat* 31a:

That which is hateful to you, do not do to your fellow...

Source: Talmud Sanhedrin 4:8 (37a):

Whoever destroys a [life], it is considered as if he destroyed an entire world. And whoever saves a life, it is considered as if he saved an entire world.

Source: Talmud Avot 2:4:

Make that His will should be your will, so that He should make your will to be as His will…

Source: Talmud *Midrash Sifre to Bamidbar* 27:

God's compassion extends to men and women; God's compassion extends to all… His works.

Source: Talmud:

Make [your] study of the word of The Eternal a fixed practice; say little and do much; and receive all countenance.

He that gives should never remember. He that receives should never forget… The highest form of wisdom is kindness… The Divine Spirit does not reside in any except the joyful heart.

Sin is sweet in the beginning, but bitter in the end.

If silence be good for the wise, how much better for fools.

Man has three friends on whose company he relies. First, "wealth" which goes with him only while good fortune lasts. Second, his "relatives" they go only as far as the grave and leave him there. The third friend, his "good deeds," go with him beyond the grave.

Who can protest an injustice but does not is an accomplice to the act.

Despise no [person] and consider nothing impossible... [for] God does not rejoice with the fall of the wicked.

Aboriginal:

We are all visitors... We are just passing through. Our purpose here is to observe, to learn, to grow, to love... and then we return home [to God].

The more you know, the less you need.

Bahaism:

Source: Bahá'u'lláh:

Blessed is he who prefer[s] his brother before himself.

Ascribe not to any soul that which [you] [would] not have ascribed to [you]... Beware lest [you] harm any soul, or make any heart to sorrow; lest [you] wound any [person] with your words...

So powerful is the light of unity that it can illuminate the whole earth.

Buddhism:

Source: Buddha:

[They] who experience the unity of life sees [their] own Self in all beings.

Source: Japanese Buddhist Proverbs. 11 April 2011. http://www.sacred-texts.com/shi/igj/igj12.htm

The future life is the all-important thing; [o]nly by reason of having died does one enter into life.

Life is a lamp-flame before a wind. Human life is like the dew of morning... The flower goes back to its root; [t]he fallen blossom never returns to the branch.

The mouth is the front-gate of all misfortune. All evil done clings to the body.

Source: Buddhist Maxims. 11 April 2011. http://oaks.nvg.org/buddhist-proverbs.html

Those who wish for divine wealth, life, glory and happiness should avoid doing all kinds of evil; [l]et [one] avoid evil as someone of great wealth avoids a dangerous road... Never does a wise [person] commit a sin for the sake of his happiness. Never will [they] discard morality, even though [they] may suffer...

[They] who [have] done meritorious deeds [rejoice] both in [t]his present life and in the hereafter. All sentient beings are seekers after happiness. [Those] who [do] not violate other persons for the sake of [their] happiness will attain happiness later.

Forbearance is the chief cause of all virtues such as morality and concentration. All other virtues increase with the development of forbearance.

Only good words should be spoken, never evil ones. Uttering good words is profitable. One who utters evil words will have to regret.

Confucianism:

Source: Confucius:

Heaven means to be one with God. The firm, the enduring, the simple, and the modest are near to virtue.

Heaven covers all without partiality; earth sustains and embraces without partiality; the sun and the moon shine upon all without partiality.

If Heaven and earth were to have no inter-communication, things would not grow and flourish as they do.

Speak the truth, do not yield to anger; give, if [you are] asked for little; by these three steps [you will attain salvation]. To practice... gravity, generosity of soul, sincerity, earnestness, and kindness... under all circumstances constitutes perfect virtue... To see and listen to the wicked is already the beginning of wickedness.

Do not impose on others what you yourself do not desire.

Learning without thought is labor lost; thought without learning is perilous; [i]gnorance is the night of the mind... a night without moon and star.

Forget injuries, never forget kindnesses. To be wronged is nothing unless you continue to remember it. When anger rises, think of the consequences. Before you embark on a journey of revenge, dig two graves.

It is not Heaven that does not deal impartially with [people], but [people who] ruin themselves... Be not like them who reject this and cling to that. Be not like them who are ruled by their likes and desires... If the will be set on virtue, there will be no... wickedness.

Perfect is the virtue which is according to the mean.

To see what is right and not to do it, is want of courage.

Notes of the same pitch respond to one another; creatures of the same nature seek one another... Things that have their origin in Heaven, tend upward.

Hinduism:

Source: Sri Sivananda. The Science Of Seven Cultures. 21 February 2005:

[7] Speak the TRUTH. Speak little. Speak kindly. Speak sweetly. [8] Do not injure anyone in thought, word or deed. Be kind to all. [9] Be sincere, straightforward and open-hearted in your talks and dealings. [10] Be honest. Earn by the sweat of your brow. Do not accept any money, things or [favor] unless earned lawfully. Develop nobility and integrity. [11]

169

Control fits of anger by serenity, patience, love, mercy and tolerance. Forget and forgive…

Source: **32 Famous Hindu Proverbs.** Special Dictionary. 2011. http://www.special-dictionary.com/proverbs/source/h/hindu_proverb/

A [person] in this world without learning is as a beast of the field.

[They] who [do] kind deeds become rich. They who give have all things; they who withhold have nothing.

North American Indian:

Cherokee:

When you were born, you cried and the world rejoiced. Live your life so that when you die, the world cries and you rejoice.

Cheyenne:

Do not judge your neighbor until you walk two moons in his moccasins.

Mourning Dove Salish (1888-1936) and Chief Seattle, Suquamish (c. 1780-1866):

…[E]verything on the earth has a purpose… We are but one thread in… the web of life… All things are bound together… All things share the same breath – the beast, the tree, the [person]… [God's] compassion is equal for [all].

Polingaysi Qoyawayma, Hopi (1892-1990):

We… are clay blended by the Master Potter, come from the kiln of Creation in many hues. How can people say one skin is colored, when each has its own coloration? What should it matter that one bowl is dark and ther other pale, if each is of good design and serves its purpose well.

Rolling Thunder, Cherokee/Shoshone (1916-1997):

[U]nderstanding begins with love and respect. It begins with respect for the Great Spirit (God) and [recognition that] the Great Spirit is the life that is in all things.

Tecumseh, Shawnee Nation (1768-1813):

…[L]ive your life that the fear of death can never enter your heart. Trouble no one; respect others in their view… Beautify all things in your life… When you arise… give thanks for the food and for the joy of living… If you see no reason for giving thanks, the fault lies only in yourself.

Shintoism:

Even the wishes of an ant reach to heaven… A single sincere prayer moves heaven… Sincerity… binds [God] and [people] in one… Come to Me daily with… [a] pure heart.

Sufism:

Source: Hazrat Inayat Khan:

"To understand all is to forgive all."

The "Luminous" Religion:

"He who speaks does not know and he who knows does not speak."

XVIII. The Book of Isaiah

Christianity/Judaism:

Isaiah 6:

[1] ... I (Isaiah) saw the Lord, high and exalted, seated on a throne; and the train of his robe filled the temple. [2] Above [H]im were seraphim, each with six wings: With two wings they covered their faces, with two they covered their feet, and with two they were flying. [3] And they were calling to one another: "Holy, holy, holy is the LORD Almighty; the whole earth is full of [H]is glory."

[4] At the sound of their voices the doorposts and thresholds shook and the temple was filled with smoke. [5] "Woe to me!" I cried. "I am ruined! For I am a man of unclean lips, and I live among a people of unclean lips, and my eyes have seen the King, the LORD Almighty."

[6] Then one of the seraphim flew to me with a live coal in his hand, which he had taken with tongs from the altar. [7] With it he touched my mouth and said, "See, this has touched your lips; your guilt is taken away and your sin atoned for." [8] Then I heard the voice of the Lord saying, "Whom shall I send? And who will go for us?" And I said, "Here am I. Send me!"

Isaiah 1:

[2] Hear me, you heavens! Listen, earth! For the LORD has spoken: [16] "Wash and make yourselves clean... [S]top doing wrong. [17] Learn to do right; seek justice. Defend the oppressed. Take up the cause of the fatherless; plead the case of the widow. [18] [Then] [t]hough your sins are like scarlet, they shall be as white as snow; though they are red as crimson, they shall be like wool. [19] If you are willing and obedient, you will eat the good things of the land..."

Isaiah 2:

[2] In the last days the mountain of the LORD's temple will be established as the highest of the mountains; it will be exalted above the hills, and all nations will stream to it. [3] Many peoples will come and say, "Come, let us go up to the mountain of the LORD... He will teach us [H]is ways, so that we may walk in [H]is paths." The law will go out [to all the world], the word of the LORD from Jerusalem.

[4] He will judge between the nations and will settle disputes for many peoples. *They will beat their swords into plowshares and their spears into pruning hooks. Nation will not take up sword against nation, nor will they train for war anymore.*

[5] Come... let us walk in the light of the LORD.

Isaiah 3:

[10] [For] the righteous it will be well... for they will enjoy the fruit of their deeds.

Isaiah 4:

[2] In that day the Branch of the LORD will be beautiful and glorious, and the fruit of the land will be the pride and glory of the survivors (the righteous). [3] [They]... will be called holy, all who are recorded among the living... [5] Then the LORD will create over all... a cloud of smoke by day and a glow of flaming fire by night; over everything the glory will be a canopy. [6] It will be a shelter and shade from the heat of the day, and a refuge and hiding place from the storm and rain.

Isaiah 7:

[13] ...Isaiah said, [14] "...[T]he Lord... will give you a sign: The virgin will conceive and give birth to a son, and will call him Immanuel. [15] He will be eating curds and honey when he knows enough to reject the wrong and choose the right... [17] The LORD will bring... a time unlike any..."

Isaiah 8:

[13] The LORD Almighty is the [O]ne you are to regard as holy, [H]e is the [O]ne you are to fear... [14] He will be a holy place...

[17] I will wait for the LORD... I will put my trust in [H]im. [18] Here am I, and the children the LORD has given me. We are signs and symbols... from the LORD Almighty...

[20] Consult God's instruction...

Isaiah 9:

[1] ...[T]here will be no more gloom for those who were in distress. [2] The people walking in darkness have seen a great light; on those living in the land of deep darkness a light has dawned. [3] You have enlarged the nation and increased their joy; they rejoice before [Y]ou as people rejoice at the harvest...

[4] For... [Y]ou have shattered the yoke that burdens them, the bar across their shoulders, the rod of their oppressor. [6] For to us a child is born, to us a son is given... [a]nd he will be called Wonderful Counselor, Mighty God, Everlasting Father, Prince of Peace.

[7] ...He will reign on David's throne and over his kingdom, establishing and upholding it with justice and righteousness from that time on and forever. The zeal of the LORD Almighty will accomplish this.

Isaiah 11:

[1] A shoot will come up from the stump of Jesse; from his roots a Branch will bear fruit. [2] The Spirit of the LORD will rest on him — the Spirit of wisdom and of understanding, the Spirit of counsel and of might, the Spirit of the knowledge and fear of the LORD — [3] and he will delight in the fear of the LORD.

He will not judge by what he sees with his eyes, or decide by what he hears with his ears; ⁴ but with righteousness he will judge the needy, with justice he will give decisions for the poor of the earth… ⁵ Righteousness will be his belt and faithfulness the sash around his waist.

⁶ The wolf will live with the lamb, the leopard will lie down with the goat, the calf and the lion and the yearling together; and a little child will lead them. ⁷ The cow will feed with the bear, their young will lie down together, and the lion will eat straw like the ox. ⁸ The infant will play near the cobra's den, the young child will put its hand into the viper's nest. ⁹ They will neither harm nor destroy on all [M]y holy mountain, for the earth will be filled with the knowledge of the LORD as the waters cover the sea.

¹⁰ In that day the Root of Jesse will stand as a banner for the peoples; the nations will rally to him, and his resting place will be glorious. ¹¹ In that day the Lord will reach out [H]is hand a second time… ¹² He will raise a banner for the nations and gather the exiles…; [H]e will assemble the scattered people… from the four quarters of the earth…

Isaiah 12:

¹ In that day you will say: "I will praise you, LORD. …[Y]ou have comforted me. ² Surely God is my salvation; I will trust and not be afraid. The LORD, the LORD [H]imself, is my strength and my defense; [H]e has become my salvation." ³ With joy you will draw water from the wells of salvation.

⁴ In that day you will say: "Give praise to the LORD, proclaim [H]is name; make known among the nations what [H]e has done, and proclaim that [H]is name is exalted. ⁵ Sing to the LORD, for [H]e has done glorious things; let this be known to all the world. ⁶ Shout aloud and sing for joy… for great is the Holy One…"

Isaiah 17:

⁷ In that day people will look to their Maker and turn their eyes to the Holy One…

Isaiah 24:

²³ …[T]he LORD Almighty will reign… with great glory.

Isaiah 25:

¹ LORD, [Y]ou are my God; I will exalt [Y]ou and praise [Y]our name, for in perfect faithfulness [Y]ou have done wonderful things, things planned long ago. ⁴ You have been a refuge for the poor, a refuge for the needy in their distress, a shelter from the storm and a shade from the heat.

⁶ On this mountain the LORD Almighty will prepare a feast of rich food for all peoples, a banquet of aged wine — the best of meats and the finest of wines. ⁸ [H]e will swallow up death forever. The Sovereign LORD will wipe away the tears from all faces…

⁹ In that day they will say, "Surely this is our God; we trusted in [H]im, and [H]e saved us. This is the LORD, we trusted in [H]im; let us rejoice and be glad in [H]is salvation."

Isaiah 26:

¹ In that day this song will be sung…: We have a strong city; God makes salvation its walls and ramparts. ² Open the gates that the righteous… may enter… ³ You will keep in perfect peace those whose minds are steadfast, because they trust in [Y]ou. ⁴ Trust in the LORD forever, for the LORD, the LORD [H]imself, is the Rock eternal.

⁷ The path of the righteous is level; [Y]ou, the Upright One, make the way of the righteous smooth. ⁸ Yes, LORD, walking in the way of [Y]our laws, we wait for [Y]ou; [Y]our name and renown are the desire of our hearts.

⁹ My soul yearns for [Y]ou in the night; in the morning my spirit longs for [Y]ou. When [Y]our judgments come upon the earth, the people of the world learn righteousness. ¹² LORD, [Y]ou establish peace for us; all that we have accomplished [Y]ou have done for us. ¹³ LORD our God… [Y]our name alone do we honor.

¹⁹ …[Y]our dead will live, LORD; their bodies will rise — let those who dwell in the dust wake up and shout for joy — your dew is like the dew of the morning; the earth will give birth to her dead.

Isaiah 27:

² In that day — "Sing about a fruitful vineyard: ³ I, the LORD, watch over it; I water it continually. I guard it day and night so that no one may harm it." ⁶ [It]… will take root, [it] will bud and blossom and fill all the world with fruit. ⁹ …[T]his will be the full fruit of the removal of… sin… ¹² In that day… [all] will be gathered up one by one. ¹³ …[A] great trumpet will sound [and all]… will come and worship the LORD on the holy mountain in Jerusalem.

⁵ "…[L]et them come to [M]e for refuge; let them make peace with [M]e, yes, let them make peace with [M]e."

Isaiah 28:

⁵ In that day the LORD Almighty will be a glorious crown, a beautiful wreath for… [H]is people. ⁶ He will be a spirit of justice… a source of strength. ¹¹ …God will speak, "This is the resting place, let the weary rest…" ¹⁴ Therefore hear the word of the LORD… ¹⁶ "See, I lay a… precious cornerstone for a sure foundation; the one who relies on it will never be stricken with panic. ¹⁷ I will make justice the measuring line and righteousness the plumb line…"

²⁹ All this… comes from the LORD Almighty, [W]hose plan is wonderful, [W]hose wisdom is magnificent.

Isaiah 29:

¹⁶ …Shall what is formed say to the One Who formed it, "You did not make me?"

²² Therefore this is what the LORD… says: ²³ When they see… the work of [M]y hands, they will keep [M]y name holy; they will acknowledge the holiness of the Holy One… and

175

will stand in awe of... God. ²⁴ Those who are wayward in spirit will gain understanding; those who complain will accept instruction."

Isaiah 30:

¹⁵ This is what the Sovereign LORD... says: "In repentance and rest is your salvation, in quietness and trust is your strength..." [Though] you would have none of it... "[b]ecause you... relied on oppression and depended on deceit... ¹⁸ ...[T]he LORD longs to be gracious to you; therefore [H]e will... show you compassion. For the LORD is a God of justice. Blessed are all who wait for [H]im!

¹⁹ ...[Y]ou will weep no more. How gracious [H]e will be when you cry for help! As soon as [H]e hears, [H]e will answer you.

²³ He will also send you rain for the seed you sow in the ground, and the food that comes from the land will be rich and plentiful. ²⁶ The moon will shine like the sun, and the sunlight will be seven times brighter, like the light of seven full days, when the LORD binds up the bruises of [H]is people and heals the[ir] wounds...

³⁰ The LORD will cause people to hear [H]is majestic voice... ²¹ Whether you turn to the right or to the left, your ears will hear a voice behind you, saying, "This is the way; walk in it." ²⁹ And you will sing...; your hearts will rejoice...

Isaiah 32:

¹ See, a king will reign in righteousness and rulers will rule with justice. ² Each one will be like a shelter from the wind and a refuge from the storm, like streams of water in the desert and the shadow of a great rock in a thirsty land. ³ Then the eyes of those who see will no longer be closed, and the ears of those who hear will listen. ⁴ The fearful heart will know and understand, and the stammering tongue will be fluent and clear.

¹⁶ The LORD's justice will dwell in the desert, [H]is righteousness live in the fertile field. ¹⁷ The fruit of that righteousness will be peace; its effect will be quietness and confidence forever. ¹⁸ My people will live in peaceful dwelling places, in secure homes, in undisturbed places of rest. ²⁰ [H]ow blessed you will be, sowing your seed by every stream, and letting your cattle and donkeys range free.

Isaiah 33:

² LORD, be gracious to us; we long for [Y]ou. Be our strength every morning, our salvation in time of distress.

⁵ The LORD is exalted, for [H]e dwells on high; [H]e will fill [you] with [H]is justice and righteousness. ⁶ He will be the sure foundation for your times, a rich store of salvation and wisdom and knowledge; the fear of the LORD is the key to this treasure.

¹⁵ Those who walk righteously and speak what is right, who reject gain from extortion and keep their hands from accepting bribes, who stop their ears against plots of murder and shut their eyes against contemplating evil — ¹⁶ they are the ones who will dwell on

the heights, whose refuge will be the mountain fortress. Their bread will be supplied, and water will not fail them.

[17] Your eyes will see the king in [H]is beauty and view a land that stretches afar... [20] ...[Y]our eyes will see Jerusalem, a peaceful abode, a tent that will not be moved; its stakes will never be pulled up, nor any of its ropes broken. [21] There the LORD will be our Mighty One. [22] For the LORD is our judge, the LORD is our lawgiver, the LORD is our king; it is [H]e who will save us.

[23] ...Then an abundance of spoils will be divided... [24] and...sins... will be forgiven.

Isaiah 35:

[1] The desert and the parched land will be glad; the wilderness will rejoice and blossom. Like the crocus, [2] it will burst into bloom; it will rejoice greatly and shout for joy. ...[T]hey will see the glory of the LORD, the splendor of our God.

[3] Strengthen the feeble hands, steady the knees that give way; [4] say to those with fearful hearts, "Be strong, do not fear; your God will come... [H]e will come to save you."

[5] Then will the eyes of the blind be opened and the ears of the deaf unstopped. [6] Then will the lame leap like a deer, and the mute tongue shout for joy. Water will gush forth in the wilderness and streams in the desert. [7] The burning sand will become a pool, the thirsty ground bubbling springs. In the haunts where jackals once lay, grass and reeds and papyrus will grow.

[8] And a highway will be there; it will be called the Way of Holiness; it will be for those who walk on that Way... [9] ...[O]nly the redeemed will walk there, [10] and those the LORD has rescued will return. They will enter... with singing; everlasting joy will crown their heads. Gladness and joy will overtake them, and sorrow and sighing will flee away.

Isaiah 40:

[3] A voice of one calling: "In the wilderness prepare the way for the LORD; make straight in the desert a highway for our God. [4] Every valley shall be raised up, every mountain and hill made low; the rough ground shall become level, the rugged places a plain. [5] And the glory of the LORD will be revealed, and all people will see it together. [8] ...[T]he word of... God endures forever."

[9] You who bring good news... go up on a high mountain. You who bring good news... lift up your voice with a shout, lift it up, do not be afraid; say..., "Here is your God!"

[10] See, the Sovereign LORD comes with power, and [H]e rules with a mighty arm. See, [H]is reward is with [H]im, and [H]is recompense accompanies [H]im. [11] He tends [H]is flock like a shepherd: He gathers the lambs in [H]is arms and carries them close to [H]is heart; [H]e gently leads those that have young.

[12] Who has measured the waters in the hollow of his hand, or with the breadth of [H]is

hand marked off the heavens? Who has held the dust of the earth in a basket, or weighed the mountains on the scales and the hills in a balance? ¹³ Who can fathom the Spirit of the LORD, or instruct the LORD as his counselor? ¹⁴ Whom did the LORD consult to enlighten [H]im, and who taught [H]im the right way? Who was it that taught [H]im knowledge, or showed [H]im the path of understanding?

¹⁵ Surely the nations are like a drop in a bucket; they are regarded as dust on the scales; [H]e weighs the islands as though they were fine dust.

¹⁸ With whom, then, will you compare God? ²² He sits enthroned above the circle of the earth…   He stretches out the heavens like a canopy, and spreads them out like a tent to live in. ²⁵ "To whom will you compare [M]e? Or who is [M]y equal?" says the Holy One. 26 Lift up your eyes and look to the heavens: Who created all these? He who brings out the starry host one by one and calls forth each of them by name. Because of [H]is great power and mighty strength, not one of them is missing.

²⁸ Do you not know? The LORD is the everlasting God, the Creator of the ends of the earth. He will not grow tired or weary, and [H]is understanding no one can fathom. ²⁹ He gives strength to the weary and increases the power of the weak. ³⁰ Even youths grow tired and weary, and [the] young stumble and fall; ³¹ but those who hope in the LORD will renew their strength. They will soar on wings like eagles; they will run and not grow weary, they will walk and not be faint.

Isaiah 41:

⁹ "I took you from the ends of the earth, from its farthest corners I called you… I have chosen you and have not rejected you. ¹⁰ So do not fear, for I am with you; do not be dismayed, for I am your God.

I will strengthen you and help you; I will uphold you with my righteous right hand. ¹³ For I am the LORD your God [W]ho takes hold of your right hand and says to you, Do not fear; I will help you. ¹⁴ Do not be afraid… for I [M]yself will help you," declares the LORD…

¹⁷ "The poor and needy search for water, but there is none; their tongues are parched with thirst. But I the LORD will answer them; I… will not forsake them. ¹⁸ I will make rivers flow on barren heights, and springs within the valleys. I will turn the desert into pools of water, and the parched ground into springs. ¹⁹ I will put in the desert the cedar and the acacia, the myrtle and the olive. I will set junipers in the wasteland, the fir and the cypress together, ²⁰ so that people may see and know, may consider and understand, that the hand of the LORD has done this, that the Holy One… has created it."

Isaiah 42:

¹ "Here is [M]y servant, whom I uphold, [M]y chosen one in whom I delight; I will put [M]y Spirit on him, and he will bring justice to the nations. ² He will not shout or cry out, or raise his voice in the streets. ³ A bruised reed he will not break, and a smoldering wick he will not snuff out. In faithfulness he will bring forth justice; ⁴ he will not falter or be discouraged till he establishes justice on earth."

⁵ This is what God the LORD says — the Creator of the heavens, [W]ho stretches them out, [W]ho spreads out the earth with all that springs from it, [W]ho gives breath to its people, and life to those who walk on it: ⁶ "I, the LORD, have called you in righteousness; I will take hold of your hand. I will keep you and will make you to be a covenant for the people... ⁷ to open eyes that are blind, to free captives from prison and to release from the dungeon those who sit in darkness. ⁸ "I am the LORD! ⁹ See, the former things have taken place, and new things I declare; before they spring into being I announce them to you."

¹⁰ Sing to the LORD a new song, [H]is praise from the ends of the earth, you who go down to the sea, and all that is in it, you islands, and all who live in them. ¹¹ Let [all] raise their voices... rejoice... [and] sing for joy; let [all] shout from the mountaintops. ¹² Let [all] give glory to the LORD and proclaim [H]is praise...

¹⁶ I will lead the blind by ways they have not known, along unfamiliar paths I will guide them; I will turn the darkness into light before them and make the rough places smooth. These are the things I will do; I will not forsake them.

Isaiah 43:

¹ But now, this is what the LORD says — [H]e who created you... [H]e who formed you: "Do not fear, for I have redeemed you; I have summoned you by name; you are [M]ine. ² ...I will be with you...³ For I am the LORD your God, the Holy One... your Savior...

⁴ Since you are precious and honored in [M]y sight, and because I love you... ⁵ Do not be afraid, for I am with you; I will bring your children from the east and gather you from the west. ⁶ I will say to the north, 'Give them up!' and to the south, 'Do not hold them back.' Bring my sons from afar and my daughters from the ends of the earth — ⁷ everyone who is called by [M]y name, whom I created for [M]y glory, whom I formed and made."

⁸ Lead out those who have eyes but are blind, who have ears but are deaf. ⁹ All the nations gather together and the peoples assemble. ¹⁰ "You are [M]y witnesses," declares the LORD, "and my servant whom I have chosen, so that you may know and believe [M]e and understand that I am [H]e. ¹¹ ...[A]part from [M]e there is no savior. ¹² I have revealed and saved and proclaimed... You are my witnesses," declares the LORD, "that I am God."

Isaiah 44:

² This is what the LORD says — [H]e who made you, [W]ho formed you in the womb, and [W]ho will help you: Do not be afraid... ³ For I will pour water on the thirsty land, and streams on the dry ground; I will pour out [M]y Spirit on your offspring, and [M]y blessing on your descendants. ⁴ They will spring up like grass in a meadow, like poplar trees by flowing streams...

⁶ "This is what the LORD says — ...I am the first and I am the last; apart from [M]e there is no God. ⁸ Do not tremble, do not be afraid. Did I not proclaim this and foretell it long ago? You are my witnesses. ²¹ ...I have made you [and]... I will not forget you. ²² I

have swept away your offenses like a cloud, your sins like the morning mist. Return to [M]e, for I have redeemed you."

²³ Sing for joy, you heavens, for the LORD has done this; shout aloud, you earth beneath. Burst into song, you mountains, you forests and all your trees, for the LORD has redeemed [us].

Isaiah 45:

³ I will give you hidden treasures, riches stored in secret places, so that you may know that I am the LORD… ⁵ I am the LORD, and there is no other… I will strengthen you… ⁷ I form the light and create darkness, I bring prosperity … I, the LORD, do all these things.

⁸ "You heavens above, rain down my righteousness; let the clouds shower it down. Let the earth open wide, let salvation spring up, let righteousness flourish with it; I, the LORD, have created it. ¹² It is I who made the earth and created mankind on it. My own hands stretched out the heavens; I marshaled their starry hosts.

¹⁷ [You] will be saved by the LORD with an everlasting salvation; you will never be put to shame or disgraced, to ages everlasting. ¹⁸ For this is what the LORD says — "[H]e who created the heavens, [H]e is God; [H]e who fashioned and made the earth, [H]e founded it; [H]e did not create it to be empty, but formed it to be inhabited" — [H]e says: "I am the LORD, and there is no other. ¹⁹ I, the LORD, speak the truth; I declare what is right."

²² "Turn to [M]e and be saved, all you ends of the earth; for I am God, and there is no other. ²³ By [M]yself I have sworn, [M]y mouth has uttered in all integrity a word that will not be revoked: Before [M]e every knee will bow… ²⁴ They will say of [M]e, 'In the LORD alone are deliverance and strength.'"

Isaiah 46:

³ "Listen to [M]e… you whom I have upheld since your birth, and have carried since you were born. ⁴ …I am [H]e, I am [H]e [W]ho will sustain you. I have made you and I will carry you; I will sustain you and I will rescue you.

⁹ Remember… I am God, and there is no other; I am God, and there is none like me. ¹⁰ I make known the end from the beginning, from ancient times, what is still to come. ¹³ I am bringing [M]y righteousness near, it is not far away; and [M]y salvation will not be delayed. I will grant [My] salvation…

Isaiah 49:

⁵ …[T]he LORD says…⁶ "I will also make you a light for the Gentiles, that [M]y salvation may reach to the ends of the earth."

⁷ Th[e]… LORD says — to him who was despised and abhorred by the nation, to the servant of rulers: "Kings will see you and stand up, princes will see and bow down, because of the LORD, [W]ho is faithful… [W]ho has chosen you.

[8] In the time of [M]y favor I will answer you, and in the day of salvation I will help you; I will keep you and will make you to be a covenant for the people, to restore the land... [9] to say to the captives, 'Come out,' and to those in darkness, 'Be free!'"

"They will feed beside the roads and find pasture on every barren hill. [10] They will neither hunger nor thirst, nor will the desert heat or the sun beat down on them. He who has compassion on them will guide them and lead them beside springs of water. [11] I will turn all [M]y mountains into roads, and [M]y highways will be raised up. [12] See, they will come from afar — some from the north, some from the west..."

[13] Shout for joy, you heavens; rejoice, you earth; burst into song, you mountains! For the LORD comforts [H]is people and will have compassion on [H]is afflicted ones. [15] "Can a mother forget the baby at her breast and have no compassion on the child she has borne? Though she may forget, I will not forget you! [18] ...As surely as I live," declares the LORD...

[22] "...See, I will beckon to the nations, I will lift up [M]y banner to the peoples... [23] [T]hose who hope in [M]e will not be disappointed. [26] ...Then all mankind will know that I, the LORD, am your Savior, your Redeemer..."

Isaiah 50:

[4] The Sovereign LORD has given me a well-instructed tongue, to know the word that sustains the weary. He wakens me morning by morning, wakens my ear to listen like one being instructed. [5] The Sovereign LORD has opened my ears; I have not been rebellious, I have not turned away.

[6] I offered my back to those who beat me, my cheeks to those who pulled out my beard; I did not hide my face from mocking and spitting. [7] Because the Sovereign LORD helps me, I will not be disgraced. Therefore have I set my face like flint, and I know I will not be put to shame.

[8] He who vindicates me is near. Who then will bring charges against me? Let us face each other! Who is my accuser? Let him confront me! [9] It is the Sovereign LORD [W]ho helps me. Who will condemn me?

[10] Who among you fears the LORD and obeys the word of his servant? Let the one who walks in the dark, who has no light, trust in the name of the LORD and rely on their God.

Isaiah 51:

[1] "Listen to me, you who pursue righteousness and who seek the LORD: Look to the rock from which you were cut and to the quarry from which you were hewn; [2] look to Abraham, your father, and to Sarah, who gave you birth. When I called him he was only one man, and I blessed him and made him many."

[3] The LORD will surely comfort... and ...look with compassion...[H]e will make [the] deserts like Eden, ...wastelands like the garden of the LORD. Joy and gladness will be

found… [and] thanksgiving and the sound of singing.

[4] "Listen to [M]e…: …[M]y justice will become a light to the nations. My righteousness draws near speedily, [M]y salvation is on the way… [6] Lift up your eyes to the heavens, look at the earth beneath; the heavens will vanish like smoke, the earth will wear out like a garment… But [M]y salvation will last forever, [M]y righteousness will never fail.

[11] Those the LORD has rescued will [live]; everlasting joy will crown their heads. Gladness and joy will overtake them, and sorrow and sighing will flee away.

[14] The cowering prisoners will soon be set free; they will not die in their dungeon, nor will they lack bread. [15] For I am the LORD your God, who stirs up the sea so that its waves roar… [16] I have put [M]y words in your mouth and covered you with the shadow of my hand — I [W]ho set the heavens in place, [W]ho laid the foundations of the earth, and [W]ho say… 'You are my people.'"

Isaiah 52:

[1] Awake, awake… clothe yourself with strength! Put on your garments of splendor… [2] Shake off your dust; rise up… Free yourself from the chains on your neck… [3] For this is what the LORD says: "You were sold for nothing, and without money you will be redeemed."

[7] How beautiful on the mountains are the feet of those who bring good news, who proclaim peace, who bring good tidings, who proclaim salvation, who say… "Your God reigns!"

[8] Listen! Your watchmen lift up their voices; together they shout for joy. When the LORD returns… they will see it with their own eyes. [9] Burst into songs of joy together… for the LORD has comforted [H]is people… [10] …[A]ll the ends of the earth will see the salvation of… God.

[13] See, my servant will act wisely; he will be raised and lifted up and highly exalted. [14] Just as there were many who were appalled at him — his appearance was so disfigured beyond that of any human being and his form marred beyond human likeness — [15] so he will sprinkle many nations, and kings will shut their mouths because of him. For what they were not told, they will see, and what they have not heard, they will understand.

Isaiah 53:

[2] He grew up before him like a tender shoot, and like a root out of dry ground. He had no beauty or majesty to attract us to him, nothing in his appearance that we should desire him. [3] He was despised and rejected by mankind, a man of suffering, and familiar with pain. Like one from whom people hide their faces he was despised, and we held him in low esteem.

[4] Surely he took up our pain and bore our suffering… [5] [H]e was pierced for our transgressions, he was crushed for our iniquities; the punishment that brought us peace was on him, and by his wounds we are healed. [6] We all, like sheep, have gone astray,

each of us has turned to our own way; and [he bore] the iniquity of us all.

[7] He was oppressed and afflicted, yet he did not open his mouth; he was led like a lamb to the slaughter, and as a sheep before its shearers is silent, so he did not open his mouth.

[8] By oppression and judgment he was taken away. Yet who of his generation protested? For he was cut off from the land of the living; for [our] transgressions he was punished. [9] He was assigned a grave with the wicked... though he had done no violence, nor was any deceit in his mouth.

[10] [H]is life [was] an offering for sin... [11] After he has suffered, he will see the light of life and be satisfied... [12] Therefore I will give him a portion among the great, and he will divide the spoils... because he poured out his life unto death, and was numbered with the transgressors. For he bore the sin of many, and made intercession for the transgressors.

Isaiah 54:

[1] "Sing, barren woman, you who never bore a child; burst into song, shout for joy, you who were never in labor; because more are the children of the desolate woman than of her who has a husband," says the LORD.

[2] "Enlarge the place of your tent, stretch your tent curtains wide, do not hold back; lengthen your cords, strengthen your stakes. [3] For you[r] [descendants] will spread out to the right and to the left..."

[4] "Do not be afraid; you will not be put to shame. Do not fear disgrace; you will not be humiliated. You will forget the shame of your youth and remember no more the reproach of your widowhood. [5] For your Maker is your husband — the LORD Almighty is [H]is name — the Holy One... is your Redeemer; [H]e is called the God of all the earth. [8] "...I will have compassion on you," says the LORD your Redeemer.

[13] "All your children will be taught by the LORD, and great will be their peace. [14] In righteousness you will be established: Tyranny will be far from you; you will have nothing to fear. Terror will be far removed; it will not come near you. [17] [N]o weapon forged against you will prevail... This is the heritage of the servants of the LORD, and this is their vindication from me," declares the LORD.

Isaiah 55:

[3] ...I will make an everlasting covenant with you... [6] Seek the LORD while [H]e may be found; call on [H]im while [H]e is near. [7] Let the wicked forsake their ways and the unrighteous their thoughts. Let them turn to the LORD, and [H]e will have mercy on them... for [H]e will freely pardon.

[8] "For my thoughts are not your thoughts, neither are your ways my ways," declares the LORD. [9] "As the heavens are higher than the earth, so are [M]y ways higher than your ways and [M]y thoughts than your thoughts."

[10] As the rain and the snow come down from heaven, and do not return to it without watering the earth and making it bud and flourish, so that it yields seed for the sower and bread for the eater, [11] so is [M]y word that goes out from [M]y mouth: It will not return to [M]e empty, but will accomplish what I desire and achieve the purpose for which I sent it.

[12] You will go out in joy and be led forth in peace; the mountains and hills will burst into song before you, and all the trees of the field will clap their hands. [13] Instead of the thorn bush will grow the juniper, and instead of briers the myrtle will grow. This will be for the LORD's renown, for an everlasting sign, that will endure forever.

Isaiah 56:

[1] This is what the LORD says: "Maintain justice and do what is right, for [M]y salvation is close at hand and [M]y righteousness will soon be revealed. [2] Blessed is the one who does this — the person who holds it fast… and keeps their hands from doing any evil."

[3] Let no foreigner who is bound to the LORD say, "The LORD will surely exclude me from [H]is people." And let no eunuch complain, "I am only a dry tree." [7] [T]hese I will bring to [M]y holy mountain and give them joy in [M]y house of prayer… "for [M]y house will be called a house of prayer for all nations."

Isaiah 57:

[1] …[T]he devout are taken away, and no one understands that the righteous are taken away to be spared from evil. [2] Those who walk uprightly enter into peace; they find rest as they lie in death.

[14] And it will be said: "Build up, build up, prepare the road! Remove the obstacles out of the way of [M]y people." [15] For this is what the high and exalted One says — [H]e who lives forever, [W]hose name is holy: "I live in a high and holy place, but also with the one who is contrite and lowly in spirit, to revive the spirit of the lowly and to revive the heart of the contrite. [18] …I will heal them; I will guide them and restore comfort to [them]… [19] creating praise on their lips. Peace, peace, to those far and near," says the LORD.

Isaiah 58:

[6] "Is not this the kind of fasting I have chosen: to loose the chains of injustice and untie the cords of the yoke, to set the oppressed free and break every yoke? [7] Is it not to share your food with the hungry and to provide the poor wanderer with shelter — when you see the naked, to clothe them, and not to turn away from your own flesh and blood?"

[8] Then your light will break forth like the dawn, and your healing will quickly appear; then your righteousness will go before you, and the glory of the LORD will be your rear guard. [9] Then you will call, and the LORD will answer; you will cry for help, and [H]e will say: Here am I.

"If you do away with the yoke of oppression, with the pointing finger and malicious talk, [10] and if you spend yourselves in behalf of the hungry and satisfy the needs of the oppressed, then your light will rise in the darkness, and your night will become like the noonday. [11] The LORD will guide you always; [H]e will satisfy your needs in a sun-scorched land and will strengthen your frame.   You will be like a well-watered garden, like a spring whose waters never fail.

[13] If you keep your feet from breaking the Sabbath and from doing as you please on [M]y holy day, if you call the Sabbath a delight and the LORD's holy day honorable, and if you honor it by not going your own way and not doing as you please or speaking idle words, [14] then you will find your joy in the LORD..." For the mouth of the LORD has spoken.

Isaiah 59:

[1] Surely the arm of the LORD is not too short to save, nor [H]is ear too dull to hear.

[19] From the west, people will fear the name of the LORD, and from the rising of the sun, they will revere [H]is glory. For... [20] "[t]he Redeemer will come... to those... who repent of their sins," declares the LORD.

[21] "As for [M]e, this is [M]y covenant with them," says the LORD. "My Spirit, [W]ho is on you, will not depart from you, and [M]y words that I have put in your mouth will always be on your lips, on the lips of your children and on the lips of their descendants — from this time on and forever," says the LORD.

Isaiah 60:

[1] "Arise, shine, for your light has come, and the glory of the LORD rises upon you. [2] See, darkness covers the earth and thick darkness is over the peoples, but the LORD rises upon you and [H]is glory appears over you. [4] Lift up your eyes and look about you...[5] Then you will look and be radiant, your heart will throb and swell with joy...

[15] ...I will make you the everlasting pride and the joy of all generations. [17] Instead of bronze I will bring you gold, and silver in place of iron. Instead of wood I will bring you bronze, and iron in place of stones. I will make peace your governor and well-being your ruler. [18] No longer will violence be [upon you], nor ruin or destruction...

[19] The sun will no more be your light by day, nor will the brightness of the moonshine on you, for the LORD will be your everlasting light, and your God will be your glory. [20] Your sun will never set again, and your moon will wane no more; the LORD will be your everlasting light, and your days of sorrow will end. [21] Then all... people will be righteous and they will possess the land forever. They are the shoot I have planted, the work of [M]y hands, for the display of [M]y splendor."

Isaiah 61:

[1] The Spirit of the Sovereign LORD is on me, because the LORD has anointed me to proclaim good news to the poor. He has sent me to bind up the brokenhearted, to proclaim freedom for the captives and release from darkness for the prisoners... [2] to comfort all who mourn, [3] and provide for those who grieve... — to bestow on them a crown of beauty instead of ashes, the oil of joy instead of mourning, and a garment of praise instead of a spirit of despair.   They will be called oaks of righteousness, a planting of the LORD for the display of [H]is splendor.

^{7} ...[Y]ou will receive a double portion... you will rejoice in your inheritance. ...[A]nd everlasting joy will be yours. ^{8} "For I, the LORD, love justice... In [M]y faithfulness I will reward [M]y people and make an everlasting covenant with them. ^{9} ...All ...will acknowledge that they are a people the LORD has blessed."

^{10} I delight greatly in the LORD; my soul rejoices in my God. For [H]e has clothed me with garments of salvation and arrayed me in a robe of [H]is righteousness, as a bridegroom adorns his head like a priest, and as a bride adorns herself with her jewels. ^{11} For as the soil makes the sprout come up and a garden causes seeds to grow, so the Sovereign LORD will make righteousness and praise spring up before all nations.

Isaiah 62:

^{3} You will be a crown of splendor in the LORD's hand, a royal diadem in the hand of your God ^{4} ...for the LORD will take delight in you... ^{5} As a young man marries a young woman... as a bridegroom rejoices over his bride, so will your God rejoice over you.

^{11} The LORD has made proclamation to the ends of the earth: "See, your Savior comes! See, [H]is reward is with [H]im, and [H]is recompense accompanies [H]im." ^{12} [All] will be called... the Redeemed of the LORD...

Isaiah 63:

^{1} Who is this coming... with his garments stained crimson? Who is this, robed in splendor, striding forward in the greatness of his strength? "It is I, proclaiming victory, mighty to save."

^{2} Why are your garments red, like those of one treading the winepress? ^{3} "I have trodden the winepress alone; from the nations no one was with me... ^{5} I looked, but there was no one to help, I was appalled that no one gave support; so my own arm achieved salvation for me..."

^{7} I will tell of the kindnesses of the LORD, the deeds for which [H]e is to be praised, according to all the LORD has done for us — according to [H]is compassion and many kindnesses. ^{8} He said, "Surely they are [M]y people, children who will be true to me" and so [H]e became their Savior. ^{9} In all their distress [H]e too was distressed, and the angel of [H]is presence saved them. In [H]is love and mercy [H]e redeemed them; [H]e lifted them up and carried them...

Isaiah 64:

^{4} Since ancient times no one has heard, no ear has perceived, no eye has seen any God besides [Y]ou, who acts on behalf of those who wait for [H]im. ^{5} You come to the help of those who gladly do right, who remember [Y]our ways.

^{8} ...[Y]ou, LORD, are our Father. We are the clay, [Y]ou are the potter; we are all the work of [Y]our hand. ^{9} Do not... remember our sins forever. Oh, look on us, we pray, for we are all [Y]our people.

Isaiah 65:

^{1} "I revealed [M]yself to those who did not ask for [M]e; I was found by those who did not seek [M]e. To a nation that did not call on [M]y name, I said, 'Here am I, here am I.' [2] All day long I have held out my hands to an obstinate people…"

[13] Therefore this is what the Sovereign LORD says: "My servants will eat… [M]y servants will drink… [M]y servants will rejoice… [14] My servants will sing out of the joy of their hearts…

[17] "See, I will create new heavens and a new earth. The former things will not be remembered, nor will they come to mind. [18] But be glad and rejoice forever in what I will create… [19] I will rejoice… and take delight in [M]y people; the sound of weeping and of crying will be heard… no more.

[20] "Never again will there be.. an infant who lives but a few days, or an old man who does not live out his years… [21] They will build houses and dwell in them; they will plant vineyards and eat their fruit. [22] …For as the days of a tree, so will be the days of [M]y people; [M]y chosen ones will long enjoy the work of their hands. [23] They will not labor in vain, nor will they bear children doomed to misfortune; for they will be a people blessed by the LORD, they and their descendants with them. [24] Before they call I will answer; while they are still speaking I will hear.

[25] The wolf and the lamb will feed together, and the lion will eat straw like the ox, and dust will be the serpent's food. They will neither harm nor destroy on all [M]y holy mountain," says the LORD.

Isaiah 66:

[1] This is what the LORD says: "These are the ones I look on with favor: those who are humble and contrite in spirit, and who tremble at [M]y word."

[9] "Do I bring to the moment of birth and not give delivery?" says the LORD. "Do I close up the womb when I bring to delivery?" says your God. [10] "Rejoice… and be glad… [11] For you will nurse and be satisfied… you will… delight in… overflowing abundance."

[12] For this is what the LORD says: [13] "As a mother comforts her child, so will I comfort you; [14] When you see this, your heart will rejoice and you will flourish like grass; the hand of the LORD will be made known to [H]is servants…

[18] And I [will]… gather the people of all nations and languages, and they will come and see [M]y glory. [19] I will set a sign among them… They will proclaim [M]y glory among the nations.

[22] As the new heavens and the new earth that I make will endure before [M]e," declares the LORD, "so will your name and descendants endure. [23] From one New Moon to another and from one Sabbath to another, all mankind will come and bow down before [M]e," says the LORD.

"The Prophet Isaiah" by Ugolino
di Nerio c. 1317-1327

Islam:

The Children of Israel 17:4-7 And [I] had made known to the children of Israel in the Book: Most certainly you will make mischief in the land twice, and most certainly you will behave insolently with great insolence. So when the promise for the first of the two came, [I] sent over (to) you [My] servants, of mighty prowess, so they went to and fro among the houses, and it was a promise to be accomplished. Then [I]... aided you with wealth and children and made you a numerous band. If you do good, you will do good for your own souls...

The Believer 40:77-78 So be patient, surely the promise of [God] is true... And certainly [I] sent apostles before you: there are some of them that [I] have mentioned to you and there are others whom [I] have not mentioned to you, and it was not meet for an apostle that he should bring a sign except with [God's] permission, but when the command of [God] came, judgment was given with truth...

Buddhism:

Source: Buddhist Prophesies Fulfilled. 13 April 2011. http://www.bci.org/prophecy-fulfilled/Buddha.htm

[God] is the Unbounded Light... the Source of Wisdom, of Virtue...

In due time [one] will arise in the world, a Holy One, a supremely enlightened One, endowed with wisdom in conduct, auspicious knowing the universe, an incomparable leader... a Master of angels and mortals. He will reveal... [and] preach... eternal truths... wholly perfect and pure... He will be known as "Maitreya," which means "He Whose Name is 'kindness.'"

~Siddhãrtha Gautama (d. c. 486-483 BC)

Unum

XIX. The Book of Jeremiah

Christianity/Judaism:

Jeremiah 1:

⁴ The word of the LORD came to me, saying, ⁵ "Before I formed you in the womb I knew you, before you were born I set you apart; I appointed you as a prophet to the nations."

⁶ "Alas, Sovereign LORD," I said, "I do not know how to speak; I am too young." ⁷ But the LORD said to me, "Do not say, 'I am too young.' You must go to everyone I send you to and say whatever I command you. ⁸ Do not be afraid of them... ¹⁹ They will fight against you but will not overcome you, for I am with you and will rescue you," declares the LORD.

⁹ Then the LORD reached out [H]is hand and touched my mouth and said to me, "I have put [M]y words in your mouth. ¹⁰ See, today I appoint you over nations... to build and to plant."

¹¹ The word of the LORD came to me: "What do you see, Jeremiah?" "I see the branch of an almond tree," I replied. ¹² The LORD said to me, "You have seen correctly, for I am watching to see that [M]y word is fulfilled... ¹⁷ "Get yourself ready!"

Jeremiah 3:

¹¹ The LORD said to me... ¹² Go, proclaim this message: "Return, faithless... I will frown on you no longer, for I am faithful... ¹⁴ Return, faithless people... for I am your husband... I will give you shepherds after [M]y own heart, who will lead you with knowledge and understanding.

¹⁶ In those days, when your numbers have increased greatly in the land," declares the LORD, "people will no longer say, 'The ark of the covenant of the LORD.' It will never enter their minds or be remembered; it will not be missed, nor will another one be made. ¹⁷ At that time... all nations will gather... to honor the name of the LORD. No longer will they follow the stubbornness of their evil hearts.

¹⁹ I myself said, 'How gladly would I treat you like [M]y children and give you... the most beautiful inheritance...' I thought you would call [M]e 'Father' and not turn away from following me. ²⁰ But like a woman unfaithful to her husband... you... have been unfaithful to [M]e," declares the LORD.

²¹ A cry is heard on the barren heights, the weeping and pleading of the people... because they have perverted their ways and have forgotten the LORD their God. ²² "Return, faithless people; I will cure you of backsliding."

"Yes, we will come to [Y]ou, for [Y]ou are the LORD our God. ²³ Surely... in the LORD our God is [our] salvation...

²⁵ Let us lie down in our shame, and let our disgrace cover us. We have sinned against the LORD our God… [W]e have not obeyed the LORD our God."

Jeremiah 4:

³ This is what the LORD says: "Break up your unplowed ground and do not sow among thorns. ⁴ Circumcise yourselves to the LORD, circumcise your hearts…"

Jeremiah 6:

¹⁶ This is what the LORD says: "Stand at the crossroads and look; ask for the ancient paths, ask where the good way is, and walk in it, and you will find rest for your souls.

Jeremiah 8:

⁷ Even the stork in the sky knows her appointed seasons, and the dove, the swift and the thrush observe the time of their migration. But my people do not know the requirements of the LORD. ⁸ How can you say, 'We are wise…?'"

Jeremiah 9:

²³ "Let not the wise boast of their wisdom or the strong boast of their strength or the rich boast of their riches, ²⁴ but let the one who boasts boast about this: that they have the understanding to know [M]e, that I am the LORD, [W]ho exercises kindness, justice and righteousness on earth, for in these I delight," declares the LORD.

Jeremiah 10:

⁶ No one is like [Y]ou, LORD; [Y]ou are great, and [Y]our name is mighty in power. ⁷ Who should not fear [Y]ou, King of the nations? This is [Y]our due. Among all the wise leaders of the nations and in all their kingdoms, there is no one like [Y]ou.

¹² …God made the earth by [H]is power; [H]e founded the world by [H]is wisdom and stretched out the heavens by [H]is understanding. ¹³ When [H]e thunders, the waters in the heavens roar; [H]e makes clouds rise from the ends of the earth. He sends lightning with the rain and brings out the wind from his storehouses.

Jeremiah 11:

¹⁸ Because the LORD revealed their plot to me, I knew it, for at that time [H]e showed me what they were doing. ¹⁹ I had been like a gentle lamb led to the slaughter; I did not realize that they had plotted against me, saying, "Let us destroy the tree and its fruit; let us cut him off from the land of the living, that his name be remembered no more." ²⁰ But [Y]ou, LORD Almighty, [W]ho judge righteously… to [Y]ou I have committed my cause.

Jeremiah 15:

¹⁹ Therefore this is what the LORD says: "If you repent, I will restore you that you may serve [M]e; if you utter worthy, not worthless, words, you will be [M]y spokesman… ²¹ I will save you from the hands of the wicked and deliver you from the grasp of the cruel."

Jeremiah 17:

[7] "...[B]lessed is the one who trusts in the LORD, whose confidence is in [H]im. [8] They will be like a tree planted by the water that sends out its roots by the stream. It does not fear when heat comes; its leaves are always green. It has no worries in a year of drought and never fails to bear fruit."

[10] "I the LORD search the heart and examine the mind, to reward each person according to their conduct, according to what their deeds deserve." [13] LORD, you are the hope of [all]... [14] Heal me, LORD, and I will be healed; save me and I will be saved, for [Y]ou are the one I praise.

Jeremiah 18:

[18] They said, "Come, let's make plans against Jeremiah; for the teaching of the law by the priest will not cease, nor will counsel from the wise, nor the word from the prophets. So come, let's attack him with our tongues and pay no attention to anything he says."

Jeremiah 20:

[7] ...I am ridiculed all day long; everyone mocks me. [8] ...[T]he word of the LORD has brought me insult and reproach all day long. [9] But if I say, "I will not mention [H]is word or speak anymore in [H]is name," [H]is word is in my heart like a fire, a fire shut up in my bones. I am weary of holding it in; indeed, I cannot.

[10] I hear many whispering, "...Denounce him! Let's denounce him!" All my friends are waiting for me to slip, saying, "Perhaps... then we will prevail over him..." [11] But the LORD is with me... so my persecutors will stumble and not prevail. They will fail and be thoroughly disgraced... [12] LORD Almighty, [Y]ou who examine the righteous and probe the heart and mind... to [Y]ou I have committed my cause.

[13] Sing to the LORD! Give praise to the LORD! He rescues the life of the needy from the hands of the wicked.

Jeremiah 21:

[11] "...Hear the word of the LORD. [12] This is what the LORD says to you...: 'Administer justice every morning; rescue from the hand of the oppressor the one who has been robbed...'"

Jeremiah 22:

[3] This is what the LORD says: "Do what is just and right. Rescue from the hand of the oppressor the one who has been robbed. Do no wrong or violence to the foreigner, the fatherless or the widow, and do not shed innocent blood..."

Jeremiah 23:

[3] "I myself will gather the remnant of my flock out of all the countries... and will bring

them back to their pasture, where they will be fruitful and increase in number. **4** I will place shepherds over them who will tend them, and they will no longer be afraid or terrified, nor will any be missing," declares the LORD.

5 "The days are coming," declares the LORD, "when I will raise up... a righteous Branch, a King who will reign wisely and do what is just and right in the land. **6** In his days [the people] will be saved and... will live in safety. This is the name by which he will be called: The LORD Our Righteous Savior."

Jeremiah 30:

1 This is the word that came to Jeremiah from the LORD: **3** "The days are coming... when I will bring my people... back from captivity and restore them... **8** In that day," declares the LORD Almighty, "I will break the yoke off their necks and will tear off their bonds... **9** [T]hey will serve the LORD their God... **10** So do not be afraid... do not be dismayed...

11 I am with you and will save you," declares the LORD. **18** "I will... have compassion [on my people]. **19** From them will come songs of thanksgiving and the sound of rejoicing. I will add to their numbers, and they will not be decreased; I will bring them honor, and they will not be disdained. **21** ...I will bring [them] near and [they] will come close to [M]e... **22** 'So you will be [M]y people, and I will be your God.' **24** ...In days to come you will understand this."

Jeremiah 31:

1 "At that time," declares the LORD, "I will be the God of all... families... and they will be [M]y people."

7 This is what the LORD says: "Sing with joy... Make your praises heard, and say, 'LORD, save your people...' **8** See, I will bring them... and gather them from the ends of the earth. Among them will be the blind and the lame, expectant mothers and women in labor; a great throng will return. **9** They will come with weeping; they will pray as I bring them back. I will lead them beside streams of water on a level path where they will not stumble, because I am [their] father...

12 They will come and shout for joy... they will rejoice in the bounty of the LORD — the grain, the new wine and the olive oil, the young of the flocks and herds. They will be like a well-watered garden, and they will sorrow no more. **13** Then young women will dance and be glad, young men and old as well. I will turn their mourning into gladness; I will give them comfort and joy instead of sorrow," declares the LORD.

15 This is what the LORD says: "A voice is heard... Rachel weeping for her children and refusing to be comforted..." **16** This is what the LORD says: "Restrain your voice from weeping and your eyes from tears, for your work will be rewarded," declares the LORD. **17** "Your children will return..."

31 "The days are coming," declares the LORD, "when I will make a new covenant... **32** It will not be like the covenant I made [before]... **33** I will put [M]y law in their minds and write it on their hearts. I will be their God, and they will be [M]y people. **34** No longer will they teach their neighbor, or say to one another, 'Know the LORD,' because they will all know [M]e, from the least of them to the greatest," declares the LORD. "For I will forgive their wickedness and will remember their sins no more."

Jeremiah 32:

³ Now Zedekiah king of Judah… imprisoned [Jeremiah], saying, "Why do you prophesy as you do?"

¹⁶ "…[Jeremiah] prayed to the LORD: ¹⁷ "Ah, Sovereign LORD, you have made the heavens and the earth by [Y]our great power and outstretched arm. Nothing is too hard for you. ¹⁸ You show love… Great and mighty God, [W]hose name is the LORD Almighty, ¹⁹ great are [Y]our purposes and mighty are [Y]our deeds. Your eyes are open to the ways of all mankind; you reward each person according to their conduct and as their deeds deserve. ²⁰ You performed signs and wonders… ²² You gave them… a land flowing with milk and honey ²³ …but they did not obey [Y]ou or follow [Y]our law; they did not do what [Y]ou commanded them to do…"

²⁶ Then the word of the LORD came to Jeremiah: ²⁷ "I am the LORD, the God of all mankind. Is anything too hard for [M]e? ³⁷ I will surely gather them from all the lands… [and] bring them back… and let them live in safety. ³⁸ They will be [M]y people, and I will be their God. ³⁹ I will give them singleness of heart and action, so that they will always fear [M]e and that all will then go well for them and for their children after them. ⁴⁰ I will make an everlasting covenant with them: I will never stop doing good to them, and I will inspire them… [to] never turn away from [M]e. ⁴¹ I will rejoice in doing them good and will assuredly plant them… with all [M]y heart and soul. ⁴² …I will give them all… prosperity…" ⁴⁴ declares the LORD.

Jeremiah 33:

¹ While Jeremiah was still confined in the courtyard of the guard, the word of the LORD came to him a second time: ⁶ "… I will bring health and healing…; I will heal my people and will let them enjoy abundant peace and security. ⁸ I will cleanse them from all the sin they have committed against [M]e and will forgive all their sins of rebellion against [M]e. ⁹ Then [they] will bring [M]e renown, joy, praise and honor before all nations on earth that hear of all the good things I do for [them]; and they will be in awe and will tremble at the abundant prosperity and peace I provide for [them]."

¹⁰ This is what the LORD says: "…[T]here will be heard once more ¹¹ the sounds of joy and gladness, the voices of bride and bridegroom, and the voices of those who bring thank offerings to the house of the LORD, saying, 'Give thanks to the LORD Almighty, for the LORD is good; [H]is love endures forever.'"

¹⁴ "The days are coming," declares the LORD, "when I will fulfill the good promise I made… ⁵ In those days and at that time I will make a righteous Branch sprout from David's line; he will do what is just and right in the land. ¹⁶ In those days [all] will be saved and… live in safety. This is the name by which it will be called: 'The LORD Our Righteous Savior.' ²⁶ …For I will…have compassion on them."

Islam:

Source: **Stories of the Prophets by Imam Ibn Kathir** and the **Quran:**

Aramaya (Jeremiah) asked [God]: "O Lord! Which of Your slaves is more lovable to You?" He answered: "Those who remember Me most away from their remembrance of My creatures; those who are not thinking of death, nor speak of eternal living; those who, when they are allured by the riches of this world, despise them, and when they lose them are happy; those have My love, indeed, and I shall reward them more than they desired."

Aramaya stood up and rent his clothes, and applied ashes to his face and fell prostrate and said: "O Lord! Would that my mother had not borne me, when You made me the last prophet..." [God] said: "Raise your head... Stand up Aramaya, and hear the news ... Before I chose you, I had made you and favored you and honored you...Go and tell them what I have told you."

"O [God]! I am weak..."

"Do you not know that all affairs are controlled by Me? I am [God] without semblance, or any like Me. I spoke to the oceans so; I am with you, and nothing shall harm you. Go to your people and tell them: [God] has remembered you, with His remembrance of our forefathers' good deeds. The animals remember their countries and return to them. But those people of yours... they have forgotten the purpose of My generosity to their forefathers and have misplaced My favors."

Aramaya said: "By your grace I have come to learn before You; how is it possible when I am weak and powerless, to speak before You? But by Your mercy You have spared me to this day."

He on High said: "...If they disobeyed [M]e I will place them among the disobedient, until I rescue them out of My Mercy... O Aramaya, I made you honored in your mother's womb and have chosen you to this day. If your people had protected the orphans, the widows, the helpless, and the stranded, I would have been their Sustainer. They would have been like a blissful garden to Me; [Still] I have been the kind shepherd to them..."

[God] the Exalted revealed to Aramaya: "I am going to reconstruct Jerusalem, so go there." He went and found it devastated. He said to himself: "Exalted be [God]! [God] told me to come to this city and that He was reconstructing it. When will [God] rebuild it? And when will He bring it back to life?"

Then [Aramaya] slept, and his donkey with him... He remained in that sleep of his until he had completed one hundred years. When [God] awoke him, he thought that he had slept no more than an hour. He had known the city as a devastated land; when he saw it rebuilt and populated, he said:

The Cow 2:269 "He grants wisdom to [W]hom He pleases, and whoever is granted wisdom, he indeed is given a great good..."

XX. Lamentations

Christianity/Judaism:

Lamentations 1:

¹ How deserted lies the city, once so full of people! How like a widow is she, who once was great among the nations! She who was queen among the provinces has now become a slave.

² Bitterly she weeps at night, tears are on her cheeks. Among all her lovers there is no one to comfort her. All her friends have betrayed her; they have become her enemies.

³ After affliction and harsh labor, Judah has gone into exile. She dwells among the nations; she finds no resting place. All who pursue her have overtaken her in the midst of her distress.

⁴ The roads to Zion mourn, for no one comes to her appointed festivals. All her gateways are desolate, her priests groan, her young women grieve, and she is in bitter anguish.

⁵ Her foes have become her masters; her enemies are at ease... grief because of her many sins. Her children have gone into exile, captive before the foe.

⁶ All the splendor has departed from Daughter Zion. Her princes are like deer that find no pasture; in weakness they have fled before the pursuer.

⁷ In the days of her affliction and wandering Jerusalem remembers all the treasures that were hers in days of old. When her people fell into enemy hands, there was no one to help her. Her enemies looked at her and laughed at her destruction.

⁸ Jerusalem has sinned greatly and so has become unclean. All who honored her despise her, for they have all seen her naked; she herself groans and turns away.

⁹ Her filthiness clung to her skirts; she did not consider her future. Her fall was astounding; there was none to comfort her. "Look, LORD, on my affliction, for the enemy has triumphed."

¹⁰ The enemy laid hands on all her treasures...

¹¹ All her people groan as they search for bread; they barter their treasures for food to keep themselves alive. "Look, LORD, and consider, for I am despised."

¹² "Is it nothing to you, all you who pass by? Look around and see. Is any suffering like my suffering that was inflicted on me?

¹⁴ "My sins have been bound into a yoke; [t]hey have been hung on my neck... [My strength is] sapped... ¹⁵ Virgin Daughter Judah [has been] trampled.

[16] "This is why I weep and my eyes overflow with tears. No one is near to comfort me, no one to restore my spirit. My children are destitute because the enemy has prevailed."

[17] Zion stretches out her hands, but there is no one to comfort her... Jerusalem has become an unclean thing among them.

[18] "The LORD is righteous, yet I rebelled against [H]is command. Listen, all you peoples; look on my suffering. My young men and young women have gone into exile.

[19] "I called to my allies but they betrayed me...

[20] "See, LORD, how distressed I am! I am in torment within, and in my heart I am disturbed, for I have been most rebellious…

[21] "People have heard my groaning, but there is no one to comfort me. All my enemies have heard of my distress; they rejoice… [22] My groans are many and my heart is faint."

Lamentations 2:

[5] …[All] destroyed her strongholds [lay in ruin]. [M]ourning and lamentation [are multiplied] for Daughter Judah. [8] [Her] ramparts and walls lament; together they [waste] away. [9] Her gates have sunk into the ground; their bars… broken and destroyed. Her king and her princes are exiled among the nations, the law is no more, and her prophets no longer find visions from the LORD.

[10] The elders of Daughter Zion sit on the ground in silence; they have sprinkled dust on their heads and put on sackcloth. The young women of Jerusalem have bowed their heads to the ground.

[11] My eyes fail from weeping, I am in torment within; my heart is poured out on the ground because my people are destroyed, because children and infants faint in the streets of the city.

[12] They say to their mothers, "Where is bread and wine?" as they faint like the wounded in the streets of the city, as their lives ebb away in their mothers' arms.

[13] What can I say for you? With what can I compare you, Daughter Jerusalem? To what can I liken you, that I may comfort you, Virgin Daughter Zion? Your wound is as deep as the sea. Who can heal you?

[15] All who pass your way clap their hands at you; they scoff and shake their heads at Daughter Jerusalem: "Is this the city that was called the perfection of beauty, the joy of the whole earth?"

[16] All your enemies open their mouths wide against you; they scoff and gnash their teeth and say, "We have swallowed her up. This is the day we have waited for; we have lived to see it."

[18] The hearts of the people cry out to the Lord. You walls of Daughter Zion, let your tears flow like a river day and night; give yourself no relief, your eyes no rest.

¹⁹ Arise, cry out in the night, as the watches of the night begin; pour out your heart like water in the presence of the Lord. Lift up your hands to [H]im for the lives of your children…

²¹ Young and old lie together in the dust of the streets…

Lamentations 3:

¹ I am the man who has seen affliction… ² [I] walk in darkness rather than light. ⁴ …[M]y skin and my flesh grow old… [my bones are] broken.   ⁵ [I am] besieged… and surrounded with bitterness and hardship. ⁶ [I] dwell in darkness like those long dead.

⁷ … I cannot escape [for] I am weighed… down with chains. ⁸ Even when I call out or cry for help, [no one hears] my prayer.   ⁹ …[M]y way [is barred] with blocks of stone; my paths [are] crooked.

¹⁴ I became the laughingstock of all my people; they mock me in song all day long. ¹⁵ [I am filled] with bitter herbs and given… gall to drink.   ¹⁶ [M]y teeth [are broken]; [I am] trampled in the dust.

¹⁷ I have been deprived of peace; I have forgotten what prosperity is. ¹⁸ So I say, "My splendor is gone and all that I had hoped from the LORD."

¹⁹ I remember my affliction and my wandering, the bitterness and the gall.   ²⁰ I well remember them, and my soul is downcast within me. ²¹ Yet this I call to mind and therefore I have hope: ²² Because of the LORD's great love we are not consumed, for [H]is compassions never fail.   ²³ They are new every morning; great is [Y]our faithfulness. ²⁴ I say to myself, "The LORD is my portion; therefore I will wait for [H]im."

²⁵ The LORD is good to those whose hope is in [H]im, to the one who seeks [H]im; ²⁶ it is good to wait quietly for the salvation of the LORD.

²⁷ It is good for a man to bear the yoke while he is young.   ²⁸ Let him sit alone in silence… ²⁹ Let him bury his face in the dust — there may yet be hope. ³⁰ Let him offer his cheek to one who would strike him, and let him be filled with disgrace. ³¹ For no one is cast off by the Lord… ³² …[H]e will show compassion, so great is [H]is unfailing love. ⁴⁰ Let us… return to the LORD. ⁴¹ Let us lift up our hearts and our hands to God in heaven, and say: ⁴² "We have sinned and rebelled…"

⁴⁶ "All our enemies have opened their mouths wide against us. ⁴⁷ We have suffered terror and pitfalls, ruin and destruction." ⁵¹ What I see brings grief to my soul because of all the women of my city. ⁴⁸ Streams of tears flow from my eyes… ⁴⁹ My eyes will flow unceasingly, without relief, ⁵⁰ until the LORD looks down from heaven and sees.

⁵² Those who were my enemies without cause hunted me like a bird. ⁵³ They tried to end my life in a pit and threw stones at me; ⁵⁴ the waters closed over my head, and I thought I was about to perish.

⁵⁵ I called on [Y]our name, LORD, from the depths of the pit. ⁵⁶ You heard my plea: "Do not close your ears to my cry for relief." ⁵⁷ You came near when I called [Y]ou, and [Y]ou

said, "Do not fear." ⁵⁸ You, Lord, took up my case; [Y]ou redeemed my life.

Lamentations 4:

¹ How the gold has lost its luster, the fine gold bec[a]me dull! The sacred gems are scattered at every street corner.

² How the precious children of Zion, once worth their weight in gold, are now considered as pots of clay, the work of a potter's hands!

³ Even jackals offer their breasts to nurse their young, but my people have become heartless like ostriches in the desert.

⁵ Those who once ate delicacies are destitute in the streets. Those brought up in royal purple now lie on ash heaps.

⁷ Their princes were brighter than snow and whiter than milk, their bodies more ruddy than rubies, their appearance like lapis lazuli.

⁸ But now they are blacker than soot; they are not recognized in the streets. Their skin has shriveled on their bones; it has become as dry as a stick.

¹² The kings of the earth did not believe, nor did any of the peoples of the world, that enemies and foes could enter the gates of Jerusalem.

¹³ But it happened because of the sins of her prophets and the iniquities of her priests…

¹⁴ Now they grope through the streets as if they were blind. They are so defiled… that no one dares to touch their garments.

¹⁵ "Go away! You are unclean!" people cry to them. "Away! Away! Don't touch us!"

¹⁶ The [people are] scattered; [t]he priests are shown no honor, the elders no favor.

¹⁷ Moreover, our eyes failed, looking in vain for help; from our towers we watched for a nation that could not save us.

¹⁸ People stalked us at every step, so we could not walk in our streets. Our end was near, our days were numbered, for our end had come.

¹⁹ Our pursuers were swifter than eagles in the sky; they chased us over the mountains and lay in wait for us in the desert.

²⁰ …[O]ur very life breath was caught in their traps.

Lamentations 5:

¹ Remember, LORD, what has happened to us; look, and see our disgrace. ² Our inheritance has been turned over to strangers, our homes to foreigners. ³ We have become fatherless, our mothers are widows.

⁴ We must buy the water we drink; our wood can be had only at a price. ⁵ Those who pursue us are at our heels; we are weary and find no rest. ⁸ ...[T]here is no one to free us from their hands.

⁹ We get our bread at the risk of our lives... ¹⁰ Our skin is hot as an oven, feverish from hunger. ¹¹ Women have been violated in Zion, and virgins in the towns of Judah. ¹² ...[E]lders are shown no respect.

¹³ Young men toil at the millstones; boys stagger under loads of wood. ¹⁴ The elders are gone from the city gate; the young men have stopped their music. ¹⁵ Joy is gone from our hearts; our dancing has turned to mourning. ¹⁶ The crown has fallen from our head. Woe to us, for we have sinned! ¹⁷ Because of this our hearts are faint, because of these things our eyes grow dim ¹⁸ for Mount Zion, which lies desolate, with jackals prowling over it.

¹⁹ You, LORD, reign forever; [Y]our throne endures from generation to generation. ²¹ Restore us to [Y]ourself, LORD, that we may return; renew our days as of old...

Islam:

The Bee 16:89 And on the day when [I] will raise up in every people a witness... from among themselves... – [I] [will] [reveal] the Book to you explaining clearly everything, and a guidance and mercy and good news for those who submit.

The Cow 2:2 This Book, there is no doubt in it, is a guide to those who guard (against evil).

The Children of Israel 17:89 And certainly [I] have explained for [people]... every kind of similitude, but most... do not consent to aught but denying.

The Cave 18:54 And certainly [I] have explained... every kind of example, and man is most of all given to contention.

The Cattle 6:114 Shall I then seek a judge other than [God]? And He it is Who has revealed to you the Book made plain; and those whom [I] have given the Book know that it is revealed by your Lord with truth, therefore you should not be of the disputers.

The Cave 18:109 Say: If the sea were ink for the words of my Lord, the sea would surely be consumed before the words of my Lord are exhausted, though We were to bring the like of that to add.

Luqman 31:27 And were every tree that is in the earth (be made into) pens and the sea (to supply [them] with ink), with seven more seas to increase it, the words of [God] would not come to an end; surely [God] is Mighty, Wise.

The Pilgrimage 22:78 And strive hard in (the way of) [God], a striving... due to Him; He has chosen you and has not laid upon you an hardship in religion; the faith of your father Ibrahim (Abraham); He named you... before and in this, that the Apostle may be a bearer of witness to you, and you may be bearers of witness to the people; therefore keep up prayer... and hold fast by [God]; He is your Guardian; how excellent the

Guardian and how excellent the Helper!

Buddhism:

Source: Buddha:

All beings tremble before violence. All fear death. All love life. See yourself in others. Then whom can you hurt? What harm can you do?

He who seeks happiness [b]y hurting those who seek happiness [w]ill never find happiness. For your brother and sister are like you. They want to be happy. Never harm them. And when you leave this life, [y]ou too will find happiness.

Sikhism:

Sri Guru Granth Sahib:

Life and death come to all who are born. Everything here gets devoured by Death… [T]he beauty of youth and flowers are guests for only a few days. Like the leaves of the water-lily, they wither and fade and finally die. Be happy… as long as your youth is fresh and delightful. But your days are few – you have grown weary, and now your body has grown old. My playful friends have gone to sleep in the graveyard…

The day dawns, and then it ends, and the night passes away. Man's life is diminishing, but he does not understand. Each day, the mouse of death is gnawing away at the rope of life… The Messenger of Death is cruel and unfeeling.

Jewels, treasures, pearls, gold and silver – all these are just dust. [T]he color of the safflower… lasts for only a few days.

Without God, there is no saving grace… No one else can save you… [P]lease save and protect me, please bless me… Without You… Lord, who else is there for me? Granting His Grace, God meets us and we [live]… All suffering and sorrow shall depart.

When you are confronted with terrible hardships, and no one offers you any support, when your friends turn into enemies, and even your relatives have deserted you, and when all support has given way, and all hope has been lost – if you then come to remember the Supreme Lord God, even the hot wind shall not touch you.

Mayan Religion:

Source: Allen J. Christensen. Popol Vuh: Literal Translation. Mesoweb Publications. 29 November 2011. http://www.mesoweb.com/publications/Christensen/PV-Literal.pdf:

[3826] Truly pity our faces! [4666] Truly we sinned… [5536] We are lost… [4790] [God] You are called upon, [4791] It will come to be… [4798] Not will be lost your names (people).

[5277-5278] Behold us, Hear us! [5279] [Do] not abandon us… [5293] Give us steadfast light [5556] [You] our provider. [6016] [You] comfort [our] hearts.

XXI. The Book of Ezekiel

Christianity/Judaism:

Ezekiel 1:

¹ ...[W]hile I was among the exiles... the heavens were opened and I saw visions of God ³ [T]he word of the LORD came to Ezekiel the priest...

Ezekiel 2:

³ He said: "...I am sending you to the [exiles]... ⁴ The people to whom I am sending you are obstinate and stubborn. Say to them, 'This is what the Sovereign LORD says.' ⁵ And whether they listen or fail to listen — ...they will know that a prophet has been among them. ⁶ And you... do not be afraid of them or their words. Do not be afraid, though briers and thorns are all around you and you live among scorpions. Do not be afraid of what they say or be terrified by them, though they are a rebellious people. ⁷ You must speak [M]y words to them..."

⁹ Then I looked, and I saw a hand stretched out to me. In it was a scroll, ¹⁰ which [H]e unrolled before me. On both sides of it were written words of lament and mourning and woe.

Ezekiel 3:

¹ And [H]e said to me, "...[E]at what is before you, eat this scroll; then go and speak to the people..." ² So I opened my mouth, and [H]e gave me the scroll to eat. ³ ...So I ate it, and it tasted as sweet as honey in my mouth.

⁴ He then said to me: "...[G]o now to the people... and speak [M]y words to them. ⁸ ...I will make you as unyielding and hardened as they are. ⁹ I will make your forehead like the hardest stone, harder than flint. Do not be afraid of them or terrified by them..."

¹² Then... I heard behind me a loud rumbling sound as the glory of the LORD rose from the place where it was standing. ¹⁴ The Spirit then lifted me up and took me away... with the strong hand of the LORD on me. ¹⁵ I came to the exiles...

Ezekiel 11:

¹⁷ "...This is what the Sovereign LORD says: 'I will gather you from the nations and bring you back from the countries where you have been scattered...'

¹⁹ I will give them an undivided heart and put a new spirit in them; I will remove from them their heart of stone and give them a heart of flesh. ²⁰ Then they will follow [M]y decrees and be careful to keep [M]y laws. They will be [M]y people, and I will be their God."

²⁴ Then the vision I had seen went up from me, ²⁵ and I told the exiles everything the LORD had shown me.

Ezekiel 12:

23 "Say to them, This is what the Sovereign LORD says: 'The days are near when every vision will be fulfilled. **25** ...I will fulfill whatever I say, declares the Sovereign LORD.'"

Ezekiel 13:

23 "...I will save [M]y people... And then [all] will know that I am the LORD."

Ezekiel 14:

6 "...Repent! Turn from... and renounce all your detestable practices!"

Ezekiel 16:

4 "On the day you were born... **5** [n]o one looked on you with pity or had compassion... Rather, you were thrown out into the open field, for on the day you were born you were despised. **6** Then I passed by and saw you... and as you lay there... I said to you, 'Live!' **7** I made you grow like a plant of the field. You grew and developed...

8 Later I passed by, and when I looked at you and saw that you were old enough for love, I spread the corner of [M]y garment over you... I gave you my solemn oath and entered into a covenant with you... and you became [M]ine.

9 I bathed you with water... and put ointments on you. **10** I clothed you with an embroidered dress and put sandals of fine leather on you. I dressed you in fine linen and covered you with costly garments. **11** I adorned you with jewelry: I put bracelets on your arms and a necklace around your neck, **12** and I put a ring on your nose, earrings on your ears and a beautiful crown on your head. **13** So you were adorned with gold and silver; your clothes were of fine linen and costly fabric and embroidered cloth. Your food was honey, olive oil and the finest flour. You became very beautiful and rose to be a queen. **14** And your fame spread among the nations on account of your beauty, because the splendor I had given you made your beauty perfect, declares the Sovereign LORD."

Ezekiel 20:

8 "But [you] rebelled against [M]e and would not listen to [M]e."

Ezekiel 16:

60 "Yet I will remember the covenant I made with you in the days of your youth, and I will establish an everlasting covenant with you. **63** Then, when I make atonement for you for all you have done, you will remember and be ashamed..., declares the Sovereign LORD."

Ezekiel 17:

22 "This is what the Sovereign LORD says: I [M]yself will take a shoot from the very top of a cedar and plant it; I will break off a tender sprig from its topmost shoots and plant it on a high and lofty mountain. ²³ …I will plant it; it will produce branches and bear fruit and become a splendid cedar. Birds of every kind will nest in it; they will find shelter in the shade of its branches. ²⁴ All the trees of the forest will know that I the LORD… make the low tree grow tall... and make the dry tree flourish. I the LORD have spoken, and I will do it."

Ezekiel 18:

⁴ "For everyone belongs to [M]e, the parent as well as the child — both alike belong to [M]e.

⁵ Suppose there is a righteous man who does what is just and right. He does not defile his neighbor's wife… ⁷ He does not oppress anyone… He does not commit robbery but gives his food to the hungry and provides clothing for the naked. ⁸ …He withholds his hand from doing wrong and judges fairly… ⁹ He follows [M]y decrees and faithfully keeps [M]y laws. …[H]e will surely live," declares the Sovereign LORD.

²¹ "…[I]f a wicked person turns away from all the sins they have committed and keeps all [M]y decrees and does what is just and right, that person will surely live… ²² None of the offenses they have committed will be remembered against them. Because of the righteous things they have done, they will live.

²⁹ Yet [many] say, 'The way of the Lord is not just.' Are [M]y ways unjust? Is it not your ways that are unjust? ³⁰ Therefore… Repent! Turn away from all your offenses… ³¹ Rid yourselves of all the offenses you have committed, and get a new heart and a new spirit… ³² For I take no pleasure in the death of anyone, declares the Sovereign LORD. Repent and live!"

Ezekiel 45:

⁹ "…You have gone far enough… Give up your violence and oppression and do what is just and right."

Ezekiel 34:

¹¹ "For this is what the Sovereign LORD says: I… will search for [M]y sheep and look after them. ¹² As a shepherd looks after his scattered flock when he is with them, so will I look after my sheep. I will rescue them from all the places where they were scattered on a day of clouds and darkness. ¹³ I will bring them out from the nations and gather them from the countries, and I will bring them into their own land. I will pasture them on the mountains… in the ravines and in all the settlements in the land. ¹⁴ I will tend them in a good pasture, and the mountain heights… will be their grazing land. There they will lie down in good grazing land, and there they will feed in a rich pasture… ¹⁵ I myself will tend my sheep and have them lie down, declares the Sovereign LORD. ¹⁶ I will search for the lost and bring back the strays. I will bind up the injured and strengthen the weak…I will shepherd the flock with justice.

²² I will save [M]y flock, and they will no longer be plundered... ²⁵ I will make a covenant of peace with them… so that they may live in the wilderness and sleep in the forests in safety. ²⁶ I will make them and the places surrounding my hill a blessing. I will send

down showers in season; there will be showers of blessing.

²⁷ The trees will yield their fruit and the ground will yield its crops; the people will be secure in their land. They will know that I am the LORD, when I break the bars of their yoke and rescue them… ²⁸ They will no longer be plundered by the nations, nor will wild animals devour them. They will live in safety, and no one will make them afraid. ²⁹ …[T]hey will no longer be victims of famine… or bear the scorn of the nations. ³⁰ Then they will know that I, the LORD their God, am with them and that they… are [M]y people, declares the Sovereign LORD. ³¹ 'You are my sheep, the sheep of [M]y pasture, and I am your God, declares the Sovereign LORD.'"

Ezekiel 36:

³³ "…On the day I cleanse you from all your sins, I will resettle your towns, and the ruins will be rebuilt. ³⁴ The desolate land will be cultivated instead of lying desolate in the sight of all who pass through it. ³⁵ They will say, 'This land that was laid waste has become like the garden of Eden; the cities that were lying in ruins… are now fortified and inhabited.' ³⁶ …I the LORD have spoken, and I will do it. ³⁷ I will make [the] people as numerous as sheep… ³⁸ So will the ruined cities be filled with flocks of people. Then [all] will know that I am the LORD."

Ezekiel 37:

¹ The hand of the LORD was on me and [H]e brought me out by the Spirit of the LORD and [He] set me in the middle of a valley; it was full of bones. ² He led me back and forth among them, and I saw a great many bones on the floor of the valley, bones that were very dry. ³ He asked me, "…[C]an these bones live?" I said, "Sovereign LORD, [Y]ou alone know."

⁴ Then [H]e said to me, "Prophesy to these bones and say to them, 'Dry bones, hear the word of the LORD! ⁵ This is what the Sovereign LORD says to these bones: I will make breath enter you, and you will come to life. ⁶ I will attach tendons to you and make flesh come upon you and cover you with skin; I will put breath in you, and you will come to life. Then you will know that I am the LORD.'"

⁷ So I prophesied as I was commanded. And as I was prophesying, there was a noise, a rattling sound, and the bones came together, bone to bone. ⁸ I looked, and tendons and flesh appeared on them and skin covered them, but there was no breath in them.

⁹ Then [H]e said to me, "Prophesy to the breath; prophesy… and say to it, 'This is what the Sovereign LORD says: Come, breath, from the four winds and breathe into [them], that they may live.'" ¹⁰ So I prophesied as [H]e commanded me, and breath entered them; they came to life and stood up on their feet — a vast [crowd].

¹¹ Then [H]e said to me: "…[T]hese bones are [of My] people. They say, 'Our bones are dried up and our hope is gone…' ¹² Therefore prophesy and say to them: 'This is what the Sovereign LORD says: My people, I am going to open your graves and bring you up from them; I will bring you back… ¹³ Then you, [M]y people, will know that I am the LORD, when I open your graves and bring you up from them. ¹⁴ I will put [M]y Spirit in you and you will live… Then you will know that I the LORD have spoken, and I have done it, declares the LORD.'"

[26] "I will make a covenant of peace with them; it will be an everlasting covenant. I will establish them and increase their numbers, and I will put [M]y sanctuary among them forever. [27] My dwelling place will be with them; I will be their God, and they will be [M]y people..."

Ezekiel 39:

[7] "I will make known [M]y holy name... and the nations will know that I the LORD am the Holy One... [27] ...I will be proved holy... in the sight of many nations. [28] Then they will know that I am the LORD their God for... [29] I will pour out my Spirit... declares the Sovereign LORD."

Ezekiel 43:

[1] Then... [2] I saw the glory of.. God.... His voice was like the roar of rushing waters, and the land was radiant with [H]is glory. [3] ...and I fell facedown. [9] "...I will live among [you] forever," [27] ...declare[d] the Sovereign LORD.

Islam:

[The Cow 2:243] Have you not considered those who went forth from their homes, for fear of death, and they were thousands [who died]... then... again He gave them life; most surely [God] is [g]racious to people...

[The Cow 2:259] ...[L]ook at the bones, how [I] set them together, then clothed them with flesh; so when it became clear to [Hizqeel] (Ezekiel), he said: I know that [God] has power over all things.

Source: Stories of the Prophets by Imam Ibn Kathir:

The people had fled... for fear of the plague and settled on a plateau... The Angel of Death called to the survivors: "Die you all," and they perished. After a long time [as] a prophet called Hizqeel, passing by, stooped over them [and] wonder[ed]... [t]here came a voice: "Do you want [God] to resurrect them while you watch?"

He said: "Yes." His idea was to marvel at the power of [God] over them. A voice said to him: "Call: 'O you bones, [God] commands you to gather up.'" The bones began to fly one to the other until they became skeletons. Then [God] revealed to him to say; "Call: 'O you bones, [God] commands you to put on flesh and blood and the clothes in which they had died.'" And a voice said: "[God] commands you to call the bodies to rise." And they rose. When they returned to life they said: "Blessed are You, O Lord, and all praises [are] Yours." Ibn 'Abbas reported that the dead who were resurrected were four thousand, while Ibn Salih said they were nine thousand.

XXII. The Book of Daniel

Christianity/Judaism:

Daniel 1:

³ ...[Nebuchadnezzar king of Babylon] ordered Ashpenaz, chief of his court officials, to bring into the king's service some of the Israelites from the royal family and the nobility — ⁴ [Ashpenaz] was to teach them the language and literature of the Babylonians. ⁶ Among those who were chosen were some from Judah [including] Daniel, Hananiah, Mishael and Azariah.

⁸ ...Daniel resolved not to defile himself with the royal food and wine, and he asked the chief official for permission not to defile himself this way. ¹⁰ [B]ut the official told Daniel, "I am afraid of my lord the king, who has assigned your food and drink. Why should he see you looking worse than the other young men your age? The king would then have my head because of you."

¹¹ Daniel then said to the guard... ¹² "Please test your servants for ten days: Give us nothing but vegetables to eat and water to drink. ¹³ Then compare our appearance with that of the young men who eat the royal food, and treat your servants in accordance with what you see." ¹⁴ So he agreed to this and tested them for ten days.

¹⁵ At the end of the ten days they looked healthier and better nourished than any of the young men who ate the royal food. ¹⁶ So the guard took away their choice food and the wine they were to drink and gave them vegetables instead.

¹⁷ To these four young men God gave knowledge and understanding of all kinds of literature and learning. And Daniel could understand visions and dreams of all kinds.

¹⁸ At the end of the time set by the king to bring them into his service, the chief official presented them to Nebuchadnezzar. ¹⁹ The king talked with them, and he found none equal to Daniel, Hananiah, Mishael and Azariah; so they entered the king's service. ²⁰ In every matter of wisdom and understanding about which the king questioned them, he found them ten times better than [everyone] in his whole kingdom. ²¹ And Daniel remained there until the first year of King Cyrus.

Daniel 2:

¹ In the second year of his reign, Nebuchadnezzar had dreams; his mind was troubled and he could not sleep. ² So the king summoned the magicians, enchanters, sorcerers and astrologers to tell him what he had dreamed. ¹⁰ The astrologers answered the king, "There is no one on earth who can do what the king asks! ¹¹ What the king asks is too difficult. No one can reveal it..."

²⁴ Then Daniel went to Arioch... and said to him, "...Take me to the king, and I will interpret his dream for him." ²⁵ Arioch took Daniel to the king at once...

²⁶ The king asked Daniel, "Are you able to tell me what I saw in my dream and interpret

it?" ²⁷ Daniel replied, "No wise man, enchanter, magician or diviner can explain to the king the mystery he has asked about, ²⁸ but there is a God in heaven who reveals mysteries... ⁴⁴ ...[T]he God of heaven will set up a kingdom that will never be destroyed, nor will it be left to another people... ⁴⁵ This is the meaning of [your] vision..."

⁴⁶ Then King Nebuchadnezzar fell prostrate before Daniel and paid him honor... ⁴⁸ [He] placed Daniel in a high position and lavished many gifts on him. He made him ruler over the entire province of Babylon and placed him in charge of all its wise men.

²⁰ "Praise be to the name of God for ever and ever; wisdom and power are [H]is. ²¹ He gives wisdom to the wise and knowledge to the discerning. ²² He reveals deep and hidden things; [H]e knows what lies in darkness, and light dwells with [H]im. ²³ I thank and praise [Y]ou, God...: You have given me wisdom and power, [Y]ou have made known to me what we asked of [Y]ou, [Y]ou have made known to us the dream of the king."

Daniel 3:

¹ King Nebuchadnezzar made an image of gold... and set it up on the plain of Dura in the province of Babylon. ⁴ Then the herald loudly proclaimed, "Nations and peoples of every language, this is what you are commanded to do: ⁵ As soon as you hear the sound of the horn, flute, zither, lyre, harp, pipe and all kinds of music, you must fall down and worship the image of gold that King Nebuchadnezzar has set up. ⁶ Whoever does not fall down and worship will immediately be thrown into a blazing furnace."

⁷ Therefore, as soon as they heard the sound of the horn, flute, zither, lyre, harp and all kinds of music, all the nations and peoples of every language fell down and worshiped the image of gold that King Nebuchadnezzar had set up.

⁸ At this time some astrologer came forward and [said], ¹² "...Shadrach, Meshach and Abednego... pay no attention to you... They neither serve your gods nor worship the image of gold you have set up."

¹³ Furious with rage, Nebuchadnezzar summoned Shadrach, Meshach and Abednego. ¹⁴ [He] said to them, "Is it true... that you do not serve my gods or worship the image of gold I have set up? ¹⁵ Now when you hear the sound of the horn, flute, zither, lyre, harp, pipe and all kinds of music, if you are ready to fall down and worship the image I made, very good. But if you do not worship it, you will be thrown immediately into a blazing furnace. Then what god will be able to rescue you from my hand?"

¹⁶ [They] replied to him, "King Nebuchadnezzar, we do not need to defend ourselves before you in this matter. ¹⁷ If we are thrown into the blazing furnace, the God we serve is able to deliver us from it... ¹⁸ But even if [H]e does not... we will not serve your gods or worship the image of gold you have set up."

¹⁹ Then Nebuchadnezzar was furious... He ordered the furnace heated seven times hotter than usual ²⁰ and commanded some of the strongest soldiers in his army to tie up Shadrach, Meshach and Abednego and throw them into the blazing furnace. ²¹ So [they]... were bound and thrown into the blazing furnace.

²⁴ Then King Nebuchadnezzar leaped to his feet in amazement and asked his advisers, "Weren't there three men that we tied up and threw into the fire?" They replied, "Certainly, Your Majesty."

²⁵ He said, "Look! I see four men walking around in the fire, unbound and unharmed..."

²⁶ Nebuchadnezzar then approached the opening of the blazing furnace and shouted, "Shadrach, Meshach and Abednego, servants of the Most High God, come out! Come here!"

So Shadrach, Meshach and Abednego came out of the fire, ²⁷ and [everyone] crowded around them. They saw that the fire had not harmed their bodies, nor was a hair of their heads singed; their robes were not scorched, and there was no smell of fire on them.

²⁸ Then Nebuchadnezzar said, "Praise be to the God of Shadrach, Meshach and Abednego, who has sent [H]is angel and rescued [H]is servants! They trusted in [H]im and defied the king's command and were willing to give up their lives rather than serve or worship any god except their own God. ³⁰ Then [He] promoted Shadrach, Meshach and Abednego in the province of Babylon.

Daniel 4:

² It is my pleasure to tell you about the miraculous signs and wonders that the Most High God has performed for me. ³ How great are [H]is signs, how mighty [H]is wonders! His kingdom is an eternal kingdom; [H]is dominion endures from generation to generation.

⁴ I, Nebuchadnezzar, was at home in my palace, contented and prosperous. ⁵ I had a dream that made me afraid. ⁹ I said, "[Daniel]... I know... no mystery is too difficult for you. Here is my dream; interpret it for me. ¹⁰ These are the visions I saw... there before me stood a tree in the middle of the land. Its height was enormous. ¹¹ The tree grew large and strong and its top touched the sky; it was visible to the ends of the earth. ¹² Its leaves were beautiful, its fruit abundant, and on it was food for all. Under it the wild animals found shelter, and the birds lived in its branches; from it every creature was fed.

¹³ ...I looked, and there before me was a holy one, a messenger, coming down from heaven. ¹⁴ He called in a loud voice: 'Cut down the tree and trim off its branches; strip off its leaves and scatter its fruit. Let the animals flee from under it and the birds from its branches. ¹⁵ But let the stump and its roots, bound with iron and bronze, remain in the ground, in the grass of the field. Let him be drenched with the dew of heaven, and let him live with the animals among the plants of the earth... ¹⁶ till seven times pass by for him.'"

¹⁹ Then Daniel ... answered, ²² "...Your Majesty, you are that tree! ²⁷ Therefore... be pleased to accept my advice: Renounce your sins by doing what is right, and your wickedness by being kind to the oppressed. It may be that then your prosperity will continue."

²⁸ All this happened to King Nebuchadnezzar. ³³ ...He ate grass like the ox. His body was drenched with the dew of heaven until his hair grew like the feathers of an eagle and his nails like the claws of a bird.

[34] At the end of that time, I, Nebuchadnezzar, raised my eyes toward heaven, and my sanity was restored. Then I praised the Most High; I honored and glorified [H]im who lives forever. His dominion is an eternal dominion; [H]is kingdom endures from generation to generation. [36] At the same time... my honor and splendor were returned to me for the glory of my kingdom. My advisers and nobles sought me out, and I was restored to my throne and became even greater than before. [37] Now I, Nebuchadnezzar, praise and exalt and glorify the King of heaven, because everything [H]e does is right and all [H]is ways are just..."

Daniel 5:

[31] ...Darius the Mede took over the kingdom, at the age of sixty-two.

Daniel 6:

[3] Now Daniel so distinguished himself... by his exceptional qualities that the king planned to set him over the whole kingdom. [4] At this, the administrators.. tried to find grounds for charges against Daniel in his conduct of government affairs, but they were unable to do so. They could find no corruption in him, because he was trustworthy and neither corrupt nor negligent. [5] Finally these men said, "We will never find any basis for charges against this man Daniel unless it has something to do with the law of his God."

[6] So [they] went as a group to the king and said: "May King Darius live forever! [7] [We] have all agreed that the king should issue an edict and enforce the decree that anyone who prays to any god or human being during the next thirty days, except to you, Your Majesty, shall be thrown into the lions' den. [8] Now, Your Majesty, issue the decree and put it in writing so that it cannot be altered — in accordance with the law of the Medes and Persians, which cannot be repealed." [9] So King Darius put the decree in writing.

[10] Now when Daniel learned that the decree had been published, he went... to his upstairs room... Three times a day he got down on his knees and prayed, giving thanks to... God, just as he had done before. [11] Then these men went as a group and found Daniel praying and asking God for help. [12] So they went to the king and spoke to him about his royal decree: "Did you not publish a decree that during the next thirty days anyone who prays to any god or human being except to you, Your Majesty, would be thrown into the lions' den?"

The king answered, "The decree stands..."

[13] Then they said to the king, "Daniel... pays no attention to you... or to the decree you put in writing. He still prays three times a day." [14] When the king heard this, he was greatly distressed; he was determined to rescue Daniel and made every effort until sundown to save him.

[15] Then the men went as a group to King Darius and said to him, "Remember, Your Majesty, that according to the law of the Medes and Persians no decree or edict that the king issues can be changed." [16] So the king gave the order, and they brought Daniel and threw him into the lions' den. The king said to Daniel, "May your God, [W]hom you serve continually, rescue you!"

¹⁷ A stone was brought and placed over the mouth of the den, and the king sealed it with his own signet ring and with the rings of his nobles, so that Daniel's situation might not be changed. ¹⁸ Then the king returned to his palace and spent the night without eating and without any entertainment being brought to him. And he could not sleep.

¹⁹ At the first light of dawn, the king got up and hurried to the lions' den. ²⁰ When he came near the den, he called to Daniel in an anguished voice, "Daniel, servant of the living God, has your God, [W]hom you serve continually, been able to rescue you from the lions?"

²¹ Daniel answered, "May the king live forever! ²² My God sent [H]is angel, and [H]e shut the mouths of the lions. They have not hurt me, because I was found innocent in [H]is sight. Nor have I ever done any wrong before you, Your Majesty."

²³ The king was overjoyed and gave orders to lift Daniel out of the den. And when Daniel was lifted from the den, no wound was found on him, because he had trusted in… God.

²⁵ Then King Darius wrote to all the nations and peoples of every language in all the earth: ²⁶ "I issue a decree that in every part of my kingdom people must fear and reverence the God of Daniel. 'For [H]e is the living God and [H]e endures forever; [H]is kingdom will not be destroyed, [H]is dominion will never end. ²⁷ He rescues and [H]e saves; [H]e performs signs and wonders in the heavens and on the earth. He has rescued Daniel from the power of the lions.'"

²⁸ So Daniel prospered during the reign of Darius and the reign of Cyrus the Persian.

Daniel 7:

¹ In the first year of Belshazzar king of Babylon, Daniel had a dream, and visions passed through his mind as he was lying in bed. He wrote down the substance of his dream.

² Daniel said: "In my vision at night I looked, and there before me were the four winds of heaven churning up the great sea. ³ Four great beasts, each different from the others, came up out of the sea. ⁴ "The first was like a lion, and it had the wings of an eagle. I watched until its wings were torn off and it was lifted from the ground so that it stood on two feet like a human being, and the mind of a human was given to it.

⁵ And there before me was a second beast, which looked like a bear. It was raised up on one of its sides, and it had three ribs in its mouth between its teeth… ⁶ After that, I looked, and there before me was another beast, one that looked like a leopard. And on its back it had four wings like those of a bird. This beast had four heads…

⁷ After that… there before me was a fourth beast — terrifying and frightening and very powerful. It had large iron teeth; it crushed and devoured its victims and trampled underfoot whatever was left. It was different from all the former beasts, and it had ten horns. ⁸ While I was thinking about the horns, there before me was another horn, a little one, which came up among them; and three of the first horns were uprooted before it. This horn had eyes like the eyes of a human being and a mouth that spoke boastfully.

⁹ As I looked, thrones were set in place, and the Ancient of Days took [H]is seat. His

clothing was as white as snow; the hair of [H]is head was white like wool. His throne was flaming with fire, and its wheels were all ablaze. ¹⁰ A river of fire was flowing, coming out from before [H]im. Thousands upon thousands attended [H]im; ten thousand times ten thousand stood before [H]im. The court was seated, and the books were opened.

¹¹ ...I kept looking until the beast was slain and its body destroyed and thrown into the blazing fire. ¹³ ...I looked, and there before me was one like a son of man, coming with the clouds of heaven. He approached the Ancient of Days and was led into [H]is presence. ¹⁴ He was given authority, glory and sovereign power; all nations and peoples of every language worshiped [H]im. His dominion is an everlasting dominion that will not pass away, and [H]is kingdom is one that will never be destroyed.

¹⁶ I approached one of those standing there and asked him the meaning of all this. So he... gave me the interpretation of these things: ¹⁷ 'The four great beasts are four kings that will rise from the earth. ¹⁸ But the holy people of the Most High will receive the kingdom and will possess it forever...'

¹⁹ Then I wanted to know the meaning of the fourth beast, which was different...and most terrifying... — the beast that crushed and devoured its victims and trampled underfoot whatever was left. ²⁰ I also wanted to know about the ten horns on its head and about the other horn that came up, before which three of them fell — the horn that looked more imposing than the others and that had eyes and a mouth that spoke boastfully. ²¹ As I watched, this horn was waging war against the holy people and defeating them, ²² until the Ancient of Days came and pronounced judgment in favor of the holy people... and the time came when they possessed the kingdom.

²³ "He gave me this explanation: 'The fourth beast is a fourth kingdom that will appear on earth. It will be different from all the other kingdoms and will devour the whole earth, trampling it down and crushing it. ²⁴ The ten horns are ten kings who will come from this kingdom. After them another king will arise, different from the earlier ones; he will subdue three kings. ²⁵ He will speak against the Most High and oppress [the] holy people and try to change the set times and the laws. The holy people will be delivered into [H]is hands for a time, times and half a time.

²⁶ But the court will sit, and his power will be taken away... ²⁷ Then the sovereignty, power and greatness of all the kingdoms under heaven will be handed over to the holy people of the Most High. His kingdom will be an everlasting kingdom, and all rulers will worship and obey [H]im."

Daniel 9:

³ ...[I]n in sackcloth and ashes, ⁴ I prayed to the LORD: "Lord, the great and awesome God, who keeps [H]is covenant of love with those who love [H]im and keep [H]is commandments, ⁵ we have sinned and done wrong. We have been wicked and have rebelled; we have turned away from [Y]our commands and laws. ⁶ We have not listened to [Y]our servants the prophets, who spoke in [Y]our name...

⁷ Lord, [Y]ou are righteous, but this day we are covered with shame — ...because of our unfaithfulness to [Y]ou. ⁸ We... have sinned against [Y]ou. ⁹ The Lord our God is

merciful and forgiving... [16] ...[I]n keeping with all [Y]our righteous acts... [17] [H]ear the prayers and petitions of [Y]our servant. For [Y]our sake, Lord, look with favor on [Y]our desolate sanctuary. [18] Give ear, our God, and hear; open [Y]our eyes and see the desolation of the city that bears [Y]our Name. We do not make requests of [Y]ou because we are righteous, but because of [Y]our great mercy. [19] Lord, listen! Lord, forgive! Lord, hear and act! For [Y]our sake, my God, do not delay..."

[20] While I was... praying, [21] ...Gabriel, the man I had seen in the earlier vision, came to me in swift flight... [22] "Daniel, I have now come to give you insight and understanding [23] ...for you are highly esteemed. Therefore... understand the vision: [25] ...From the time the word goes out to restore and rebuild Jerusalem until the Anointed One... there will be seven 'sevens,' and sixty-two 'sevens...' [26] After the sixty-two 'sevens,' the Anointed One will be put to death..."

Daniel 12:

[1] "...There will be a time [when]... everyone whose name is found written in the book — will be delivered. [2] Multitudes who sleep in the dust of the earth will awake... [3] Those who are wise will shine like the brightness of the heavens, and those who lead many to righteousness, like the stars for ever and ever. [4] But you, Daniel, roll up and seal the words of the scroll until the time of the end..."

[8] I heard, but I did not understand. So I asked, "My [L]ord, what will the outcome of all this be?" [9] He replied, "Go your way, Daniel, because the words are rolled up and sealed until the time of the end.

[10] Many will be purified, made spotless and refined... [though only] those who are wise will understand. [12] Blessed is the one who waits for and reaches the end... [13] As for you, go your way till the end. You will rest, and then at the end of the days you will rise to receive your allotted inheritance."

Islam:

Source: **Stories of the Prophets by Imam Ibn Kathir:**

Ibn Abi Al-Dunya narrated the following... N[e]buchadnezzar captured the two lions and threw them into a pit. He then brought Daniel and threw him at them; yet they did not pounce at him [...the lion and lioness began to lick him and did not harm him]; he remained as [God] wished... [Daniel] said: "And so my Lord has remembered me[!] Praise be to [God] Who never forgets those who appeal to Him! And Praise be to Him Who compensates good with good, rewards patience with safety, dispels harm after distress, assures us when we are overwhelmed, and is our hope when skill fails us."

The Cave 18:83-89 And they ask you about Zulqarnain (King Cyrus of Persia). Say: I will recite to you an account of him. Surely [I] established him in the land and granted him means of access to every thing. So he followed a course. Until when he reached the place where the sun set, he found it going down into a black sea, and found by it a people. ...[F]or him who believes and does good, he shall have goodly reward, and [I] will speak

212

to him an easy word of [My] command. Then he followed (another) course.

^{The Cave 18:90-98} Until when he reached the land of the rising of the sun, he found it rising on a people to whom [I] had given no shelter from It; Even so! [A]nd [I] had a full knowledge of what he had. Then he followed (another) course. Until when he reached (a place) between the two mountains, he found on that side of them a people who could hardly understand a word. They said: O Zulqarnain! [S]urely Gog and Magog make mischief in the land. Shall we then pay you a tribute on condition that you should raise a barrier between us and them. He said: That in which my Lord has established me is better, therefore you only help me with workers, I will make a fortified barrier between you and them… So they were not able to scale it nor could they make a hole in it. He said: This is a mercy from my Lord… and the promise of my Lord is ever true.

^{The Believer 40:78} And certainly [I] sent apostles before you: there are some of them that [I] have mentioned to you and there are others whom [I] have not mentioned to you, and it was not meet for an apostle that he should bring a sign except with [God's] permission, but when the command of [God] came, judgment was given with truth…

XXIII. The Minor Prophets I

Christianity/Judaism:

Hosea 1:

^{1} The word of the LORD… came to Hosea… during the reign of Jeroboam…

Hosea 2:

^{16} "In that day," declares the LORD, "you will call me 'my husband;' you will no longer call me 'my master.' ^{18} In that day I will make a covenant for them with the beasts of the field, the birds in the sky and the creatures that move along the ground. Bow and sword and battle I will abolish from the land, so that all may lie down in safety.

^{19} I will betroth you to [M]e forever; I will betroth you in righteousness and justice, in love and compassion. ^{20} I will betroth you in faithfulness, and you will acknowledge the LORD. ^{21} In that day I will respond," declares the LORD — "I will respond to the skies, and they will respond to the earth; ^{22} and the earth will respond to the grain, the new wine and the olive oil… ^{23} …I will say to those called 'Not my people, 'You are my people;' [and show them love] and they will say, 'You are my God.'"

Hosea 3:

^{5} [The people] will return and seek the LORD their God… They will come trembling to the LORD and to [H]is blessings in the last days.

Hosea 10:

^{2} Sow righteousness for yourselves, reap the fruit of unfailing love… for it is time to seek the LORD, until [H]e comes and showers [H]is righteousness on you.

Hosea 11:

^{1} "When [they were] child[ren], I loved [them]… ^{2} But the more they were called, the more they went away from [M]e. ^{3} It was I who taught [them] to walk, taking them by the arms; but they did not realize it was I who healed them. ^{4} I led them with cords of human kindness, with ties of love. To them I was like one who lifts a little child to the cheek, and I bent down to feed them.

^{7} [Yet] My people are determined to turn from [M]e… ^{8} [But] all my compassion is aroused… ^{9} For I am God… the Holy One among you. ^{10} They will follow the LORD; [H]e will roar like a lion. When [H]e roars, [H]is children will come trembling from the west. ^{11} They will come from Egypt, trembling like sparrows, from Assyria, fluttering like doves. I will settle them in their homes," declares the LORD.

Hosea 12:

^{6} …[Y]ou must return to your God; maintain love and justice, and wait for your God always.

214

Hosea 13:

[14] "I will deliver [My] people from the power of the grave; I will redeem them from death. Where, O death, are your plagues? Where, O grave, is your destruction?"

Hosea 14:

[1] Return... to the LORD your God. [2] ...Say to [H]im: "Forgive all our sins and receive us graciously, that we may offer the fruit of our lips. [3] ...[F]or in [Y]ou the fatherless find compassion."

[4] "I will heal their waywardness and love them freely... [8] ...I am like a flourishing juniper; your fruitfulness comes from [M]e." [9] Who is wise? Let them realize these things. Who is discerning? Let them understand. The ways of the LORD are right; the righteous walk in them...

Joel 1:

[2] Hear this... listen, all who live in the land. Has anything like this ever happened in your days or in the days of your ancestors? [3] Tell it to your children, and let your children tell it to their children, and their children to the next generation....

[8] Mourn like a virgin in sackcloth grieving for the betrothed of her youth. [14] Declare a holy fast; call a sacred assembly... [A]ll who live in the land... cry out to the LORD. [15] ...For the day of the LORD is near...

Joel 2:

[1] Blow the trumpet... Let all who live in the land tremble, for the day of the LORD is coming. [11] ...The day of the LORD is great...

[12] "Even now," declares the LORD, "return to [M]e with all your heart, with fasting and weeping and mourning." [13] Rend your heart and not your garments. Return to the LORD your God, for [H]e is gracious and compassionate, slow to anger and abounding in love...

[15] Blow the trumpet... declare a holy fast, call a sacred assembly. [16] Gather the people, consecrate the assembly; bring together the elders, gather the children... Let the bridegroom leave his room and the bride her chamber. [17] Let the priests, who minister before the LORD, weep between the portico and the altar.

[18] Then the LORD... took pity on [H]is people. [19] The LORD replied: "I am sending you grain, new wine and olive oil, enough to satisfy you fully; never again will... you [be] an object of scorn to the nations."

[21] ...[B]e glad and rejoice. [23] Be glad... rejoice in the LORD your God... because [H]e is faithful. [26] You will have plenty to eat, until you are full, and you will praise the name of the LORD your God, [W]ho has worked wonders for you; never again will [M]y people be shamed. [27] Then you will know that... I am the LORD your God, and that there is no other... [28] "And afterward, I will pour out [M]y Spirit on all people...

[30] I will show wonders in the heavens and on the earth... [32] And everyone who calls on the name of the LORD will be saved; for... there will be deliverance, as the LORD has

said..."

Joel 3:

[16] The LORD... will be a refuge for [H]is people...

Amos 4:

[13] He who forms the mountains, [W]ho creates the wind, and [W]ho reveals [H]is thoughts to mankind... the LORD God Almighty is [H]is name.

Amos 5:

[4] This is what the LORD says...: "Seek [M]e and live; [14] Seek good, not evil... Then the LORD God Almighty will be with you... [15] Hate evil, love good; maintain justice..."

Amos 9:

[13] "The days are coming," declares the LORD, "when the reaper will be overtaken by the plowman and the planter by the one treading grapes.   New wine will drip from the mountains and flow from all the hills, [14] and I will bring [M]y people... back from exile. They will rebuild the ruined cities and live in them. They will plant vineyards and drink their wine; they will make gardens and eat their fruit..."

Obadiah 1:

[17] ...[O]n Mount Zion will be deliverance; it will be holy... [21] And the kingdom will be the LORD's.

Islam:

Source: Stories of the Prophets by Imam Ibn Kathir:

Wahb Ibn Munbah reported that when sin increased, [God] revealed to an Israelite prophet called Mamia (Amos) that he should stand before his people and admonish them that they are hard-headed, blind, and deaf and tell them: "I [God] remember their forefathers, and that makes Me merciful with them. And ask them about My bounty: '[C]an any of them benefit from disobeying Me? And does any suffer who obeys Me?'"

Sikhism:

Sri Guru Granth Sahib:

The Fearless Lord is forever Merciful; He takes care of all. God, the Merciful, has bestowed His mercy...

O God, You are the Hope of all. All beings are Yours. You are the Wealth of all. O God, none return from You empty-handed...

XXIV. The Minor Prophets II

Christianity/Judaism:

Jonah 1:

[1] The word of the LORD came to Jonah... [2] "Go to the great city of Nineveh and preach against it, because its wickedness has come up before me." [3] But Jonah ran away from the LORD and headed for Tarshish...

[4] Then... a violent storm arose that the ship threatened to break up. [5] All the sailors were afraid ... [7] Then the sailors said, "Come, let us cast lots to find out who is responsible for this calamity." They cast lots and the lot fell on Jonah. [10] This terrified them and they asked, "What have you done?" (They knew he was running away from the LORD, because he had already told them so).

[12] "Pick me up and throw me into the sea," [Jonah] replied, "and it will become calm. I know that it is my fault that this great storm has come upon you." [13] Instead, the men did their best to row back to land. But they could not, for the sea grew even wilder than before. [14] Then they cried out to the LORD, "Please, LORD, do not let us die for taking this man's life. Do not hold us accountable for killing an innocent man..." [15] Then they took Jonah and threw him overboard, and the raging sea grew calm. [16] At this the [sailors] greatly feared the LORD...

[17] [A] huge fish [then] swallow[ed] Jonah, and Jonah was in the belly of the fish three days and three nights.

Jonah 2:

[1] From inside the fish Jonah prayed... [2] "In my distress I called to the LORD, and [H]e answered me. From deep in the realm of the dead I called for help, and [Y]ou listened to my cry... [4] I said, 'I have been banished from [Y]our sight; yet I will look again...' [5] The engulfing waters threatened me, the deep surrounded me... [6] To the roots of the mountains I sank down; the earth beneath barred me in forever. But [Y]ou, LORD my God, brought my life up from the pit. [7] When my life was ebbing away, I remembered [Y]ou, LORD, and my prayer rose to [Y]ou... [9] ...What I [vow] I will make good. I will say, 'Salvation comes from the LORD.'"

[10] And the LORD commanded the fish, and it vomited Jonah onto dry land.

Jonah 3:

[1] Then the word of the LORD came to Jonah a second time: [2] "Go to the great city of Nineveh and proclaim to it the message I give you."

[3] Jonah obeyed the word of the LORD and went to Nineveh. Now Nineveh was a very large city; it took three days to go through it. [4] Jonah began by going a day's journey into the city, proclaiming, "Forty more days and Nineveh will be overthrown." [5] The Ninevites believed God. A fast was proclaimed, and all of them, from the greatest to the least, put

on sackcloth.

[6] When Jonah's warning reached the king of Nineveh, he rose from his throne, took off his royal robes, covered himself with sackcloth and sat down in the dust. [7] This is the proclamation he issued in Nineveh: "By the decree of the king and his nobles: Do not let people or animals, herds or flocks, taste anything; do not let them eat or drink. [8] But let people and animals be covered with sackcloth. Let everyone call urgently on God. Let them give up their evil ways and their violence.

[10] When God saw what they did and how they turned from their evil ways, [Nineveh was spared through [His] compassion].

Greek Orthodox Icon of Jonah

Islam:

Jonah 10:98 And wherefore was there not a town which should believe so that their belief should have profited them but the people of Yunus (Jonah)? When they believed, [I]... gave them provision...

The Rangers 37:139-148 And Yunus was most surely of the apostles. When he ran away to a ship completely laden... he shared (with them), but was of those who are cast off. So the fish swallowed him while he did that for which he blamed himself. But had it not been that he was of those who glorify (Me), [h]e would certainly have tarried in its belly to the day when they are raised. Then [I] cast him on to the vacant surface of the earth while he was sick. And [I] caused to grow up for him a gourdplant. And [I] sent him to a hundred thousand, rather they exceeded. And they believed, so [I] gave them provision...

The Prophets 21:87-88 And Yunus, when he went away in wrath, so he thought that [I] would not strai[gh]ten him, so he called out among afflictions: There is no [G]od but [You], glory be to [You]; surely I am of those who make themselves to suffer loss. So [I] responded to him and delivered him from the grief and thus do [I] deliver the believers.

218

XXV. The Minor Prophets III

Christianity/Judaism:

Micah 2:

[7] "Do not [M]y words do good to the one whose ways are upright? [12] I will surely gather all of you... I will bring [all] together like sheep... [T]he place will throng with people. [13] ...Their King will pass through before them, the LORD at their head."

Micah 4:

[1] In the last days the mountain of the LORD's temple will be established as the highest of the mountains; it will be exalted above the hills, and peoples will stream to it. [2] Many nations will come and say, "Come, let us go up to the mountain of the LORD... He will teach us [H]is ways, so that we may walk in [H]is paths."

[3] He will judge between many peoples and will settle disputes... [4] Everyone will sit under their own vine and under their own fig tree, and no one will make them afraid, for the LORD Almighty has spoken. [6] "In that day," declares the LORD, "I will gather the lame; I will assemble the exiles... [7] The LORD will rule over them... from that day and forever."

Micah 5:

[2] "But you, Bethlehem... though you are small... out of you will come for [M]e one who will be ruler... whose origins are from of old, from ancient times. [4] He will stand and shepherd his flock in the strength of the LORD, in the majesty of the name of the LORD his God. And they will live securely, for then his greatness will reach to the ends of the earth." [5] And he will be our peace... [6] He will deliver us...

Micah 7:

[8] ...Though I have fallen, I will rise. Though I sit in darkness, the LORD will be my light. [9] ...He will bring me out into the light; I will see [H]is righteousness.

[14] Shepherd [Y]our people with your staff, the flock of [Y]our inheritance... [18] Who is a God like you, [W]ho pardons sin and forgives the transgression... [Who] delight[s] to show mercy[?] [19] You will... have compassion on us; [Y]ou will tread our sins underfoot and hurl all our iniquities into the depths of the sea. [20] You will be faithful... and show love...

Nahum 1:

[7] The LORD is good, a refuge in times of trouble. He cares for those who trust in [H]im...

Habakkuk 3:

[3] [When] God came... His glory covered the heavens and [H]is praise filled the earth. [4]

His splendor was like the sunrise; rays flashed from [H]is hand, where [H]is power was hidden. **¹¹** Sun and moon stood still in the heavens…

¹⁸ …I will rejoice in the LORD, I will be joyful in God my Savior. **¹⁹** The Sovereign LORD is my strength; [H]e makes my feet like the feet of a deer, [H]e enables me to tread on the heights.

Zephaniah 2:

³ Seek the LORD, all you humble of the land, you who do what [H]e commands. Seek righteousness, seek humility…

Zephaniah 3:

⁹ "…I will purify the lips of the peoples, that all of them may call on the name of the LORD and serve [H]im… **¹⁰** …[M]y worshipers, [M]y scattered people, will bring me offerings. **¹¹** On that day you… will not be put to shame for all the wrongs you have done… **¹²** [All] will trust in the name of the LORD. **¹³** They will do no wrong; they will tell no lies… They will eat and lie down and no one will make them afraid.

¹⁴ …Be glad and rejoice with all your heart… **¹⁵** The LORD… is with you; never again will you fear any harm. **¹⁷** …He will take great delight in you; in [H]is love [H]e will… rejoice over you with singing."

¹⁹ …I will rescue the lame; I will gather the exiles. I will give them praise and honor… **²⁰** At that time I will gather you; at that time I will bring you home. I will give you honor and praise among all the peoples of the earth…

Haggai 1:

⁷ This is what the LORD Almighty says: "Give careful thought to your ways. **⁸** Go up into the mountains and bring down timber and build my house, so that I may take pleasure in it and be honored," says the LORD. **¹²** …[All] obeyed the voice of the LORD their God and the message of the prophet Haggai…

¹³ Then Haggai… gave this message of the LORD to the people: "I am with you," declares the LORD. **¹⁴** So the LORD stirred up the spirit [in everyone]. They came and began to work on the house of the LORD Almighty, their God…

Haggai 2:

⁶ "This is what the LORD Almighty says: 'In a little while… I will fill this house with glory. **⁹** 'The glory of this present house will be greater than the glory of the former house,' says the LORD Almighty. 'And in this place I will grant peace,' declares the LORD Almighty. **¹⁹** '…From this day on I will bless you.'"

XXVI. The Book of Zechariah

Christianity/Judaism:

Zechariah 1:

¹ ...[T]he LORD came to the prophet Zechariah: ³ "This is what the LORD Almighty says: 'Return to me... and I will return to you. ⁴ ...Turn from your evil ways and your evil practices.'" ⁶ Then they repented...

¹⁶ [The]... LORD [also] sa[id]: "I will return to Jerusalem with mercy, and there [M]y house will be rebuilt. And the measuring line will be stretched out over Jerusalem... ¹⁷ My towns will again overflow with prosperity, and the LORD will again comfort [His] people."

Zechariah 2:

¹ Then I looked up, and there before me was a man with a measuring line in his hand. ² I asked, "Where are you going?"   He answered me, "To measure Jerusalem, to find out how wide and how long it is."

³ While the angel who was speaking to me was leaving, another angel came to meet him ⁴ and said to him: "Run, tell that young man, 'Jerusalem will be a city without walls because of the great number of people and animals in it. ⁵ And I myself will be a wall of fire around it,' declares the LORD, 'and I will be its glory within.'"

¹⁰ "Shout and be glad...   For I am coming, and I will live among you," declares the LORD. ¹¹ Many nations will be joined with the LORD in that day and will become [His] people.

Zechariah 3:

¹ Then he showed me Joshua the high priest... ³ [He] was dressed in filthy clothes as he stood before the angel. ⁴ The angel said to those who were standing before him, "Take off his filthy clothes."   Then he said to Joshua, "See, I have taken away your sin, and I will put fine garments on you."

⁶ The angel of the LORD gave this charge to Joshua: ⁷ "This is what the LORD Almighty says: 'If you will walk in obedience to [M]e and keep [M]y requirements, then you will govern [M]y house and have charge of [M]y courts, and I will give you a place among these standing here.'"

⁸ "Listen... I am going to bring [M]y servant, the Branch ⁹ ...and I will remove the sin of this land in a single day. ¹⁰ In that day each of you will invite your neighbor to sit under your vine and fig tree," declares the LORD Almighty.

Zechariah 4:

¹ Then the angel who talked with me returned and woke me up... ² He asked me, "What

do you see?" I answered, "I see a solid gold lampstand with a bowl at the top and seven lamps on it, with seven channels to the lamps. ³ Also there are two olive trees by it, one on the right of the bowl and the other on its left. ⁴ …What are these?"

⁸ Then the word of the LORD came to me: ⁹ "The hands of Zerubbabel have laid the foundation of this temple; his hands will also complete it… ¹⁰ …[T]he seven eyes of the LORD that range throughout the earth will rejoice when they see the chosen capstone…"

¹¹ Then I asked the angel, "What are these two olive trees on the right and the left of the lampstand?" ¹⁴ …[H]e said, "These are the two who are anointed to serve the Lord of all the earth."

Zechariah 6:

¹ I looked up again, and there before me were four chariots coming out from between two mountains — mountains of bronze. ² The first chariot had red horses, the second black, ³ the third white, and the fourth dappled — all of them powerful. ⁴ I asked the angel who was speaking to me, "What are these, my lord?" ⁵ The angel answered me, "These are the four spirits of heaven, going out from standing in the presence of the Lord of the whole world. ⁶ The one with the black horses is going toward the north country, the one with the white horses toward the west, and the one with the dappled horses toward the south."

⁷ When the powerful horses went out, they were straining to go throughout the earth. And he said, "Go throughout the earth!" So they went throughout the earth. ⁸ Then he called to me, "Look, those going toward the north country have given my Spirit rest in the land of the north."

⁹ The word of the LORD came to me: ¹² Tell [Joshua] this is what the LORD Almighty says: 'Here is the man whose name is the Branch, and he will branch out from his place and build the temple of the LORD. ¹³ It is he who will build the temple of the LORD, and he will be clothed with majesty and will sit and rule on his throne. And he will be a priest on his throne. And there will be harmony…

¹⁵ Those who are far away will come and help to build the temple of the LORD, and you will know that the LORD Almighty has sent me to you. This will happen if you diligently obey the LORD your God."

Zechariah 7:

⁸ And the word of the LORD came again to Zechariah: ⁹ "This is what the LORD Almighty said: 'Administer true justice; show mercy and compassion to one another. ¹⁰ Do not oppress the widow or the fatherless, the foreigner or the poor. Do not plot evil against each other.'"

Zechariah 8:

³ This is what the LORD says: "I will return… and dwell in Jerusalem. Then Jerusalem will be called the Faithful City, and the mountain of the LORD Almighty will be called the Holy Mountain."

[4] This is what the LORD Almighty says: "Once again men and women of ripe old age will sit in the streets of Jerusalem, each of them with cane in hand because of their age. [5] The city streets will be filled with boys and girls playing there."

[7] This is what the LORD Almighty says: "I will save [M]y people... [8] I will bring them back...; they will be [M]y people, and I will be faithful and righteous to them as their God."

[9] This is what the LORD Almighty says: "Let your hands be strong so that the temple may be built. [12] The seed will grow well, the vine will yield its fruit, the ground will produce its crops, and the heavens will drop their dew. I will give all these things as an inheritance to [My] people. [13] ...I will save you, and you will be a blessing. Do not be afraid, but let your hands be strong.

[16] These are the things you are to do: Speak the truth to each other, and render true and sound judgment in your courts; [17] do not plot evil against each other, and do not love to swear falsely. I hate all this," declares the LORD. [19] "...Therefore love truth and peace."

Zechariah 9:

[9] Rejoice greatly, Daughter Zion! Shout, Daughter Jerusalem! See, your king comes to you, righteous and victorious, lowly and riding on a donkey, on a colt, the foal of a donkey.

[10] ...[T]he battle bow will be broken. He will proclaim peace to the nations. His rule will extend from sea to sea... to the ends of the earth.

[11] As for you, because of... [M]y covenant with you, I will free your prisoners from the waterless pit. [12] Return... you prisoners of hope; even now I announce that I will restore twice as much to you.

[16] The LORD... God will save [H]is people... as a shepherd saves his flock. They will sparkle in [H]is land like jewels in a crown. [17] How attractive and beautiful they will be! Grain will make the young men thrive, and new wine the young women.

Zechariah 10:

[1] Ask the LORD for rain in the springtime; it is the LORD who sends the thunderstorms. He gives showers of rain to all people, and plants of the field to everyone. [3] ...[T]he LORD Almighty will care for [H]is flock...

[6] "I will restore them because I have compassion on them... for I am the LORD their God and I will answer them. [7] ...[T]heir hearts will rejoice in the LORD. [8] ...Surely I will redeem them... [12] ...[I]n [My] name they will live securely," declares the LORD.

Zechariah 12:

[10] "And I will pour out... a spirit of grace and supplication. They will look on me, the one they have pierced, and they will mourn for him as one mourns for an only child, and grieve bitterly for him as one grieves for a firstborn son. [11] On that day the weeping in Jerusalem will be... great... [12] The land will mourn...

Zechariah 13:

[1] "On that day a fountain will be opened... to cleanse them from sin and impurity. [9] ...They will call on [M]y name and I will answer them; I will say, 'They are [M]y people,' and they will say, 'The LORD is our God.'"

Zechariah 14:

[1] A day of the LORD is coming... [6] On that day there will be neither sunlight nor cold, frosty darkness. [7] It will be a unique day — a day known only to the LORD — with no distinction between day and night. When evening comes, there will be light.

[8] On that day living water will flow out... [9] The LORD will be king over the whole earth...

XXVII. The Books of Malachi and The Maccabees

Christianity/Judaism:

Malachi 1:

² "I have loved you," says the LORD.

Malachi 2:

⁵ "...[L]ife and peace... I gave them to [Levi]; this called for reverence and he revered [M]e and stood in awe of [M]y name. ⁶ True instruction was in his mouth and nothing false was found on his lips. He walked with [M]e in peace and uprightness, and turned many from sin.

⁷ For the lips of a priest ought to preserve knowledge, because he is the messenger of the LORD Almighty and people seek instruction from his mouth."

¹⁰ Do we not all have one Father? Did not one God create us? ¹⁵ Has not the one God made you? You belong to him in body and spirit. ...[D]o not be unfaithful...

Malachi 3:

¹ "I will send my messenger, who will prepare the way before [M]e. Then suddenly the Lord you are seeking will come to [H]is temple...," says the LORD Almighty.

¹⁶ Then those who feared the LORD talked with each other, and the LORD listened and heard. A scroll of remembrance was written... concerning those who feared the LORD and honored [H]is name. ¹⁷ "...[T]hey will be my treasured possession... I will [have]... compassion..."

Malachi 4:

² "...[F]or you who revere [M]y name, the sun of righteousness will rise with healing in its rays. And you will go out and frolic like well-fed calves.

1 Maccabees 1:

⁴¹ Then the king (Antiochus) wrote to his whole kingdom that all should be one people, ⁴² and that all should give up their particular customs. ⁴³ All the Gentiles accepted the command of the king. Many even from Israel gladly adopted his religion; they sacrificed to idols and profaned the [S]abbath. ⁴⁴ And the king sent letters by messengers to Jerusalem and the towns of Judah; he directed them to... to profane [S]abbaths and festivals, ⁴⁶ to defile the sanctuary and the priests, ⁴⁷ to build altars and sacred precincts and shrines for idols, to sacrifice swine and other unclean animals, ⁴⁸ and to leave their sons uncircumcised. They were to make themselves abominable by everything unclean and profane, ⁴⁹ so that they would forget the law and change all the ordinances.

2 Maccabees 10:

¹ Now Maccabeus and his followers, the Lord leading them on, recovered the temple and

the city... [3] They purified the sanctuary... and they offered incense and lighted lamps and set out the bread of the Presence. [4] When they had done this, they fell prostrate and implored the Lord that they might never again fall into such misfortunes... [6] They celebrated... for eight days with rejoicing, in the manner of the festival of booths, remembering how not long before, during the festival of booths, they had been wandering in the mountains and caves like wild animals.

Judaism:

[Babylonian Talmud. Shabbat 21b]:

What is the reason for Chanukah? For our Rabbis taught: On the twenty-fifth day of Kislev the eight days of Chanukah begin, during which lamentation for the dead and fasting are forbidden. For [after the] Temple [and]... all the oils therein [were defiled], and when the [Temple was recovered by the Maccabees], they made search and found only one cruse of oil which lay with the seal of the High Priest, but which contained sufficient [oil] for one day's lighting only; yet a miracle was wrought therein and they lit the lamp therewith for eight days...

Maimonides the Laws of Chanukkah, ch. 3 Halachah 3:

"It is because of this... that these eight days, beginning on the twenty fifth of Kislev, should be days of joy and praise, and candles are lit each evening in the doorway of the home, in order to show and reveal the miracle."

Al Ha-Nissim (recited in the Amidah and Birkat Ha-Mazon Prayers):

"[We thank [Y]ou] for the miracles and for the salvation... [Y]ou in [Y]our great mercy stood up for [Your people] in the time of their distress. You took up their grievance, judged their claim... For Yourself, You made a great and holy name in Your world, and for Your people... You [brought] salvation... Thereafter, Your children came to the Holy of Holies of Your House, cleansed your Temple, purified the site of Your holiness and kindled lights in the courtyards of Your sanctuary; and they established these eight days of Chanukah to express thanks and praise to Your great name."

Maoz Tzur:

O mighty stronghold of my salvation, to praise You is a delight. Restore my House of Prayer and there we will bring a thanksgiving offering. ...Then I shall complete with a song of hymn the dedication of the Altar.

My soul had been sated with troubles, my strength has been consumed with grief. They had embittered my life with hardship, with the calf-like kingdom's bondage. But with His great power He brought forth the treasured ones...

To the holy abode of His Word He brought me. But there, too, I had no rest [a]nd an oppressor came and exiled me. ...[T]hen in Hasmonean days, [t]hey breached the walls of my towers and they defiled all the oils; [a]nd from the one remnant of the flasks a miracle was wrought for the roses. [People] of insight — eight days established for song and jubilation.

XXVIII. The Gospels: Jesus the Christ

Christianity:

John 1:

¹ In the beginning was the Word, and the Word was with God, and the Word was God. ² He was with God in the beginning. ³ Through [H]im all things were made; without [H]im nothing was made... ⁴ In [H]im was life, and that life was the light of all mankind. ⁵ The light shines in the darkness, and the darkness has not overcome it.

⁶ There was a man sent from God whose name was John. ⁷ He came as a witness to testify concerning that light, so that through him all might believe. ⁸ He himself was not the light; he came only as a witness to the light.

⁹ The true light that gives light to everyone was coming into the world. ¹⁰ He was in the world, and though the world was made through [H]im, the world did not recognize [H]im. ¹¹ He came to that which was [H]is own, but [H]is own did not receive [H]im. ¹² Yet to all who did receive [H]im, to those who believed in [H]is name, [H]e gave the right to become children of God — ¹³ children born not of natural descent, nor of human decision or a husband's will, but born of God.

¹⁴ The Word became flesh and made [H]is dwelling among us... the one and only Son, who came from the Father, full of grace and truth.

¹⁵ (John testified concerning him. He cried out, saying, "This is the one I spoke about when I said, 'He who comes after me has surpassed me because [H]e was before me'").

Luke 1:

⁵ In the time of Herod king of Judea there was a priest named Zechariah, who belonged to the priestly division of Abijah; his wife Elizabeth was also a descendant of Aaron. ⁶ Both of them were righteous in the sight of God, observing all the Lord's commands and decrees blamelessly. ⁷ But they were childless because Elizabeth was not able to conceive, and they were both very old.

⁸ ... Zechariah... ⁹ was chosen by lot, according to the custom of the priesthood, to go into the temple of the Lord and burn incense. ¹⁰ And when the time for the burning of incense came, all the assembled worshipers were praying outside.

¹¹ Then an angel of the Lord appeared to him, standing at the right side of the altar of incense. ¹² When Zechariah saw him, he was startled and was gripped with fear.

¹³ But the angel said to him: "Do not be afraid, Zechariah; your prayer has been heard. Your wife Elizabeth will bear you a son, and you are to call him John. ¹⁴ He will be a joy and delight to you, and many will rejoice because of his birth, ¹⁵ for he will be great in the sight of the Lord. ...[H]e will be filled with the Holy Spirit even before he is born. ¹⁶ He will bring back many of the people... to the Lord their God. ¹⁷ And he will go on before the Lord, in the spirit and power of Elijah, to turn the hearts of the parents to their children

and the disobedient to the wisdom of the righteous — to make ready a people prepared for the Lord."

[18] Zechariah asked the angel, "How can I be sure of this? I am an old man and my wife is well along in years."

[19] The angel said to him, "I am Gabriel. I stand in the presence of God, and I have been sent to speak to you and to tell you this good news. [20] And now you will be silent and not able to speak until the day this happens, because you did not believe my words, which will come true at their appointed time."

[21] Meanwhile, the people were waiting for Zechariah and wondering why he stayed so long in the temple. [22] When he came out, he could not speak to them. They realized he had seen a vision in the temple, for he kept making signs to them but remained unable to speak.

[23] When his time of service was completed, he returned home. [24] After this his wife Elizabeth became pregnant and for five months remained in seclusion. [25] "The Lord has done this for me," she said.

[26] In the sixth month of Elizabeth's pregnancy, God sent the angel Gabriel to Nazareth, a town in Galilee, [27] to a virgin pledged to be married to a man named Joseph, a descendant of David. The virgin's name was Mary. [28] The angel went to her and said, "Greetings, you who are highly favored! The Lord is with you."

[29] Mary was greatly troubled at his words and wondered what kind of greeting this might be. [30] But the angel said to her, "Do not be afraid, Mary; you have found favor with God. [31] You will conceive and give birth to a son, and you are to call him Jesus. [32] He will be great and will be called the Son of the Most High. The Lord God will give him the throne of his father David, [33] and he will reign... forever; his kingdom will never end."

[34] "How will this be," Mary asked the angel, "since I am a virgin?" [35] The angel answered, "The Holy Spirit will come on you, and the power of the Most High will overshadow you. So the holy one to be born will be called the Son of God. [37] For no word from God will ever fail."

[38] "I am the Lord's servant," Mary answered. "May your word to me be fulfilled." Then the angel left her.

[39] At that time Mary got ready and hurried to a town in the hill country of Judea, [40] where she entered Zechariah's home and greeted Elizabeth. [41] When Elizabeth heard Mary's greeting, the baby leaped in her womb, and Elizabeth was filled with the Holy Spirit. [42] In a loud voice she exclaimed: "Blessed are you among women, and blessed is the child you will bear! [43] But why am I so favored, that the mother of my Lord should come to me? [44] As soon as the sound of your greeting reached my ears, the baby in my womb leaped for joy. [45] Blessed is she who has believed that the Lord would fulfill his promises to her!"

[46] And Mary said: "My soul glorifies the Lord [47] and my spirit rejoices in God my Savior, [48] for [H]e has been mindful of the humble state of [H]is servant. From now on all

generations will call me blessed, [49] for the Mighty One has done great things for me — holy is [H]is name.

The Annunciation by Fra Angelico c. 1430

[50] His mercy extends to those who fear [H]im, from generation to generation. [51] He has performed mighty deeds with [H]is arm... [52] He has... lifted up the humble. [53] He has filled the hungry with good things... [54] He has helped [H]is servant... remembering to be merciful... [55] just as [H]e promised our ancestors."

[56] Mary stayed with Elizabeth for about three months and then returned home.

[57] When it was time for Elizabeth to have her baby, she gave birth to a son. [58] Her neighbors and relatives heard that the Lord had shown her great mercy, and they shared her joy. [59] On the eighth day they came to circumcise the child, and they were going to name him after his father Zechariah, [60] but his mother spoke up and said, "No! He is to be called John."

[61] They said to her, "There is no one among your relatives who has that name." [62] Then they made signs to his father, to find out what he would like to name the child. [63] He asked for a writing tablet, and to everyone's astonishment he wrote, "His name is John." [64] Immediately his mouth was opened and his tongue set free, and he began to speak, praising God. [65] All the neighbors were filled with awe... [66] Everyone who heard this wondered about it, asking, "What then is this child going to be?" For the Lord's hand was with him.

[67] His father Zechariah was filled with the Holy Spirit and prophesied: [68] "Praise be to the Lord, [our] God... because [H]e has come to [H]is people and redeemed them. [69] He has raised up a horn of salvation for us... [71] salvation from our enemies and from the hand of all who hate us — [72] to show mercy to our ancestors and to remember [H]is holy covenant... [74] ...to enable us to serve [H]im without fear [75] in holiness and righteousness before [H]im all our days.

[76] And you, my child, will be called a prophet of the Most High; for you will go on before the Lord to prepare the way for [H]im, [77] to give [H]is people the knowledge of salvation through the forgiveness of their sins, [78] because of the tender mercy of our God, by

which the rising sun will come to us from heaven [79] to shine on those living in darkness and in the shadow of death, to guide our feet into the path of peace."

[80] And the child grew and became strong in spirit; and he lived in the wilderness until he appeared publicly....

Matthew 1:

[18] This is how the birth of Jesus the Messiah came about: His mother Mary was pledged to be married to Joseph, but before they came together, she was found to be pregnant through the Holy Spirit. [19] Because Joseph her husband was faithful to the law, and... did not want to expose her to public disgrace, he had in mind to divorce her quietly.

[20] But after he had considered this, an angel of the Lord appeared to him in a dream and said, "Joseph... do not be afraid to take Mary home as your wife, because what is conceived in her is from the Holy Spirit. [21] She will give birth to a son, and you are to give him the name Jesus, because he will save his people from their sins."

[22] All this took place to fulfill what the Lord had said through the prophet: [23] "The virgin will conceive and give birth to a son, and they will call him Immanuel" (which means "God with us").

[24] When Joseph woke up, he did what the angel of the Lord had commanded him and took Mary home as his wife. [25] But he did not consummate their marriage until she gave birth to a son. And he gave him the name Jesus.

Luke 2:

[1] In those days Caesar Augustus issued a decree that a census should be taken of the entire Roman world. [3] And everyone went to their own town to register. [4] So Joseph also went up from the town of Nazareth... [to] Bethlehem... because he belonged to the house and line of David. [5] He went there to register with Mary, who was pledged to be married to him and was expecting a child. [6] While they were there, the time came for the baby to be born, [7] and she gave birth to her firstborn, a son. She wrapped him in cloths and placed him in a manger, because there was no guest room available for them.

[8] And there were shepherds living out in the fields nearby, keeping watch over their flocks at night. [9] An angel of the Lord appeared to them, and the glory of the Lord shone around them... [10] [T]he angel said to them, "...I bring you good news that will cause great joy for all the people. [11] Today... a Savior has been born to you; he is the Messiah, the Lord. [12] This will be a sign to you: You will find a baby wrapped in cloths and lying in a manger."

[13] Suddenly a great company of the heavenly host appeared with the angel, praising God and saying, [14] "Glory to God in the highest heaven, and on earth peace to those on whom [H]is favor rests."

[15] When the angels had left them and gone into heaven, the shepherds said to one another, "Let's go to Bethlehem and see this thing that has happened, which the Lord has told us about." [16] So they hurried off and found Mary and Joseph, and the baby, who was lying in the manger. [17] When they had seen him, they spread the word

concerning what had been told them about this child, [18] and all who heard it were amazed at what the shepherds said to them. [19] But Mary treasured up all these things and pondered them in her heart. [20] The shepherds returned, glorifying and praising God for all the things they had heard and seen, which were just as they had been told.

Nativity by Fra Angelico c. 1439-1443

[21] On the eighth day, when it was time to circumcise the child, he was named Jesus, the name the angel had given him before he was conceived.

[22] When the time came for the purification rites required by the Law of Moses, Joseph and Mary took him to Jerusalem to present him to the Lord [23] (as it is written in the Law of the Lord, "Every firstborn male is to be consecrated to the Lord"), [24] and to offer a sacrifice in keeping with what is said in the Law of the Lord: "a pair of doves or two young pigeons."

[25] Now there was a man in Jerusalem called Simeon, who was righteous and devout. He was waiting for the consolation of [the people], and the Holy Spirit was on him. [26] It had been revealed to him by the Holy Spirit that he would not die before he had seen the Lord's Messiah. [27] Moved by the Spirit, he went into the temple courts. When the parents brought in the child Jesus to do for him what the custom of the Law required, [28] Simeon took him in his arms and praised God, saying: [29] "Sovereign Lord, as [Y]ou have promised, [Y]ou may now dismiss [Y]our servant in peace. [30] For my eyes have seen [Y]our salvation, [31] which [Y]ou have prepared in the sight of all nations: [32] a light for revelation… and… glory…"

[33] The child's father and mother marveled at what was said about him. [34] Then Simeon blessed them and said to Mary, his mother: "This child is destined to cause the falling and rising of many… and to be a sign that will be spoken against, [35] so that the thoughts of many hearts will be revealed. And a sword will pierce your own soul too."

[36] There was also a prophet, Anna… She was very old; she had lived with her husband seven years after her marriage, [37] and then was a widow until she was eighty-four. She never left the temple but worshiped night and day, fasting and praying. [38] Coming up to them at that very moment, she gave thanks to God and spoke about the child to all who were looking forward to the redemption of Jerusalem.

Matthew 2:

¹ After Jesus was born in Bethlehem… during the time of King Herod, Magi from the east came to Jerusalem ² and asked, "Where is the one who has been born king? We saw his star when it rose and have come to worship him."

³ When King Herod heard this he was disturbed… ⁴ When he had called together all the people's chief priests and teachers of the law, he asked them where the Messiah was to be born. ⁵ "In Bethlehem in Judea," they replied, "for this is what the prophet has written:

⁶ 'But you, Bethlehem, in the land of Judah, are by no means least among the rulers of Judah; for out of you will come a ruler who will shepherd [M]y people…'"

⁷ Then Herod called the Magi secretly and found out from them the exact time the star had appeared. ⁸ He sent them to Bethlehem and said, "Go and search carefully for the child. As soon as you find him, report to me, so that I too may go and worship him."

⁹ After they had heard the king, they went on their way, and the star they had seen when it rose went ahead of them until it stopped over the place where the child was. ¹⁰ When they saw the star, they were overjoyed.

Adoration of the Magi by Fra Angelico and
Fra Filippo Lippi c. 1440-1460

¹¹ On coming to the house, they saw the child with his mother Mary, and they bowed down and worshiped him. Then they opened their treasures and presented him with gifts of gold, frankincense and myrrh. ¹² And having been warned in a dream not to go back to Herod, they returned to their country by another route.

¹³ When they had gone, an angel of the Lord appeared to Joseph in a dream. "Get up," he said, "take the child and his mother and escape to Egypt. Stay there until I tell you, for Herod is going to search for the child to kill him."

¹⁴ So he got up, took the child and his mother during the night and left for Egypt, ¹⁵ where he stayed until the death of Herod. And so was fulfilled what the Lord had said through the prophet: "Out of Egypt I called my son." ¹⁹ After Herod died, an angel of the Lord appeared in a dream to Joseph in Egypt ²⁰ and said, "Get up, take the child and his

mother and go to the land of Israel..."

[21] So he got up, took the child and his mother and went to the land of Israel. [22] But when he heard that Archelaus was reigning in Judea in place of his father Herod, he was afraid to go there. Having been warned in a dream, he withdrew to the district of Galilee, [23] and he went and lived in a town called Nazareth. So was fulfilled what was said through the prophets, that he would be called a Nazarene.

Luke 2:

[40] And the child grew and became strong; he was filled with wisdom, and the grace of God was on him.

[41] Every year Jesus' parents went to Jerusalem for the Festival of the Passover. [42] When he was twelve years old, they went up to the festival, according to the custom. [43] After the festival was over, while his parents were returning home, the boy Jesus stayed behind in Jerusalem, but they were unaware of it. [44] Thinking he was in their company, they traveled on for a day. Then they began looking for him among their relatives and friends.

[45] When they did not find him, they went back to Jerusalem to look for him. [46] After three days they found him in the temple courts, sitting among the teachers, listening to them and asking them questions. [47] Everyone who heard him was amazed at his understanding and his answers. [48] When his parents saw him, they were astonished. His mother said to him, "Son, why have you treated us like this? Your father and I have been anxiously searching for you."

[49] "Why were you searching for me?" he asked. "Didn't you know I had to be in my Father's house?" [50] But they did not understand what he was saying to them. [51] Then he went down to Nazareth with them and was obedient to them. But his mother treasured all these things in her heart. [52] And Jesus grew in wisdom and stature, and in favor with God and man.

Matthew 3:

[1] In those days John the Baptist came, preaching in the wilderness of Judea [2] and saying, "Repent, for the kingdom of heaven has come near." [3] This is he who was spoken of through the prophet Isaiah: "A voice of one calling in the wilderness, 'Prepare the way for the Lord, make straight paths for him.'"

Mark 1:

[4] And so John the Baptist appeared in the wilderness, preaching a baptism of repentance for the forgiveness of sins.

Matthew 3:

[5] People went out to him from Jerusalem and all Judea and the whole region of the Jordan. [6] Confessing their sins, they were baptized by him in the Jordan River.

Luke 3:

[10] "What should we do then?" the crowd asked. [11] John answered, "Anyone who has

two shirts should share with the one who has none, and anyone who has food should do the same." [12] Even tax collectors came to be baptized. "Teacher," they asked, "what should we do?" [13] "Don't collect any more than you are required to," he told them. [14] Then some soldiers asked him, "And what should we do?" He replied, "Don't extort money and don't accuse people falsely — be content with your pay."

John 1:

[20] ...[John] confessed freely, "I am not the Messiah." [25] "Why then do you baptize if you are not the Messiah, nor Elijah, nor the Prophet?" [he was asked].

Matthew 3:

[11] "I baptize you with water for repentance. But after me comes one who is more powerful than I, whose sandals I am not worthy to carry. He will baptize you with the Holy Spirit..."

John 1:

[29] The next day John saw Jesus coming toward him and said, "Look, the Lamb of God, who takes away the sin of the world! [30] This is the one I meant when I said, 'A man who comes after me has surpassed me because he was before me.' [31] I myself did not know him, but the reason I came baptizing with water was that he might be revealed..."

Matthew 3:

[13] Then Jesus came from Galilee to the Jordan to be baptized by John. [14] But John tried to deter him, saying, "I need to be baptized by you, and... you come to me?" [15] Jesus replied, "Let it be so now; it is proper for us to do this to fulfill all righteousness." Then John consented.

[16] As soon as Jesus was baptized, he went up out of the water. At that moment heaven was opened, and he saw the Spirit of God descending like a dove and alighting on him. [17] And a voice from heaven said, "This is [M]y Son, whom I love; with him I am well pleased."

Baptism of Christ by Fra Angelico c. 1425

Luke 3:

[23] Now Jesus himself was about thirty years old when he began his ministry.

Matthew 4:

[1] Then Jesus was led by the Spirit into the wilderness to be tempted by the devil. [2] After fasting forty days and forty nights, he was hungry.

Luke 4:

[3] The devil said to him, "If you are the Son of God, tell this stone to become bread." [4] Jesus answered, "It is written: 'Man shall not live on bread alone.'"

[5] The devil led him up to a high place and showed him in an instant all the kingdoms of the world. [6] And he said to him, "I will give you all their authority and splendor; it has been given to me, and I can give it to anyone I want to. [7] If you worship me, it will all be yours." [8] Jesus answered, "It is written: 'Worship the Lord your God and serve [H]im only.'"

[9] The devil led him to Jerusalem and had him stand on the highest point of the temple. "If you are the Son of God," he said, "throw yourself down from here. [10] For it is written: 'He will command his angels concerning you to guard you carefully; [11] they will lift you up in their hands, so that you will not strike your foot against a stone.'" [12] Jesus answered, "It is said: 'Do not put the Lord your God to the test.'"

[13] When the devil had finished all this tempting, he left him until an opportune time.

John 1:

[35] The next day John was there again with two of his disciples. [36] When he saw Jesus passing by, he said, "Look, the Lamb of God!" [37] When the two disciples heard him say this, they followed Jesus. [38] Turning around, Jesus saw them following and asked, "What do you want?" They said, "Rabbi" (which means "Teacher"), "where are you staying?" [39] "Come," he replied, "and you will see." So they went and saw where he was staying, and they spent that day with him. It was about four in the afternoon.

[40] Andrew, Simon Peter's brother, was one of the two who heard what John had said and who had followed Jesus. [41] The first thing Andrew did was to find his brother Simon and tell him, "We have found the Messiah." [42] And he brought him to Jesus. Jesus looked at him and said, "You are Simon son of John. You will be called Cephas" (which, when translated, is Peter).

[43] The next day Jesus decided to leave for Galilee. Finding Philip, he said to him, "Follow me." [44] Philip, like Andrew and Peter, was from the town of Bethsaida. [45] Philip found Nathanael and told him, "We have found the one Moses wrote about in the Law, and about whom the prophets also wrote — Jesus of Nazareth, the son of Joseph."

[46] "Nazareth! Can anything good come from there?" Nathanael asked. "Come and see," said Philip. [47] When Jesus saw Nathanael approaching, he said of him, "Here truly is an

Israelite in whom there is no deceit." ⁴⁸ "How do you know me?" Nathanael asked. Jesus answered, "I saw you while you were still under the fig tree before Philip called you."

⁴⁹ Then Nathanael declared, "Rabbi, you are the Son of God; you are the king of Israel." ⁵⁰ Jesus said, "You believe because I told you I saw you under the fig tree. You will see greater things than that." ⁵¹ He then added, "Very truly I tell you, you will see 'heaven open, and the angels of God ascending and descending on' the Son of Man."

John 2:

¹ On the third day a wedding took place at Cana in Galilee. Jesus' mother was there, ² and Jesus and his disciples had also been invited to the wedding. ³ When the wine was gone, Jesus' mother said to him, "They have no more wine."

⁴ "[W]hy do you involve me?" Jesus replied. "My hour has not yet come." ⁵ His mother said to the servants, "Do whatever he tells you."

⁶ Nearby stood six stone water jars, the kind used… for ceremonial washing, each holding from twenty to thirty gallons. ⁷ Jesus said to the servants, "Fill the jars with water;" so they filled them to the brim. ⁸ Then he told them, "Now draw some out and take it to the master of the banquet."

They did so, ⁹ and the master of the banquet tasted the water that had been turned into wine. He did not realize where it had come from, though the servants who had drawn the water knew. Then he called the bridegroom aside ¹⁰ and said, "Everyone brings out the choice wine first and then the cheaper wine after the guests have had too much to drink; but you have saved the best till now."

¹¹ What Jesus did here in Cana of Galilee was the first of the signs through which he revealed his glory; and his disciples believed in him.

¹² After this he went down to Capernaum with his mother and brothers and his disciples. There they stayed for a few days.

¹³ When it was almost time for the Jewish Passover, Jesus went up to Jerusalem. ¹⁴ In the temple courts he found people selling cattle, sheep and doves, and others sitting at tables exchanging money. ¹⁵ So he… drove all from the temple courts, both sheep and cattle; he scattered the coins of the money changers and overturned their tables. ¹⁶ To those who sold doves he said, "Get these out of here! Stop turning my Father's house into a market!" ¹⁷ His disciples remembered that it is written: "Zeal for [Y]our house will consume me."

¹⁸ The [crowd] then [asked], "What sign can you show us to prove your authority to do all this?" ¹⁹ Jesus answered them, "Destroy this temple, and I will raise it again in three days."

²⁰ They replied, "It has taken forty-six years to build this temple, and you are going to raise it in three days?" ²¹ But the temple he had spoken of was his body. ²² After he was raised from the dead, his disciples recalled what he had said.

23 Now while he was in Jerusalem at the Passover Festival, many people saw the signs he was performing and believed in his name.

John 3:

1 Now there was a Pharisee, a man named Nicodemus who was a member of the Jewish ruling council. 2 He came to Jesus at night and said, "Rabbi, we know that you are a teacher who has come from God. For no one could perform the signs you are doing if God were not with him." 3 Jesus replied, "Very truly I tell you, no one can see the kingdom of God unless they are born again."

4 "How can someone be born when they are old?" Nicodemus asked. "Surely they cannot enter a second time into their mother's womb to be born!" 5 Jesus answered, "Very truly I tell you, no one can enter the kingdom of God unless they are born of water and the Spirit. 6 Flesh gives birth to flesh, but the Spirit gives birth to spirit. 7 You should not be surprised at my saying, 'You must be born again.' 8 The wind blows wherever it pleases. You hear its sound, but you cannot tell where it comes from or where it is going. So it is with everyone born of the Spirit.

14 …[T]he Son of Man must be lifted up, 15 that everyone who believes may have eternal life in him." 16 For God so loved the world that [H]e gave [H]is one and only Son, that whoever believes in him shall not perish but have eternal life. 17 For God did not send [H]is Son into the world to condemn the world, but to save the world through him. 18 Whoever believes in him is not condemned… 19 Light has come into the world… 21 [W]hoever lives by the truth comes into the light, so that it may be seen plainly that what they have done has been done in the sight of God.

22 After this, Jesus and his disciples went out into the Judean countryside, where he spent some time with them, and baptized. 23 Now John also was baptizing at Aenon near Salim, because there was plenty of water, and people were coming and being baptized. 25 An argument developed between some of John's disciples and a certain [person] over the matter of ceremonial washing. 26 They came to John and said, "…[T]hat man who was with you on the other side of the Jordan — the one you testified about — look, he is baptizing, and everyone is going to him."

27 To this John replied, "A person can receive only what is given them from heaven. 28 You yourselves can testify that I said, 'I am not the Messiah but am sent ahead of him.' 29 The bride belongs to the bridegroom. The friend who attends the bridegroom waits and listens for him, and is full of joy when he hears the bridegroom's voice. That joy is mine, and it is now complete. 30 He must become greater; I must become less."

31 …The one who comes from heaven is above all. 13 No one has ever gone into heaven except the one who came from heaven — the Son of Man. 35 The Father loves the Son and has placed everything in his hands. 36 Whoever believes in the Son has eternal life…

John 4:

3 [Jesus] left Judea and went back once more to Galilee. 4 Now he had to go through Samaria. 5 So he came to a town… Sychar… 6 Jacob's well was there, and Jesus, tired

as he was from the journey, sat down by the well. It was about noon. [7] When a Samaritan woman came to draw water, Jesus said to her, "Will you give me a drink?" [8] (His disciples had gone into the town to buy food).

[9] The Samaritan woman said to him, "You are a Jew and I am a Samaritan woman. How can you ask me for a drink?" (For Jews do not associate with Samaritans). [10] Jesus answered her, "If you knew the gift of God and who it is that asks you for a drink, you would have asked him and he would have given you living water."

[11] "Sir," the woman said, "you have nothing to draw with and the well is deep. Where can you get this living water?" [13] Jesus answered, "Everyone who drinks this water will be thirsty again, [14] but whoever drinks the water I give them will never thirst. Indeed, the water I give them will become in them a spring of water welling up to eternal life."

[15] The woman said to him, "Sir, give me this water so that I won't get thirsty and have to keep coming here to draw water."

[21] "Woman," Jesus replied, "believe me, a time is coming when you will worship the Father neither on this mountain nor in Jerusalem. [23] [A] time is coming and has now come when the true worshipers will worship the Father in the Spirit and in truth… [24] God is spirit, and [H]is worshipers must worship in the Spirit and in truth."

[25] The woman said, "I know that [the] Messiah is coming. When he comes, he will explain everything to us." [26] Then Jesus declared, "I, the one speaking to you — I am he."

[27] Just then his disciples returned and were surprised to find him talking with a woman. But no one asked, "What do you want?" or "Why are you talking with her?"

[28] Then, leaving her water jar, the woman went back to the town and said to the people, [29] "Come, see a man who told me everything I ever did. Could this be the Messiah?" [30] They came out of the town and made their way toward him.

[31] Meanwhile his disciples urged him, "Rabbi, eat something." [32] But he said to them, "I have food to eat that you know nothing about."

[33] Then his disciples said to each other, "Could someone have brought him food?" [34] "My food," said Jesus, "is to do the will of [H]im who sent me and to finish [H]is work. [35] …I tell you, open your eyes and look at the fields! They are ripe for harvest. [36] Even now the one who reaps draws a wage and harvests a crop for eternal life, so that the sower and the reaper may be glad together. [37] Thus the saying 'One sows and another reaps' is true. [38] I sent you to reap what you have not worked for. Others have done the hard work, and you have reaped the benefits of their labor."

[39] Many of the Samaritans from that town believed in him because of the woman's testimony… [40] So when the Samaritans came to him, they urged him to stay with them, and he stayed two days. [41] And because of his words many more became believers.

[42] They said to the woman, "We no longer believe just because of what you said; now we have heard for ourselves, and we know that this man really is the Savior of the world."

⁴³ After the two days he left for Galilee. ⁴⁵ When he arrived in Galilee, the Galileans welcomed him… ⁴⁶ Once more he visited Cana…, where he had turned the water into wine. And there was a certain royal official whose son lay sick at Capernaum. ⁴⁷ When this man heard that Jesus had arrived in Galilee from Judea, he went to him and begged him to come and heal his son, who was close to death. ⁴⁹ The royal official said, "Sir, come down before my child dies."

⁵⁰ "Go," Jesus replied, "your son will live." The man took Jesus at his word and departed. ⁵¹ While he was still on the way, his servants met him with the news that his boy was living. ⁵² When he inquired as to the time when his son got better, they said to him, "Yesterday, at one in the afternoon, the fever left him." ⁵³ Then the father realized that this was the exact time at which Jesus had said to him, "Your son will live." So he and his whole household believed. ⁵⁴ This was the second sign Jesus performed after coming from Judea to Galilee.

Mark 1:

¹⁴ After John was put in prison, Jesus went into Galilee, proclaiming the good news of God. ¹⁵ "The time has come," he said. "The kingdom of God has come near. Repent and believe the good news!"

¹⁶ As Jesus walked beside the Sea of Galilee, he saw Simon and his brother Andrew casting a net into the lake, for they were fishermen. ¹⁷ "Come, follow me," Jesus said, "and I will send you out to fish for people." ¹⁸ At once they left their nets and followed him.

¹⁹ When he had gone a little farther, he saw James son of Zebedee and his brother John in a boat, preparing their nets. ²⁰ Without delay he called them, and they left their father Zebedee in the boat with the hired men and followed him.

Luke 4:

¹⁴ Jesus returned to Galilee in the power of the Spirit, and news about him spread through the whole countryside. ¹⁵ He was teaching in their synagogues, and everyone praised him.

¹⁶ He went to Nazareth, where he had been brought up, and on the Sabbath day he went into the synagogue, as was his custom. He stood up to read, ¹⁷ and the scroll of the prophet Isaiah was handed to him. Unrolling it, he found the place where it is written:

¹⁸ "The Spirit of the Lord is on me, because he has anointed me to proclaim good news to the poor. He has sent me to proclaim freedom for the prisoners and recovery of sight for the blind, to set the oppressed free, ¹⁹ to proclaim the year of the Lord's favor."

²⁰ Then he rolled up the scroll, gave it back to the attendant and sat down. The eyes of everyone in the synagogue were fastened on him. ²¹ "Today this scripture is fulfilled in your hearing," [Jesus said].

Mark 1:

²¹ They went to Capernaum, and when the Sabbath came, Jesus went into the

synagogue and began to teach. [22] The people were amazed at his teaching, because he taught them as one who had authority… [23] Just then a man in their synagogue who was possessed by an impure spirit cried out, [24] "What do you want with us, Jesus of Nazareth? Have you come to destroy us? I know who you are — the Holy One of God!"

[25] "Be quiet!" said Jesus sternly. "Come out of him!" [26] The impure spirit shook the man violently and came out of him with a shriek. [27] The people were all so amazed that they asked each other, "What is this? A new teaching — and with authority! He even gives orders to impure spirits and they obey him." [28] News about him spread quickly over the whole region of Galilee.

Matthew 8:

[14] When Jesus came into Peter's house, he saw Peter's mother-in-law lying in bed with a fever. [15] He touched her hand and the fever left her, and she got up and began to wait on him.

Luke 4:

[40] At sunset, the people brought to Jesus all who had various kinds of sickness, and laying his hands on each one, he healed them.

Matthew 8:

[17] This was to fulfill what was spoken through the prophet Isaiah: "He took up our infirmities and bore our diseases."

Matthew 4:

[23] Jesus went throughout Galilee, teaching in their synagogues, proclaiming the good news of the kingdom, and healing every disease and sickness among the people. [24] News about him spread all over… and people brought to him all who were ill with various diseases, those suffering severe pain, the demon-possessed, those having seizures, and the paralyzed; and he healed them. [25] Large crowds from [all over]… followed him.

Mark 1:

[35] Very early in the morning, while it was still dark, Jesus got up, left the house and went off to a solitary place, where he prayed. [36] Simon and his companions went to look for him, [37] and when they found him, they exclaimed: "Everyone is looking for you!"

[38] Jesus replied, "Let us go… to the nearby villages so I can preach there also. That is why I have come." [39] So he traveled throughout Galilee, preaching in their synagogues and driving out demons.

Luke 5:

[1] One day as Jesus was standing by the Lake of Gennesaret, the people were crowding around him and listening to the word of God. [2] He saw at the water's edge two boats, left there by the fishermen, who were washing their nets. [3] He got into one of the boats, the one belonging to Simon, and asked him to put out a little from shore. Then he sat down and taught the people from the boat.

⁴ When he had finished speaking, he said to Simon, "Put out into deep water, and let down the nets for a catch." ⁵ Simon answered, "Master, we've worked hard all night and haven't caught anything. But because you say so, I will let down the nets."

⁶ When they had done so, they caught such a large number of fish that their nets began to break. ⁷ So they signaled their partners in the other boat to come and help them, and they came and filled both boats so full that they began to sink. ⁸ When Simon Peter saw this, he fell at Jesus' knees and said, "Go away from me, Lord; I am a sinful man!" ⁹ For he and all his companions were astonished at the catch of fish they had taken, ¹⁰ and so were James and John, the sons of Zebedee, Simon's partners.

Then Jesus said to Simon, "...[F]rom now on you will fish for people." ¹¹ So they pulled their boats up on shore, left everything and followed him.

Matthew 8:

¹ When Jesus came down from the mountainside, large crowds followed him. ² A man with leprosy came and knelt before him and said, "Lord, if you are willing, you can make me clean."

Mark 1:

⁴¹ [Jesus] reached out his hand and touched the man. "I am willing," he said. "Be clean!" ⁴² Immediately the leprosy left him and he was cleansed.

⁴³ Jesus sent him away at once with a strong warning: ⁴⁴ "See that you don't tell this to anyone. But go, show yourself to the priest... as a testimony..." ⁴⁵ Instead he went out and... spread the news. As a result, Jesus could no longer enter a town openly but stayed outside in lonely places. Yet the people still came to him from everywhere.

Matthew 9:

¹ Jesus stepped into a boat, crossed over and came to [Capernaum].

Mark 2:

² They gathered in such large numbers that there was no room left, not even outside the door, and he preached the word to them. ³ Some men came, bringing to him a paralyzed man, carried by four of them. ⁴ Since they could not get him to Jesus because of the crowd, they made an opening in the roof above Jesus by digging through it and then lowered the mat the man was lying on. ⁵ When Jesus saw their faith, he said to the paralyzed man, "Son, your sins are forgiven."

Luke 5:

²¹ [Some religious leaders and teachers] began thinking to themselves, "...Who can forgive sins but God alone?"

Matthew 9:

⁴ Knowing their thoughts, Jesus [asked]... ⁵ Which is easier: to say, 'Your sins are forgiven,' or to say, 'Get up and walk'? ⁶ But I want you to know that the Son of Man has

authority on earth to forgive sins." So he said to the paralyzed man, "Get up, take your mat and go home."

Luke 5:

^{25} Immediately he stood up in front of them, took what he had been lying on and went home praising God.

Matthew 9:

^{8} When the crowd saw this, they were filled with awe; and they praised God...

^{9} As Jesus went on from there, he saw a man named Matthew sitting at the tax collector's booth. "Follow me," he told him, and Matthew got up and followed him. ^{10} [Then] [w]hile Jesus was having dinner at Matthew's house, many tax collectors and sinners came and ate with him and his disciples. ^{11} When the [religious leaders] saw this, they asked his disciples, "Why does your teacher eat with tax collectors and sinners?"

Mark 2:

^{17} On hearing this, Jesus said to them, "It is not the healthy who need a doctor, but the sick. I have not come to call the righteous, but sinners."

Matthew 9:

^{14} Then John's disciples came and asked him, "How is it that we and the Pharisees fast often, but your disciples do not fast?" ^{15} Jesus answered, "How can the guests of the bridegroom mourn while he is with them? The time will come when the bridegroom will be taken from them; then they will fast."

^{16} "No one sews a patch of unshrunk cloth on an old garment, for the patch will pull away from the garment, making the tear worse. ^{17} Neither do people pour new wine into old wineskins. If they do, the skins will burst; the wine will run out and the wineskins will be ruined. No, they pour new wine into new wineskins, and both are preserved."

Mark 2:

^{23} One Sabbath Jesus was going through the grainfields, and as his disciples walked along, they began to pick some heads of grain. ^{24} The [religious leaders] said to him, "Look, why are they doing what is unlawful on the Sabbath?"

Matthew 12:

^{3} He answered, "Haven't you read what David did when he and his companions were hungry? ^{4} He entered the house of God, and he and his companions ate the consecrated bread — which was not lawful for them to do, but only for the priests.

Mark 2:

^{27} Then he said to them, "The Sabbath was made for man, not man for the Sabbath."

Matthew 12:

^{6} " I desire mercy, not sacrifice."

Mark 2:

[8] "…[T]he Son of Man is Lord even of the Sabbath."

Luke 6:

[6] On another Sabbath he went into the synagogue and was teaching, and a man was there whose right hand was shriveled.

Matthew 12:

[10] …Looking for a reason to bring charges against Jesus, [several] asked him, "Is it lawful to heal on the Sabbath?" [11] He said to them, "If any of you has a sheep and it falls into a pit on the Sabbath, will you not take hold of it and lift it out? [12] How much more valuable is a person than a sheep! Therefore it is lawful to do good on the Sabbath." [13] Then he said to the man, "Stretch out your hand." So he stretched it out and it was completely restored, just as sound as the other.

Luke 6:

[11] [T]he [religious leaders] and the teachers of the law were furious and began to discuss with one another what they might do to Jesus.

Matthew 12:

[5] Aware of this, Jesus withdrew from that place. A large crowd followed him, and he healed all who were ill. [16] He warned them not to tell others about him. [17] This was to fulfill what was spoken through the prophet Isaiah:

[18] "Here is [M]y servant whom I have chosen, the one I love, in whom I delight; I will put [M]y Spirit on him, and he will proclaim justice to the nations. [19] He will not quarrel or cry out; no one will hear his voice in the streets. [20] A bruised reed he will not break… [21] In his name the nations will put their hope."

Luke 6:

[12] One of those days Jesus went out to a mountainside to pray, and spent the night praying to God. [13] When morning came, he called his disciples to him and chose twelve of them, whom he also designated apostles: [14] Simon (whom he named Peter), his brother Andrew, James, John, Philip, Bartholomew, [15] Matthew, Thomas, James son of Alphaeus, Simon who was called the Zealot, [16] Judas son of James, and Judas Iscariot, who became a traitor.

Matthew 5:

[1] Now when Jesus saw the crowds, he went up on a mountainside and sat down. His disciples came to him, [2] and he began to teach them. He said:

[3] "Blessed are the poor in spirit, for theirs is the kingdom of heaven. [4] Blessed are those who mourn, for they will be comforted. [5] Blessed are the meek, for they will inherit the earth. [6] Blessed are those who hunger and thirst for righteousness, for they will be filled. [7] Blessed are the merciful, for they will be shown mercy. [8] Blessed are the pure in heart,

for they will see God. [9] Blessed are the peacemakers, for they will be called children of God. [10] Blessed are those who are persecuted because of righteousness, for theirs is the kingdom of heaven. [11] Blessed are you when people insult you, persecute you and falsely say all kinds of evil against you because of me. [12] Rejoice and be glad, because great is your reward in heaven..."

[3] "You have heard that it was said, 'Love your neighbor and hate your enemy.' [44] But I tell you, love your enemies and pray for those who persecute you..."

Thomas:

[25] "[and] [l]ove your friends like your own soul, protect them like the pupil of your eye."

Luke 6:

[29] If someone slaps you on one cheek, turn to them the other also. If someone takes your coat, do not withhold your shirt from them. [30] Give to everyone who asks you, and if anyone takes what belongs to you, do not demand it back. [31] Do to others as you would have them do to you.

Sermon on the Mount by Fra Angelico c. 1440

[32] "If you love those who love you, what credit is that to you? Even sinners love those who love them. [33] And if you do good to those who are good to you, what credit is that to you? Even sinners do that. [34] And if you lend to those from whom you expect repayment, what credit is that to you? Even sinners lend to sinners, expecting to be repaid in full. [35] But love your enemies, do good to them, and lend to them without expecting to get anything back. Then your reward will be great, and you will be children of the Most High... [36] Be merciful, just as your Father is merciful."

Matthew 5:

[14] "You are the light of the world. A town built on a hill cannot be hidden. [15] Neither do people light a lamp and put it under a bowl. Instead they put it on its stand, and it gives light to everyone in the house. [16] In the same way, let your light shine before others, that they may see your good deeds and glorify your Father in heaven.

[17] "Do not think that I have come to abolish the Law or the Prophets; I have not come to abolish them but to fulfill them.

[23] [I]f you are offering your gift at the altar and there remember that your brother or sister has something against you, [24] leave your gift there in front of the altar. First go and be reconciled to them; then come and offer your gift.

[37] All you need to say is simply 'Yes' or 'No.'"

Matthew 6:

[1] "Be careful not to practice your righteousness in front of others to be seen by them... [2] So when you give to the needy, do not announce it with trumpets... and on the streets, to be honored by others. [3] But when you give to the needy, do not let your left hand know what your right hand is doing, [4] so that your giving may be in secret. Then your Father, who sees what is done in secret, will reward you.

[6] [W]hen you pray, go into your room, close the door and pray to your Father, who is unseen. Then your Father, who sees what is done in secret, will reward you.

Luke 11:2, 4 / Matthew 6:11:

[1] One day Jesus was praying in a certain place. When he finished, one of his disciples said to him, "Lord, teach us to pray..." [2] He said to them, "When you pray, say:

'Father, hallowed be your name, your kingdom come. [11] Give us today our daily bread. [4] Forgive us our sins, for we also forgive everyone who sins against us. And lead us not into temptation.'"

Matthew 6:

[14] For if you forgive other people when they sin against you, your heavenly Father will also forgive you.

[16] "When you fast, do not look somber... to show others [you] are fasting... [17] But when you fast, put oil on your head and wash your face, [18] so that it will not be obvious to others that you are fasting, but only to your Father, who is unseen; and your Father, who sees what is done in secret, will reward you."

[19] "Do not store up for yourselves treasures on earth, where moths and vermin destroy, and where thieves break in and steal. [20] But store up for yourselves treasures in heaven, where moths and vermin do not destroy, and where thieves do not break in and steal. [21] For where your treasure is, there your heart will be also."

[24] "No one can serve two masters. Either you will hate the one and love the other, or you will be devoted to the one and despise the other. You cannot serve both God and money."

Luke 11:

[33] "No one lights a lamp and puts it in a place where it will be hidden, or under a bowl. Instead they put it on its stand, so that those who come in may see the light. [34] Your eye is the lamp of your body. When your eyes are healthy, your whole body also is full of light. But when they are unhealthy, your body also is full of darkness. [35] See to it, then, that the light within you is not darkness. [36] Therefore, if your whole body is full of light,

and no part of it dark, it will be just as full of light as when a lamp shines its light on you."

Luke 12:

23 For life is more than food, and the body more than clothes. 24 Consider the ravens: They do not sow or reap, they have no storeroom or barn; yet God feeds them. And how much more valuable you are than birds! 25 Who of you by worrying can add a single hour to your life? 26 Since you cannot do this very little thing, why do you worry about the rest?

27 "Consider how the wild flowers grow. They do not labor or spin. Yet I tell you, not even Solomon in all his splendor was dressed like one of these. 28 If that is how God clothes the grass of the field… how much more will [H]e clothe you! 29 And do not set your heart on what you will eat or drink; do not worry about it. 30 For… your Father knows that you need them. 31 But seek his kingdom, and these things will be given to you as well.

32 "Do not be afraid, little flock, for your Father has been pleased to give you the kingdom. 33 Sell your possessions and give to the poor. Provide purses for yourselves that will not wear out, a treasure in heaven that will never fail, where no thief comes near and no moth destroys. 34 For where your treasure is, there your heart will be also.

Luke 6:

39 "…Can the blind lead the blind? Will they not both fall into a pit?"

37 "Do not judge, and you will not be judged. Do not condemn, and you will not be condemned. Forgive, and you will be forgiven. 38 Give, and it will be given to you… For with the measure you use, it will be measured to you.

Matthew 7:

3 "Why do you look at the speck of sawdust in your brother's eye and pay no attention to the plank in your own eye? 4 How can you say to your brother, 'Let me take the speck out of your eye,' when all the time there is a plank in your own eye? 5 …[F]irst take the plank out of your own eye, and then you will see clearly to remove the speck from your brother's eye."

Luke 11:

5 Then Jesus said to them, "Suppose you have a friend, and you go to him at midnight and say, 'Friend, lend me three loaves of bread; 6 a friend of mine on a journey has come to me, and I have no food to offer him.' 7 And suppose the one inside answers, 'Don't bother me. The door is already locked, and my children and I are in bed. I can't get up and give you anything.' 8 I tell you, even though he will not get up and give you the bread because of friendship, yet because of your shameless audacity he will surely get up and give you as much as you need.

9 So I say to you: Ask and it will be given to you; seek and you will find; knock and the door will be opened to you. 10 For everyone who asks receives; the one who seeks finds; and to the one who knocks, the door will be opened.

11 "Which of you fathers, if your son asks for a fish, will give him a snake instead? 12 Or if he asks for an egg, will give him a scorpion? 13 If you then, though you are [sinful], know

how to give good gifts to your children, how much more will your Father in heaven give the Holy Spirit to those who ask [H]im!"

Luke 6:

3 "No good tree bears bad fruit, nor does a bad tree bear good fruit. 44 Each tree is recognized by its own fruit. People do not pick figs from thornbushes, or grapes from briers. 45 A good man brings good things out of the good stored up in his heart, and an evil man brings evil things out of the evil stored up in his heart. For the mouth speaks what the heart is full of.

Matthew 7:

24 "Therefore everyone who hears these words of mine and puts them into practice is like a wise man who built his house on the rock. 25 The rain came down, the streams rose, and the winds blew and beat against that house; yet it did not fall, because it had its foundation on the rock."

Matthew 8:

5 When Jesus had entered Capernaum, a centurion came to him, asking for help. 6 "Lord," he said, "my servant lies at home paralyzed, suffering terribly." 7 Jesus said to him, "Shall I come and heal him?"

8 The centurion replied, "Lord, I do not deserve to have you come under my roof. But just say the word, and my servant will be healed. 9 For I myself am a man under authority, with soldiers under me. I tell this one, 'Go,' and he goes; and that one, 'Come,' and he comes. I say to my servant, 'Do this,' and he does it."

Luke 7:

9 When Jesus heard this, he was amazed at him, and turning to the crowd following him, he said, "I tell you, I have not found such great faith…"

Matthew 8:

13 Then Jesus said to the centurion, "Go! Let it be done just as you believed it would." And his servant was healed at that moment.

Luke 7:

10 Then the men who had been sent returned to the house and found the servant well.

11 Soon afterward, Jesus went to a town called Nain, and his disciples and a large crowd went along with him. 12 As he approached the town gate, a dead person was being carried out — the only son of his mother, and she was a widow. And a large crowd from the town was with her. 13 When the Lord saw her, his heart went out to her and he said, "Don't cry."

14 Then he went up and touched the bier they were carrying him on, and the bearers stood still. He said, "Young man, I say to you, get up!" 15 The dead man sat up and began to talk, and Jesus gave him back to his mother.

16 They were all filled with awe and praised God. "A great prophet has appeared among

us," they said. "God has come to help [H]is people." [17] This news about Jesus spread throughout Judea and the surrounding country.

Matthew 11:

[2] When John [the Baptist], who was in prison, heard about the deeds of the Messiah, he sent his disciples [3] to ask him, "Are you the one who is to come, or should we expect someone else?"

[4] Jesus replied, "Go back and report to John what you hear and see: [5] The blind receive sight, the lame walk, those who have leprosy are cleansed, the deaf hear, the dead are raised, and the good news is proclaimed to the poor."

Luke 7:

[27] "This is the one about whom it is written: 'I will send my messenger ahead of you, who will prepare your way before you.'"

[36] When one of the Pharisees invited Jesus to have dinner with him, he went to the Pharisee's house and reclined at the table. [37] A woman in that town who lived a sinful life learned that Jesus was eating at the Pharisee's house, so she came there with an alabaster jar of perfume. [38] As she stood behind him at his feet weeping, she began to wet his feet with her tears. Then she wiped them with her hair, kissed them and poured perfume on them.

[39] When the Pharisee who had invited him saw this, he said to himself, "If this man were a prophet, he would know who is touching him and what kind of woman she is — that she is a sinner." [40] Jesus answered him, "...I have something to tell you." "Tell me, teacher," he said.

[41] "Two people owed money to a certain moneylender. One owed him five hundred denarii, and the other fifty. [42] Neither of them had the money to pay him back, so he forgave the debts of both. Now which of them will love him more?"

[43] [He] replied, "I suppose the one who had the bigger debt forgiven." "You have judged correctly," Jesus said. [44] Then he turned toward the woman and said... "Do you see this woman? I came into your house. You did not give me any water for my feet, but she wet my feet with her tears and wiped them with her hair. [45] You did not give me a kiss, but this woman, from the time I entered, has not stopped kissing my feet. [46] You did not put oil on my head, but she has poured perfume on my feet. [47] Therefore, I tell you, her many sins have been forgiven — as her great love has shown. [48] Then Jesus said to her, "Your sins are forgiven. [50] Your faith has saved you; go in peace."

Luke 11:

[14] Jesus was driving out a demon [from a man] that was mute. When the demon left, the man who had been mute spoke, and the crowd was amazed.

Matthew 12:

[25] Jesus knew their thoughts and said to them, "Every kingdom divided against itself will be ruined, and every city or household divided against itself will not stand. [26] If Satan drives out Satan, he is divided against himself. How then can his kingdom stand? [28] But

if it is by the Spirit of God that I drive out demons, then the kingdom of God has come upon you."

³¹ "And so I tell you, every kind of sin and slander can be forgiven, but blasphemy against the Spirit will not be forgiven. ³² Anyone who speaks a word against the Son of Man will be forgiven, but anyone who speaks against the Holy Spirit will not be forgiven, either in this age or in the age to come."

³⁵ "A good man brings good things out of the good stored up in him…"

⁵⁰ "[W]hoever does the will of my Father in heaven is my brother and sister and mother."

Luke 11:

²⁷ As Jesus was saying these things, a woman in the crowd called out, "Blessed is the mother who gave you birth and nursed you." ²⁸ He replied, "Blessed rather are those who hear the word of God and obey it."

Matthew 13:

¹ That same day Jesus went out of the house and sat by the lake. ² Such large crowds gathered around him that he got into a boat and sat in it, while all the people stood on the shore. ³ Then he told them many things in parables, saying: "A farmer went out to sow his seed. ⁴ As he was scattering the seed, some fell along the path, and the birds came and ate it up. ⁵ Some fell on rocky places, where it did not have much soil. It sprang up quickly, because the soil was shallow. ⁶ But when the sun came up, the plants were scorched, and they withered because they had no root. ⁷ Other seed fell among thorns, which grew up and choked the plants. ⁸ Still other seed fell on good soil, where it produced a crop — a hundred, sixty or thirty times what was sown."

Luke 8:

¹¹ "This is the meaning of the parable: The seed is the word of God. ¹² Those along the path are the ones who hear, and then the devil comes and takes away the word from their hearts… ¹³ Those on the rocky ground are the ones who receive the word with joy when they hear it, but they have no root. They believe for a while, but in the time of testing they fall away. ¹⁴ The seed that fell among thorns stands for those who hear, but as they go on their way they are choked by life's worries, riches and pleasures, and they do not mature. ¹⁵ But the seed on good soil stands for those with a noble and good heart, who hear the word, retain it, and by persevering produce a crop."

Mark 4:

²¹ He said to them, "Do you bring in a lamp to put it under a bowl or a bed? Instead, don't you put it on its stand? ²² For whatever is hidden is meant to be disclosed, and whatever is concealed is meant to be brought out into the open. ²³ If anyone has ears to hear, let them hear. ²⁴ Consider carefully what you hear," he continued. "With the measure you use, it will be measured to you — and even more. ²⁵ Whoever has will be given more; whoever does not have, even what they have will be taken from them."

Matthew 13:

³¹ He told them another parable: "The kingdom of heaven is like a mustard seed, which a

man took and planted in his field. ^{32} Though it is the smallest of all seeds, yet when it grows, it is the largest of garden plants and becomes a tree, so that the birds come and perch in its branches."

^{34} Jesus spoke all these things to the crowd in parables; he did not say anything to them without using a parable. ^{35} So was fulfilled what was spoken through the prophet: "I will open my mouth in parables, I will utter things hidden since the creation of the world."

^{44} "The kingdom of heaven is like treasure hidden in a field. When a man found it, he hid it again, and then in his joy went and sold all he had and bought that field. ^{45} Again, the kingdom of heaven is like a merchant looking for fine pearls. ^{46} When he found one of great value, he went away and sold everything he had and bought it."

Luke 8:

^{22} One day Jesus said to his disciples, "Let us go over to the other side of the lake." So they got into a boat and set out. ^{23} As they sailed, he fell asleep. A squall came down on the lake, so that the boat was being swamped, and they were in great danger.

^{24} The disciples went and woke him, saying, "Master, Master, we're going to drown!" He got up and rebuked the wind and the raging waters; the storm subsided, and all was calm. ^{25} "Where is your faith?" he asked his disciples.

Mark 5:

^{1} They went across the lake to the region of the Gerasenes. ^{2} When Jesus got out of the boat, a man with an impure spirit came from the tombs to meet him. ^{3} This man lived in the tombs, and no one could bind him anymore, not even with a chain. ^{4} For he had often been chained hand and foot, but he tore the chains apart and broke the irons on his feet. No one was strong enough to subdue him. ^{5} Night and day among the tombs and in the hills he would cry out and cut himself with stones.

^{6} When he saw Jesus from a distance, he ran and fell on his knees in front of him. ^{7} He shouted at the top of his voice, "What do you want with me, Jesus, Son of the Most High God? In God's name don't torture me!" ^{8} For Jesus had said to him, "Come out of this man, you impure spirit!"

Luke 8:

^{30} Jesus asked him, "What is your name?" "Legion," he replied, because many demons had gone into him. ^{31} And they begged Jesus repeatedly not to order them to go into the Abyss.

^{32} A large herd of pigs was feeding there on the hillside. The demons begged Jesus to let them go into the pigs, and he gave them permission. ^{33} When the demons came out of the man, they went into the pigs, and the herd rushed down the steep bank into the lake and was drowned.

Matthew 9:

^{18} While [Jesus was speaking], a synagogue leader came and knelt before him and said, "My daughter has just died. But come and put your hand on her, and she will live." ^{19}

Jesus got up and went with him, and so did his disciples.

Luke 8:

⁴² ...As Jesus was on his way, the crowds almost crushed him. ⁴³ And a woman was there who had been subject to bleeding for twelve years, but no one could heal her. ⁴⁴ She came up behind him and touched the edge of his cloak, and immediately her bleeding stopped.

⁴⁵ "Who touched me?" Jesus asked.

Mark 5:

³¹ "You see the people crowding against you," his disciples answered, "and yet you can ask, 'Who touched me?'"

Luke 8:

⁴⁶ But Jesus said, "Someone touched me; I know that power has gone out from me."

⁴⁷ Then the woman, seeing that she could not go unnoticed, came trembling and fell at his feet. In the presence of all the people, she told why she had touched him and how she had been instantly healed.

Mark 5:

³⁴ He said to her, "Daughter, your faith has healed you. Go in peace and be freed from your suffering."

Matthew 9:

²³ When Jesus entered the synagogue leader's house and saw the noisy crowd and people playing pipes, ²⁴ he said, "Go away. The girl is not dead but asleep." But they laughed at him.

Mark 5:

⁴⁰ ...After he put them all out, he took the child's father and mother and the disciples who were with him, and went in where the child was. ⁴¹ He took her by the hand and said to her, *"Talitha koum!"* (which means "Little girl, I say to you, get up!"). ⁴² Immediately the girl stood up and began to walk around (she was twelve years old). At this they were completely astonished.

Luke 8:

⁵⁵ ...Then Jesus told them to give her something to eat.

Mark 5:

³ He gave strict orders not to let anyone know about [it]...

Matthew 9:

²⁷ As Jesus went on from there, two blind men followed him, calling out, "Have mercy on

us, Son of David!" ²⁸ When he had gone indoors, the blind men came to him, and he asked them, "Do you believe that I am able to do this?" "Yes, Lord," they replied.

²⁹ Then he touched their eyes and said, "According to your faith let it be done to you;" ³⁰ and their sight was restored. Jesus warned them sternly, "See that no one knows about this." ³¹ But they went out and spread the news about him all over that region.

³² While they were going out, a man who was demon-possessed and could not talk was brought to Jesus. ³³ And when the demon was driven out, the man who had been mute spoke. The crowd was amazed and said, "Nothing like this has ever been seen…"

Matthew 13:

⁵³ When Jesus had finished these parables, he moved on from there. ⁵⁴ Coming to his hometown, he began teaching the people in their synagogue, and they were amazed. "Where did this man get this wisdom and these miraculous powers?" they asked. ⁵⁵ "Isn't this the carpenter's son Isn't his mother's name Mary, and aren't his brothers James, Joseph, Simon and Judas? ⁵⁶ Aren't all his sisters with us? Where then did this man get all these things?" ⁵⁷ And they took offense at him. But Jesus said to them, "A prophet is not without honor except in his own town and in his own home."

Mark 6:

⁵ He could not do any miracles there, except lay his hands on a few sick people and heal them

Matthew 13:

⁵⁸ …because of their lack of faith.

John 5:

¹ Some time later, Jesus went up to Jerusalem for one of the Jewish festivals. ² Now there is in Jerusalem near the Sheep Gate a pool, which in Aramaic is called Bethesda and which is surrounded by five covered colonnades. ³ Here a great number of disabled people used to lie — the blind, the lame, the paralyzed. ⁵ One who was there had been an invalid for thirty-eight years. ⁶ When Jesus saw him lying there and learned that he had been in this condition for a long time, he asked him, "Do you want to get well?"

⁷ "Sir," the invalid replied, "I have no one to help me into the pool… While I am trying to get in, someone else goes down ahead of me." ⁸ Then Jesus said to him, "Get up! Pick up your mat and walk."

⁹ At once the man was cured; he picked up his mat and walked. The day on which this took place was a Sabbath, ¹⁰ and so the [religious] leaders said to the man who had been healed, "It is the Sabbath; the law forbids you to carry your mat." ¹¹ But he replied, "The man who made me well said to me, 'Pick up your mat and walk.'"

¹² So they asked him, "Who is this fellow who told you to pick it up and walk?" ¹⁵ The man… told the[m]… it was Jesus who had made him well.

¹⁶ So, because Jesus was doing these things on the Sabbath, the [religious] leaders began to persecute him. ¹⁷ In his defense Jesus said, "My Father is always at [H]is work to this very day, and I too am working." ¹⁸ For this reason they tried all the more to kill

him; not only was he breaking the Sabbath, but he was even calling God his own Father...

19 Jesus gave them this answer: "Very truly I tell you, the Son can do nothing by himself; he can do only what he sees his Father doing, because whatever the Father does the Son also does. 20 For the Father loves the Son and shows him all he does. Yes, and he will show him even greater works than these, so that you will be amazed. 21 For just as the Father raises the dead and gives them life, even so the Son gives life... 22 Moreover, the Father judges no one, but has entrusted all judgment to the Son, 23 that all may honor the Son just as they honor the Father...

24 Very truly I tell you, whoever hears my word and believes [H]im who sent me has eternal life and will not be judged but has crossed over from death to life. 25 Very truly I tell you, a time is coming and has now come when the dead will hear the voice of the Son of God and those who hear will live. 26 For as the Father has life in [H]imself, so [H]e has granted the Son also to have life in himself.

28 Do not be amazed at this, for a time is coming when all who are in their graves will hear his voice 29 and come out... — those who have done what is good will rise to live...

Matthew 9:

35 Jesus went through all the towns and villages, teaching in their synagogues, proclaiming the good news of the kingdom and healing every disease and sickness. 37 Then he said to his disciples, "The harvest is plentiful but the workers are few. 38 Ask the Lord of the harvest, therefore, to send out workers into his harvest field."

Matthew 10:

1 Jesus called his twelve disciples to him and gave them authority to drive out impure spirits and to heal every disease and sickness. 5 These twelve Jesus sent out with the following instructions: 6 "Go... to the lost sheep... 7 As you go, proclaim this message: 'The kingdom of heaven has come near.' 8 Heal the sick, raise the dead, cleanse those who have leprosy, drive out demons. Freely you have received; freely give.

9 Do not get any gold or silver or copper to take with you in your belts — 10 no bag for the journey or extra shirt or sandals or a staff, for the worker is worth his keep. 11 Whatever town or village you enter, search there for some worthy person and stay at their house until you leave. 12 As you enter the home, give it your greeting. 13 If the home is deserving, let your peace rest on it; if it is not, let your peace return to you. 14 If anyone will not welcome you or listen to your words, leave that home or town and shake the dust off your feet.

16 I am sending you out like sheep among wolves. Therefore be as shrewd as snakes and as innocent as doves. 17 Be on your guard; you will be handed over to the local councils and be flogged... 18 On my account you will be brought before governors and kings... 19 But when they arrest you, do not worry about what to say or how to say it. At that time you will be given what to say, 20 for it will not be you speaking, but the Spirit of your Father speaking through you.

22 You will be hated by everyone because of me, but the one who stands firm to the end will be saved. 23 When you are persecuted in one place, flee to another. Truly I tell you,

you will not finish going through the towns... before the Son of Man comes. [26] So do not be afraid of them, for there is nothing concealed that will not be disclosed, or hidden that will not be made known.

[28] Do not be afraid of those who kill the body but cannot kill the soul. Rather, be afraid of the One who can destroy both soul and body... [29] Are not two sparrows sold for a penny? Yet not one of them will fall to the ground outside your Father's care. [30] And even the very hairs of your head are all numbered. [31] So don't be afraid; you are worth more than many sparrows. [32] Whoever acknowledges me before others, I will also acknowledge before my Father in heaven."

[40] "Anyone who welcomes you welcomes me, and anyone who welcomes me welcomes the one who sent me. [41] Whoever welcomes a prophet as a prophet will receive a prophet's reward, and whoever welcomes a righteous person as a righteous person will receive a righteous person's reward. [42] And if anyone gives even a cup of cold water to one of these little ones who is my disciple, truly I tell you, that person will certainly not lose their reward."

Luke 9:

[6] So they set out and went from village to village, proclaiming the good news and healing people everywhere.

Matthew 11:

[1] After Jesus had finished instructing his twelve disciples, he went on from there to teach and preach in the towns of Galilee.

Luke 9:

[9] But Herod said, "...Who, then, is this I hear such things about?" And he tried to see [Jesus].

Matthew 14:

[13] When Jesus heard... he withdrew by boat privately to a solitary place. Hearing of this, the crowds followed him on foot from the towns.

Mark 6:

[34] When Jesus landed and saw a large crowd, he had compassion on them, because they were like sheep without a shepherd. So he began teaching them many things.

Luke 9:

[12] Late in the afternoon the Twelve came to him and said, "Send the crowd away so they can go to the surrounding villages and countryside and find food and lodging, because we are in a remote place here."

[13] He replied, "You give them something to eat." They answered, "We have only five loaves of bread and two fish — unless we go and buy food for all this crowd." [14] (About five thousand men were there.) But he said to his disciples, "Have them sit down in groups of about fifty each." [15] The disciples did so...

John 6:

 ¹⁰ …There was plenty of grass in that place, and they sat down…

Luke 9:

¹⁶ Taking the five loaves and the two fish and looking up to heaven, he gave thanks and broke them. Then he gave them to the disciples to distribute to the people. ¹⁷ They all ate and were satisfied, and the disciples picked up twelve basketfuls of broken pieces that were left over.

John 6:

¹⁴ After the people saw the sign Jesus performed, they began to say, "Surely this is the Prophet who is to come into the world." ¹⁵ Jesus, knowing that they intended to come and make him king by force, withdrew again to a mountain by himself.

¹⁶ When evening came, his disciples went down to the lake, ¹⁷ where they got into a boat and set off across the lake for Capernaum. By now it was dark, and Jesus had not yet joined them. ¹⁸ A strong wind was blowing and the waters grew rough. ¹⁹ When they had rowed about three or four miles, they saw Jesus approaching the boat, walking on the water; and they were frightened.

Mark 6:

⁴⁹ [W]hen they saw him walking on the lake, they thought he was a ghost…

John 6:

²⁰ But he said to them, "It is I; don't be afraid."

Matthew 14:

⁸ "Lord, if it's you," Peter replied, "tell me to come to you on the water." ²⁹ "Come," he said. Then Peter got down out of the boat, walked on the water and came toward Jesus. ³⁰ But when he saw the wind, he was afraid and, beginning to sink, cried out, "Lord, save me!" ³¹ Immediately Jesus reached out his hand and caught him. "You of little faith," he said, "why did you doubt?"

³² And when they climbed into the boat, the wind died down. ³³ Then those who were in the boat… [declared], "Truly you are the Son of God."

³⁴ When they had crossed over, they landed at Gennesaret.

Mark 6:

⁵⁴ As soon as they got out of the boat, people recognized Jesus. ⁵⁵ They ran throughout that whole region and carried the sick on mats to wherever they heard he was

Matthew 14:

³⁶ and begged him to let the sick just touch the edge of his cloak, and all who touched it were healed.

John 6:

²² The next day the crowd that had stayed on the opposite shore of the lake realized that only one boat had been there, and that Jesus had not entered it with his disciples, but that they had gone away alone. ²³ Then some boats from Tiberias landed near the place where the people had eaten the bread after the Lord had given thanks. ²⁴ Once the crowd realized that neither Jesus nor his disciples were there, they got into the boats and went to Capernaum in search of Jesus.

²⁵ When they found him on the other side of the lake, they asked him, "[W]hen did you get here?" ²⁶ Jesus answered, "Very truly I tell you, you are looking for me, not because you saw the signs I performed but because you ate the loaves and had your fill. ²⁷ Do not work for food that spoils, but for food that endures to eternal life, which the Son of Man will give you. For on him God the Father has placed his seal of approval."

²⁸ Then they asked him, "What must we do to do the works God requires?" ²⁹ Jesus answered, "The work of God is this: to believe in the one he has sent."

³⁰ So they asked him, "What sign then will you give that we may see it and believe you? What will you do? ³¹ Our ancestors ate the manna in the wilderness; as it is written: 'He gave them bread from heaven to eat.'" ³² Jesus said to them, "Very truly I tell you, it is not Moses who has given you the bread from heaven, but it is my Father who gives you the true bread from heaven. ³³ For the bread of God is the bread that comes down from heaven and gives life to the world."

³⁴ "Sir," they said, "always give us this bread." ³⁵ Then Jesus declared, "I am the bread of life. Whoever comes to me will never go hungry, and whoever believes in me will never be thirsty. ³⁷ All those the Father gives me will come to me, and whoever comes to me I will never drive away. ³⁸ For I have come down from heaven not to do my will but to do the will of [H]im [W]ho sent me. ³⁹ And this is the will of [H]im [W]ho sent me, that I shall lose none of all those [H]e has given me, but raise them up at the last day. ⁴⁰ For my Father's will is that everyone who… believes… shall have eternal life, and I will raise them up at the last day."

⁴⁵ It is written in the Prophets: 'They will all be taught by God.' Everyone who has heard the Father and learned from [H]im comes to me. ⁴⁶ No one has seen the Father except the one who is from God; only he has seen the Father. ⁴⁷ Very truly I tell you, the one who believes has eternal life. ⁴⁸ I am the bread of life. ⁵¹ I am the living bread that came down from heaven. Whoever eats this bread will live forever. This bread is my flesh, which I will give for the life of the world."

⁵⁴ Whoever eats my flesh and drinks my blood has eternal life, and I will raise them up at the last day. ⁵⁵ For my flesh is real food and my blood is real drink. ⁵⁶ Whoever eats my flesh and drinks my blood remains in me, and I in them. ⁵⁷ Just as the living Father sent me and I live because of the Father, so the one who feeds on me will live because of me. ⁵⁸ This is the bread that came down from heaven. [W]hoever feeds on this bread will live forever."

⁶⁶ From this time many of his disciples turned back and no longer followed him. ⁶⁷ "You do not want to leave too, do you?" Jesus asked the Twelve. ⁶⁸ Simon Peter answered him, "Lord, to whom shall we go? You have the words of eternal life. ⁶⁹ We have come to

believe and to know that you are the Holy One of God."

Mark 7:

[5] [One day some] asked Jesus, "Why don't your disciples live according to the tradition of the elders instead of eating their food with defiled hands?"

Matthew 15:

[10] Jesus called the crowd to him and said, "Listen and understand. [11] What goes into someone's mouth does not defile them, but what comes out of their mouth, that is what defiles them." [15] Peter [asked], "Explain... to us."

Mark 7:

[18] "Don't you see that nothing that enters a person from the outside can defile them? [19] For it doesn't go into their heart but into their stomach, and then out of the body." [20] He went on: "What comes out of a person is what defiles them. [21] For it is from within, out of a person's heart, that evil thoughts come... [23] All these... come from inside and defile a person."

Matthew 15:

[21] Leaving that place, Jesus withdrew to the region of Tyre and Sidon.

Mark 7:

[25] ...[A]s soon as she heard... a woman whose little daughter was possessed by an impure spirit came and fell at his feet. [26] The woman was a Greek, born in Syrian Phoenicia. She begged Jesus to drive the demon out of her daughter.

[27] "First let the children eat all they want," he told her, "for it is not right to take the children's bread and toss it to the dogs." [28] "Lord," she replied, "even the dogs under the table eat the children's crumbs."

Matthew 15:

[28] Then Jesus said to her, "Woman, you have great faith! Your request is granted." And her daughter was healed at that moment.

[29] Jesus left there and went along the Sea of Galilee. Then he went up on a mountainside and sat down. [30] Great crowds came to him, bringing the lame, the blind, the crippled, the mute and many others, and laid them at his feet; and he healed them. [31] The people were amazed when they saw the mute speaking, the crippled made well, the lame walking and the blind seeing. And they praised... God...

[32] Jesus [then] called his disciples to him and said, "I have compassion for these people; they have already been with me three days and have nothing to eat. I do not want to send them away hungry, or they may collapse on the way."

[33] His disciples answered, "Where could we get enough bread in this remote place to feed such a crowd?" [34] "How many loaves do you have?" Jesus asked. "Seven," they

replied, "and a few small fish."

³⁵ He told the crowd to sit down on the ground. ³⁶ Then he took the seven loaves and the fish, and when he had given thanks, he broke them and gave them to the disciples, and they in turn to the people.

Mark 8:

⁸ The people ate and were satisfied. Afterward the disciples picked up seven basketfuls of broken pieces that were left over.

Matthew 15:

³⁸ The number of those who ate was four thousand men, besides women and children. ³⁹ After Jesus had sent the crowd away, he got into the boat and went to the vicinity of Magadan.

Matthew 16:

¹³ When Jesus came to the region of Caesarea Philippi, he asked his disciples,

Mark 8:

²⁷ "Who do people say I am?"

Matthew 16:

¹⁴ They replied, "Some say John the Baptist; others say Elijah; and still others, Jeremiah or one of the prophets." ¹⁵ "But… [w]ho do you say I am?" [he asked]. ¹⁶ Simon Peter answered, "You are the Messiah, the Son of the living God." ¹⁷ Jesus replied, "Blessed are you, Simon son of Jonah, for this was not revealed to you by flesh and blood, but by my Father in heaven."

Luke 9:

²¹ Jesus strictly warned them not to tell this to anyone.

Matthew 16:

²⁴ Then Jesus said to his disciples, "Whoever wants to be my disciple must deny themselves and take up their cross and follow me. ²⁵ For whoever wants to save their life will lose it, but whoever loses their life for me will find it."

Mark 9:

² After six days Jesus took Peter, James and John with him and led them up a high mountain, where they were all alone. There he was transfigured before them. ³ His clothes became dazzling white, whiter than anyone in the world could bleach them.

The Transfiguration by Fra Angelico
c. 1440

Matthew 17:

³ Just then there appeared before them Moses and Elijah, talking with Jesus. ⁴ Peter said to Jesus, "Lord, it is good for us to be here. If you wish, I will put up three shelters — one for you, one for Moses and one for Elijah."

⁵ While he was still speaking, a bright cloud covered them, and a voice from the cloud said, "This is my Son, whom I love; with him I am well pleased. Listen to him!" ⁶ When the disciples heard this, they fell facedown to the ground, terrified. ⁷ But Jesus came and touched them. "Get up," he said. "Don't be afraid." ⁸ When they looked up, they saw no one except Jesus.

⁹ As they were coming down the mountain, Jesus instructed them, "Don't tell anyone what you have seen, until the Son of Man has been raised from the dead."

Mark 9:

¹⁰ They kept the matter to themselves, discussing what "rising from the dead" meant.

Matthew 17:

²⁰ "...Truly I tell you, if you have faith as small as a mustard seed, you can say to this mountain, 'Move from here to there,' and it will move. Nothing will be impossible for you."

²² When they came together in Galilee, he said to them, "The Son of Man is going to be delivered into the hands of men. ²³ They will kill him, and on the third day he will be raised to life." And the disciples were filled with grief.

Matthew 18:

¹ At that time the disciples came to Jesus and asked, "Who, then, is the greatest in the kingdom of heaven?"

Mark 9:

³⁵ Sitting down, Jesus called the Twelve and said, "Anyone who wants to be first must be

the very last, and the servant of all."

[36] He took a little child whom he placed among them. Taking the child in his arms, he said to them, [37] "Whoever welcomes one of these little children in my name welcomes me; and whoever welcomes me does not welcome me but the one who sent me."

Matthew 18:

[4] "Therefore, whoever takes the lowly position of this child is the greatest in the kingdom of heaven."

Thomas:

[39] "[B]e… as simple as [a] dove."

Mark 9:

[38] "Teacher," said John, "we saw someone driving out demons in your name and we told him to stop, because he was not one of us."

Luke 9:

[50] "Do not stop him," Jesus said, "for whoever is not against you is for you."

Mark 9:

[41] "Truly I tell you, anyone who gives you a cup of water in my name… will certainly not lose their reward."

John 7:

[14] Not until halfway through the festival did Jesus go up to the temple courts and begin to teach. [15] The Jews there were amazed and asked, "How did this man get such learning without having been taught?" [16] Jesus answered, "My teaching is not my own. It comes from the one who sent me."

[25] At that point some of the people of Jerusalem began to ask, "Isn't this the man they are trying to kill? [26] Here he is, speaking publicly, and they are not saying a word to him. Have the authorities really concluded that he is the Messiah? [27] But we know where this man is from; when the Messiah comes, no one will know where he is from."

[28] Then Jesus, still teaching in the temple courts, cried out, "Yes, you know me, and you know where I am from. I am not here on my own authority, but [H]e who sent me is true. You do not know [H]im, [29] but I know [H]im because I am from [H]im and [H]e sent me."

[30] At this they tried to seize him, but no one laid a hand on him, because his hour had not yet come. [31] Still, many in the crowd believed in him.

[33] Jesus said, "I am with you for only a short time, and then I am going to the one who sent me. [34] You will look for me, but you will not find me; and where I am, you cannot come."

³⁷ On the last and greatest day of the festival, Jesus stood and said in a loud voice, "Let anyone who is thirsty come to me and drink. ³⁸ Whoever believes in me, as Scripture has said, rivers of living water will flow from within them."

⁴⁰ On hearing his words, some of the people said, "Surely this man is the Prophet." ⁴¹ Others said, "He is the Messiah."   Still others asked, "How can the Messiah come from Galilee? ⁴² Does not Scripture say that the Messiah will come from David's descendants and from Bethlehem, the town where David lived?" ⁴³ Thus the people were divided because of Jesus. ⁴⁴ Some wanted to seize him, but no one laid a hand on him.

⁵³ Then they all went home,

John 8:

¹ [B]ut Jesus went to the Mount of Olives.

² At dawn he appeared again in the temple courts, where all the people gathered around him, and he sat down to teach them.

³ The teachers of the law and the [religious leaders] brought in a woman caught in adultery. They made her stand before the group ⁴ and said to Jesus, "Teacher, this woman was caught in the act of adultery. ⁵ In the Law, Moses commanded us to stone such women. Now what do you say?" ⁶ They were using this question as a trap, in order to have a basis for accusing him.

But Jesus bent down and started to write on the ground with his finger. ⁷ When they kept on questioning him, he straightened up and said to them, "Let any one of you who is without sin be the first to throw a stone at her." ⁸ Again he stooped down and wrote on the ground.

⁹ At this, those who heard began to go away one at a time, the older ones first, until only Jesus was left, with the woman still standing there. ¹⁰ Jesus straightened up and asked her, "Woman, where are they? Has no one condemned you?" ¹¹ "No one, sir," she said. "Then neither do I condemn you," Jesus declared. "Go now and leave your life of sin."

¹² When Jesus spoke again to the people, he said, "I am the light of the world. Whoever follows me will never walk in darkness, but will have the light of life."

²⁰ He spoke these words while teaching in the temple courts near the place where the offerings were put. Yet no one seized him, because his hour had not yet come.

²¹ Once more Jesus said to them, "I am going away, and you will look for me… Where I go, you cannot come."

²⁸ So Jesus said, "When you have lifted up the Son of Man, then you will know that I am he and that I do nothing on my own but speak just what the Father has taught me. ²⁹ The one who sent me is with me; [H]e has not left me alone, for I always do what pleases [H]im." ³⁰ [As] he spoke, many believed in him.

³¹ To [those] who had believed him, Jesus said, "If you hold to my teaching, you are

really my disciples. ³² Then you will know the truth, and the truth will set you free." ³³ They answered him, "We are Abraham's descendants and have never been slaves of anyone. How can you say that we shall be set free?"

³⁴ Jesus replied, "Very truly I tell you, everyone who sins is a slave to sin. ³⁵ Now a slave has no permanent place in the family, but a son belongs to it forever. ³⁶ So if the Son sets you free, you will be free indeed."

⁴⁹ "…I honor my Father…" [Jesus said]. ⁵⁰ I am not seeking glory for myself; but there is one who seeks it, and [H]e is the judge. ⁵¹ Very truly I tell you, whoever obeys my word will never see death."

⁵² At this they exclaimed, "…Abraham died and so did the prophets, yet you say that whoever obeys your word will never taste death. ⁵³ Are you greater than our father Abraham? He died, and so did the prophets. Who do you think you are?"

⁵⁴ Jesus replied, "If I glorify myself, my glory means nothing. My Father… your God, is the one who glorifies me. ⁵⁵ Though you do not know [H]im, I know [H]im. If I said I did not, I would be a liar… but I do know [H]im and obey [H]is word. ⁵⁶ Your father Abraham rejoiced at the thought of seeing my day; he saw it and was glad."

⁵⁷ "You are not yet fifty years old," they said to him, "and you have seen Abraham!" ⁵⁸ "Very truly I tell you," Jesus answered, "before Abraham was born, I am!" ⁵⁹ At this, they picked up stones to stone him, but Jesus… slipp[ed] away from the temple grounds.

John 9:

¹ As [Jesus] went along, he saw a man blind from birth. ² His disciples asked him, "Rabbi, who sinned, this man or his parents, that he was born blind?"

³ "Neither this man nor his parents sinned," said Jesus, "but this happened so that the works of God might be displayed in him. ⁴ As long as it is day, we must do the works of [H]im [W]ho sent me. Night is coming, when no one can work. ⁵ While I am in the world, I am the light of the world."

⁶ After saying this, [Jesus healed] the man's eyes. ⁷ "Go," he told him, "wash in the Pool of Siloam." So the man went and washed, and came home seeing. ⁸ His neighbors and those who had formerly seen him begging asked, "Isn't this the same man who used to sit and beg?" ⁹ Some claimed that he was. Others said, "No, he only looks like him." But he himself insisted, "I am the man."

¹⁰ "How then were your eyes opened?" they asked. ¹¹ He replied, "The man they call Jesus made some mud and put it on my eyes. He told me to go to Siloam and wash. So I went and washed, and then I could see."

¹³ They brought to the Pharisees the man who had been blind. ¹⁴ Now the day on which Jesus had… opened the man's eyes was a Sabbath. ¹⁶ Some… said, "This man is not from God, for he does not keep the Sabbath." But others asked, "How can a sinner perform such signs?" So they were divided.

¹⁷ Then they turned again to the blind man, "What have you to say about him? It was

your eyes he opened." The man replied, "He is a prophet."

¹⁸ They still did not believe that he had been blind and had received his sight until they sent for the man's parents. ¹⁹ "Is this your son?" they asked. "Is this the one you say was born blind? How is it that now he can see?"

²⁰ "We know he is our son," the parents answered, "and we know he was born blind. ²¹ But how he can see now, or who opened his eyes, we don't know. Ask him. He is of age; he will speak for himself." ²² His parents said this because they were afraid of the [religious] leaders…

²⁴ A second time they summoned the man who had been blind. "Give glory to God by telling the truth," they said. "We know this man is a sinner." ²⁵ He replied, "Whether he is a sinner or not, I don't know. One thing I do know. I was blind but now I see!"

²⁶ Then they asked him, "What did he do to you? How did he open your eyes?" ²⁷ He answered, "I have told you already and you did not listen. Why do you want to hear it again? Do you want to become his disciples too?"

²⁸ Then they hurled insults at him and said, "You are this fellow's disciple! We are disciples of Moses! ²⁹ We know that God spoke to Moses, but as for this fellow, we don't even know where he comes from."

³⁰ The man answered, "Now that is remarkable! You don't know where he comes from, yet he opened my eyes. ³¹ We know that God does not listen to sinners. He listens to the godly person who does [H]is will. ³² Nobody has ever heard of opening the eyes of a man born blind. ³³ If this man were not from God, he could do nothing."

³⁴ To this they replied, "…[H]ow dare you lecture us!" And they threw him out.

³⁵ [When] Jesus heard that they had thrown him out.. he found him, [and] said, "Do you believe in the Son of Man?" ³⁶ "Who is he, sir?" the man asked. "Tell me so that I may believe in him." ³⁷ Jesus said, "You have now seen him; in fact, he is the one speaking with you." ³⁸ Then the man said, "Lord, I believe," and he worshiped him.

John 10:

¹ "Very truly I tell you… anyone who does not enter the sheep pen by the gate, but climbs in by some other way, is a thief and a robber. ² The one who enters by the gate is the shepherd of the sheep. ³ The gatekeeper opens the gate for him, and the sheep listen to his voice. He calls his own sheep by name and leads them out. ⁴ When he has brought out all his own, he goes on ahead of them, and his sheep follow him because they know his voice.

⁷ Very truly I tell you, I am the gate for the sheep. ⁹ I am the gate; whoever enters through me will be saved. They will come in and go out, and find pasture. ¹⁰ The thief comes only to steal and kill and destroy; I have come that they may have life, and have it to the full.

¹¹ "I am the good shepherd. The good shepherd lays down his life for the sheep. ¹² The

hired hand is not the shepherd and does not own the sheep. So when he sees the wolf coming, he abandons the sheep and runs away. Then the wolf attacks the flock and scatters it. [13] The man runs away because he is a hired hand and cares nothing for the sheep.

[14] "I am the good shepherd; I know my sheep and my sheep know me — [15] just as the Father knows me and I know the Father — and I lay down my life for the sheep. [16] I have other sheep that are not of this sheep pen. I must bring them also. They too will listen to my voice, and there shall be one flock and one shepherd. [17] The reason my Father loves me is that I lay down my life — only to take it up again. [18] No one takes it from me, but I lay it down of my own accord. I have authority to lay it down and authority to take it up again. This command I received from my Father." [19] The [people] who heard these words were… divided.

Luke 9:

[56] Then he and his disciples went to another village.

Matthew 11:

[27] "All things have been committed to me by my Father. No one knows the Son except the Father, and no one knows the Father except the Son and those to whom the Son chooses to reveal [H]im. [28] "Come to me, all you who are weary and burdened, and I will give you rest. [29] Take my yoke upon you and learn from me, for I am gentle and humble in heart, and you will find rest for your souls. [30] For my yoke is easy and my burden is light."

Luke 10:

[20] "…[R]ejoice that your names are written in heaven."

[25] On one occasion an expert in the law stood up to test Jesus. "Teacher," he asked, "what must I do to inherit eternal life?" [26] "What is written in the Law?" he replied. "How do you read it?"

[27] He answered, "Love the Lord your God with all your heart and with all your soul and with all your strength and with all your mind;" and "Love your neighbor as yourself." [28] "You have answered correctly," Jesus replied. "Do this and you will live."

[29] But he wanted to justify himself, so he asked Jesus, "And who is my neighbor?" [30] In reply Jesus said: "A man was going down from Jerusalem to Jericho, when he was attacked by robbers. They stripped him of his clothes, beat him and went away, leaving him half dead.

[31] A priest happened to be going down the same road, and when he saw the man, he passed by on the other side. [32] So too, a Levite, when he came to the place and saw him, passed by on the other side. [33] But a Samaritan, as he traveled, came where the man was; and when he saw him, he took pity on him. [34] He went to him and bandaged his wounds, pouring on oil and wine. Then he put the man on his own donkey, brought him to an inn and took care of him. [35] The next day he took out two denarii and gave them to the innkeeper. 'Look after him,' he said, 'and when I return, I will reimburse you for any extra expense you may have.' [36] "Which of these three do you think was a neighbor to the man who fell into the hands of robbers?"

[37] The expert in the law replied, "The one who had mercy on him." Jesus told him, "Go and do likewise."

Luke 10:

[35] "Be dressed ready for service and keep your lamps burning, [36] like servants waiting for their master to return from a wedding banquet, so that when he comes and knocks they can immediately open the door for him. [37] It will be good for those servants whose master finds them watching when he comes. Truly I tell you, he will dress himself to serve, will have them recline at the table and will come and wait on them. [38] It will be good for those servants whose master finds them ready, even if he comes in the middle of the night or toward daybreak. [39] But understand this: If the owner of the house had known at what hour the thief was coming, he would not have let his house be broken into. [40] You also must be ready, because the Son of Man will come at an hour when you do not expect him."

[41] Peter asked, "Lord, are you telling this parable to us, or to everyone?" [42] The Lord answered, "Who then is the faithful and wise manager, whom the master puts in charge of his servants to give them their food allowance at the proper time? [43] It will be good for that servant whom the master finds doing so when he returns. [44] Truly I tell you, he will put him in charge of all his possessions. [48] [For] [f]rom everyone who has been given much, much will be demanded; and from the one who has been entrusted with much, much more will be asked."

Luke 13:

[10] On a Sabbath Jesus was teaching in one of the synagogues, [11] and a woman was there who had been crippled... for eighteen years. She was bent over and could not straighten up at all. [12] When Jesus saw her, he called her forward and said to her, "Woman, you are set free from your infirmity." [13] Then he put his hands on her, and immediately she straightened up and praised God.

[24] "Make every effort to enter through the narrow door, because many, I tell you, will try to enter and will not be able to."

[29] People will come from east and west and north and south, and will take their places at the feast in the kingdom of God. [30] Indeed there are those who are last who will be first, and first who will be last."

[31] At that time some Pharisees came to Jesus and said to him, "Leave this place and go somewhere else. Herod wants to kill you." [32] He replied, "Go tell that fox, 'I will keep on driving out demons and healing people today and tomorrow, and on the third day I will reach my goal.' [33] In any case, I must press on today and tomorrow and the next day — for surely no prophet can die outside Jerusalem!

[34] "Jerusalem, Jerusalem... how often I have longed to gather your children together, as a hen gathers her chicks under her wings... [35] ...I tell you, you will not see me again until you say, 'Blessed is he who comes in the name of the Lord.'"

Luke 14:

[1] One Sabbath, when Jesus went to eat in the house of a prominent Pharisee, he was

being carefully watched. [2] There in front of him was a man suffering from abnormal swelling of his body. [3] Jesus asked the Pharisees and experts in the law, "Is it lawful to heal on the Sabbath or not?" [4] But they remained silent. So taking hold of the man, he healed him and sent him on his way.

[5] Then he asked them, "If one of you has a child or an ox that falls into a well on the Sabbath day, will you not immediately pull it out?" [6] And they had nothing to say.

[7] When he noticed how the guests picked the places of honor at the table, he told them this parable: [8] "When someone invites you to a wedding feast, do not take the place of honor, for a person more distinguished than you may have been invited. [9] If so, the host who invited both of you will come and say to you, 'Give this person your seat.' Then, humiliated, you will have to take the least important place. [10] But when you are invited, take the lowest place, so that when your host comes, he will say to you, 'Friend, move up to a better place.' Then you will be honored in the presence of all the other guests. [11] For all those who exalt themselves will be humbled, and those who humble themselves will be exalted."

[12] Then Jesus said to his host, "When you give a luncheon or dinner, do not invite your friends, your brothers or sisters, your relatives, or your rich neighbors; if you do, they may invite you back and so you will be repaid. [13] But when you give a banquet, invite the poor, the crippled, the lame, the blind, [14] and you will be blessed. Although they cannot repay you, you will be repaid at the resurrection of the righteous."

Luke 15:

[1] Now the tax collectors and sinners were all gathering around to hear Jesus. [2] But the Pharisees and the teachers of the law muttered, "This man welcomes sinners and eats with them." [3] Then Jesus told them this parable:

Matthew 18:

[11] For the Son of Man has come to save that which was lost. [12] "What do you think? If a man owns a hundred sheep, and one of them wanders away, will he not leave the ninety-nine on the hills and go to look for the one that wandered off? [13] And if he finds it, truly I tell you, he is happier about that one sheep than about the ninety-nine that did not wander off."

Luke 15:

[5] "And when he finds it, he joyfully puts it on his shoulders [6] and goes home. Then he calls his friends and neighbors together and says, 'Rejoice with me; I have found my lost sheep.' [7] I tell you that in the same way there will be more rejoicing in heaven over one sinner who repents than over ninety-nine righteous persons who do not need to repent."

Matthew 18:

[14] "In the same way your Father in heaven is not willing that any of these little ones should perish."

Luke 15:

[8] "Or suppose a woman has ten silver coins and loses one. Doesn't she light a lamp,

sweep the house and search carefully until she finds it? ⁹ And when she finds it, she calls her friends and neighbors together and says, 'Rejoice with me; I have found my lost coin.' ¹⁰ In the same way, I tell you, there is rejoicing in the presence of the angels of God over one sinner who repents."

¹¹ Jesus continued: "There was a man who had two sons. ¹² The younger one said to his father, '[G]ive me my share of the estate.' So he divided his property between them.

¹³ Not long after that, the younger son got together all he had, set off for a distant country and there squandered his wealth in wild living. ¹⁴ After he had spent everything, there was a severe famine in that whole country, and he began to be in need. ¹⁵ So he went and hired himself out to a citizen of that country, who sent him to his fields to feed pigs. ¹⁶ He longed to fill his stomach with the pods that the pigs were eating, but no one gave him anything.

¹⁷ When he came to his senses, he said, 'How many of my father's hired servants have food to spare, and here I am starving to death! ¹⁸ I will set out and go back to my father and say to him: Father, I have sinned against heaven and against you. ¹⁹ I am no longer worthy to be called your son; make me like one of your hired servants.' ²⁰ So he got up and went to his father.

But while he was still a long way off, his father saw him and was filled with compassion for him; he ran to his son, threw his arms around him and kissed him. ²¹ The son said to him, 'Father, I have sinned against heaven and against you. I am no longer worthy to be called your son.'

²² But the father said to his servants, 'Quick! Bring the best robe and put it on him. Put a ring on his finger and sandals on his feet. ²³ Bring the fattened calf and kill it. Let's have a feast and celebrate. ²⁴ For this son of mine was dead and is alive again; he was lost and is found.' So they began to celebrate.

²⁵ Meanwhile, the older son was in the field. When he came near the house, he heard music and dancing. ²⁶ So he called one of the servants and asked him what was going on. ²⁷ 'Your brother has come,' he replied, 'and your father has killed the fattened calf because he has him back safe and sound.'

²⁸ The older brother became angry and refused to go in. So his father went out and pleaded with him. ²⁹ But he answered his father, 'Look! All these years I've been slaving for you and never disobeyed your orders. Yet you never gave me even a young goat so I could celebrate with my friends. ³⁰ But when this son of yours who has squandered your property… comes home, you kill the fattened calf for him!'

³¹ 'My son,' the father said, 'you are always with me, and everything I have is yours. ³² But we had to celebrate and be glad, because this brother of yours was dead and is alive again; he was lost and is found.'"

Luke 17:

³ "If your brother or sister sins against you, rebuke them; and if they repent, forgive them. ⁴ Even if they sin against you seven times in a day and seven times come back to you saying 'I repent,' you must forgive them."

Matthew 18:

²¹ Then Peter came to Jesus and asked, "Lord, how many times shall I forgive my brother or sister who sins against me? Up to seven times?" ²² Jesus answered, "I tell you, not seven times, but seventy-seven times."

²³ "Therefore, the kingdom of heaven is like a king who wanted to settle accounts with his servants. ²⁴ As he began the settlement, a man who owed him ten thousand bags of gold was brought to him. ²⁵ Since he was not able to pay, the master ordered that he and his wife and his children and all that he had be sold to repay the debt.

²⁶ At this the servant fell on his knees before him. 'Be patient with me,' he begged, 'and I will pay back everything.' ²⁷ The servant's master took pity on him, canceled the debt and let him go.

²⁸ But when that servant went out, he found one of his fellow servants who owed him a hundred silver coins. He grabbed him and began to choke him. 'Pay back what you owe me!' he demanded. ²⁹ "His fellow servant fell to his knees and begged him, 'Be patient with me, and I will pay it back.'

³⁰ But he refused. Instead, he went off and had the man thrown into prison until he could pay the debt. ³¹ When the other servants saw what had happened, they were outraged and went and told their master everything that had happened.

³² Then the master called the servant in. 'You wicked servant,' he said, 'I canceled all that debt of yours because you begged me to. ³³ Shouldn't you have had mercy on your fellow servant just as I had on you?' ³⁴ In anger his master handed him over to the jailers… until he should pay back all he owed.

³⁵ This is how my heavenly Father will treat each of you unless you forgive your brother or sister from your heart."

Luke 17:

⁵ The apostles said to the Lord, "Increase our faith!" ⁶ He replied, "If you have faith as small as a mustard seed, you can say to this mulberry tree, 'Be uprooted and planted in the sea,' and it will obey you."

¹¹ Now on his way to Jerusalem, Jesus traveled along the border between Samaria and Galilee. ¹² As he was going into a village, ten men who had leprosy met him. They stood at a distance ¹³ and called out in a loud voice, "Jesus, Master, have pity on us!"

¹⁴ When he saw them, he said, "Go, show yourselves to the priests." And as they went, they were cleansed.

¹⁵ One of them, when he saw he was healed, came back, praising God in a loud voice. ¹⁶ He threw himself at Jesus' feet and thanked him… ¹⁷ Jesus asked, "Were not all ten cleansed? Where are the other nine? ¹⁸ Has no one returned to give praise to God except this foreigner?" ¹⁹ Then he said to him, "Rise and go; your faith has made you well."

[20] Once, on being asked… when the kingdom of God would come, Jesus replied, "The coming of the kingdom of God is not something that can be observed, [21] nor will people say, 'Here it is,' or 'There it is,' because the kingdom of God is in your midst."

[22] Then he said to his disciples, "The time is coming when you will long to see one of the days of the Son of Man, but you will not see it. [25] But first he must suffer many things and be rejected by this generation."

Luke 18:

[9] To some who were confident of their own righteousness and looked down on everyone else, Jesus told this parable: [10] "Two men went up to the temple to pray, one a Pharisee and the other a tax collector. [11] The Pharisee stood by himself and prayed: 'God, I thank you that I am not like other people — robbers, evildoers, adulterers — or even like this tax collector. [12] I fast twice a week and give a tenth of all I get.'

[13] But the tax collector stood at a distance. He would not even look up to heaven, but beat his breast and said, 'God, have mercy on me, a sinner.' [14] "I tell you that this man, rather than the other, went home justified before God. For all those who exalt themselves will be humbled, and those who humble themselves will be exalted."

Matthew 19:

[13] Then people brought little children to Jesus for him to place his hands on them and pray for them. But the disciples rebuked them. [14] Jesus said, "Let the little children come to me, and do not hinder them, for the kingdom of heaven belongs to such as these."

Mark 10:

[16] And he took the children in his arms, placed his hands on them and blessed them.

Matthew 19:

[16] Just then a man came up to Jesus and asked, "Teacher, what good thing must I do to get eternal life?" [17] "Why do you ask me about what is good?" Jesus replied. "There is only One who is good. If you want to enter life, keep the commandments."

[18] "Which ones?" he inquired. Jesus replied, "'You shall not murder, you shall not commit adultery, you shall not steal, you shall not give false testimony, [19] honor your father and mother,' and 'love your neighbor as yourself.'"

[20] "All these I have kept," the young man said. "What do I still lack?"

[21] Jesus answered, "If you want to be perfect, go, sell your possessions and give to the poor, and you will have treasure in heaven. Then come, follow me." [22] When the young man heard this, he went away sad, because he had great wealth.

Mark 10:

[23] Jesus looked around and said to his disciples, "How hard it is for the rich to enter the

kingdom of God! ^{25} It is easier for a camel to go through the eye of a needle than for someone who is rich to enter the kingdom of God." ^{26} The disciples… said to each other, "Who then can be saved?"

Matthew 19:

^{26} Jesus looked at them and said, "With man this is impossible, but with God all things are possible."

Matthew 20:

^{1} "For the kingdom of heaven is like a landowner who went out early in the morning to hire workers for his vineyard. ^{2} He agreed to pay them a denarius for the day and sent them into his vineyard.

^{3} About nine in the morning he went out and saw others standing in the marketplace doing nothing. ^{4} He told them, 'You also go and work in my vineyard, and I will pay you whatever is right.' ^{5} So they went. He went out again about noon and about three in the afternoon and did the same thing. ^{6} About five in the afternoon he went out and found still others standing around. He asked them, 'Why have you been standing here all day long doing nothing?' ^{7} 'Because no one has hired us,' they answered. He said to them, 'You also go and work in my vineyard.'

^{8} When evening came, the owner of the vineyard said to his foreman, 'Call the workers and pay them their wages, beginning with the last ones hired and going on to the first.'

^{9} The workers who were hired about five in the afternoon came and each received a denarius. ^{10} So when those came who were hired first, they expected to receive more. But each one of them also received a denarius. ^{11} When they received it, they began to grumble against the landowner. ^{12} 'Th[o]se who were hired last worked only one hour,' they said, 'and you have made them equal to us who have borne the burden of the work and the heat of the day.'

^{13} But he answered, 'I am not being unfair to you, friend. Didn't you agree to work for a denarius? ^{14} Take your pay and go. I want to give the one who was hired last the same as I gave you. ^{15} Don't I have the right to do what I want with my own money? Or are you envious because I am generous?' ^{16} So the last will be first, and the first will be last."

John 10:

^{27} My sheep listen to my voice; I know them, and they follow me. ^{28} I give them eternal life, and they shall never perish; no one will snatch them out of my hand. ^{29} My Father, who has given them to me, is greater than all; no one can snatch them out of my Father's hand. ^{30} I and the Father are one."

^{31} [H]is… opponents [then] picked up stones to stone him, ^{32} but Jesus said to them, "I have shown you many good works from the Father. For which of these do you stone me?" ^{33} "We are not stoning you for any good work," they replied. ^{39} [T]hey tried to seize [Jesus], but he escaped their grasp.

John 11:

^{1} Now a man named Lazarus was sick. He was from Bethany, the village of Mary and her sister Martha. ³ So the sisters sent word to Jesus, "Lord, the one you love is sick." ⁴ When he heard this, Jesus said, "This sickness will not end in death. No, it is for God's glory so that God's Son may be glorified through it." ⁵ Now Jesus loved Martha and her sister and Lazarus. ⁶ So when he heard that Lazarus was sick, he stayed where he was two more days, ⁷ and then he said to his disciples, "Let us go back to Judea. ¹¹ ...Our friend Lazarus has fallen asleep; but I am going there to wake him up."

¹² His disciples replied, "Lord, if he sleeps, he will get better." ¹⁴ So then he told them plainly, "Lazarus is dead."

¹⁷ On his arrival, Jesus found that Lazarus had... been in the tomb for four days. ¹⁸ Now...¹⁹ many... had come to Martha and Mary to comfort them in the loss of their brother. ²⁰ When Martha heard that Jesus was coming, she went out to meet him...

²¹ "Lord," Martha said to Jesus, "if you had been here, my brother would not have died. ²² But I know that even now God will give you whatever you ask." ²³ Jesus said to her, "Your brother will rise again." ²⁴ Martha answered, "I know he will rise again in the resurrection at the last day."

²⁵ Jesus said to her, "I am the resurrection and the life. The one who believes in me will live, even though they die; ²⁶ and whoever lives by believing in me will never die. Do you believe this?" ²⁷ "Yes, Lord," she replied, "I believe that you are the Messiah, the Son of God, who is to come into the world."

²⁸ After she had said this, she went back and called her sister Mary... "The Teacher is here," she said... ²⁹ When Mary heard this, she got up quickly and went to him. ³⁰ Now Jesus had not yet entered the village, but was still at the place where Martha had met him. ³¹ When the [crowd] who had been with Mary in the house, comforting her, noticed how quickly she got up and went out, they followed her, supposing she was going to the tomb to mourn there.

³² When Mary reached the place where Jesus was and saw him, she fell at his feet and said, "Lord, if you had been here, my brother would not have died."

³³ When Jesus saw her weeping, and the [crowd] who had come along with her also weeping, he was deeply moved... ³⁴ "Where have you laid him?" he asked. "Come and see, Lord," they replied. ³⁵ Jesus wept.

³⁶ Then the [people] said, "See how he loved him!" ³⁷ But some of them said, "Could not he who opened the eyes of the blind man have kept this man from dying?"

³⁸ Jesus, once more deeply moved, came to the tomb... ³⁹ "Take away the stone," he said. "But, Lord," said Martha... "by this time there is a bad odor, for he has been there four days." ⁴⁰ Then Jesus said, "Did I not tell you that if you believe, you will see the glory of God?"

⁴¹ So they took away the stone. Then Jesus looked up and said, "Father, I thank you that you have heard me. ⁴² I kn[o]w that you always hear me, but I said this for the benefit of the people standing here, that they may believe that you sent me."

⁴³ When he had said this, Jesus called in a loud voice, "Lazarus, come out!" ⁴⁴ The dead man came out, his hands and feet wrapped with strips of linen, and a cloth around his face. Jesus [then] said to them, "Take off the grave clothes and let him go."

⁴⁵ Therefore many… who had come to visit Mary, and had seen what Jesus did, believed in him. ⁴⁶ But some of them went to the Pharisees and told them what Jesus had done. ⁴⁷ Then the chief priests and the Pharisees called a meeting of the Sanhedrin. "What are we accomplishing?" they asked. "Here is this man performing many signs. ⁴⁸ If we let him go on like this, everyone will believe in him, and then the Romans will come and take away both our temple and our nation."

The Raising of Lazarus by Fra Angelico c. 1438-1445

⁴⁹ Then one of them, named Caiaphas, who was high priest that year, spoke up, "You know nothing at all! ⁵⁰ You do not realize that it is better for you that one man die for the people than that the whole nation perish." ⁵³ So from that day on they plotted to take his life. ⁵⁴ Therefore Jesus no longer moved about publicly among the people of Judea. Instead he withdrew to a region near the wilderness, to a village called Ephraim, where he stayed with his disciples.

Matthew 20:

¹⁷ Now Jesus was going up to Jerusalem. On the way, he took the Twelve aside and said to them, ¹⁸ "We are going up to Jerusalem, and the Son of Man will be delivered over to the chief priests and the teachers of the law. They will condemn him to death ¹⁹ and will hand him over… to be mocked and flogged and crucified. On the third day he will be raised to life!"

Mark 10:

³⁵ [One day] James and John, the sons of Zebedee, came to him. "Teacher, we want you to do for us whatever we ask." ³⁶ "What do you want me to do for you?" he asked. ³⁷ They replied, "Let one of us sit at your right and the other at your left in your glory."

³⁸ "You don't know what you are asking," Jesus said. "Can you drink the cup I drink or be baptized with the baptism I am baptized with?" ³⁹ "We can," they answered. Jesus said to them, "You will drink the cup I drink and be baptized with the baptism I am baptized

with, ⁴⁰ but to sit at my right or left is not for me to grant. These places belong to those for whom they have been prepared.

⁴³ ...[W]hoever wants to become great among you must be your servant, ⁴⁴ and whoever wants to be first must be slave of all. ⁴⁵ For even the Son of Man did not come to be served, but to serve, and to give his life as a ransom for many."

Matthew 20:

²⁹ As Jesus and his disciples were leaving Jericho, a large crowd followed him. ³⁰ [A] blind [man] (Bartimaeus) [was] sitting by the roadside, and when [he] heard that Jesus was going by, [he] shouted, "Lord, Son of David, have mercy on [me]!"

³¹ The crowd rebuked [him] and told [him] to be quiet, but [he] shouted all the louder, "Lord, Son of David, have mercy on [me]!" ³² Jesus stopped and called [him]. "What do you want me to do for you?" he asked. ³³ "Lord," [he] answered, "[I] want... sight."

Luke 18:

⁴² Jesus said to him, "Receive your sight; your faith has healed you." ⁴³ Immediately he received his sight and followed Jesus, praising God. When all the people saw it, they also praised God.

Luke 19:

¹ Jesus entered Jericho and was passing through. ² A man was there by the name of Zacchaeus; he was a chief tax collector and was wealthy. ³ He wanted to see who Jesus was, but because he was short he could not see over the crowd. ⁴ So he ran ahead and climbed a sycamore-fig tree to see him, since Jesus was coming that way.

⁵ When Jesus reached the spot, he looked up and said to him, "Zacchaeus, come down immediately. I must stay at your house today." ⁶ So he came down at once and welcomed him gladly. ⁷ All the people saw this and began to mutter, "He has gone to be the guest of a sinner."

⁸ But Zacchaeus stood up and said to the Lord, "Look, Lord! Here and now I give half of my possessions to the poor, and if I have cheated anybody out of anything, I will pay back four times the amount." ⁹ Jesus said to him, "Today salvation has come to this house, because this man, too, is a son of Abraham. ¹⁰ For the Son of Man came to seek and to save the lost."

John 12:

¹ Six days before the Passover, Jesus came to Bethany, where Lazarus lived, whom Jesus had raised from the dead. ² Here a dinner was given in Jesus' honor. Martha served, while Lazarus was among those reclining at the table with him. ³ Then Mary took about a pint of pure nard, an expensive perfume; she poured it on Jesus' feet and wiped his feet with her hair. And the house was filled with the fragrance of the perfume.

⁴ [O]ne of his disciples, Judas Iscariot, who was later to betray him, objected, ⁵ "Why wasn't this perfume sold and the money given to the poor? It [is] worth a year's wages." ⁶ He did not say this because he cared about the poor but because he was a thief...

[7] "Leave her alone," Jesus replied. "It was intended that she should save this perfume for the day of my burial."

Matthew 21:

[1] As they approached Jerusalem… Jesus sent two disciples, [2] saying to them, "Go to the village ahead of you, and at once you will find a donkey tied there, with her colt by her. Untie them and bring them to me."

Luke 19:

[33] As they were untying the colt, its owners asked them, "Why are you untying the colt?" [34] They replied, "The Lord needs it." [35] They brought it to Jesus, threw their cloaks on the colt and put Jesus on it.

Matthew 21:

[4] This took place to fulfill what was spoken through the prophet: [5] "Say to Daughter Zion, 'See, your king comes to you, gentle and riding on a donkey, and on a colt, the foal of a donkey.'"

[8] A very large crowd spread their cloaks on the road, while others cut branches from the trees and spread them on the road. [9] The crowds that went ahead of him and those that followed shouted, "Hosanna to the Son of David! Blessed is he who comes in the name of the Lord! Hosanna in the highest heaven!"

[10] When Jesus entered Jerusalem, the whole city was stirred and asked, "Who is this?" [11] The crowds answered, "This is Jesus, the prophet from Nazareth in Galilee."

Luke 19:

[41] As [Jesus] approached Jerusalem and saw the city, he wept over it [42] and said, "If you, even you, had only known on this day what would bring you peace — but now it is hidden from your eyes."

Entry into Jerusalem by
Fra Angelico c. 1450

Matthew 21:

¹² Jesus entered the temple courts and drove out all who were buying and selling there. He overturned the tables of the money changers and the benches of those selling doves. ¹³ "It is written," he said to them, "'My house will be called a house of prayer,' but you are making it 'a den of robbers.'"

¹⁴ The blind and the lame came to him at the temple, and he healed them. ¹⁵ But when the chief priests and the teachers of the law saw the wonderful things he did and the children shouting in the temple courts, "Hosanna to the Son of David," they were indignant.

¹⁶ "Do you hear what these children are saying?" they asked him. "Yes," replied Jesus, "have you never read, 'From the lips of children and infants [Y]ou, Lord, have called forth your praise?'" ¹⁷ And he left them and went out of the city to Bethany, where he spent the night.

Mark 11:

²² "Have faith in God," Jesus [urged]. ²³ "Truly I tell you, if anyone says to this mountain, 'Go, throw yourself into the sea,' and does not doubt in their heart but believes that what they say will happen, it will be done for them. ²⁴ Therefore I tell you, whatever you ask for in prayer, believe that you have received it, and it will be yours. ²⁵ And when you stand praying, if you hold anything against anyone, forgive them, so that your Father in heaven may forgive you your sins."

Matthew 21:

⁴² Jesus said to them… "The stone the builders rejected has become the cornerstone; the Lord has done this, and it is marvelous in our eyes."

Mark 12:

¹³ Later… some [came] to Jesus to catch him in his words.

Matthew 22:

¹⁶ "Teacher," they said, "we know that you are a man of integrity and that you teach the way of God in accordance with the truth. You aren't swayed by others, because you pay no attention to who they are."

Luke 20:

²² "Is it right for us to pay taxes to Caesar or not?"

Matthew 22:

¹⁸ But Jesus, knowing their… intent, said, ¹⁹ "Show me the coin used for paying the tax." They brought him a denarius, ²⁰ and he asked them, "Whose image is this? And whose inscription?" ²¹ "Caesar's," they replied. Then he said to them, "So give back to Caesar what is Caesar's, and to God what is God's."

Luke 20:

²⁷ Some of the Sadducees, who say there is no resurrection, came to Jesus…

Matthew 22:

³¹ "…[A]about the resurrection of the dead — have you not read what God said to you, ³² 'I am the God of Abraham, the God of Isaac, and the God of Jacob?' He is not the God of the dead but of the living."

Luke 20:

³⁹ Some of the teachers of the law responded, "Well said, teacher!" ⁴⁰ And no one dared to ask him any more questions.

Mark 12:

²⁸ One of the teachers of the law came and… asked [Jesus], "Of all the commandments, which is the most important?" ²⁹ "The most important one," answered Jesus, "is… 'The Lord our God, the Lord is one. ³⁰ Love the Lord your God with all your heart and with all your soul and with all your mind and with all your strength.' ³¹ The second is… 'Love your neighbor as yourself.' There is no commandment greater than these."

³² "Well said.. " the man replied. "You are right in saying that God is one and there is no other but [H]im. ³³ To love [H]im with all your heart, with all your understanding and with all your strength, and to love your neighbor as yourself is more important than all burnt offerings and sacrifices." ³⁴ When Jesus saw that he had answered wisely, he said… "You are not far from the kingdom of God."

Luke 21:

¹ As Jesus looked up, he saw the rich putting their gifts into the temple treasury. ² He also saw a poor widow put in two very small copper coins. ³ "Truly I tell you," he said, "this poor widow has put in more than all the others. ⁴ All these people gave their gifts out of their wealth; but she out of her poverty put in all she had to live on."

Matthew 24:

¹ Jesus left the temple and was walking away when his disciples came up to him to call his attention to its buildings. ² "Do you see all these things?" he asked. "Truly I tell you, not one stone here will be left on another; every one will be thrown down… ¹³ [B]ut the one who stands firm to the end will be saved. ¹⁴ [The] gospel of the kingdom will be preached in the whole world as a testimony to all nations, and then the end will come. ³⁰ Then will appear the sign of the Son of Man… coming on the clouds of heaven, with power and great glory. ³¹ And he will send his angels with a loud trumpet call, and they will gather his elect from the four winds, from one end of the heavens to the other.

³⁶ "But about that day or hour no one knows, not even the angels in heaven, nor the Son, but only the Father. ⁴² Therefore keep watch, because you do not know on what day your Lord will come. ⁴⁴ So you also must be ready, because the Son of Man will come at an hour when you do not expect him."

Matthew 25:

³¹ "When the Son of Man comes in his glory, and all the angels with him, he will sit on his glorious throne. ³² All the nations will be gathered before him…

³⁴ "Then the King will say... 'Come, you who are blessed by my Father; take your inheritance, the kingdom prepared for you since the creation of the world. ³⁵ For I was hungry and you gave me something to eat, I was thirsty and you gave me something to drink, I was a stranger and you invited me in, ³⁶ I needed clothes and you clothed me, I was sick and you looked after me, I was in prison and you came to visit me.'"

³⁷ "Then the righteous will answer him, 'Lord, when did we see you hungry and feed you, or thirsty and give you something to drink? ³⁸ When did we see you a stranger and invite you in, or needing clothes and clothe you? ³⁹ When did we see you sick or in prison and go to visit you?'"

⁴⁰ "The King will reply, 'Truly I tell you, whatever you did for one of the least of these brothers and sisters of mine, you did for me.'"

John 12:

²³ Jesus [said], "The hour has come for the Son of Man to be glorified. ²⁴ Very truly I tell you, unless a kernel of wheat falls to the ground and dies, it remains only a single seed. But if it dies, it produces many seeds. ²⁵ Anyone who loves their life will lose it, while anyone who hates their life in this world will keep it for eternal life. ²⁶ Whoever serves me must follow me; and where I am, my servant also will be. My Father will honor the one who serves me."

²⁷ "Now my soul is troubled, and what shall I say? 'Father, save me from this hour?' No, it was for this very reason I came to this hour. ²⁸ Father, glorify your name!" Then a voice came from heaven, "I have glorified it, and will glorify it again."

³⁰ Jesus said, ³¹ "Now is the time for judgment on this world; now the prince of this world will be driven out. ³² And... when I am lifted up from the earth, will draw all people to myself." ³³ He said this to show the kind of death he was going to die.

³⁴ The crowd spoke up, "We have heard from the Law that the Messiah will remain forever, so how can you say, 'The Son of Man must be lifted up?' Who is this 'Son of Man?'"

³⁵ Then Jesus told them, "You are going to have the light just a little while longer. Walk while you have the light, before darkness overtakes you... ³⁶ Believe in the light while you have the light, so that you may become children of light. ⁴⁴ Whoever believes in me does not believe in me only, but in the one who sent me. ⁴⁵ The one who looks at me is seeing the one who sent me. ⁴⁶ I have come into the world as a light, so that no one who believes in me should stay in darkness."

⁴⁹ "...I did not speak on my own, but the Father [W]ho sent me commanded me to say all that I have spoken. ⁵⁰ I know that [H]is command leads to eternal life. So whatever I say is just what the Father has told me to say."

Matthew 26:

¹ When Jesus had finished saying all these things, he said to his disciples, ² "As you

know, the Passover is two days away — and the Son of Man will be handed over to be crucified."

³ Then the chief priests and the elders of the people assembled in the palace of the high priest, whose name was Caiaphas, ⁴ and they schemed to arrest Jesus secretly and kill him.

¹⁴ Then one of the Twelve — Judas Iscariot — went to the chief priests ¹⁵ and asked, "What are you willing to give me if I deliver him over to you?" So they counted out for him thirty pieces of silver. ¹⁶ From then on Judas watched for an opportunity to hand him over.

¹⁷ On the first day of the Festival of Unleavened Bread, the disciples came to Jesus and asked, "Where do you want us to make preparations for you to eat the Passover?"

Luke 22:

¹⁰ He replied, "As you enter the city, a man carrying a jar of water will meet you. Follow him to the house that he enters, ¹¹ and say to the owner of the house, 'The Teacher asks: Where is the guest room, where I may eat the Passover with my disciples?' ¹² He will show you a large room upstairs, all furnished. Make preparations there."

Matthew 26:

¹⁹ So the disciples did as Jesus had directed them and prepared the Passover.

²⁰ When evening came, Jesus was reclining at the table with the Twelve. ²¹ And while they were eating, he said, "Truly I tell you, one of you will betray me."

²² They were very sad and began to say to him one after the other, "Surely you don't mean me, Lord?" ²³ Jesus replied, "The one who has dipped his hand into the bowl with me will betray me. ²⁴ The Son of Man will go just as it is written about him…"

²⁵ Then Judas, the one who would betray him, said, "Surely you don't mean me, Rabbi?" Jesus answered, "You have said so."

²⁶ While they were eating, Jesus took bread, and when he had given thanks, he broke it and gave it to his disciples, saying, "Take and eat; this is my body."

²⁷ Then he took a cup, and when he had given thanks, he gave it to them, saying, "Drink from it, all of you. ²⁸ This is my blood of the covenant, which is poured out for many for the forgiveness of sins. ²⁹ I tell you, I will not drink from this fruit of the vine from now on until that day when I drink it new with you in my Father's kingdom."

Communion of the Apostles by Fra Angelico
c. 1451-1453

John 13:

¹ It was just before the Passover Festival. Jesus knew that the hour had come for him to leave this world and go to the Father. Having loved his own who were in the world, he loved them to the end.

³ Jesus knew that the Father had put all things under his power, and that he had come from God and was returning to God; ⁴ so he got up from the meal, took off his outer clothing, and wrapped a towel around his waist. ⁵ After that, he poured water into a basin and began to wash his disciples' feet, drying them with the towel that was wrapped around him.

⁶ He came to Simon Peter, who said to him, "Lord, are you going to wash my feet?" ⁷ Jesus replied, "You do not realize now what I am doing, but later you will understand."

⁸ "No," said Peter, "you shall never wash my feet." Jesus answered, "Unless I wash you, you have no part with me."

⁹ "Then, Lord," Simon Peter replied, "not just my feet but my hands and my head as well!"

¹⁰ Jesus answered, "Those who have had a bath need only to wash their feet; their whole body is clean. And you are clean, though not every one of you." ¹¹ For he knew who was going to betray him, and that was why he said not every one was clean.

¹² When he had finished washing their feet, he put on his clothes and returned to his place. "Do you understand what I have done for you?" he asked them. ¹³ "You call me 'Teacher' and 'Lord,' and rightly so, for that is what I am. ¹⁴ Now that I, your Lord and Teacher, have washed your feet, you also should wash one another's feet. ¹⁵ I have set you an example that you should do as I have done for you. ¹⁶ Very truly I tell you, no servant is greater than his master, nor is a messenger greater than the one who sent him. ¹⁷ Now that you know these things, you will be blessed if you do them."

[31] When [Judas] was gone, Jesus said, "Now the Son of Man is glorified and God is glorified in him... [33] "My children, I will be with you only a little longer... [34] A new command I give you: Love one another. As I have loved you, so you must love one another. [35] By this everyone will know that you are my disciples, if you love one another."

Matthew 26:

[30] When they had sung a hymn, they went out to the Mount of Olives. [31] Then Jesus told them, "This very night you will all fall away on account of me, for it is written: 'I will strike the shepherd, and the sheep of the flock will be scattered.' [32] But after I have risen, I will go ahead of you into Galilee."

[33] Peter replied, "Even if all fall away on account of you, I never will." [34] "Truly I tell you," Jesus answered, "this very night, before the rooster crows, you will disown me three times." [35] But Peter declared, "Even if I have to die with you, I will never disown you." And all the other disciples said the same.

[36] Then Jesus went with his disciples to a place called Gethsemane, and he said to them, "Sit here while I go over there and pray."

Luke 22:

[37] "It is written: 'And he was numbered with the transgressors;' and I tell you that this must be fulfilled in me. Yes, what is written about me is reaching its fulfillment."

John 14:

[1] "Do not let your hearts be troubled... [2] My Father's house has many rooms; if that were not so, would I have told you that I am going there to prepare a place for you? [3] And if I go and prepare a place for you, I will come back and take you to be with me that you also may be where I am. [4] You know the way to the place where I am going."

[5] Thomas said to him, "Lord, we don't know where you are going, so how can we know the way?" [6] Jesus answered, "I am the way and the truth and the life. No one comes to the Father except through me..."

[8] Philip said, "Lord, show us the Father and that will be enough for us." [9] Jesus answered: "Don't you know me, Philip, even after I have been among you such a long time? Anyone who has seen me has seen the Father.

[10] ...The words I say to you I do not speak on my own authority. Rather, it is the Father, living in me, [W]ho is doing [H]is work. [11] Believe me when I say that I am in the Father and the Father is in me; or at least believe on the evidence of the works themselves. [12] Very truly I tell you, whoever believes in me will do the works I have been doing, and they will do even greater things than these, because I am going to the Father. [13] And I will do whatever you ask in my name, so that the Father may be glorified in the Son. [14] You may ask me for anything in my name, and I will do it.

[15] "If you love me, keep my commands. [16] And I will ask the Father, and [H]e will give you another advocate to help you and be with you forever — [17] the Spirit of truth... [18] I will not leave you as orphans; I will come to you. [19] Before long, the world will not see me anymore, but you will see me. Because I live, you also will live. [20] On that day you will realize that I am in my Father, and you are in me, and I am in you. [21] Whoever has my

commands and keeps them is the one who loves me. The one who loves me will be loved by my Father, and I too will love them and show myself to them."

²⁵ "All this I have spoken while still with you. ²⁶ But the Advocate, the Holy Spirit, whom the Father will send in my name, will teach you all things and will remind you of everything I have said to you. ²⁷ Peace I leave with you; my peace I give you. I do not give to you as the world gives. Do not let your hearts be troubled and do not be afraid."

²⁸ "You heard me say, 'I am going away and I am coming back to you.' If you loved me, you would be glad that I am going to the Father, for the Father is greater than I. ²⁹ I have told you now before it happens, so that when it does happen you will believe."

John 15:

¹ "I am the true vine... ⁴ Remain in me, as I also remain in you. No branch can bear fruit by itself; it must remain in the vine. Neither can you bear fruit unless you remain in me.

⁵ I am the vine; you are the branches. If you remain in me and I in you, you will bear much fruit... ⁷ If you remain in me and my words remain in you, ask whatever you wish, and it will be done for you. ⁸ This is to my Father's glory, that you bear much fruit, showing yourselves to be my disciples.

⁹ As the Father has loved me, so have I loved you. Now remain in my love. ¹⁰ If you keep my commands, you will remain in my love, just as I have kept my Father's commands and remain in [H]is love. ¹² My command is... Love each other as I have loved you. ¹³ Greater love has no one than this: to lay down one's life for one's friends. ¹⁴ You are my friends if you do what I command. ¹⁵ I no longer call you servants, because a servant does not know his master's business. Instead, I have called you friends, for everything that I learned from my Father I have made known to you. ¹⁶ You did not choose me, but I chose you and appointed you so that you might go and bear fruit — fruit that will last — and so that whatever you ask in my name the Father will give you. ¹⁷ This is my command: Love each other.

¹⁸ If the world hates you, keep in mind that it hated me first. ¹⁹ If you belonged to the world, it would love you as its own. As it is, you do not belong to the world, but I have chosen you out of the world. That is why the world hates you. ²⁰ Remember what I told you: 'A servant is not greater than his master.' If they persecuted me, they will persecute you also..."

The Dialogue of the Savior:

Mary [Magadalene] said, "...[T]he laborer is worthy of his food."

John 16:

¹³ [Jesus then went on to say,] "[When] the Spirit of truth, comes, he will guide you into all the truth. He will not speak on his own; he will speak only what he hears, and he will tell you what is yet to come... ¹⁶ In a little while you will see me no more, and then after a little while you will see me... ²⁰ Very truly I tell you, you will weep and mourn... You will grieve, but your grief will turn to joy. ²² ...I will see you again and you will rejoice, and no one will take away your joy.

25 Though I have been speaking figuratively, a time is coming when I... will tell you plainly about my Father.

32 A time is coming and in fact has come when you will be scattered, each to your own home. You will leave me all alone. Yet I am not alone, for my Father is with me. 33 "I have told you these things, so that in me you may have peace... [T]ake heart! I have overcome the world."

John 17:

1 After Jesus said this, he looked toward heaven and prayed: "Father, the hour has come. Glorify [Y]our Son, that [Y]our Son may glorify [Y]ou. 2 For [Y]ou granted him authority over all people that he might give eternal life to all those [Y]ou have given him. 4 I have brought [Y]ou glory on earth by finishing the work [Y]ou gave me to do. 5 And now, Father, glorify me in [Y]our presence with the glory I had with [Y]ou before the world began.

15 My prayer is... that [Y]ou... 17 [s]anctify them by the truth; [Y]our word is truth. 18 As [Y]ou sent me into the world, I have sent them into the world. 19 For them I sanctify myself, that they too may be truly sanctified. 24 Father, I want those [Y]ou have given me to be with me where I am, and to see my glory, the glory [Y]ou have given me because [Y]ou loved me before the creation of the world."

Matthew 26:

36 Then Jesus went with his disciples to a place called Gethsemane, and he said to them, "Sit here while I go over there and pray." 37 He took Peter and the two sons of Zebedee along with him, and he began to be sorrowful and troubled.

Luke 22:

41 He withdrew about a stone's throw beyond them, knelt down and prayed, 42 "Father, if [Y]ou are willing, take this cup from me; yet not my will, but [Y]ours be done." 43 An angel from heaven appeared to him and strengthened him. 44 And being in anguish, he prayed more earnestly, and his sweat was like drops of blood falling to the ground.

Matthew 26:

40 Then he returned to his disciples and found them sleeping. "Couldn't you... keep watch with me for one hour?" he asked Peter. 41 "Watch and pray so that you will not fall into temptation. The spirit is willing, but the flesh is weak."

42 He went away a second time and prayed, "My Father, if it is not possible for this cup to be taken away unless I drink it, may [Y]our will be done."

43 When he came back, he again found them sleeping, because their eyes were heavy.

44 So he left them and went away once more and prayed the third time, saying the same thing.

45 Then he returned to the disciples and said to them, "Are you still sleeping and resting? Look, the hour has come, and the Son of Man is delivered into the hands of sinners. 46 Rise! Let us go! Here comes my betrayer!" 47 While he was still speaking, Judas...

arrived. With him was a large crowd armed with swords and clubs... [48] Now the betrayer had arranged a signal with them: "The one I kiss is the man; arrest him." [49] Going at once to Jesus, Judas said, "Greetings, Rabbi!" and kissed him.

John 18:

[4] Jesus, knowing all that was going to happen to him, went out and asked them, "Who is it you want?" [5] "Jesus of Nazareth," they replied. "I am he," Jesus said. [6] When Jesus said, "I am he," they drew back and fell to the ground.

[7] Again he asked them, "Who is it you want?" "Jesus of Nazareth," they said. [8] Jesus answered, "I told you that I am he. If you are looking for me, then let these men go." [9] This happened so that the words he had spoken would be fulfilled: "I have not lost one of those [Y]ou gave me."

Mark 14:

[46] The men seized Jesus and arrested him. [47] Then one of those standing near drew his sword and struck the servant of the high priest, cutting off his ear.

Matthew 26:

[52] "Put your sword back in its place," Jesus said to him, "for all who draw the sword will die by the sword. [53] Do you think I cannot call on my Father, and he will at once put at my disposal more than twelve legions of angels? [54] But how then would the Scriptures be fulfilled that say it must happen in this way?"

Luke 22:

[51] ...And he touched the man's ear and healed him.

Mark 14:

[48] "Am I leading a rebellion," said Jesus, "that you have come out with swords and clubs to capture me? [49] Every day I was with you, teaching in the temple courts, and you did not arrest me. But the Scriptures must be fulfilled." [50] Then [his disciples] deserted him and fled.

Matthew 26:

[57] Those who had arrested Jesus took him to Caiaphas the high priest, where the teachers of the law and the elders had assembled. [58] But Peter followed him at a distance, right up to the courtyard... He entered and sat down with the guards to see the outcome.

[59] The chief priests and the whole Sanhedrin were looking for false evidence against Jesus so that they could put him to death. [60] But they did not find any, though many false witnesses came forward. Finally two came forward [61] and declared, "This fellow said, 'I am able to destroy the temple of God and rebuild it in three days.'"

[62] Then the high priest stood up and said to Jesus, "Are you not going to answer? What is this testimony that these men are bringing against you?" [63] But Jesus remained silent.

The high priest said to him, "I charge you under oath by the living God: Tell us if you are the Messiah, the Son of God." [64] "You have said so," Jesus replied. "But I say to all of you: From now on you will see the Son of Man sitting at the right hand of the Mighty One and coming on the clouds of heaven." [65] Then the high priest tore his clothes and said, "He has spoken blasphemy! Why do we need any more witnesses? Look, now you have heard the blasphemy. [66] What do you think?" "He is worthy of death," they answered.

Luke 22:

[63] The men who were guarding Jesus began mocking and beating him. [64] They blindfolded him and demanded, "Prophesy! Who hit you?"

Matthew 26:

[69] Now Peter was sitting out in the courtyard, and a servant girl came to him. "You also were with Jesus of Galilee," she said. [70] But he denied it before them all. "I don't know what you're talking about," he said. [71] Then he went out to the gateway, where another servant girl saw him and said to the people there, "This fellow was with Jesus of Nazareth." [72] He denied it again, with an oath: "I don't know the man!"

[73] After a little while, those standing there went up to Peter and said, "Surely you are one of them; your accent gives you away." [74] Then he began to call down curses, and he swore to them, "I don't know the man!" Immediately a rooster crowed. [75] Then Peter remembered the word Jesus had spoken: "Before the rooster crows, you will disown me three times." And he went outside and wept bitterly.

Matthew 27:

[1] Early in the morning, all the chief priests and the elders of the people made their plans... to have Jesus executed. [2] So they bound him, led him away and handed him over to Pilate the governor.

[3] When Judas, who had betrayed him, saw that Jesus was condemned, he was seized with remorse and returned the thirty pieces of silver to the chief priests and the elders. [4] "I have sinned," he said, "for I have betrayed innocent blood." "What is that to us?" they replied. "That's your responsibility." [5] So Judas threw the money into the temple... [6] The chief priests picked up the coins and said, "It is against the law to put this into the treasury, since it is blood money." [7] So they decided to use the money to buy the potter's field as a burial place for foreigners. [9] [W]hat was spoken by Jeremiah the prophet was fulfilled: "They took the thirty pieces of silver, the price set on him by the people... [10] and they used them to buy the potter's field..."

John 18:

[28] Then [they] took Jesus from Caiaphas to the palace of the Roman governor. By now it was early morning, and to avoid ceremonial uncleanness they did not enter the palace, because they wanted to be able to eat the Passover. [29] So Pilate came out to them and asked, "What charges are you bringing against this man?"

[30] "If he were not a criminal," they replied, "we would not have handed him over to you."

Luke 23:

² And they began to accuse him, saying, "We have found this man subverting our nation. He opposes payment of taxes to Caesar and claims to be [the] Messiah, a king."

John 18:

³³ Pilate then went back inside the palace [and] summoned Jesus.

Luke 23:

³ So Pilate asked Jesus, "Are you the king of the Jews?"

Matthew 27:

¹¹ "You have said so," Jesus replied.

John 18:

³⁵ "Your own people... handed you over to me. What is it you have done?" ³⁶ Jesus said, "My kingdom is not of this world. If it were, my servants would fight to prevent my arrest... But now my kingdom is from another place." ³⁷ "You are a king, then!" said Pilate. Jesus answered, "You say that I am a king. In fact, the reason I was born and came into the world is to testify to the truth. Everyone on the side of truth listens to me."

Matthew 27:

¹³ Pilate asked him, "Don't you hear the testimony they are bringing against you?" ¹⁴ But Jesus made no reply, not even to a single charge — to the great amazement of the governor.

Luke 23:

⁴ Then Pilate announced... "I find no basis for a charge against this man." ⁵ But they insisted, "He stirs up the people all over Judea by his teaching. He started in Galilee and has come all the way here."

⁶ On hearing this, Pilate asked if the man was a Galilean. ⁷ When he learned that Jesus was under Herod's jurisdiction, he sent him to Herod, who was also in Jerusalem at that time. ⁸ When Herod saw Jesus, he was greatly pleased, because for a long time he had been wanting to see him. From what he had heard about him, he hoped to see him perform a sign of some sort. ⁹ He plied him with many questions, but Jesus gave him no answer. ¹¹ Then Herod and his soldiers ridiculed and mocked him [and] sent him back to Pilate.

Matthew 27:

¹⁵ Now it was [a] custom... to release a prisoner chosen by the crowd [at the festival]. ¹⁶ At that time they had a well-known prisoner whose name was Barabbas. ¹⁹ While Pilate was sitting on the judge's seat, his wife sent him this message: "Don't have anything to do with that innocent man, for I have suffered a great deal today in a dream because of him."

¹⁷ So when the crowd had gathered, Pilate asked them, "Which one do you want me to release to you: Barabbas, or Jesus who is called the Messiah?" ²⁰ But the chief priests and the elders persuaded the crowd to ask for Barabbas…

Mark 15:

¹² "What shall I do, then, with the one you call the king of the Jews?" Pilate asked them. ¹³ "Crucify him!" they shouted. ¹⁴ "Why? What crime has he committed?" asked Pilate. But they shouted all the louder, "Crucify him!"

Matthew 27:

²⁴ When Pilate saw that he was getting nowhere, but that instead an uproar was starting, he took water and washed his hands in front of the crowd. "I am innocent of this man's blood," he said. "It is your responsibility!" ²⁵ All the people answered, "His blood is on us and on our children!"

John 19:

¹ Then Pilate took Jesus and had him flogged. ² The soldiers twisted together a crown of thorns and put it on his head. They clothed him in a purple robe ³ and went up to him again and again, saying, "Hail, king of the Jews!" And they slapped him in the face.

⁴ Once more Pilate came out and said to the [crowd] gathered there, "Look, I am bringing him out to you to let you know that I find no basis for a charge against him." ⁵ When Jesus came out wearing the crown of thorns and the purple robe, Pilate said to them, "Here is the man!" ⁶ As soon as the chief priests and their officials saw him, they shouted, "Crucify [him]! Crucify [him]!" But Pilate answered, "You take him and crucify him." ⁷ [They] insisted, "We have a law, and according to that law he must die, because he claimed to be the Son of God."

⁸ When Pilate heard this, he was even more afraid, ⁹ and he went back inside the palace. "Where do you come from?" he asked Jesus, but Jesus gave him no answer. ¹⁰ "Do you refuse to speak to me?" Pilate said. "Don't you realize I have power either to free you or to crucify you?" ¹¹ Jesus answered, "You would have no power over me if it were not given to you from above…" ¹² From then on, Pilate tried to set Jesus free, but the [crowd] kept shouting, "If you let this man go, you are no friend of Caesar. Anyone who claims to be a king opposes Caesar." ¹³ When Pilate heard this, he brought Jesus out… "Here is your king," Pilate said… ¹⁵ But they shouted, "Take him away! Take him away! Crucify him!"

"Shall I crucify your king?" Pilate asked. "We have no king but Caesar," [they] answered.

¹⁶ Finally Pilate handed him over… to be crucified.

Luke 23:

²⁶ As the soldiers led him away, they seized Simon from Cyrene, who was on his way in from the country, and put the cross on him and made him carry it behind Jesus. ²⁷ A large number of people followed him, including women who mourned and wailed for him.

[28] Jesus turned and said to them, "Daughters of Jerusalem, do not weep for me…"

Mark 15:

[22] They brought Jesus to the place called Golgotha (which means "the place of the skull").

John 19:

[18] There they crucified him… with… two others — one on each side and Jesus in the middle.

Luke 23:

[34] Jesus said, "Father, forgive them, for they do not know what they… [do]."

John 19:

[23] When the soldiers crucified Jesus, they took his clothes, dividing them into four shares, one for each of them, with the undergarment remaining. This garment was seamless, woven in one piece from top to bottom. [24] "Let's not tear it," they said to one another. "Let's decide by lot who will get it." This happened that the scripture might be fulfilled that said, "They divided my clothes among them and cast lots for my garment."

Matthew 27:

[36] And sitting down, they kept watch over him...

Luke 23:

[35] The people stood watching, and the rulers even sneered at him.

Matthew 27:

[40] "You who are going to destroy the temple and build it in three days, save yourself! Come down from the cross, if you are the Son of God!" [42] "He saved others," they said, "but he can't save himself! …Let him come down now from the cross, and we will believe in him. [43] He trusts in God. Let God rescue him now if [H]e wants him, for he said, 'I am the Son of God.'

Luke 23:

[39] One of the criminals who [was crucified with Jesus] hurled insults at him: "Aren't you the Messiah? Save yourself and us!" [40] But the other criminal rebuked him. "Don't you fear God," he said, "since you are under the same sentence? [41] We are punished justly, for we are getting what our deeds deserve. But this man has done nothing wrong." [42] Then he said, "Jesus, remember me when you come into your kingdom." [43] Jesus answered him, "Truly I tell you, today you will be with me in paradise."

Matthew 27:

[55] Many women were there, watching from a distance. They had followed Jesus from Galilee to care for his needs.

John 19:

²⁵ Near the cross of Jesus stood his mother, his mother's sister, Mary the wife of Clopas, and Mary Magdalene. ²⁶ When Jesus saw his mother there, and [a] disciple whom he loved standing nearby, he said to her, "…[H]ere is your son," ²⁷ and to the disciple, "Here is your mother." From that time on, this disciple took her into his home.

Mark 15:

³³ At noon, darkness came over the whole land until three in the afternoon. ³⁴ And at three in the afternoon Jesus cried out in a loud voice, *"Eloi, Eloi, lema sabachthani?"* (which means "My God, my God, why have you forsaken me?").

Matthew 27:

⁴⁷ When some of those standing there heard this, they said, "He's calling Elijah." ⁴⁹ Let's see if Elijah comes to save him," [they said].

John 19:

²⁸ Later, knowing that everything had now been finished, and so that Scripture would be fulfilled, Jesus said, "I… [thirst]." ²⁹ A jar of wine vinegar was there, so they soaked a sponge in it, put the sponge on a stalk of the hyssop plant, and lifted it to Jesus' lips. ³⁰ When he had received the drink, Jesus said, "It is finished."

Luke 23:

⁴⁶ "Father, into your hands I [commend] my spirit."   When he had said this…

John 19:

³⁰ …he bowed his head… gave up his spirit [and]

Luke 23:

…breathed his last.

Crucified Christ with Saint John the Evangelist,
the Virgin, and Saints Dominic and Jerome
by Fra Angelico c. 1439-1443

288

Matthew 27:

⁵¹ At that moment the curtain of the temple was torn in two from top to bottom. The earth shook, the rocks split ⁵² and the tombs broke open. The bodies of many holy people who had died were raised to life [and] ⁵³ appeared to many people. ⁵⁴ When the centurion and those... who were guarding Jesus saw the earthquake and all that had happened, they... exclaimed, "Surely he was the Son of God!"

Luke 23:

⁴⁸ When all the people who had gathered... saw what took place, they beat their breasts and went away.

John 19:

³¹ Now it was the day of Preparation, and the next day was to be a special Sabbath. Because the [religious] leaders did not want the bodies left on the crosses during the Sabbath, they asked Pilate to have the legs broken and the bodies taken down. ³² The soldiers therefore came and broke the legs of the first man who had been crucified with Jesus, and then those of the other. ³³ But when they came to Jesus and found that he was already dead, they did not break his legs. ³⁴ Instead, one of the soldiers pierced Jesus' side with a spear, bringing a sudden flow of blood and water. ³⁶ These things happened so that the scripture would be fulfilled: "Not one of his bones will be broken," ³⁷ and... "They will look on the one they have pierced."

³⁸ Later, Joseph of Arimathea [a secret disciple] asked Pilate for the body of Jesus. With Pilate's permission, he came and took the body away. ³⁹ He was accompanied by Nicodemus, the man who earlier had visited Jesus at night. Nicodemus brought a mixture of myrrh and aloes, about seventy-five pounds. ⁴⁰ Taking Jesus' body, the two of them wrapped it, with the spices, in strips of linen. This was in accordance with Jewish burial customs.

⁴¹ At the place where Jesus was crucified, there was a garden, and in the garden a new tomb, in which no one had ever been laid. ⁴² Because it was the Jewish day of Preparation and since the tomb was nearby, they laid Jesus there.

Matthew 27:

⁶⁰ [They then] rolled a big stone in front of the entrance to the tomb and went away.

⁶² [Now] [t]he... chief priests and the Pharisees went to Pilate. ⁶³ "Sir," they said, "we remember that while he was still alive [he] said, 'After three days I will rise again.' ⁶⁴ So give the order for the tomb to be made secure until the third day. Otherwise, his disciples may come and steal the body and tell the people that he has been raised from the dead. This last deception will be worse than the first." ⁶⁵ "Take a guard," Pilate answered. "Go, make the tomb as secure as you know how." ⁶⁶ So they went and made the tomb secure by putting a seal on the stone and posting the guard.

Mark 16:

¹ When the Sabbath was over, Mary Magdalene, Mary the mother of James, and Salome

bought spices so that they might go to anoint Jesus' body.

Nicodemus XIII:

[Before sunrise] an angel descend[ed] from heaven, and he rolled away the stone from the mouth of the cave…

Mark 16:

[2] Very early on the first day of the week, just after sunrise, they were on their way to the tomb [3] and they asked each other, "Who will roll the stone away from the entrance of the tomb?"

[4] But when they looked up, they saw that the stone, which was very large, had been rolled away. [5] As they entered the tomb, they saw a young man dressed in a white robe sitting on the right side…

Matthew 28:

[3] His appearance was like lightning, and his clothes were white as snow.

Matthew 28:

[5] The angel said to the women, "Do not be afraid, for I know that you are looking for Jesus, who was crucified.

Luke 24:

[5] "[But] [w]hy do you look for the living among the dead? [6] He is not here; he has risen! [7] 'The Son of Man [had to] delivered over to the hands of sinners, be crucified and on the third day be raised again.'"

Matthew 28:

[7] "[G]o quickly and tell his disciples: 'He has risen from the dead and is going ahead of you into Galilee. There you will see him.'" [8] So the women hurried away from the tomb, afraid yet filled with joy, and ran to tell his disciples.

John 20:

[2] So [they] came running to Simon Peter and the other disciple… and said, "They have taken the Lord out of the tomb, and we don't know where they have put him!" [3] So Peter and the other disciple started for the tomb. [4] Both were running, but the other disciple outran Peter and reached the tomb first. [5] He bent over and looked in at the strips of linen lying there but did not go in. [6] Then Simon Peter came along behind him and went straight into the tomb. He saw the strips of linen lying there, [7] as well as the cloth that had been wrapped around Jesus' head. The cloth was still lying in its place, separate from the linen. [8] Finally the other disciple, who had reached the tomb first, also went inside. He saw and believed.

Mark 16:

[9] When Jesus rose early on the first day of the week, he appeared first to Mary Magdalene…

John 20:

[11] Now Mary stood outside the tomb crying. As she wept, she bent over to look into the tomb [12] and saw two angels in white, seated where Jesus' body had been, one at the head and the other at the foot. [13] They asked her, "Woman, why are you crying?" "They have taken my Lord away," she said, "and I don't know where they have put him."

[16] Jesus said to her, "Mary." She turned toward him and cried out in Aramaic, "Rabboni!" (which means "Teacher"). [17] Jesus said, "Do not hold on to me, for I have not yet ascended to the Father. Go instead to my brothers and tell them, 'I am ascending to my Father and your Father, to my God and your God.'"

Dialogue of the Savior:

Mary said, "Lord, you are fearful and wonderful..."

John 20:

[18] [She then] went to the disciples with the news: "I have seen the Lord!"

The Resurrection of Christ and the Women
at the Tomb by Fra Angelico c. 1440-1441

Mark 16:

[11] When they heard that Jesus was alive and that she had seen him, they did not believe it.

Mary Magdalene 5:

[1] [T]hey were grieved [and] wept greatly...

Luke 24:

[13] Now that same day two of them were going to a village called Emmaus, about seven miles from Jerusalem. [14] They were talking with each other about everything that had happened. [15] As they talked and discussed these things with each other, Jesus himself came up and walked along with them... [17] He asked them, "What are you discussing

together as you walk along?" They stood still, their faces downcast. [18] One of them, named Cleopas, asked him, "Are you the only one visiting Jerusalem who does not know the things that have happened there in these days?"

[19] "What things?" he asked. "About Jesus of Nazareth," they replied. "He was a prophet, powerful in word and deed before God and all the people. [20] [He was] handed... over to be sentenced to death, and they crucified him; [21] but we had hoped that he was the one who was going to redeem [us]. ...[I]t is the third day since all this took place.

[22] In addition, some of our women amazed us. They went to the tomb early this morning [23] but didn't find his body. They came and told us that they had seen a vision of angels, who said he was alive. [24] Then some of our companions went to the tomb and found it just as the women had said, but they did not see Jesus." [25] He said to them, "How foolish you are, and how slow to believe... [26] Did not the Messiah have to suffer these things and then enter his glory?" [27] And beginning with Moses and all the Prophets, he explained to them what was said in all the Scriptures concerning himself.

[28] As they approached the village to which they were going...[29] they urged him strongly, "Stay with us, for it is nearly evening; the day is almost over." So he went in to stay with them. [30] When he was at the table with them, he took bread, gave thanks, broke it and began to give it to them. [31] Then their eyes were opened and they recognized him, and he disappeared from their sight. [32] They asked each other, "Were not our hearts burning within us while he talked with us on the road and opened the Scriptures to us?"

[33] They got up and returned at once to Jerusalem. There they found the Eleven and those with them, assembled together [34] and saying, "It is true! The Lord has risen and has appeared to Simon." [35] Then the two told what had happened on the way, and how Jesus was recognized by them when he broke the bread.

[36] While they were still talking about this, Jesus himself stood among them and said to them, "Peace be with you." [37] They were startled... thinking they saw a ghost. [38] He said to them, "Why are you troubled, and why do doubts rise in your minds? [39] Look at my hands and my feet. It is I myself! Touch me and see; a ghost does not have flesh and bones, as you see I have." [40] When he had said this, he showed them his hands and feet.

John 20:

[20] ...The disciples were overjoyed when they saw the Lord.

Luke 24:

[41] [H]e asked them, "Do you have anything here to eat?" [42] They gave him a piece of broiled fish, [43] and he took it and ate it in their presence. [44] He said to them, "This is what I told you while I was still with you: Everything must be fulfilled... [46] The Messiah will suffer and rise from the dead on the third day, [47] and repentance for the forgiveness of sins will be preached in his name to all nations, beginning at Jerusalem. [48] You are witnesses of these things."

John 20:

[21] [Then] Jesus said, "As the Father has sent me, I am sending you." [22] And with that he breathed on them and said, "Receive the Holy Spirit."

[24] Now Thomas (also known as Didymus), one of the Twelve, was not with the disciples when Jesus came. [25] So the other disciples told him, "We have seen the Lord!" But he said to them, "Unless I see the nail marks in his hands and put my finger where the nails were, and put my hand into his side, I will not believe."

[26] A week later his disciples were in the house again, and Thomas was with them. Though the doors were locked, Jesus came and stood among them and said, "Peace be with you!" [27] Then he said to Thomas, "Put your finger here; see my hands. Reach out your hand and put it into my side. Stop doubting and believe." [28] Thomas said to him, "My Lord and my God!" [29] Then Jesus told him, "Because you have seen me, you have believed; blessed are those who have not seen and yet have believed." [30] Jesus performed many other signs in the presence of his disciples, which are not recorded…

John 21:

[1] Afterward Jesus appeared again to his disciples, by the Sea of Galilee. It happened this way: [3] "I'm going out to fish," Simon Peter told [the other disciples], and they said, "We'll go with you." So they went out and got into the boat, but that night they caught nothing.

[4] Early in the morning, Jesus stood on the shore, but the disciples did not realize that it was Jesus. [5] He called out to them, "Friends, haven't you any fish?" "No," they answered. [6] He said, "Throw your net on the right side of the boat and you will find some." When they did, they were unable to haul the net in because of the large number of fish.

[7] Then [a] disciple… said to Peter, "It is the Lord!" As soon as Simon Peter heard him say, "It is the Lord," he… jumped into the water. [8] The other disciples followed in the boat, towing the net full of fish, for they were not far from shore, about a hundred yards. [9] When they landed, they saw a fire of burning coals there with fish on it, and some bread. [10] Jesus said to them, "Bring some of the fish you have just caught." [11] So Simon Peter climbed back into the boat and dragged the net ashore. It was full of large fish, 153, but even with so many the net was not torn. [12] Jesus said to them, "Come and have breakfast." [13] Jesus came, took the bread and gave it to them, and did the same with the fish.

[15] When they had finished eating, Jesus said to Simon Peter, "Simon son of John, do you love me more than these?" "Yes, Lord," he said, "you know that I love you." Jesus said, "Feed my lambs." [16] Again Jesus said, "Simon son of John, do you love me?" He answered, "Yes, Lord, you know that I love you." Jesus said, "Take care of my sheep." [17] The third time he said to him, "Simon son of John, do you love me?" Peter was hurt because Jesus asked him the third time, "Do you love me?" He said, "Lord, you know all things; you know that I love you." Jesus said, "Feed my sheep." Then he said… "Follow me!"

Luke 24:

[50] When [Jesus] had led [the disciples]… to the vicinity of Bethany, he lifted up his hands and blessed them.

James:

"I shall ascend to the place from which I have come… Now [that] I have said my last word[s] to you, I shall part from you…"

Acts 1:

[9] After… this, he was taken up before their very eyes, and a cloud hid him from their sight. [10] They were looking intently up into the sky as he was going, when suddenly two men dressed in white stood beside them. [11] "Men of Galilee," they said, "why do you stand here looking into the sky? This same Jesus, who has been taken from you into heaven, will come back in the same way you have seen him go into heaven."

The Ascension by Giotto c. 1305-1306

James:

[Then they] saw with [their] eyes and heard with [their] ears hymns and angelic praises and angelic jubilation… [They] knelt down… and gave thanks…

Luke 24:

[52] Then they worshiped him and returned to Jerusalem with great joy.

Mary Magdalene 5:

[5] [At one point,] Peter said to Mary [Magdalene]… "[W]e know that the Savior loved you…"

Philip:

[Jesus was] the companion of… Mary Magdalene… [and] loved her… and used to kiss her often… [and she] always walked with the Lord…

The Dialogue of the Savior:

She… understood [him] completely.

Mary Magdalene 5:

[6] "Tell us the words of the Savior [when you saw him], which you remember, which you know, but we do not…" [7] Mary answered: [8] [T]he Lord… said to me, [9] "Blessed are you that you did not waver at the sight of [m]e…"

294

Jesus Appearing to [Mary] Magdalene
by Fra Angelico c. 1440-1441

Mary Magdalene 9:

[6] Levi answered: [8] [T]he savior knows her very well. [9] That is why He love[s] her… Let us be ashamed… and [go] as [h]e commanded… and preach the gospel…

Mark 16:

[20] [Afterwards] the disciples went out and preached everywhere, and the Lord worked with them and confirmed his word by the signs that accompanied it.

Christian Orthodox Tradition:

<u>Source:</u> **The Book of James 12:10-14, 14:1-4, 9-12:**

Mary said to Joseph, "Take me down from the ass, for that which is in me presses to come forth."

But Joseph replied, "[Where] shall I take [you]? For this place is a desert."

Then said Mary… "Take me down, for that which is within me mightily presses me." And Joseph took her down. And he found there a cave and led her into it…

Then I [Joseph] beheld a woman coming down from the mountains and she said to me, "Where [are] [you] going, O man?"

And I said to her, "I go to [i]nquire for a Hebrew midwife."

She replied… "Where is the woman that is to be delivered?"

And I answered, "in the cave…" And the midwife went along with him and stood in the cave. Then a bright light overshadowed the cave… On a sudden the cloud became a great light in the cave so their eyes could not bear it. But the light gradually decreased, until the infant appeared…

[T]he midwife said, "This day my soul is magnified for mine eyes have seen surprising things, and salvation is brought forth..."

Judaism:

Source: Targum to Yesha'yahu 11:1 in the Tanakh:

"A king shall come forth from the sons of Jesse, and the Messiah shall grow up from his sons' sons."

Source: Targum to Z'kharyah 6:12 in the Tanakh:

"Thus says the L~rd of Hosts, saying, 'Behold the Man whose name is the Messiah who shall be revealed.'"

Source: Targum to Yirmeyahu 23:5 in the Tanakh:

"Behold the days come says the L~rd that I will raise up unto David a righteous Messiah and he shall reign as King and understand."

Source: Jerusalem Talmud, Berakoth 5a:

"The King Messiah... from where does he come forth? From the royal city of Bethlehem in Judah."

Source: Zohar III, Shemoth 7b, 8b, 220a; Otzar Midrashim, 466:

"The Messiah... will arise in the land of Galilee... the Messiah shall reveal himself in the land of Galilee because in this part of the Holy Land the desolation first began, therefore he will manifest himself there first."

Source: Pesikta Rabbati, Piska 36.1; Zohar II. 212a:

"The Holy One, blessed be He, will tell [the Messiah] in detail what will befall him... their sins will cause you to bend down as under a yoke of iron and make you like a calf whose eyes grow dim with suffering and will choke your spirit as with a yoke, and because of their sins your tongue will cleave to the roof of your mouth. Are you willing to endure such things?... The Messiah will say: 'Master of the universe with joy in my soul and gladness in my heart I take this suffering upon myself provided that not one person... shall perish, so that not only those who are alive be saved in my days, but also those who are dead, who died from the days of Adam up to the time of redemption.'"

Source: Midrash Ruth Rabbah, 2.14:

"Dip your morsel of bread in the vinegar... 'He was pierced through for our transgressions, he was bruised for our iniquities.'"

Source: Babylonian Talmud, Sanhedrin 98:

"Rabbi Yochanan said, 'The Messiah - what is his name?'... And our Rabbis said, 'the pale one... is his name,' as it is written 'Surely he took up our infirmities and carried our sorrows - yet we considered him stricken by G~d, smitten by him and afflicted.'"

Source: Babylonian Talmud, Sukkah 52a:

"What is the cause of the mourning? It is well according to him who explains that the cause is the slaying of Messiah, the son of Joseph, as it is written, 'And they shall look upon me whom they have pierced; and they shall mourn for him as one mourneth for his only son.'"

<u>Source:</u> Zohar 2:172b:

"...[A]ll the nations of the world will gather around King Messiah..."

<u>Source:</u> Antiquities of the Jews, book 18, chapter 3, paragraph 3; Yosef ben Mattityahu "Josephus" and Tanakh, Yesha'yahu 53:

"Who has believed what we have heard? To whom is the arm of Adonai (God) revealed? For before Him he grew up like a young plant, like a root out of dry ground. He had no form or beauty. We saw him, but his appearance did not attract us. He was despised and shunned by men, a man of pains and familiar with illness; like one from whom we would hide our faces. He was despised and we had no regard for him. In truth, it was our infirmities he bore, and our pains that he suffered; yet we regarded him as punished and afflicted by G~d. He was wounded because of our sins and crushed because of our iniquities. The chastisement he bore made us whole, and through his wounds we are healed. We all like sheep went astray; we turned, each one, to his own way. Yet [God] laid on him the guilt of all of us... [H]e exposed himself to death and was numbered among the sinners. For he bore the sin of many, and made intercession for the transgressors."

"Now there was about this time, Yeshua (Jesus), a wise man, if it be lawful to call him a man, for he was a doer of wonderful works, a teacher of such men as receive the truth with pleasure. He drew over to him both many of the Jews and many of the Gentiles. He was Mashiach (the Messiah); and when Pilate, at the suggestion of the principal men among us, had condemned him to the cross, those that loved him at the first did not forsake him, for he appeared to them alive again the third day, as the divine prophets had foretold these and ten thousand other wonderful things concerning him..."

<u>Source:</u> Babylonian Talmud, Sanhedrin 43a:

"On the eve of Passover they hanged [crucified] Yeshu [Jesus]... For forty days before the execution took place, a herald went forth and cried, 'He is going forth to be stoned. Any one who can say anything in his favor, let him come forward and plead on his behalf.' But since nothing was brought forward in his favor he was hanged on the eve of the Passover!"

<u>Source:</u> Babylonian Talmud, Shabbath 104b (Revised):

"She who was the descendant of princes and governors [married a carpenter. Miriam [was a virgin].... Yeshu was a [miracle worker] and [wise like the prophets].

<u>Source:</u> Babylonian Talmud, Yebamoth 49b, Sanhedrin 106a,b, Shabbath 116b and Sanhedrin 107b (Revised):

"Yeshu was... born of [a virgin]... Yeshu was [the Son of Man]... Jesus the Nazarene [who] [performed miracles] and led Israel [to God]."

<u>Source:</u> Dead Sea Scrolls Fragment 4Q521:

"[The hea]vens and the earth will listen to His Messiah, and none therein will stray from the commandments of the holy ones. Seekers of the Lord, strengthen yourselves in His service! ...For the Lord will consider the pious and call the righteous by name. Over the poor His spirit will hover and will renew the faithful with His power. And He will glorify the pious on the throne of the eternal Kingdom. He who liberates the captives, restores sight to the blind, straightens the b[ent]... in His mercy... And the fr[uit...] will not be delayed for anyone. And the Lord will accomplish glorious things which have never been [seen]... F*or He will heal the wounded, and revive the dead and bring good news to the poor* ...He will lead the uprooted and [bring] knowledge..."

Source: Dead Sea Scrolls Fragment 1Q28a:

"[T]he Messiah... shall stretch out his hands over the bread."

Source: Dead Sea Scrolls Fragment 4Q285:

"A shoot will arise from the roots of Jesse, and a branch from his roots will bear fruit... The branch of David will be put to death"

Source: Dead Sea Scrolls (Gabriel's Vision):

"Blessed be the glory of... the Lord... In just a little while, I will shake the heavens and the earth... By three days you shall know that, thus said the Lord of Hosts... the evil has been broken by righteousness... By three days, live (be resurrected), I Gabriel, command you, prince of princes... Then you will stand... in... eternity."

Source: Dead Sea Scrolls Fragment 4Q458:

"...and he will ascend to the height..."

Islam:

The Family of Imran 3:42-43 And... the angels said: O Marium (Mary)! [S]urely [God] has chosen you and purified you and chosen you above the women of the world. O Marium! [K]eep to obedience to your Lord and humble yourself, and bow down with those who bow.

The Family of Imran 3:45-47 When the angels said: O Marium, surely [God] gives you good news with a Word from Him whose name is the 'Messiah,' Isa (Jesus) son of Marium, worthy of regard in this world and the hereafter and of those who are made near (to [God]). And he shall speak to the people... and (he shall be) one of the good ones. She said: My Lord! when shall there be a son (born) to me, and man has not touched me? He said: Even so, [God] creates what He pleases; when He has decreed a matter, He only says to it, Be, and it is.

The Believers 23:50 And [I] made the son of Marium and his mother a sign, and [I] gave them a shelter on a lofty ground having meadows and springs.

The Prohibition 66:12 And Marium, the daughter of Imran (Joachim), who guarded her chastity, so [I] breathed into her of [My] inspiration and she accepted the truth of the words of her Lord and His books, and she was of, the obedient ones.

Marium 19:16-22, 31 And mention Marium in the Book when she drew aside from her family to an eastern place; So she took a veil (to screen herself) from them; then [I] sent to her [My] spirit, and there appeared to her a well-made man (the Angel Gabriel)... He said: I am only a messenger of your Lord: That I will give you a pure boy. She said: [How] shall I have a boy and no mortal has yet touched me, nor have I been unchaste? He said: Even so; your Lord says: It is easy to Me: and that [I] [will] make him a sign to [people] [as] a mercy from [Me], and it is a matter which has been decreed. So she conceived him… And [God] has… blessed [Marium] wherever [she] may be…

The Women 4:171 [T]he Messiah [is] Isa son of Marium…

Marium 19:30-31, 33 [Isa] said, "I am the servant of [my Father]. He has given me the Scripture… And He has made me blessed wherever I am and has enjoined upon me prayer… And peace is on me the day I was born and the day I will die and the day I am raised alive."

The Family of Imran 3:48-49 And He will teach him the Book and the wisdom… And (make him) an apostle to [his children]: That I have come to you with a sign from your Lord, that I determine for you out of dust like the form of a bird, then I breathe into it and it becomes a bird with [God's] permission and I heal the blind and the leprous, and bring the dead to life with [God's] permission…

The Family of Imran 3:51 Surely [God] is my Lord and your Lord, therefore serve Him; this is the right path. The Cow 2:253 [I] have made some of these apostles to excel… and [I] gave clear miracles to Isa son of Marium, and strengthened him with the holy spirit.

The Dinner Table 5:110-115 [God] [said]: O Isa son of Marium! Remember My favor on you and on your mother, when I strengthened you I with the [H]oly Spirit, you spoke to the people… and when I taught you the Book and the wisdom and the Taurat (Torah) and the Injeel (Gospel of John, Luke, Mark, and Matthew); and when you determined out of clay a thing like the form of a bird by My permission, then you breathed into it and it became a bird by My permission, and you healed the blind and the leprous by My permission; and when you brought forth the dead by My permission… And when I revealed to the disciples, saying, Believe in Me and My apostle, they said: We believe and bear witness that we submit. When the disciples said: O Isa son of Marium! [W]ill your Lord consent to send down to us food from heaven? He said: Be careful of (your duty to) [God]… They said: We desire that we should eat of it and that our hearts should be at rest, and that we may know that you have indeed spoken the truth to us and that we may be of the witnesses to it. Isa the son of Marium said: O [God], our Lord! [S]end… [I] down [as] food from heaven which should be to us an ever-recurring happiness, to the first of us and to the last of us, and a sign from [You], and grant us means of subsistence, and [You are] the best of the Providers. [God] said: Surely I will [do it]…

The Ranks 61:6, 14 And when Isa son of Marium said: O children… surely I am the apostle of [God] to you, verifying that which is before me of the Taurat… [some] said: This is clear magic. O you who believe! [B]e helpers of [God], as Isa son of Marium said to (his) disciples: Who are my helpers in the cause of [God]? The disciples said: We are helpers (in the cause) of [God]. So [some] believed and [others] disbelieved…

The Ranks 61:12 He will forgive you your faults and cause you to enter into gardens, beneath which rivers flow, and goodly dwellings in gardens of perpetuity…

The Family of Imran 3:55, 57 And… [God] said: O Isa, I am going to terminate the period of your stay and cause you to ascend unto Me… The Iron 57:27 …[I]… sent Isa son of Marium… and [I] gave him the Injeel, and [I] put in the hearts of those who followed him kindness and mercy…

^{Marium 19:33-34} And peace on me on the day I was born, and on the day I die, and on the day I am raised to life. Such is Isa, son of Marium... ^{The Women 4:157-158} And their saying: Surely we have killed the Messiah, Isa son of Marium, the apostle of [God]; and they did not kill him... Nay! [God] took him up to Himself...

Buddhism:

Source: **Shinran Shonin. <u>Project Gutenberg EBook of Buddhist Psalms.</u> 2004.**

⁵⁴ He who is of [God]... ⁷¹ [the] Lord that was made flesh... ⁵⁴ ordain[ed] that His saving grace should be made manifest. ¹²⁶ ...[T]hrough [Him] we attain... the final deliverance that destroyed... sin.

Sikhism:

Sri Guru Granth Sahib:

The Lord... dyes us in the color of His Love (the blood of Jesus)... [D]rinking [of] [His water], thirst is quenched... The tongue... [that] tastes [it] remains forever imbued with the Lord's love.

The "Luminous" Religion:

Sources: **<u>Jesus Sutras</u>, Robert Hutchinson, <u>Lost Jesus Sutras Reveal Ancient Chinese Christianity</u>. 20 August 2009, Martin Palmer. <u>The Jesus Sutras</u> (Ballantine Wellspring, New York, 2001), and Jay G. Williams. <u>The Secret Sayings of Ye Su: A Silk Road Gospel.</u> (iUniverse, Lincoln, NE, 2004):**

The Lord of Heaven sent the Pure Wind (Holy Spirit) to a girl named Mo Yen (Mary). It entered her womb and at the moment she conceived. The Lord of Heaven did this to show that conception could take place without a husband. He knew there was no man near her and that people who saw it would say, "How great is the power of the Lord of Heaven." ... Mo Yen became pregnant and gave birth to a son named Ye Su (Jesus)...

...When Ye Su Messiah was born, the world saw clear signs in heaven and earth. A new star that could be seen everywhere appeared in heaven above. The star was as big as a cart wheel and shown brightly...

[A]fter five years he began to preach... From the time the Messiah was 12 until he was 32 years old, he sought out people with bad karma and directed them to turn around... After the Messiah had gathered 12 disciples, he concerned himself with the suffering of others. Those who had died were made to live. The blind were made to see. The deformed were healed and the sick were cured... He showed love to all around him...

One day as Ye Su taught his disciples, Peter left to quiet [the] children who were playing in [a nearby] courtyard... Ye Su asked, "Where are you going?" Peter replied, "To make the children be quiet. Ye Su said, "Do not do that... Behold the kingdom is like this, full of joy and gladness..."

[At another time] Ye Su said, "...[T]he seeds of the kingdom are planted in both women and men... [I]n the kingdom there is no difference... [W]hen I appear in glory, Mary (Magdalene) [will] see me first. She is my beloved disciple." Mary said, "I love you Ye Su."

300

...For the sake of all living beings and to show us that a human life is as frail as a candle flame, the Messiah gave... up his life. ...After the Messiah had accepted death, his enemies... took him to... "the place of skulls," which was called golgotha. They bound him to a pole and placed two highway robbers to the right and left of him... They bound him at dawn and when the sun set in the west the sky became black in all four directions, the earth quaked and the hills trembled. Tombs all over the world opened and the dead came to life...

[Joseph of Arimathea] wrapped him in a new cloth and buried him in a fresh graveyard where a new tomb had been carved into the side of a mountain. A huge stone was rolled in front of the tomb and a seal stamped on it. The [people] also placed a guard... [that] guarded the tomb for three days... By the tomb stood a[n] [angel]... dressed in white, as white as snow. He appeared by the guards coming down from Heaven to stand beside the great stone. The [angel] told them to go and tell the [people] what they had seen... [They] spoke of... what they had seen... that the Messiah had risen from the dead.

Some women followers... came to where the tomb was. A number of Jews also came at dawn on the third day to the same place. It shone with a bright light and the Messiah had gone... The women went to tell all... what they had witnessed... The stone [had] rolled away and the beautiful cloth that hung there was ripped in two from top to bottom... Everyone who saw it went away talking of this.

[Ye Su] came to [the disciples] at their place of prayer so that... [they], and then the whole world, should know the truth... [Ye Su] was with [his disciples] for fourteen days in one month. Not a single day passed without them seeing him... He told them "Go out and teach everyone, baptize them in water and sign them in the name of the Father, Son, and the Pure Wind to observe everything I have taught..."

It was revealed that the Messiah remained here for thirty days after he had risen from the earth... He promised that the Pure Wind would come from Heaven on those that asked. He was [then] seen in a bright light and... he went into Heaven... [Ye Su] ascended to immortality... Ten days after the Messiah ascended to Heaven, he sent the Pure Wind upon the disciples... It came as fire upon them and [they] were... created anew... They were inspired to go out and take the... faith... to all...

"[The Messiah], 'the raft of salvation and compassion,' suffered terrible woes so that all should be freed from karma. All of us are saved by his works... [H]e will not leave you without *qi* (life)... So have no fear, not even of death; you will live as the Messiah lives... raised after death... [There] will be such joy and happiness, nothing will pass and nothing change..."

"[T]he Heavenly Honored One sends the [Pure Wind] to all places to save everyone. It goes to all that live and teach the truth..."

"...Compassionate Joyous Lamb, [l]oving all who suffer, [f]earless as [y]ou strive for us, [f]ree us of the karma of our lives, [b]ring us back to our original nature [d]elivered from all danger."

"Knock on the door and it will be opened for you. Whatever you seek, you will obtain from [God]. Kno[ck] on the door and it will be opened for you... Don't hesitate when you pray. Ask first for forgiveness for your sins and at the same time forgive those who have sinned against you. The Heavenly Ruler above will forgive you as you forgive others."

"Look at the birds in the air. They don't plant or harvest, they have no barns or cellars. In the wildnerness, [God] provided for the people and will also provide for you. You are more important than the birds and should not worry… Do not pile up treasures on the ground where they will rot or be stolen. Treasures must be stored in Heaven where they will not decay or rot."

"Look for the best in others and correct what is worst in yourself. Otherwise it is as if you were trying to take a speck of dust out of someone else's eye while all the time you had a great beam of wood in your own. …[G]et rid of the beam in your eye."

"Think not of the faults in others… for no one has achieved true righteousness… Forgive, always forgive."

"Practice… universal loving kindness that is directed toward everyone. Never seek praise for what you do… Act toward others as you would have them act toward you, and do for others what you would have them do for you…"

"If someone is hungry, even if he is your enemy, care for him, forgive and forget… Clothe the naked… If a poor person begs… give generously; [I]f you have no money, have the courtesy to explain why you can give only a little help. If someone is seriously ill or handicapped do not mock…"

"Trust in the kingdom… If you trust in the kingdom, you will not fear death… In death, life is born… The kingdom… is everlasting."

Mormonism:

The Book of Mormon:

1 Nephi 11:13,15 And it came to pass that I looked and beheld the great city of Jerusalem, and also other cities. And I beheld the city of Nazareth; and in the city of Nazareth I beheld a virgin… [a] virgin, most beautiful… 1 Nephi 11:18,20 And he said unto me: Behold, the virgin whom [you] see is the mother of the Son of God, after the manner of the flesh. And I looked and beheld the virgin… bearing a child in her arms.

Alma 5:48 …[He came]… full of grace, and mercy, and truth… to take away the sins of the world…

The Testimony of the Three Witnesses Be it known unto all nations, kindreds, tongues, and people… that… Alma 12:25 …there was a plan of redemption laid, [to] bring to pass the resurrection of the dead…

2 Nephi 2:8 …[T]hrough… merits, and mercy, and grace… the Holy Messiah… [laid] down his life… and [took] it again by the power of the Spirit, that he may bring to pass the resurrection of the dead… The Testimony of the Three Witnesses [that we may]… dwell with him eternally in the heavens.

3 Nephi 10:9-11 And it came to pass that thus did the three days pass away. And it was in the morning, and the darkness dispersed from off the face of the land, and the earth did cease to tremble, and the rocks did cease to rend, and the dreadful groanings did cease, and all the tumultuous noises did pass away. And the earth did cleave together again,

302

that it stood; and the mourning, and the weeping, and the wailing of the people who were spared alive did cease; and their mourning was turned into joy, and their lamentations into… praise and thanksgiving… And thus… were the scriptures fulfilled which had been spoken by the prophets.

Mosiah 16:8 …[T]he sting of death [was] swallowed up in Christ.

3 Nephi 8-12 And it came to pass, as they understood they cast their eyes up… towards heaven; and behold, they saw a [m]an descending out of heaven; and he was clothed in a white robe; and he came down and stood in the midst of them… [H]e stretched forth his hand and sp[o]ke [to] the people, saying: "Behold, I am [he] whom the prophets testified shall come into the world. …I am the light and the life of the world; and I have drunk out of that bitter cup which the Father ha[d] given me, and have glorified the Father in taking upon me the sins of the world, in the which I have suffered the will of the Father in all things from the beginning." And it came to pass that when Jesus had spoken these words the whole multitude fell to the earth; for they remembered that it had been prophesied among them that [the] Christ [w]ould show himself unto them after his ascension into heaven.

Mosiah 4:2-3 …And they all cried aloud with one voice, saying: O have mercy, and apply the atoning blood of Christ that we may receive forgiveness of our sins, and our hearts may be purified… And it came to pass that after they had spoken these words the Spirit of the Lord came upon them, and they were filled with joy, having received a remission of their sins…

Hinduism:

Ithareya Upanishad 1:

1.3 After creating the sky, waters, and the earth… the Lord almighty thought, "I created the worlds. Now to provide for and to save these worlds I have to [send] a savior." Thinking thus He gave birth to a man of Himself.

Sama Veda, part 2 (Thandiya Maha Brahmanam):

God is the ruler of people. He will offer [H]is body as a sacrifice, for [H]is people…

Rig Veda 10:

125 …The cause… of all creation, who protects and saves… He [H]imself appeared upon the earth wrapped in a body that [was] [h]oly and without sin.

Bhavishya Purana 19:

23 …[T]he Son of God… [was] born of a virgin.

Rig Veda 10:

90:7.15 The sacrificial victim is to be crowned with a crown made of thorny vines…

Brhadaranyaka Upanishad 3:

[7.28] His hands and legs are to be bound to a yoopa (wooden pole) causing bloodshed.

Yajurveda 31:

Before death he should be given a drink… None of his bones [will] be broken.

Ithareya Brahmanam:

After death, [h]is clothes are to be divided…

Maha Brahmanam 4:

[15] …When we were perishing, [God] came to save us by offering… [H]is own body on our behalf.

North American Indian:

Black Elk's, Oglala (1863-1950) and Sun Bear's, Ogibwe (1929-1992) "Christ" Analogy:

The *Wanekia* ("One who makes live"), the son of the Great Spirit (God)… taught, "You must not hurt anybody or do harm to anyone… Do right always." He could make animals talk… He was killed… [He] returned [and spoke of the] new world (Paradise) coming… like a cloud [with the] return of all living things [that] had vanished… [A]ll the dead… were alive… under [the Great Spirit (God)]. Black, White, Red, Yellow… all [were] one… brothers [and sisters]… liv[ing] together… embraced with love…

Mayan Religion:

Source: Allen J. Christensen. **Popol Vuh: Literal Translation.** Mesoweb Publications. **29 November 2011. http://www.mesoweb.com/publications/Christensen/PV-Literal.pdf:**

[2806] We were to have died, [2807] We were to have been lost… [4256-4257] [He] Descended, Ascended… [4263] Because of this not we died… [4477] Dead now therefore… death [4601] Do not be afraid…

Addendum Est:

Source: **The Report of Pontius Pilate/Letter to Tiberius:**

To the most mighty, venerable [emperor]… I have to report… [that] while… discharging my duties… [a] multitude [of people]… delivered to me a certain man named Jesus, bringing against him many… groundless charges… And that man wrought many cures, in addition to good works. He made the blind see; he cleansed lepers; he healed paralytics; he raised the dead… [H]e raised up a dead man, Lazarus, who had been dead four days, by a single word… [A]lthough his body was already corrupted by the worms… that ill-smelling body… came forth out of the tomb, filled with exceeding fragrance… [T]he miracles done by him were greater than any which the gods whom we worship could do.

Had I not been afraid... perhaps this man would still have been alive to us... I did not according to my strength resist... And as many were exciting an insurrection against me, I ordered him to be crucified.

And when he had been crucified, there was darkness over the whole earth... as I suppose your reverence is not ignorant of, because in all the world they lighted lamps from the sixth hour until evening. And the moon being like blood, did not shine the whole night... And the stars also, and Orion, made a lament... on account of [what] had been done.

And on the first of the week, about the third hour of the night, the sun was seen such as it had never at any time shone, and all the heaven was lighted up. [A]n innumerable multitude of angels cr[ied] out... saying: Glory in the highest to God, and on earth peace, among [people] of goodwill: come up out of Hades, ye who have been kept in slavery... And at their voice all the mountains and hills were shaken, and the rocks were burst asunder... [a]nd there were seen... [the] dead raised up... And all the multitude walked about, and sang praises to God... saying: The Lord our God that has risen from the dead has brought to life all the dead, and has plundered Hades, and put him to death.

All that night... the light ceased not... [A]t that same hour... being in perplexity and seized with much trembling... I ordered what had been done... to be written; and I have reported it to thy mightiness.

XXIX. Posterus Evangelium I

Christianity:

Acts 2:

[1] When the day of Pentecost came, they were all together in one place. [2] Suddenly a sound like the blowing of a violent wind came from heaven and filled the whole house where they were sitting. [3] They saw what seemed to be tongues of fire that separated and came to rest on each of them. [4] All of them were filled with the Holy Spirit and began to speak in other tongues as the Spirit enabled them.

[5] Now there were staying in Jerusalem God-fearing [people] from every nation under heaven. [6] When they heard this sound, a crowd came together in bewilderment, because each one heard their own language being spoken. [7] Utterly amazed, they asked: "Aren't all these who are speaking Galileans? [8] Then how is it that each of us hears them in our native language? [9] Parthians, Medes and Elamites; residents of Mesopotamia, Judea and Cappadocia, Pontus and Asia, [10] Phrygia and Pamphylia, Egypt and the parts of Libya near Cyrene; visitors from Rome; [11] Cretans and Arabs — we hear them declaring the wonders of God in our own tongues!" [12] [They were] [a]mazed…

Pentecost by Tiziano Vecelli (Titian)
c. 16th Century

Acts 3:

[1] One day Peter and John were going up to the temple at the time of prayer… [2] Now a man who was lame from birth was being carried to the temple… [3] When he saw Peter and John about to enter, he asked them for money. [4] Peter looked straight at him, as did John. Then Peter said, "Look at us!" [5] So the man gave them his attention, expecting to get something from them.

[6] Then Peter said, "Silver or gold I do not have, but what I do have I give you. In the name of Jesus Christ of Nazareth, walk." [7] Taking him by the right hand, he helped him up, and instantly the man's feet and ankles became strong. [8] He jumped to his feet and began to walk. Then he went with them into the temple courts... praising God.

[9] When all the people saw him walking and praising God, [10] they recognized him as the same man who used to sit begging at the temple gate... and they were filled with... amazement...

[12] When Peter saw this, he said... "[W]hy does this surprise you? Why do you stare at us as if by our own power or godliness we had made this man walk?"

Acts 4:

[10] "[K]now this...: It is by the name of Jesus Christ of Nazareth, whom... God raised from the dead, that this man stands before you healed."

[31] After they prayed... they were all filled with the Holy Spirit and spoke the word of God boldly. [32] All the believers were one in heart and mind. No one claimed that any of their possessions was their own, but they shared everything they had.

Acts 5:

[12] The apostles performed many signs and wonders among the people... [14] [M]ore and more men and women believed in the Lord and were added to their number.

[15] As a result, people brought the sick into the streets and laid them on beds and mats so that at least Peter's shadow might fall on some of them as he passed by. [16] Crowds gathered also from the towns around Jerusalem, bringing their sick and those tormented by impure spirits, and all of them were healed.

Acts 9:

[1] Meanwhile, Saul was still [seeking] the Lord's disciples. He went to the high priest [2] and asked him for letters to the synagogues in Damascus, so that if he found any there... whether men or women, he might take them as prisoners to Jerusalem. [3] As he neared Damascus on his journey, suddenly a light from heaven flashed around him. [4] He fell to the ground and heard a voice say to him, "Saul, Saul, why do you persecute me?"

[5] "Who are you?" Saul asked. "I am Jesus, whom you are persecuting," he replied. [6] "Now get up and go into the city, and you will be told what you must do."

[7] The men traveling with Saul stood there speechless; they heard the sound but did not see anyone. [8] Saul got up from the ground, but when he opened his eyes he could see nothing. So they led him by the hand into Damascus. [9] For three days he was blind, and did not eat or drink anything.

[10] In Damascus there was a disciple named Ananias. The Lord called to him in a vision, "Ananias!" "Yes, Lord," he answered.

[11] The Lord told him, "Go... ask for a man from Tarsus named Saul, for he is praying. [13] "Lord," Ananias answered, "I have heard many reports about this man and all the harm he has done to your holy people... [14] And he has come here with authority from the chief priests to arrest all who call on [Y]our name."

[15] But the Lord said to Ananias, "Go! This man is my chosen instrument to proclaim my name to the Gentiles and their kings and to the people of Israel..."

[17] Then Ananias went... Placing his hands on Saul, he said, "Brother Saul, the Lord — Jesus, who appeared to you on the road as you were coming here — has sent me so that you may see again and be filled with the Holy Spirit." [18] Immediately, something like scales fell from Saul's eyes, and he could see again. He got up and was baptized, [19] and after taking some food, he regained his strength.

Saul spent several days with the disciples in Damascus. [20] At once he began to preach... that Jesus is the Son of God. [21] All those who heard him were astonished...

Acts 10:

[34] Peter [spoke]: "I [know] how true it is that God does not show favoritism [35] but accepts from every nation the one who fears [H]im and does what is right.

[36] You know... [38] how God anointed Jesus of Nazareth with the Holy Spirit and power, and how he went around doing good and healing all who were under the power of the devil, because God was with him. [39] We are witnesses of everything he did... [He was killed] on a cross, [40] but God raised him from the dead on the third day and caused him to be seen. [42] He commanded us to preach to the people and to testify that he is the one whom God appointed as judge of the living and the dead. [43] All the prophets testify about him that everyone who believes in him receives forgiveness of sins through his name."

[44] While Peter was still speaking these words, the Holy Spirit came on all who heard the message. [45] The circumcised believers who had come with Peter were astonished that the gift of the Holy Spirit had been poured out even on Gentiles. [46] For they heard them speaking in tongues and praising God. Then Peter said, [47] "Surely no one can stand in the way of their being baptized with water. They have received the Holy Spirit just as we have." [48] So he ordered that they be baptized in the name of Jesus Christ.

Acts 11:

[1] The apostles and the believers throughout Judea heard that the Gentiles also had received the word of God. [2] So when Peter went up to Jerusalem, the circumcised believers criticized him.

[4] Peter told them... [15] "As I began to speak, the Holy Spirit came on them as he had come on us at the beginning. [16] Then I remembered what the Lord had said: 'John baptized with water, but you will be baptized with the Holy Spirit.' [17] So if God gave them the same gift he gave us who believed in the Lord Jesus Christ, who was I to think that I could stand in God's way?"

[18] When they heard this, they had no further objections and praised God, saying, "So then, even to Gentiles God has granted repentance that leads to life."

Acts 12:

[1] It was about this time that King Herod arrested... [3] Peter... This happened during the Festival of Unleavened Bread. [4] After arresting him, he put him in prison, handing him over to be guarded by four squads of four soldiers each. Herod intended to bring him out for public trial after the Passover.

[5] So Peter was kept in prison, but the church was earnestly praying to God for him.

[6] The night before Herod was to bring him to trial, Peter was sleeping between two soldiers, bound with two chains, and sentries stood guard at the entrance. [7] Suddenly an angel of the Lord appeared and a light shone in the cell. He struck Peter on the side and woke him up. "Quick, get up!" he said, and the chains fell off Peter's wrists.

[8] Then the angel said to him, "Put on your clothes and sandals." And Peter did so. "Wrap your cloak around you and follow me," the angel told him.

[9] Peter followed him out of the prison, but he had no idea that what the angel was doing was really happening; he thought he was seeing a vision. [10] They passed the first and second guards and came to the iron gate leading to the city. It opened for them by itself, and they went through it. When they had walked the length of one street, suddenly the angel left him.

[11] Then Peter came to himself and said, "Now I know without a doubt that the Lord has sent his angel and rescued me from Herod's clutches..."

[12] When this had dawned on him, he went to the house of Mary the mother of John, also called Mark, where many people had gathered and were praying. [13] Peter knocked at the outer entrance, and a servant named Rhoda came to answer the door. [16] [W]hen they... saw him, they were astonished. [17] Peter... described how the Lord had brought him out of prison. "Tell James and the other brothers and sisters about this," he said, and then he left for another place.

Acts 13:

[16] Standing up, Paul... said: [38] "...[M]y friends, I want you to know that through Jesus the forgiveness of sins is proclaimed to you. [39] Through him everyone who believes is set free from every sin."

[46] Then Paul and Barnabas [added]: [47] "[T]he Lord has commanded us: 'I have made you a light for the [world], that you may bring salvation to the ends of the earth.'"

[48] When the [crowd] heard this, they were glad and honored the word of the Lord... [49] [which] spread through the whole region.

Acts 14:

[8] In Lystra there sat a man who was lame. He had been that way from birth and had

309

never walked. ⁹ He listened to Paul as he was speaking. Paul looked directly at him, saw that he had faith to be healed ¹⁰ and called out, "Stand up on your feet!" At that, the man jumped up and began to walk.

¹¹ When the crowd saw what Paul had done, they shouted…"The gods have come down to us in human form!" ¹² Barnabas they called Zeus, and Paul they called Hermes because he was the chief speaker.

¹⁴ But when the apostles Barnabas and Paul heard of this, they tore their clothes and rushed out into the crowd, shouting: ¹⁵ "Friends, why are you doing this? We too are only human, like you. We are bringing you good news, telling you to turn… to the living God, [W]ho made the heavens and the earth and the sea and everything in them."

Acts 16:

⁹ During the night Paul had a vision of a man of Macedonia standing and begging him, "Come over to Macedonia and help us." ¹⁰ After Paul had seen the vision, [he and Silas] got ready at once to leave for Macedonia… ¹² [where they] stayed there several days.

¹³ On the Sabbath [they] …sat down and began to speak to the [people]… ¹⁴ One of those listening was a woman… Lydia… She was a worshiper of God. The Lord opened her heart to respond to Paul's message. ¹⁵ [S]he and the members of her household were baptized…

¹⁶ Once when [they] were going to the place of prayer, [they] were met by a female… [possessed by] a spirit… ¹⁷ She followed [them]… shouting, "These men are servants of the Most High God, who are telling you the way to be saved." ¹⁸ She kept this up for many days. Finally Paul became so annoyed that he turned around and said to the spirit, "In the name of Jesus Christ I command you to come out of her!" At that moment the spirit left her.

²² The crowd [turned] against Paul and Silas, and the magistrates ordered them to be stripped and beaten with rods. ²³ After they had been severely flogged, they were thrown into prison, and the jailer was commanded to guard them carefully. ²⁴ When he received these orders, he put them in the inner cell and fastened their feet in the stocks.

²⁵ About midnight Paul and Silas were praying and singing hymns to God, and the other prisoners were listening to them. ²⁶ Suddenly there was such a violent earthquake that the foundations of the prison were shaken. At once all the prison doors flew open, and everyone's chains came loose. ²⁷ The jailer woke up, and when he saw the prison doors open, he drew his sword and was about to kill himself because he thought the prisoners had escaped. ²⁸ But Paul shouted, "Don't harm yourself! We are all here!"

²⁹ The jailer called for lights, rushed in and fell trembling before Paul and Silas. ³⁰ He then brought them out and asked, "Sirs, what must I do to be saved?"

³¹ They replied, "Believe in the Lord Jesus, and you will be saved — you and your household." ³² Then they spoke the word of the Lord to him and to all the others in his house. ³³ At that hour of the night the jailer took them and washed their wounds; then immediately he and all his household were baptized. ³⁴ The jailer brought them into his house and set a meal before them; he was filled with joy because he had come to

believe in God — he and his whole household.

³⁵ When it was daylight, the magistrates sent their officers to the jailer with the order: "Release those men." ³⁶ The jailer told Paul, "The magistrates have ordered that you and Silas be released. Now you can leave. Go in peace."

³⁷ But Paul said to the officers: "They beat us publicly without a trial, even though we are Roman citizens, and threw us into prison. ...Let them come themselves and escort us out."

³⁸ The officers reported this to the magistrates, and when they heard that Paul and Silas were Roman citizens, they were alarmed. ³⁹ They came... and escorted them from the prison, requesting them to leave the city. ⁴⁰ After Paul and Silas came out of the prison, they went to Lydia's house, where they met with the brothers and sisters and encouraged them. Then they left.

Acts 17:

²⁹ "...[W]e are God's offspring..."

Acts 18:

¹ ...Paul... went to Corinth. ⁸ ...[M]any of the Corinthians who heard Paul believed and were baptized.

⁹ One night the Lord spoke to Paul in a vision: "Do not be afraid; keep on speaking, do not be silent. ¹⁰ For I am with you, and no one is going to attack and harm you, because I have many people in this city." ¹¹ So Paul stayed in Corinth for a year and a half, teaching them the word of God.

²⁴ Meanwhile a [man] named Apollos, a native of Alexandria, came to Ephesus. He was a learned man, with a thorough knowledge of the Scriptures. ²⁵ He had been instructed in the way of the Lord, and he spoke with great fervor and taught about Jesus accurately, though he knew only the baptism of John. ²⁶ He [spoke] boldly... When Priscilla and Aquila heard him, they invited him to their home and explained to him the way of God more adequately.

²⁷ When Apollos wanted to go to Achaia, the brothers and sisters encouraged him and wrote to the disciples there to welcome him. When he arrived, he was a great help to those who by grace had believed. ²⁸ For he vigorously refuted his... opponents in public debate, proving from the Scriptures that Jesus was the Messiah.

Acts 19:

¹ While Apollos was at Corinth, Paul took the road through the interior and arrived at Ephesus. There he found some disciples ⁵ [and] baptized [them] in the name of the Lord Jesus. ⁶ When Paul placed his hands on them, the Holy Spirit came on them, and they spoke in tongues and prophesied.

¹¹ God did extraordinary miracles through Paul, ¹² so that even handkerchiefs and

aprons that had touched him were taken to the sick, and their illnesses were cured and the evil spirits left them.

Acts 20:

⁷ On the first day of the week [they] came together to break bread. Paul spoke to the people and, because he intended to leave the next day, kept on talking until midnight. ⁹ Seated in a window was a young man named Eutychus, who [fell] into a deep sleep… When he was sound asleep, he fell to the ground from the third story and was picked up dead. ¹⁰ Paul went down, threw himself on the young man and put his arms around him. "Don't be alarmed," he said. "He's alive!" ¹² The people [then] took the young man home alive and were greatly comforted.

¹⁷ From Miletus, Paul sent to Ephesus for the elders of the church. ¹⁸ When they arrived, he said to them: "You know how I lived the whole time I was with you, from the first day I came into the province of Asia. ¹⁹ I served the Lord with great humility and with tears and in the midst of severe testing by the plots of my… opponents. ²⁰ You know that I have not hesitated to preach anything that would be helpful to you but have taught you publicly and from house to house. ²¹ I have declared to [all] that they must turn to God in repentance and have faith in our Lord Jesus.

²² "And now, compelled by the Spirit, I am going to Jerusalem, not knowing what will happen to me there. ²³ I only know that in every city the Holy Spirit warns me that prison and hardships are facing me. ²⁴ However, I consider my life worth nothing to me; my only aim is to finish the race and complete the task the Lord Jesus has given me — the task of testifying to the good news of God's grace.

²⁵ "Now I know that none of you among whom I have gone about preaching the kingdom will ever see me again. ²⁸ Keep watch over yourselves and all the flock of which the Holy Spirit has made you overseers. Be shepherds of… God…

³² "Now I commit you to God and to the word of [H]is grace, which can build you up and give you an inheritance among all those who are sanctified. ³³ I have not coveted anyone's silver or gold or clothing. ³⁵ In everything I did, I showed you that by… hard work we must help the weak, remembering the words the Lord Jesus himself said: 'It is more blessed to give than to receive.'"

³⁶ When Paul had finished speaking, he knelt down with all of them and prayed. ³⁷ They all wept as they embraced him and kissed him. ³⁸ What grieved them most was his statement that they would never see his face again. Then they accompanied him to the ship.

Acts 21:

¹⁰ After we had been [in Caesarea] a number of days, a prophet named Agabus came down from Judea. ¹¹ Coming over to us, he took Paul's belt, tied his own hands and feet with it and said, "The Holy Spirit says, 'In this way the… leaders in Jerusalem will bind the owner of this belt and will hand him over…'"

¹² When [everyone] heard this, …the people… pleaded with Paul not to go up to Jerusalem. ¹³ Then Paul answered, "Why are you weeping and breaking my heart? I am

ready not only to be bound, but also to die in Jerusalem for the name of the Lord Jesus."

¹⁷ When [Paul] arrived at Jerusalem... ³⁰ [t]he whole city [became] aroused, and the people came running from all directions. Seizing Paul, they dragged him from the temple... ³¹ While they were trying to kill him, news reached the commander of the Roman troops [who]... ³³ came up and arrested him...

Acts 22:

³⁰ The commander wanted to find out exactly why Paul was being accused... So the next day he released him and ordered the chief priests and all the members of the Sanhedrin to assemble. Then he brought Paul and had him stand before them.

Acts 23:

⁶ "My brothers... I [am here] because of the hope of the resurrection of the dead." ⁷ When [Paul] said this, a dispute broke out between the Pharisees and the Sadducees, and the assembly was divided. ⁹ [The] Pharisees stood up and argued vigorously. "We find nothing wrong with this man," they said. "What if a spirit or an angel has spoken to him?"

¹⁰ The dispute became so violent that the commander was afraid Paul would be torn to pieces... He ordered the troops to go down... and bring him [back] into the barracks.

¹¹ The following night the Lord stood near Paul and said, "Take courage! As you have testified about me in Jerusalem, so you must also testify in Rome."

Acts 27:

¹ When it was decided that [they] would sail for Italy, Paul and some other prisoners were handed over to a centurion named Julius, who belonged to the Imperial Regiment. ² [Everyone] boarded a ship...

³ The next day [they] landed at Sidon; and Julius, in kindness to Paul, allowed him to go to his friends so they might provide for his needs. ⁴ From there [they] put out to sea again... ⁵ [and] landed at Myra in Lycia. ⁶ There the centurion found an Alexandrian ship sailing for Italy and put [them] on board. ⁷ ...When the wind did not allow [them] to hold... course, [they] sailed to... Crete...

⁹ Much time had been lost, and sailing had already become dangerous... ¹⁰ "Men, I can see that our voyage is going to be disastrous and bring great loss to ship and cargo, and to our own lives also," [Paul said]. ¹¹ But the centurion, instead of listening to what Paul said, followed the advice of the pilot and of the owner of the ship ¹² [and] decided [to] sail on...

¹³ When a gentle south wind began to blow, they saw their opportunity; so they weighed anchor and sailed along the shore of Crete. ¹⁴ Before very long, a wind of hurricane force... swept down from the island. ¹⁵ The ship was caught by the storm...

¹⁷ Then... [b]ecause they were afraid they would run aground on the sandbars of Syrtis,

they lowered the sea anchor and let the ship be driven along. [18] [T]hey [also threw] the cargo overboard.

[20] When neither sun nor stars appeared for many days and the storm continued raging, [all except Paul] gave up hope of being saved.

[21] After they had gone a long time without food, Paul stood up before them and said: "Men, you should have taken my advice not to sail; then you would have spared yourselves this damage and loss. [22] But now I urge you to keep up your courage, because not one of you will be lost; only the ship will be destroyed. [23] Last night an angel of... God... stood beside me [24] and said, 'Do not be afraid, Paul. You must stand trial before Caesar; and God has graciously given you the lives of all who sail with you.' [25] So keep up your courage, men, for I have faith in God that it will happen just as he told me. [26] Nevertheless, we must run aground on some island."

[27] On the fourteenth night... [at] about midnight the sailors sensed they were approaching land. [29] Fearing [they] would be dashed against the rocks, they dropped four anchors from the stern and prayed for daylight.

[30] In an attempt to escape from the ship, the sailors let the lifeboat down into the sea, pretending they were going to lower some anchors from the bow. [31] Then Paul said to the centurion and the soldiers, "Unless these men stay with the ship, you cannot be saved." [32] So the soldiers cut the ropes that held the lifeboat and let it drift away.

[33] Just before dawn Paul urged them all to eat. "For the last fourteen days," he said, "you... have gone without food... [34] Now I urge you to take some food. You need it to survive. Not one of you will lose a single hair from his head." [35] After he said this, he took some bread and gave thanks to God in front of them all. Then he broke it and began to eat.

[36] They were all encouraged and ate some food themselves. [38] When they had eaten as much as they wanted, they lightened the ship by throwing the grain into the sea.

[39] When daylight came, they... saw a bay with a sandy beach, where they decided to run the ship aground if they could. [40] Cutting loose the anchors... [untying] the ropes that held the rudders [and] hoist[ing] the foresail to the wind [they] made for the beach. [41] But the ship struck a sandbar and ran aground. The bow stuck fast and would not move, and the stern was broken to pieces by the pounding of the surf.

[43] [T]he centurion... ordered those who could swim to jump overboard first and get to land. [44] The rest were to get there on planks or on other pieces of the ship. In this way everyone reached land safely.

Acts 28:

[1] Once safely on shore, [they] found [they were on] the island... called Malta. [2] The islanders showed [them] unusual kindness. They built a fire and welcomed [everyone] because it was raining and cold.

[7] There was an estate nearby that belonged to Publius, the chief official of the island. He

welcomed [everyone] to his home and showed [all] generous hospitality for three days. [8] His father was sick in bed, suffering from fever and dysentery. Paul went in to see him and, after prayer, placed his hands on him and healed him. [9] When this had happened, the rest of the sick on the island came and were cured.

[11] After three months [they] put out to sea [for Rome]... [16] When [they] got to Rome, Paul was allowed to live by himself, with a soldier to guard him.

[17] Three days later he called together the local... leaders. When they had assembled, Paul said to them: "My brothers, although I have done nothing against our people or against the customs of our ancestors, I was arrested in Jerusalem and handed over to the Romans. [18] They examined me and wanted to release me, because I was not guilty of any crime deserving death. [19] The [people] objected, so I was compelled to make an appeal to Caesar. [20] For this reason I have asked to see you and talk with you. It is because of the hope of [all] that I am bound with this chain."

[21] They replied, "We have not received any letters from Judea concerning you, and... [no one there has] said anything bad about you. [22] But we want to hear what your views are..."

[23] They arranged to meet Paul on a certain day, and came in even larger numbers to the place where he was staying. He witnessed to them from morning till evening, explaining about the kingdom of God... he tried to persuade them about Jesus.

[30] For two whole years Paul stayed there in his own rented house and welcomed all who came to see him. [31] He proclaimed the kingdom of God and taught about the Lord Jesus Christ — with all boldness and without hindrance!

Romans 1:

[7] To all in Rome who are loved by God and called to be [H]is holy people: Grace and peace to you from God our Father and from the Lord Jesus Christ, [Paul said].

[8] First, I thank my God through Jesus Christ for all of you, because your faith is being reported all over the world. [9] God, [W]hom I serve in my spirit in preaching the gospel of [H]is Son, is my witness how constantly I remember you [10] in my prayers at all times; and I pray that now at last by God's will the way may be opened for me to come to you.

[11] I long to see you so that I may impart to you some spiritual gift to make you strong — [12] that is, that you and I may be mutually encouraged by each other's faith.

[14] I am obligated both to Greeks and non-Greeks, both to the wise and the foolish. [15] That is why I am so eager to preach the gospel also to you who are in Rome.

[16] For I am not ashamed of the gospel, because it is the power of God that brings salvation to everyone who believes... [17] For in the gospel the righteousness of God is revealed — a righteousness that is by faith from first to last, just as it is written: "The righteous will live by faith."

20 For since the creation of the world God's invisible qualities — [H]is eternal power and divine nature — have been clearly seen…

Romans 2:

10 [G]lory, honor and peace [belong to] everyone who does good…**11** [f]or God does not show favoritism. **13** For it is not those who hear the law who are righteous in God's sight, but it is those who obey the law who will be declared righteous.

29 …[A] [just] person is… [one] who[m] is [righteous] inwardly; and circumcision is circumcision of the heart, by the Spirit… Such a person's praise is… from God.

Romans 3:

9 What shall we conclude then? Do[es] [anyone] have [an] advantage? Not at all! …[A]ll [are] under the power of sin.

21 …[T]he righteousness of God has been made known [through] the Law and the Prophets… **22** This righteousness is given through faith in Jesus Christ… There is no difference between [people], **23** for all have sinned and fall short of the glory of God, **24** and all are justified freely by [H]is grace through the redemption that came by Christ Jesus.

28 …[A] person is justified by faith… **29** …[for] God [is] the God of [all].

Romans 4:

7 "Blessed are those whose transgressions are forgiven, whose sins are covered. **8** Blessed is the one whose sin the Lord will never count against them."

13 It was not through the law that Abraham and his offspring received the promise that he would be heir of the world, but through the righteousness that comes by faith. **16** Therefore, the promise comes by faith, so that it may be by grace and may be guaranteed to all Abraham's offspring… He is the father of… all. **17** As it is written: "I have made you a father of many nations." He is our father in the sight of God, in [W]hom he believed — the God [W]ho gives life to the dead and calls into being things that were not.

20 [Abraham] did not waver through unbelief regarding the promise of God, but was strengthened in his faith and gave glory to God, **21** being fully persuaded that God had power to do what [H]e had promised. **22** This is why "it was credited to him as righteousness." **23** The words "it was credited to him" were written not for him alone, **24** but also for us, to whom God will credit righteousness — for us who believe in [H]im who raised Jesus our Lord from the dead. **25** He was delivered over to death for our sins and was raised to life for our justification.

Romans 5:

1 Therefore, since we have been justified through faith, we have peace with God through our Lord Jesus Christ, **2** through whom we have gained access by faith into this grace in which we now stand. And we boast in the hope of the glory of God. **3** …[W]e also glory in

316

our sufferings, because we know that suffering produces perseverance; ⁴ perseverance, character; and character, hope. ⁵ And hope does not put us to shame, because God's love has been poured out into our hearts through the Holy Spirit, who has been given to us.

⁸ …God demonstrates [H]is own love for us in this: While we were still sinners, Christ died for us.

¹² Therefore, just as sin entered the world through one man, and death through sin… ¹⁸ one righteous act resulted in justification and life for all people. ¹⁹ For just as through the disobedience of the one man the many were made sinners, so also through the obedience of the one man the many will be made righteous. ²⁰ [Thus] where sin increased, grace increased all the more, ²¹ so that, just as sin reigned in death, so also grace might reign through righteousness to bring eternal life through Jesus Christ our Lord.

Romans 6:

³ …[A]ll of us who were baptized into Christ Jesus were baptized into his death? ⁴ We were therefore buried with him through baptism into death in order that, just as Christ was raised from the dead through the glory of the Father, we too may live a new life.

⁵ For if we have been united with him in a death like his, we will certainly also be united with him in a resurrection like his. ⁶ For we know that our old self was crucified with him so that the body ruled by sin might be done away with, that we should no longer be slaves to sin — ⁷ because anyone who has died has been set free from sin.

⁸ Now if we died with Christ, we believe that we will also live with him. ⁹ For we know that since Christ was raised from the dead, he cannot die again; death no longer has mastery over him. ¹⁰ The death he died, he died to sin once for all; but the life he lives, he lives to God.

¹¹ In the same way, count yourselves dead to sin but alive to God in Christ Jesus. ¹² Therefore do not let sin reign in your mortal body so that you obey its evil desires. ¹³ …[O]ffer yourselves to God as those who have been brought from death to life; and offer every part of yourself to [H]im as an instrument of righteousness. ¹⁴ For sin shall no longer be your master, because you are… under grace.

¹⁸ You have been set free from sin… ¹⁹ …[O]ffer yourselves as slaves to righteousness leading to holiness. ²² …[T]he benefit you reap… is eternal life.

Romans 8:

¹ [T]here is… no condemnation for those who are in Christ Jesus, ² because through Christ Jesus the law of the Spirit who gives life has set you free from… sin and death. ¹⁰ …[I]f Christ is in you, then even though your body is subject to death because of sin, the Spirit gives life because of righteousness. ¹¹ And if the Spirit of [H]im who raised Jesus from the dead is living in you, [H]e who raised Christ from the dead will also give life to your mortal bodies because of [H]is Spirit [W]ho lives in you. ¹² Therefore… we have an obligation — to live according to [the Spirit] ¹³ [f]or if you live… by the Spirit… you will

[not die].

¹⁴ For those who are led by the Spirit of God are the children of God. ¹⁵ The Spirit you received… brought about your adoption… And by him we cry, *"Abba,* Father." ¹⁷ Now if we are children, then we are heirs — heirs of God and co-heirs with Christ, if indeed we share in his sufferings in order that we may also share in his glory. ²⁸ And we know that in all things God works for the good of those who love [H]im…

Romans 10:

⁹ If you declare with your mouth, "Jesus is Lord," and believe in your heart that God raised him from the dead, you will be saved. ¹⁰ For it is with your heart that you believe and are justified, and it is with your mouth that you profess your faith and are saved. ¹¹ As Scripture says, "Anyone who believes in him will never be put to shame." ¹² For there is no difference between [people] — the same Lord is Lord of all and richly blesses all who call on [H]im, ¹³ for, "Everyone who calls on the name of the Lord will be saved."

Romans 12:

¹ I urge you… in view of God's mercy, to offer your bodies as a living sacrifice, holy and pleasing to God… ² Do not conform to the pattern of this world…

³ …[T]hink of yourself with sober judgment, in accordance with the faith God has distributed to each of you. ⁴ For just as each of us has one body with many members, and these members do not all have the same function, ⁵ so in Christ we, though many, form one body, and each member belongs to all the others. ⁶ We have different gifts, according to the grace given to each of us...

⁹ Love must be sincere. Hate what is evil; cling to what is good. ¹⁰ Be devoted to one another in love… ¹² Be joyful in hope, patient in affliction, faithful in prayer. ¹⁴ Bless those who persecute you; bless and do not curse. ¹⁵ Rejoice with those who rejoice; mourn with those who mourn. ¹⁶ Live in harmony with one another. …Do not be conceited.

¹⁷ Do not repay anyone evil for evil. Be careful to do what is right in the eyes of everyone. ¹⁸ If it is possible… live at peace with everyone. ¹⁹ Do not take revenge… ²⁰ On the contrary: "If your enemy is hungry, feed him; if he is thirsty, give him something to drink." ²¹ Do not be overcome by evil, but overcome evil with good.

Romans 13:

⁸ …[L]ove is the fulfillment of the law. ¹⁴ [Therefore], clothe yourselves with the Lord Jesus Christ…

Romans 14:

¹¹ It is written: "As surely as I live," says the Lord, "every knee will bow before me; every tongue will acknowledge God." ¹² …[E]ach of us will give an account of ourselves to God. ¹³ Therefore let us stop passing judgment on one another. Instead, make up your mind not to put any stumbling block or obstacle in the way of a brother or sister.

Romans 15:

[2] Each of us should [build up our] neighbors for their good… [7] Accept one another…

[13] May the God of hope fill you with all joy and peace as you trust in [H]im, so that you may overflow with hope by the power of the Holy Spirit [9] and… God for [H]is mercy.

Christian Orthodox Tradition:

Source: St. Mary Magdalene, Myrrh-Bearer and Equal of the Apostles. Antiochian Orthodox Church in North America. 26 January 2012. http://www.antiochian.org/node/19008 and The Great Synaxaristes of the Orthodox Church. (Holy Apostles Convent, Buena Vista, CO. 2002):

[W]hen the Apostles departed from Jerusalem to preach to all the ends of the earth, Mary Magdalene also went with them. She went beyond her native borders to preach in… Rome. Everywhere she proclaimed to people about Christ and His teachings. When many did not believe that Christ was risen, she repeated to them what she had said to the Apostles on the… morning of the Resurrection: "I have seen the Lord!"

On [one] occasion, when Mary Magdalene and Galatia (the Hebrew wife of Onesimos, who with her husband served as a guide and protector during Mary Magdalene's stay in Rome) were alone… Galatia, needing to rest and sit down, showed Mary Magdalene her swollen and blackened legs with protruding veins. Mary Magdalene [then said], "In the name of our Lord and God and Savior, my Jesus… be healed." Galatia [immediately] [a]rose… completely [healed].

Source: Synaxarion of the Lenten Triodion and Pentecostarion. Edited by Fr. David Kidd and Sr. Gabriella Ursache (HDM Press, Rives Junction, MI, 2005):

Mary Magdalene [even] had an audience with the Roman Emperor… She picked up an egg from the table and used it as a symbol of new life, proclaiming, "Christ is Risen!" Tiberius exclaimed, "How can someone rise from the dead? It is just as likely that Christ rose from the dead as it is that the egg you are holding will turn red." Immediately then, the egg turned a brilliant red [and many came to believe].

XXX. Posterus Evangelium II

Christianity:

1 Corinthians 1:

[18] …[T]he message of the cross… to us who are being saved… is the power of God.

1 Corinthians 2:

[7] God's wisdom [is] a mystery that has been hidden… for our glory before time began. [8] None of the rulers… understood it, for if they had, they would not have crucified the Lord of glory. [9] However, as it is written: "What no eye has seen, what no ear has heard, and what no human mind has conceived" — the things God has prepared for those who love [H]im…

1 Corinthians 3:

[16] Don't you know that you yourselves are God's temple and that God's Spirit dwells in your midst? God's temple is sacred, and you together are that temple.

1 Corinthians 9:

[19] Though I am free and belong to no one, I have made myself a slave to everyone, to win as many as possible. [22] …I have become all things to all people so that by all possible means I might save some. [23] I do all this for the sake of the gospel, that I may share in its blessings.

1 Corinthians 9:

[23] "I have the right to do anything," you say — but not everything is beneficial. "I have the right to do anything" — but not everything is constructive. [24] No one should seek their own good, but the good of others.

1 Corinthians 12:

[12] Just as a body, though one, has many parts… so it is with Christ. [13] For we were all baptized by one Spirit so as to form one body… and we were all given the one Spirit to drink. [15] Now if the foot should say, "Because I am not a hand, I do not belong to the body," it would not for that reason stop being part of the body. [16] And if the ear should say, "Because I am not an eye, I do not belong to the body," it would not for that reason stop being part of the body. [17] If the whole body were an eye, where would the sense of hearing be? If the whole body were an ear, where would the sense of smell be? [18] But in fact God has placed the parts in the body, every one of them, just as [H]e wanted them to be. [19] If they were all one part, where would the body be? [20] As it is, there are many parts, but one body.

[21] The eye cannot say to the hand, "I don't need you!" And the head cannot say to the feet, "I don't need you!" [24] …God has put the body together… [25] so that there should be no division in the body, but that its parts should have equal concern for each other. [26] If one part suffers, every part suffers with it; if one part is honored, every part rejoices with it. [27] Now you are the body of Christ, and each one of you is a part of it.

320

1 Corinthians 13:

[4] Love is patient, love is kind. It does not envy, it does not boast, it is not proud. [5] It does not dishonor others, it is not self-seeking, it is not easily angered, it keeps no record of wrongs. [6] Love does not delight in evil but rejoices with the truth. [7] It always protects, always trusts, always hopes, always perseveres. [13] [Out of] faith, hope and love... the greatest of these is love.

1 Corinthians 15:

[9] ...I am the least of the apostles and do not even deserve to be called an apostle, because I persecuted the church of God. [10] But by the grace of God I am what I am, and [H]is grace to me was not without effect. No, I worked harder than all of them — yet not I, but the grace of God that was with me. [11] Whether, then, it is I or they, this is what we preach, and this is what you believed.

[12] But if it is preached that Christ has been raised from the dead, how can some of you say that there is no resurrection of the dead? [13] If there is no resurrection of the dead, then not even Christ has been raised. [14] And if Christ has not been raised, our preaching is useless and so is your faith. [15] More than that, we are then found to be false witnesses about God, for we have testified about God that he raised Christ from the dead. But [H]e did not raise him if in fact the dead are not raised. [16] For if the dead are not raised, then Christ has not been raised either. [17] And if Christ has not been raised, your faith is futile... [18] Then those also who have fallen asleep in Christ are lost. [19] If only for this life we have hope in Christ, we are of all people most to be pitied.

[20] But Christ has indeed been raised from the dead, the first fruits of those who have fallen asleep. [21] For since death came through a man, the resurrection of the dead comes also through a man. [22] For as in Adam all die, so in Christ all will be made alive. [23] But each in turn: Christ, the first fruits; then, when he comes, those who belong to him. [24] Then the end will come, when he hands over the kingdom to God the Father... [25] For he must reign until... [26] death [is destroyed]. [28] When he has done this, then the Son himself will be made subject to [H]im who put everything under him, so that God may be all in all.

[35] But someone will ask, "How are the dead raised? With what kind of body will they come?" [36] How foolish! What you sow does not come to life unless it dies. [37] When you sow, you do not plant the body that will be, but just a seed, perhaps of wheat or of something else. [42] So will it be with the resurrection of the dead. The body that is sown is perishable, it is raised imperishable; [43] it is sown in dishonor, it is raised in glory; it is sown in weakness, it is raised in power; [44] it is sown a natural body, it is raised a spiritual body.

[52] ...[T]he trumpet will sound, the dead will be raised imperishable, and we will be changed. [53] For the perishable must clothe itself with the imperishable, and the mortal with immortality.

[54] When the perishable has been clothed with the imperishable, and the mortal with immortality, then the saying that is written will come true: "Death has been swallowed up in victory." [55] "*Where, O death, is your victory? Where, O death, is your sting?*"

⁵⁷ [T]hanks be to God! He gives us the victory through our Lord Jesus Christ. ⁵⁸ Therefore... stand firm... because... your labor in the Lord is not in vain.

2 Corinthians 4:

¹⁴ ...[W]e know that the [O]ne who raised the Lord Jesus from the dead will also raise us with Jesus... ¹⁶ Therefore we do not lose heart. ¹⁷ For our... momentary troubles are achieving for us an eternal glory that far outweighs [everything]. ¹⁸ So we fix our eyes not on what is seen, but on what is unseen, since what is seen is temporary, but what is unseen is eternal.

2 Corinthians 6:

¹⁶ "I will live with them and walk among them, and I will be their God, and they will be [M]y people. ¹⁸ And, I will be a Father to you, and you will be [M]y sons and daughters," says the Lord Almighty.

2 Corinthians 9:

⁶ Whoever sows sparingly will also reap sparingly, and whoever sows generously will also reap generously. ⁹ As it is written: "They have freely scattered their gifts to the poor; their righteousness endures forever." ¹⁰ Now [H]e who supplies seed to the sower and bread for food will also supply and increase your store of seed and will enlarge the harvest of your righteousness. ¹¹ You will be enriched in every way so that you can be generous on every occasion...

2 Corinthians 10:

¹⁷ "Let the one who boasts boast in the Lord."

Galatians 3:

²⁶ [I]n Christ Jesus... all [are] children of God through faith, ²⁷ for all... who were baptized into Christ have clothed [them]selves with Christ. ²⁸ ...[A]ll [are] one in Christ Jesus ²⁹ ...and heirs according to the promise.

Galatians 5:

¹³ ...[U]se your freedom to... ¹⁴ "Love your neighbor as yourself."

Galatians 6:

² Carry each other's burdens, and in this way you will fulfill the law of Christ. ⁹ Let us not become weary in doing good, for at the proper time we will reap a harvest if we do not give up. ¹⁰ Therefore, as we have opportunity, let us do good to all people...

Ephesians 2:

⁴ [B]ecause of [H]is great love for us, God, [W]ho is rich in mercy, ⁵ made us alive with Christ even when we were dead... it is by grace [we] have been saved... ⁹ not by works... ⁸ ...[I]t is the gift of God — ¹⁰ For we are God's handiwork, created in Christ Jesus to do good works, which God prepared in advance for us to do.

Ephesians 4:

[2] Be completely humble and gentle; be patient, bearing with one another in love.

[3] Make every effort to keep the unity of the Spirit through the bond of peace. [4] There is one body and one Spirit, just as you were called to one hope when you were called; [5] one Lord, one faith, one baptism; [6] one God and Father of all, who is over all and through all and in all. [7] [T]o each one of us grace has been given... [8] This is why it says: "When he ascended on high, he took many captives and gave gifts to his people."

Ephesians 5:

[1] Follow God's example... [2] and walk in the way of love... [8] ...Live as children of light [9] (for the fruit of the light consists in all goodness, righteousness and truth). [13] [E]verything exposed by the light becomes visible — and everything that is illuminated becomes a light. [14] This is why it is said: "Wake up, sleeper, rise from the dead, and Christ will shine on you."

Philippians 2:

[3] [I]n humility value others above yourselves, [4] not looking to your own interests but each of you to the interests of the others. [5] In your relationships with one another, have the same mindset as Christ Jesus: [6] Who, being in very nature God, did not consider equality with God something to be used to his own advantage; [7] rather, he made himself nothing by taking the very nature of a servant, being made in human likeness. [8] And being found in appearance as a man, he humbled himself by becoming obedient to death — even death on a cross! [9] Therefore God exalted him to the highest place and gave him the name that is above every name, [10] that at the name of Jesus every knee should bow, in heaven and on earth and under the earth, [11] and every tongue acknowledge that Jesus Christ is Lord, to the glory of God the Father.

Philippians 3:

[20] [O]ur citizenship is in heaven. And we eagerly await... Jesus Christ, [21] who... will transform our lowly bodies so that they will be like his glorious body.

Philippians 4:

[4] Rejoice in the Lord always... [6] Do not be anxious about anything, but in every situation, by prayer and petition, with thanksgiving, present your requests to God. [5] ...The Lord is near. [13] I can do [everything] through [H]im [W]ho gives me strength.

The "Luminous" Religion:

Source: Martin Palmer. The Jesus Sutras (Ballantine Wellspring, New York, 2001):

There was no other way to free us from sins but for [Ye Su] (Jesus) to enter this world.

XXXI. Posterus Evangelium III

Christianity:

Colossians 1:

[15] The Son is the image of the invisible God, the firstborn over all creation. [16] For in him all things were created: things in heaven and on earth, visible and invisible...; all things have been created through him and for him. [17] He is before all things, and in him all things hold together. [18] And... he is the beginning and the firstborn from among the dead... [19] For God was pleased to have all [H]is fullness dwell in him, [20] and through him to reconcile to himself all things, whether things on earth or things in heaven, by making peace through his blood, shed on the cross.

1 Thessalonians 4:

[7] ...[L]ive a holy life.

1 Thessalonians 5:

[9] ...God did not appoint us to suffer wrath but to receive salvation through our Lord Jesus Christ. [10] He died for us so that, whether we are awake or asleep, we may live together with him.

1 Timothy 3:

[16] ...[T]he mystery from which true godliness springs is great: He appeared in the flesh, was vindicated by the Spirit, was seen by angels, was preached among the nations, was believed... in the world, was taken up in glory.

1 Timothy 4:

[8] ...[G]odliness has value for all things, holding promise for both the present life and the life to come.

2 Timothy 2:

[8] Remember Jesus Christ, raised from the dead... [11] "If we died with him, we will also live with him; [12] if we endure, we will also reign with him... [13] [I]f we are faithless, he remains faithful, for he cannot disown himself.

2 Timothy 4:

[6] ...I am already being poured out like a drink offering, and the time for my departure is near. [7] I have fought the good fight, I have finished the race, I have kept the faith. [8] Now there is in store for me the crown of righteousness, which the Lord, the righteous Judge, will award to me on that day — and not only to me, but also to all who have longed for [H]is appearing.

XXXII. Posterus Evangelium IV

Christianity:

Titus 3:

[4] [W]hen the kindness and love of God... appeared, [5] [H]e saved us, not because of righteous things we had done, but because of [H]is mercy. He saved us through the washing of rebirth and renewal by the Holy Spirit, [6] whom [H]e poured out on us generously through Jesus Christ our Savior, [7] so that, having been justified by his grace, we might become heirs having the hope of eternal life.

Hebrews 1:

[3] The Son is the radiance of God's glory and the exact representation of [H]is being, sustaining all things by his powerful word. After he had provided purification for sins, he sat down at the right hand of the Majesty in heaven.

Hebrews 2:

[11] ...Jesus is not ashamed to call [people] brothers and sisters. [12] He says, "I will declare [Y]our name to my brothers and sisters..." [13] And again he says, "Here am I, and the children God has given me." [14] Since the children have flesh and blood, [Jesus] shared in their humanity so that by his death he might break the power of... death.

Hebrews 3:

[15]"Today, if you hear his voice, do not harden your hearts..."

Hebrews 4:

[14] [S]ince we have a great high priest who has ascended into heaven, Jesus the Son of God, let us hold firmly to the faith we profess. [15] For we do not have a high priest who is unable to empathize with our weaknesses, but we have one who has been tempted in every way, just as we are — yet he did not sin. [16] Let us then approach God's throne of grace with confidence, so that we may receive mercy and find grace to help us in our time of need.

Hebrews 5:

[5] ...Christ did not take on himself the glory of becoming a high priest. But God said to him, "You are my Son; today I have become your Father. [6] You are a priest forever, in the order of Melchizedek."

[7] During the days of Jesus' life on earth, he offered up prayers and petitions with fervent cries and tears to the [O]ne [W]ho could save him from death, and he was heard because of his reverent submission. [8] Son though he was, he learned obedience from what he suffered [9] and, once made perfect, he became the source of eternal salvation for all who obey him...

Hebrews 6:

[10] God... will not forget your work and the love you have shown [H]im.

Hebrews 9:

[11] ...[W]hen Christ came as high priest... he went through the greater and more perfect tabernacle... [12] He... entered the Most Holy Place once for all by his own blood... obtaining eternal redemption. [13] The blood of goats and bulls and the ashes of a heifer sprinkled on those who are ceremonially unclean sanctify them so that they are outwardly clean. [14] How much more, then, will the blood of Christ, who through the eternal Spirit offered himself unblemished to God, cleanse our consciences from acts that lead to death, so that we may serve the living God!

[15] For this reason Christ is the mediator of a new covenant, that [all] may receive the promised eternal inheritance...

[26] ...[H]e... appeared once for all... to do away with sin by the sacrifice of himself. [27] Just as people are destined to die once... [28] so Christ was sacrificed once to take away the sins of many; and he will appear a second time... to bring salvation to those who are waiting for him.

Hebrews 12:

[22] ...[Y]ou have come... to the city of the living God, the heavenly Jerusalem. You have come to thousands upon thousands of angels in joyful assembly... [23] ...You have come to God, the Judge of all, to the spirits of the righteous made perfect, [24] to Jesus the mediator of a new covenant...

[25] See to it that you do not refuse him who speaks... [28] Therefore, since we are receiving a kingdom that cannot be shaken, let us be thankful, and so worship God acceptably with reverence and awe...

Hebrews 13:

[1] Keep on loving one another as brothers and sisters. [2] Do not forget to show hospitality to strangers, for by so doing some people have shown hospitality to angels without knowing it. [3] Continue to remember those in prison as if you were together with them in prison, and those who are mistreated as if you yourselves were suffering.

[5] ...[B]e content with what you have, because God has said, "Never will I leave you; never will I forsake you." [6] So we say with confidence, "The Lord is my helper; I will not be afraid. What can mere mortals do to me?"

[7] Remember... [8] Jesus Christ is the same yesterday and today and forever. [15] Through Jesus, therefore, let us continually offer to God a sacrifice of praise... [16] And do not forget to do good and to share with others, for with such sacrifices God is pleased.

James 1:

[2] Consider it pure joy, my brothers and sisters, whenever you face trials of many kinds, [3] because you know that the testing of your faith produces perseverance. [12] Blessed is the one who perseveres under trial because, having stood the test, that person will receive the crown of life that the Lord has promised to those who love [H]im.

[19] ...Everyone should be quick to listen, slow to speak and slow to become angry, [20] because human anger does not produce the righteousness that God desires. [26]

…[K]eep a tight rein on [your] [tongue]…

²⁵ …[W]hoever looks intently into the perfect law that gives freedom, and continues in it — not forgetting what they have heard, but doing it — they will be blessed in what they do. ²⁷ [The] [r]eligion that God our Father accepts as pure and faultless is this: to look after orphans and widows in their distress and to keep oneself from being polluted by the world.

James 2:

¹ …[Do] not show favoritism. ⁸ [Instead] "Love your neighbor as yourself."

¹² Speak and act as those who are going to be judged by the law that gives freedom, ¹³ because judgment without mercy will be shown to anyone who has not been merciful. Mercy triumphs over judgment.

¹⁴ What good is it… if someone claims to have faith but has no deeds? ¹⁵ Suppose a brother or a sister is without clothes and daily food. ¹⁶ If one of you says to them, "Go in peace; keep warm and well fed," but does nothing about their physical needs, what good is it? ¹⁷ In the same way, faith by itself, if it is not accompanied by action, is dead. ²⁶ As the body without the spirit is dead, so faith without deeds is dead.

James 3:

⁹ With the tongue we praise our Lord and Father, and with it we curse human beings, who have been made in God's likeness. ¹⁰ Out of the same mouth come praise and cursing. …[T]his should not be.

¹³ Who is wise and understanding? Let them show it by their good life, by deeds done in the humility that comes from wisdom. ¹⁷ [For] the wisdom that comes from heaven is… pure; …peace-loving, considerate, submissive, full of mercy and good fruit, impartial and sincere. ¹⁸ Peacemakers who sow in peace reap a harvest of righteousness.

James 4:

⁷ Submit [yourself]… to God. ⁸ Come near to God and [H]e will come near to you. Wash your hands… and purify your hearts… ¹⁰ Humble [yourself] before the Lord, and [H]e will lift you up.

James 5:

⁷ Be patient… ¹⁰ in the face of suffering… ¹¹ [for] [t]he Lord is full of compassion and mercy.

1 Peter 1:

⁵ [J]ust as he who called you is holy, so be holy in all you do; ¹⁶ for it is written: "Be holy, because I am holy."

¹⁷ Since you call on a Father who judges each person's work impartially, live out your time as foreigners here in reverent fear. ¹⁸ For you know that it was not with perishable things such as silver or gold that you were redeemed… ¹⁹ but with the precious blood of Christ, a lamb without blemish or defect.

²² ...[H]ave sincere love for each other, love one another deeply, from the heart. ²³ For you have been born again, not of perishable seed, but of imperishable, through the living and enduring word of God. ²⁴ For, "All people are like grass, and all their glory is like the flowers of the field; the grass withers and the flowers fall, ²⁵ but the word of the Lord endures forever."

1 Peter 2:

² Like newborn babies, crave pure spiritual milk, so that by it you may grow up in your salvation, ³ now that you have tasted that the Lord is good.

⁴ As you come to him, the living Stone — rejected by humans but chosen by God and precious to [H]im — ⁵ you also, like living stones, are being built into a spiritual house... ⁶ For in Scripture it says: "See, I lay a stone... a chosen and precious cornerstone, and the one who trusts in him will never be put to shame."

⁹ [Y]ou are a chosen people... called... into [God's] wonderful light.

²⁰ ...[I]f you suffer for doing good and you endure it, this is commendable before God. ²¹ ...because Christ suffered for you, leaving you an example, that you should follow in his steps. ²² "He committed no sin, and no deceit was found in his mouth. ²³ "When they hurled their insults at him, he did not retaliate; when he suffered, he made no threats. Instead, he entrusted himself to [H]im who judges justly. ²⁴ He himself bore our sins in his body on the cross, so that we might die to sins and live for righteousness; "by his wounds you have been healed."

1 Peter 3:

⁸ [B]e like-minded, be sympathetic, love one another, be compassionate and humble. ⁹ Do not repay evil with evil or insult with insult. On the contrary, repay evil with blessing, because to this you were called so that you may inherit a blessing. ¹⁰ For, "Whoever would love life and see good days must keep their tongue from evil and their lips from deceitful speech. ¹¹ They must turn from evil and do good; they must seek peace and pursue it. ¹² For the eyes of the Lord are on the righteous and [H]is ears are attentive to their prayer..." ¹⁷ [I]t is better... to suffer for doing good than for doing evil.

1 Peter 4:

⁸ Above all, love each other deeply, because love covers over a multitude of sins.

¹³ ...[R]ejoice... as you participate in the sufferings of Christ, so that you may be overjoyed when his glory is revealed. ¹⁹ [T]hose who suffer... should commit themselves to their faithful Creator and continue to do good. ¹⁴ If you are insulted because of the name of Christ, you are blessed, for the Spirit of glory and of God rests on you.

2 Peter 1:

⁵ ...[M]ake every effort to add to your faith goodness; and to goodness, knowledge; ⁶ and to knowledge, self-control; and to self-control, perseverance; and to perseverance, godliness; ⁷ and to godliness, mutual affection; and to mutual affection, love.

2 Peter 3:

[8] …With the Lord a day is like a thousand years, and a thousand years are like a day. [9] The Lord is not slow in keeping [H]is promise… Instead [H]e is patient with you, not wanting anyone to perish, but everyone to come to repentance. [15] [The] Lord's patience means salvation…

[10] …[T]he day of the Lord will come like a thief… [14] …[M]ake every effort to be found spotless, blameless and at peace with [H]im. [13] …[Look] forward to a new heaven and a new earth, where righteousness dwells. [17] Therefore… be on your guard …and [18] grow in the grace and knowledge of [the] Lord and Savior Jesus Christ.

1 John 1:

[5] …God is light; in [H]im there is no darkness… [7] …[I]f we walk in the light… [H]is Son, purifies us from all sin. [9] If we confess our sins, [H]e is faithful and just and will forgive us our sins and purify us from all unrighteousness.

1 John 2:

[9] Anyone who claims to be in the light but hates a brother or sister is still in the darkness. [10] Anyone who loves their brother and sister lives in the light…

1 John 3:

[1] …[W]hat great love the Father has lavished on us, that we should be called children of God!

[7] [L]et us love one another, for love comes from God. Everyone who loves has been born of God and knows God [8] …because God is love. [9] This is how God showed [H]is love among us: He sent [H]is one and only Son into the world that we might live through him. [10] This is love: not that we loved God, but that [H]e loved us and sent [H]is Son as an atoning sacrifice for our sins. [11] …[S]ince God so loved us, we also ought to love one another. [12] No one has ever seen God; but if we love one another, God lives in us and [H]is love is made complete in us. [16] …Whoever lives in love lives in God, and God in them.

Jude 1:

[21] [K]eep yourselves in God's love as you wait for the mercy of our Lord Jesus Christ to bring you to eternal life.

Mary Magdalene 4:

[34] The Son of Man is [with] you. [36] Those who seek him will find him.

Revelation 1:

[7] "Look, he is coming with the clouds," and "every eye will see him, even those who pierced him…"

[8] "I am the Alpha and the Omega," says the Lord God, "[W]ho is, and [W]ho was, and [W]ho is to come, the Almighty."

[17] "Do not be afraid. I am the First and the Last. [18] I am the Living One; I was dead, and now look, I am alive for ever and ever!"

The Letter of Peter to Philip:

"I am with you forever."

Revelation 1:

[18] "And I hold the keys of death and Hades."

Gospel of Truth:

He labored even on the Sabbath for the sheep which [had] fallen into the pit. He saved the life of that sheep… He… anoint[ed] [it] with [his blood]… [which] is the pity of the Father… He [did] the will of the One who called him… *Each one's name comes to him.*

The Treatise on the Resurrection ("The Letter to Rheginos"):

[W]e are saved. We have received salvation from end to end.

Revelation 4:

[8] "Holy, holy, holy is the Lord God Almighty, [W]ho was, and is, and is to come. [11] "You are worthy, our Lord and God, to receive glory and honor and power…"

Hinduism:

Bhagavad Gita 7:

6:10.20 "…I am the beginning, the middle, and the end of all things."

Sikhism:

Sri Guru Granth Sahib:

The True Creator Lord is, and shall always be. He was not born; He shall not die.

Mayan Religion:

Source: **Tortuguero Tablet c. AD 670 and Comalcalco Brick c. AD 500-700:**

He will descend from the sky.

XXXIII. Compendium

Christianity:

Revelation 13:

¹⁰ [Let there be] patient endurance and faithfulness on the part of God's people.

¹⁸ Let the person who has insight [refuse] the number of the beast…That number is 666.

Islam:

^{Abraham 14:23 and The Women 4:122} And those who believe and do good are made to enter gardens, beneath which rivers flow, to abide in them [forever] by their Lord's permission; their greeting therein is, Peace. ([I]t is) a promise of [God], true (indeed), and who is truer of word than [God]?

^{The Counsel 42:5} The… angels sing the praise of their Lord and ask forgiveness for those on earth; now surely [God] is the Forgiving, the Merciful. ^{The Cow 2:268} [God] promises you forgiveness… and abundance; and [God] is Ample-giving… ^{The Family of Imran 3:133} And hasten to forgiveness from your Lord; [for] a Garden, the extensiveness of which is (as) the heavens and the earth… is prepared for [His people].

^{The Pilgrimage 22:50} ([F]or) those who believe and do good, they shall have forgiveness and an honorable sustenance. ^{Sahih Muslim 35:6523} O people, seek repentance from [God]. Verily, I seek repentance from Him a hundred times a day.

^{The Cow 2:73} …[God] brings the dead to life…

^{The Family of Imran 3:15} Say: Shall I tell you what is better than these? For those who guard (against evil) are gardens with their Lord, beneath which rivers flow, to abide in them…

^{Muhammad 47:15} A parable of the garden which those guarding (against evil) are promised: Therein are rivers of water that does not alter, and rivers of milk the taste whereof does not change, and rivers of drink delicious to those who drink, and rivers of honey clarified and for them therein are all fruits and protection from their Lord…

^{The Family of Imran 3:145} …[W]hoever desires the reward of the hereafter I shall give him of it, and I will reward the grateful.

Source: Sahih Bukhari, Book 76: Number 572:

…[A] place equal to a foot in Paradise is better than the whole world and whatever is in it.

Judaism:

1 Enoch:

^{90:23} All… in Heaven will bless [God], and [those] who dwell in the garden of life.

[104:2,4] Be hopeful, because formerly you have pined away through evil and toil. But now you will shine like the lights of heaven, and you shall be seen, and the windows of heaven will be opened for you... [Y]ou are about to be making a great rejoicing like the angels of heaven.

Source: Talmud Yalkut Shimoni, Bereshit 20:

[Paradise] has two gates of ruby, by which stand sixty varieties of pure servants. The luster of the face of each of them glistens like the splendor of the firmament. When a righteous [person] arrives, they remove [the] clothes in which [they] had been buried, and clothe [them] in white robes of the clouds of glory.

Source: Talmud Avot 4:17:

Better is one hour of bliss in the world to come than the whole life in this world.

Mormonism:

Alma 24:

[14] And the great God has had mercy on us... that we might not perish... [H]e love[s] our souls as well as he love[s] our children... [15] Oh, how merciful is our God!

Sikhism:

Sri Guru Granth Sahib:

O Creator Lord, all are in Your power. You are [my God] – what else do I need? ...Lord, You save me. There is no other for me at all... You are the Cherisher of all beings... As our Lord... keeps us, so do we exist... I exist only by Your Power... May I never forget You, Lord. This soul, body and breath are Yours... I sing Your Glorious Praises... Songs of Joy.

Without You, there is no other... All things are Your Doing; we can do nothing ourselves.

He... weighs with the scale, perfect is the weighing of the Perfect One... He administers righteous Justice... True is [His] Justice...

The... Lord is the Giver of all; He Himself bestows all blessings. [The Lord] bestow[s] [His] Gifts, even if we do not ask for them... There is no other as great as He... [T]here is no one like [You]... Forever and ever, night and day, I praise the Greatness of Your Goodness.

[T]he Diamond of the Lord [is] His Kindness and Compassion. ...He... forgives and unites. [He] is merciful... [He is the] Destroyer of sin... [He is] the 'Redeemer of sinners.' ...He protects the poor and the lost souls... [The saved] are [made] immaculate and pure... Dear Lord, please show Mercy to me... [and] [g]rant me the wisdom to worship and adore You...

Which is the swan, and which is the crane? It is only by [God's] grace... a crow... is transformed... into a swan.

The Lord God is my Friend and Companion. God shall be my Helper and Support... [He] is the Giver, the Lover of [all] His [people]... He bears True Love for His [people].

[He has] saved me from drowning... God has showered His Perfect Mercy upon [His people].

So many of Your beings and creatures praise You day and night... With each and every breath, I dwell upon You; I shall never forget You... In suffering and in comfort, I meditate on You... When I dwell upon [the Lord] in my soul, all my sorrows depart.

Remain immersed forever in the Love of God... Pen and ink shall pass away, along with what has been written... [T]he love of [God] shall never perish.

Without virtue... human life [is] in vain... [T]he one who lives righteously rejoices... Blessed... are the humble servants of the Lord... Blessed is that heart, within which the Lord's Glorious Praises are sung. Beautiful is that land, where the Lord's humble servants dwell.

Make [your] body the field and plant the seed of good actions. Water it with the Name of the Lord... Let... the Lord... sprout in your heart... Make good deeds the soil... let the Word... be the seed, irrigate it continually with the water of Truth... Serve the Lord each and every instant. ...[F]aith will sprout... bring[ing] knowledge of heaven.

[The] Lord is [my] Gardener... [Nothing] is exempt from His Care. As is the fragrance which He bestows, so is the fragrant flower known.... [He] is the fruit-bearing tree... Fruitful are the lives of those who walk in harmony with the Will of [God].

My Lord... is Perfect; His throne is Eternal and Immovable... He is... the Most Perfect of the Perfect... the Truest of the True... O Lord, nothing is beyond You.

The [p]alace of the Lord God is beautiful. Within it there are gems, rubies, pearls and flawless diamonds. A fortress of gold surrounds the [s]ource of [n]ectar (tree of life). There... anxiety and anguish are ended... There is no... death there.

Going to the world hereafter, everyone shall realize that without [God], it is all useless... [for He is] the Light of the Soul... [T]he Lord alone can save us... remov[ing] the pains of death... He... revives... He preserves our soul... The Messenger of Death is conquered... I place all my faith in You... [T]ake me into Your Embrace.

O mortal, you shall be saved by remembering the Lord... [You shall] find the gate of salvation... [Y]ou shall be blessed with eternal life... All place their hopes in [the Lord].

God... has given me His Hand... [He] has made me His Own... All my fears have been erased... The Savior Lord has saved me... He has erased... death... He has destroyed the city of sorrow... God gave me His Hand and saved me; He has blessed me with eternal life.

The Lord... gives [His] people a seat in the eternal home... The fear of... death has been dispelled.